THE 'UNIVERSAL PRAYER' IN THE ANCIENT LATIN LITURGIES

STUDIA TRADITIONIS THEOLOGIAE

EXPLORATIONS IN EARLY AND MEDIEVAL THEOLOGY

VOLUME 56

The 'Universal Prayer' in the Ancient Latin Liturgies

Patristic Evidence and Liturgical Texts

PAUL DE CLERCK

Translated into English by
JENNIFER R. O'BRIEN

BREPOLS

Translated from Paul De Clerck, *La "prière universelle" dans les liturgies latines anciennes. Témoignages patristiques et textes liturgiques (Liturgiewissenschaftliche Quellen und Forschungen, 62)* © Aschendorff Verlag, Münster, 1977.

Cover illustration: *Tabula Peutingeriana* © ÖNB Vienna Cod. 324, Segm. VIII + IX

D/2024/0095/211
ISBN 978-2-503-60681-1
eISBN 978-2-503-60718-4
DOI 10.1484/M.STT-EB.5.134616
ISSN 2294-3617
eISSN 2566-0160

Printed in the EU on acid-free paper.

Table of Contents

Preface to the English Translation

It is highly exceptional in the current academic landscape that a study dating from about half a century ago is translated and thus republished. The very fact, however, that a significant monograph originally written in French, moreover with numerous and extensive Latin quotations, is now made available in an English edition, is as important as it is indeed extraordinary. Clearly, the same cannot and must not be done with any book. Yet that it happens with Paul De Clerck's noted study on the role and the shape of the liturgical unit known as 'universal prayer' is all the more telling. I am convinced that the arduous work of Jennifer O'Brien, who patiently but very skillfully translated the entire manuscript, is a precious gift for liturgical scholars today and for many generations to come. There at least three reasons for that.

First, there is no doubt about the tremendous importance of the universal prayer in the course of the celebration of the Eucharist. If one reads De Clerck's work, and realizes the unbridled variety of forms and wordings of the universal prayer in the Western liturgical traditions, one really wonders how it came that for so many centuries it was omitted. That seems an almost unforgivable mistake, which was happily overcome eventually by the incentive Vatican II gave to restore it, prompted as it was by sound arguments and decent scholarship developed in the bosom of the 20th century Liturgical Movement.

Furthermore, De Clerck's investigations and reflections demonstrate that the importance of the universal prayer extend beyond the restoration of a liturgical unit in the ritual scenario underlying the Roman Catholic mass. The universal prayer entails a whole pedagogy of Christian prayer and thereby contributes essentially to the Eucharist and even to the Church's entire liturgical life. If and inasmuch as it is true that today we are painfully confronted with a life-liturgy gap, the universal prayer obviously has the first fiddle to play. For it teaches what one can pray for, how one prays, which script and structure of prayer is reliable, who is addressed and how to do that appropriately, etc. Henceforth, in the context of a wide-ranging ecclesial crisis, which is not only an internal affair of the clergy, let alone a matter of revising procedures for decision-making, but also a crisis of prayer, piety and spirituality, a study about Christians' universal prayer as thorough as De Clerck's is more than welcome.

Second, there is a great deal to learn from De Clerck's approach. De Clerck himself stands in a long and solid tradition of doing research in liturgical studies on the basis of meticulous textual investigations and comparisons. De Clerck offers an outstanding example of what is means to study in-depth a file — a 'dossier' as they say in French — to leave nothing out of sight, to consult all the primary sources available, to plough through elaborate commentaries and select from them what is relevant in view of the initial question, and to slowly develop one's own original and always nuanced opinion about the subject matter. De Clerck's method is not unlike a lawyer who keenly dives into a complex yet intriguing case, who needs to know everything about it, and whose vision is incomplete until the last stone has been turned over. Was it, by the way, not Romano Guardini who in a seminal article defended the idea that *Liturgiewissenschaft* operates not unlike *Rechtswissenschaft*? Whatever the case may be, although there are sometimes doubts today about a purely text-oriented method in liturgical research, a study like De Clerck's amply convinces us that such an approach is still extremely valuable, and thus that the baby should not be thrown out with the bathwater.

Third, De Clerck's groundbreaking research about the universal prayer should remind us of the reality that the scholarship undertaken by the major representatives of the Liturgical Movement was truly international, in a time long before internationalization became a buzzword in academic policy plans. Learning from different academic cultures is today as pertinent as it was fifty years ago. Contemporary researchers in the field of liturgy and theology can benefit enormously from Paul De Clerck, whose work is typical of a French and francophone style of theologizing. In addition, the translation of the present volume opens up a wealth of material which is rarely consulted among contemporary anglophone-centered research in liturgy. It is to be hoped that through this work many more valuable resources in liturgy will be (re)discovered. His tour de force alone in the first part, where the prehistory of 'universal prayer' is sketched with great accuracy, can serve as an example for many other syntheses of liturgical history.

A final reason for being grateful that this book is published is connected to the person of Paul De Clerck, who has been an dedicated teacher and respected professor for many. I am sure that he would be happy and proud that this translation of his magnum opus now appears, even if modesty prevents him from saying that explicitly and in public. More than he himself may realize, De Clerck is both heir and testator of a grand tradition of research in liturgical studies, with unlimited potential for the future. An eye for detail, knowledge of (classical) languages, thorough familiarity with primary and secondary literature, vision, boldness, theological ingenuity — these remain crucial characteristics for researchers in liturgical scholarship. I wish that the example set by De Clerck in this book may become a quality standard and, even more so, a source of inspiration for much future research and reflection.

Joris Geldhof
Liturgical Institute, KU Leuven
Feast of Saint Patrick, March 17, 2023

Foreword to the English Translation

When this work was originally published in 1977 more than a decade had passed since the conclusion of the Second Vatican Council and the liturgical revisions called for by this momentous gathering were being experienced in Roman Rite celebrations throughout the world. One of the most interesting decisions of the Council was to restore the 'common prayer' or 'prayer of the faithful', placing it after the gospel and homily, so that 'intercession might be made for holy Church, for the civil authorities, for those oppressed by various needs, for all humankind, and for the salvation of the entire world' (*SC* 51).

The research undertaken by Fr Paul De Clerck on the precise nature of this prayer, its appropriate title, and its origins and development within the Roman Rite resulted in the book that has for over forty years been the leading reference in this area. That it was not translated into English during this time remains a mystery, but when I was asked to undertake this task, I was very happy to oblige. It has been a labour of love to extend the fruits of De Clerck's research to English-speaking liturgists and a personal tribute to a colleague whom I came to know through Societas Liturgica and who on several occasions took the time and effort to correspond with me on matters liturgical, especially on the question of the Universal Prayer.

The wide range of texts from both East and West that allowed De Clerck to support or reject conclusions reached by previous scholars revealed the subtle and varied ways in which liturgical texts and their accompanying practices can and are modified over time as they are transported from one geographical region to another and incorporated into liturgical and social conditions at variance with that of their origins. The conflict between retaining an established text and amending or composing a new one for new circumstances is certainly evident as the 'Universal Prayer' of the faithful emerged in different guises in different places.

The theological significance of this prayer in identifying the important role of the Assembly within the celebration of the Eucharist has not, in my opinion, been sufficiently understood by many within the ranks of the clergy and certainly a good proportion of the lay faithful themselves. This translation of Paul De Clerck's work into English will, I hope, go some way to remedying that situation.

Jennifer R. O'Brien
Office for Worship, Adelaide, South Australia
Feast of Our Lady Help of Christians, May 24, 2022.

Preface

While the conciliar Constitution on the Sacred Liturgy reinstituted the Universal Prayer into the Roman Mass, this decision was supported by the research of a group of first rate historians. Here you have a young scholar re-examining the documents and modifying on several important points the conclusions that were taken for granted.

First of all are those that concern the link between the Universal Prayer and the titles 'Prayer of the Faithful' and 'Common Prayer'. Fr Paul De Clerck shows that the expression 'Prayer of the Faithful', attributed by Felix III to the Greek penitential canons, is considered neither by the Greeks, nor by St Augustine, nor in Rome, as a specific designation of the Universal Prayer, but generally refers to the prayer of the baptized as opposed to that of penitents or catechumens. Likewise with Cyprian and Augustine the *oratio communis* is the Our Father, even if the expression can have a more general scope. It is therefore without historical basis that article 53 of the Constitution on the Sacred Liturgy uses these titles, and that 'Universal Prayer', which appears in the new Roman Missal, is preferable.

The *Deprecatio Gelasii* occupies a central place in the history of the Roman Universal Prayer since Edmund Bishop restored its origin to Pope Gelasius and Dom Bernard Capelle linked it to the history of the *Kyrie*. Paul De Clerck confirms attribution of the text to Gelasius, but gives it a new place in the history of the Latin litanic formularies for the Universal Prayer. Amongst these formularies he distinguishes two groups: first, the group of translations from Greek (late 4th–5th c), the *Dicamus omnes* from the Stowe Missal and the *Divinae pacis* from the Ambrosian books; then the group of adaptations (from the end of the 5th c), with the *Deprecatio Gelasii* in the first place. He considers it possible that the two litanies from the first group may be of pre-Gelasian Roman origin, but the possibility of a Northern Italian provenance cannot be excluded either.

Lastly, and above all, the usage of the Kyrie in these litanies appears in a new light; it is used for the first time, not as a response but as a triple invocation standing alone at the end of the *Divinae pacis*. In the *Deprecatio Gelasii* there is no Kyrie, and Dom Capelle was incorrect in wanting to include it as part of the history of the Kyrie of the Mass. As a response repeated after each of the intentions, the Kyrie is found for the first time in the Milanese *Dicamus omnes* that Paul De Clerck considers to be from the 6th c. (and perhaps Roman), but that I would situate well before 476, on account of the prayer for the emperor. As for the rest, I believe that the conclusions reached are right and well-merited.

B. Capelle and especially A. Chavasse have tried to clarify the journey of the litany at the beginning of the Mass. Here Paul De Clerck underlines the fragility of their argument, perhaps to excess with regard to the *oratio super sindonem* — without, for his own part, shedding any real new light on the matter. To go further, I believe that is necessary to research in two directions. On the one hand, that of the Litany of the Saints, already witnessed to in the Gelasian sacramentary, and constituting a third wave following the solemn orations and the litanic prayers so excellently studied by Paul De Clerck. On the other hand it would be vital to study in a comparative fashion the anticipation of the litanic prayer in the Roman Mass and the Byzantine Mass. What the *Typicon de la grande Eglise* of Constantinople is able to inform us of the great *ektenia* in the processions before the Mass, or independently of it, is comparable to what Paul De Clerck has discovered in the Latin processionals.

In conclusion I would like to emphasise the theological importance of two facts that Paul De Clerck alludes to in passing, but which merit further study for their own sake: first, the distinction — not juridical, I dare to say, but sacramental — between the prayer of the baptized (notably the Our Father and the Universal Prayer) and that of the non-baptised. And second, the conviction, so strong in the early centuries, of the power of ecclesial prayer and its role in the history of salvation. It is from that that, ultimately, the Universal Prayer derives its meaning and its necessity.

P.-M. Gy OP
Director of the Institut Supérieur de Liturgie, Paris

Foreword

On 4 December 1963, Pope Paul VI promulgated the Constitution *De Sacra Liturgia*, by which the Fathers of the Second Vatican Council re-established the use of the Universal Prayer in the Roman liturgy. The great success of this conciliar decision has encouraged us to undertake the study of this prayer in the first centuries. A draft of this work, directed by Mons Canon Houssiau, served as Licentiate thesis within the faculty of theology of the Catholic University of Louvain in 1967. We were able to complete it at the Institut Supérieur de Liturgie in Paris, under the direction of Dom B. Botte, and present it for the degrees of Doctorate in Theology and Masters in Liturgy, in June 1970. Teaching commitments have prevented us from publishing until now.

We would like to thank all those who helped us bring this work to fruition. First of all, the library staffs of Mont César Abbey in Leuven, the Bibliothèque Nationale et Mazarine in Paris, the Bibliothèques Municipales of Autun, Besançon, Cambrai, Rouen and Verdun, the Bibliothèque Royale and that of the Bollandist Fathers in Brussels, the Stiftsbibliothek of Saint-Gall and the Abbey of Solesmes, who happily put their treasures at our disposal, as well as the librarians of Corpus Christi College, Cambridge, the Biblioteca Civica of Bergamo and the Biblioteca Nacional of Madrid who provided us with photographs of their manuscripts. The Institut de Recherché et d'Histoire des Textes in Paris allowed us to examine the microfilms of numerous manuscripts. The Centre for Analysis and Patristic Documentation of the University of Strasbourg provided us with the references for the commentaries of the Fathers of the Church on 1 Tim 2:1–4.

We want to thank in particular those who in many ways have provided help and encouragement: Frs Botte and Gy, Canon Houssiau, Fr Kannengiesser, Fr Molin, M. Huglo among others. Finally, we are most grateful to Fr Heiming, who did us the honour of accepting this work into the collection of which he is Director, and to his successor, Fr Heckenbah, who ensured revision of the manuscript. Thanks also to the editor for the care with which he as carried out the work, and to the University Foundation of Belgium which covered part of the publishing costs.

At the point of delivering this study to the public, our wish is that it will not only serve liturgical historians but will also provide help, however minimal, to those who are actively working for the profound renewal of the liturgy that our world is currently experiencing.

Brussels, 4 January 1974.

Introduction

The *Universal Prayer* refers to the prayer of petition that, in the Mass, comes after the homily, between the readings and the Liturgy of the Eucharist. The priest or deacon who leads it is joined directly with the assembly; thus it belongs to the liturgical genre of 'common prayer', constructed in such a way as to enable the participation of the faithful. Liturgical historians generally call it the *oratio fidelium*, which can be translated into English as 'Prayer of the Faithful'. We will see that the origin of this term leads us to reject it nowadays. It is also called 'Common Prayer', an inadequate and unimaginative expression.

The title of this work indicates two restrictions on this study of the Universal Prayer. The first is geographic. In effect, this rite features in all the Christian liturgies, but due to the immensity of the field and the complexity of the problems it raises, we have lowered our sights and limited ourselves to the Latin domain. In other words, we are focusing on the West, viewed as emanating from the Roman liturgy, and have only cited the Eastern parallels of the Latin texts in order to provide proof, if any still be needed, that the content of our formularies as well as their liturgical form comes from the East.

Next there is the time frame. Our title remains indeterminate in this regard; it is rather difficult to give precise chronological limits, since many liturgical facts can only be known from much later sources. Let us say that, by and large, we do not go beyond the Carolingian reform. It is only the facts prior to Gregory the Great that we have studied with precision, and since we believe that the *oratio fidelium* disappears towards the middle of the 6th century, we could call our study a 'history of the universal prayer at Rome (and in the West) during the first six centuries'.

The impetus for this study was the recent restoration of the *oratio fidelium*. The Constitution of the Sacred Liturgy of the Second Vatican Council, promulgated by Pope Paul VI, on 4 December 1963 effectively foresaw in paragraph 53 the re-establishment of the *oratio communis seu fidelium*. This echoed a wish repeated many times by those in the Liturgical Movement and brought to fruition such scholars of liturgical history as Probst, Bäumer, Duchesne, Bishop, Meyer, and more recently Capelle, Chavasse and Molin.

The conciliar decision was met with great success and liturgical journals have published numerous articles on the subject. All of these pick up the work of the masters we have just cited. Since many points still remained unclear, it seemed useful to us to re-examine the question and provide further support, however minimal, to liturgical practice.

The aim of this research is to trace the history of the Universal Prayer in the West, especially in the Roman liturgy. It will consist of two parts. The first is dedicated to the pre-history of the Universal Prayer. It will reflect critically on the literary evidence that the Fathers and ecclesiastical writers have offered us since the (possible) Jewish origins and Clement of Rome up to the end of the fifth century. It will consider the earliest evidence without any geographical limits, so as not to miss any precious material, and then discern any traces of the *oratio fidelium* in the Churches of Africa, Rome, Milan and Gaul. The information gathered will be summarized in the conclusions.

The second part consists of the formularies that have been preserved and edited by us on the basis of a large number of manuscripts. It provides commentary on them and attempts to situate them in place and time. This calls for the preliminary development of an analysis tool, a technical vocabulary that makes it possible to describe with precision the liturgical forms used, the elements of which they are composed, and how they function.

The first text with which we will deal is none other than the wonderful *Orationes sollemnes* of Good Friday. We will then distinguish between two waves of litanies that appear in the East. The first, which extends across the first three quarters of the fifth century, consists of translated Eastern formularies; in this we have included the *Dicamus omnes* of the Stowe Missal and the *Divinae pacis* of the Milanese liturgy. The second wave, which begins in the final quarter of the fifth century, revises these materials with regard to their stylistic form and their content. Their flagship is the *Deprecatio Gelasii* but also in this wave are two Franco-Gallican texts, the second Milanese litany, and a highly altered text which nowadays figures in the canon of the Stowe Missal.

In order to provide as complete a record as possible, we will also present the Gallican and Hispanic *orationes paschales* which have retained the themes of the ancient litanies in the liturgical form of the 'Solemn Prayers'.

We also describe the evolutions undergone by these texts; by the addition of psalm verses they were transformed into *preces* of all genres. The litanies of the saints also made use of the same materials, using them to come before the invocations to the saints.

Before concluding this second part, a more synthetic section attempts to define the relationships that exist, in the Roman liturgy, between the *oratio fidelium,* the *Kyrie eleison,* and the *oratio super sindonem.* The conclusions summarise these relationships.

Finally we come to the general conclusions and the assessment of the work.

Rather than give the impression of mastering all the aspects of the problems dealt with, we prefer to honestly acknowledge the steps we have carried out, the inevitable gaps that appear on each page, and the paths that we could not follow either due to lack of competence or lack of time. We hope, however, to have at least facilitated the task of the critic and of those who seek to continue on with this work.

Part One

Examination of the Patristic Evidence

Introduction

The aim of this research is to clarify the prehistory of the *oratio fidelium*. Many authors have cited parts of sentences, even a few words taken from the Fathers of the Church, and claim to see in them evidence of the Universal Prayer. These citations piqued our curiosity and, in collating them, we were surprised to find on some occasions quite convincing traces of our prayer, and on others to note that the context pointed to something else entirely.

This study seems to us to reflect a fourfold interest. First, did the *oratio fidelium* really exist in those earliest centuries, as so many are happy to claim? Secondly, did the various local Churches all use the same literary form for the Universal Prayer, or was there a certain variety in the structure and content of the prayer? Thirdly, do these vestiges lead us to suspect the existence of fixed formularies now lost, or do they conceal a freer form of prayer in which spontaneity had its place? Finally, does the vocabulary used by these early texts have ties with the prayer texts we know today?

In the first section we will group together the very earliest sources of interest to our study. We will then classify the texts according to their geographical origin: Africa, Rome, Milan and Gaul.

Here are the principal studies that provide a list of relevant passages, both closely associated with and quite removed from the *oratio fidelium*[1]:

F. Probst, *Liturgie der drei ersten christlichen Jahrhunderte*, Tübingen, 1870.

______ *Liturgie des vierten Jahrhunderts und deren Reform*, Munster, 1893.

______ *Die abendländische Messe vom fünften bis zum achten Jahrhundert*, Munster, 1896.

E. von der Goltz, *Das Gebet in der ältesten Christenheit*, Leipzig, 1901.

R. H. Connolly, *Liturgical Prayers of Intercession. I. The Good Friday Orationes Sollemnes*, JTS, vol. 21 (1920), 219–232.

F. Cabrol, 'Litanies', in DACL 9, 1540–71.

L. Biehl, *Das liturgische Gebet für Kaiser und Reich*, Paderborn, 1937.

V. L. Kennedy, *The Saints of the Canon of the Mass*, Rome, 1963.

O. Dietz, 'Das allgemeine Kirchengebet', in *Leiturgia*, vol. 2, Cassel, 1955, 417–451.

C. A. Bouman, *Communis oratio*, Utrecht-Anvers, 1959.

---

1 We must also add the *Reliquiae liturgicae vetustissimae* of Dom Cabrol and Dom Leclercq, vol. 1, Paris, 1900–1902, which, at pp. 52–271 gives the liturgical 'fragments' drawn from the writings of the Fathers.

Amongst the numerous articles on pastoral liturgy that have appeared since the Second Vatican Council, see A. Nocent, *La prière commune des fidèles*, NRT, vol. 86 (1964), 948–964.

G. G. Willis, *Essays in Early Roman Liturgy*, London, 1964, 1–48.
Consilium, *De oratione communi seu fidelium*, Vatican City, 1965.

Section One

The Earliest Evidence

A Jewish Origin?

Nowadays it is fashionable in the world of liturgists to seek Jewish sources for Christian euchology. In this, liturgical research is only taking its cue from exegesis which, having pointed out the Hellenistic influences on the New Testament, prefers today to show its Jewish roots. Thus the relationship between the Universal Prayer and the Eighteen Benedictions has been frequently highlighted. These Benedictions (*šemonèh — 'èśréh berākôt*) together with the *ŝema'Israel*, constitute the principal part of Jewish daily prayer. Recited three times a day, it is also known as '*amidāh*, because it was held above everything else, *tephillāh*, prayer (par excellence).[1]

Should we see here the ancestor or archetype of the *oratio fidelium*? C. A. Bouman[2] has made the best study of the question. The first thing he notes is the fluctuations in the place that this prayer has occupied. Recent rabbinical books have placed it after the readings and the profession of faith (*ŝema'Israel*). If it had been there in the 1st and 2nd centuries, the parallel with the Christian synaxe would be perfect, but early evidence suggests that, in the morning of the Sabbath and festival days, an ancient form of *šemonèh — 'èśréh* preceded the readings. The content of the Eighteen Benedictions was equally varied: different sources from the period indicate this or that particular intention. But the professor from Nijmegen is convinced that the 'Eighteen' have exercised an influence on ancient Christian prayer, notably on chapters 9–10 of the Didache and on the first Letter of Clement of Rome. We shall return to this later.

We do not have the competence necessary to make a judgement in this very specialized domain. However, we think that we should exercise caution in making connections in this regard. Certainly, the Eighteen Benedictions form a kind of litany; the faithful respond each time with *Amen*. But the literary genre seems to us to be very different from that of the Universal Prayer: the 'Eighteen' are, above all, blessings, giving praise to God. Prayers of intercession are attached to them, but they do not constitute the basis of the prayer as is the case with an *oratio fidelium*. Moreover, on the Sabbath day praying for material needs was not

1 There are various versions of these in Hänggi and Pahl (1968), 41–51, or in Bonsirven (1955), 2; see also Bouyer (1968), 70–78.

2 Bouman (1959), 6–12.

permitted. These benedictions seem to us more like *preces* composed of scriptural verses than the Universal Prayer.

In this regard we have consulted Abbot Hryby, a specialist in rabbinic literature. He is skeptical about these links, notably because Christianity developed in strong opposition to Judaism. Proof would only be possible if we were to find texts with the same construction and using the same vocabulary. Without that, he suggests, any superficial similarities must be regarded with suspicion.

Since such texts do not exist, it is not possible to locate the origin of the Universal Prayer in the Jewish liturgy with any precision.

The New Testament

Must we, then, look for its provenance in the New Testament? The principal text is that from the first chapter of Timothy:

T 1 First of all, then, I urge that supplications, prayers, intercessions and thanksgivings be made for everyone, for kings and all who are in high positions, so that we may lead a quiet and peaceable life in all godliness and dignity.[3]

We certainly do not claim that in making this recommendation the author of the Letter to Timothy instituted the Universal Prayer in the technical sense of this term; that would simply be impossible, considering the embryonic state of Christian worship in that period. We cite this passage here because the entire tradition has made reference to it and seen in it the scriptural basis for its practice. Commentators on the Epistle are all of the opinion that we should not seek a particular meaning for the four terms used to describe the prayer, except perhaps the last one (thanksgiving). They point out that Jewish piety was familiar with prayer for the authorities, even if they were pagan (Baruch 1:11). What seems to them more characteristically Christian is the universal nature of this prayer ('for all people') and that this is founded on the universality of salvation, clearly affirmed in verse 4.

Less eloquent, but frequently cited nevertheless by the Fathers in connection with the Universal Prayer, is this passage from the Sermon on the Mount:

T 2 But I say to you, 'Love your enemies and pray for those who persecute you'.[4]

It is impossible to see there any reference to a particular liturgical rite; the verse indicates only one dimension of Christian prayer.

3 1 Tim 2:1–2: Παρακαλῶ οὖν πρῶτον πάντων ποιεῖσθαι δεήσεις, προσευχάς, ἐντεύξεις, εὐχαριστίας, ὑπὲρ πάντων ἀνθρώπων, ὑπὲρ βασιλέων καὶ πάντων τῶν ἐν ὑπεροχῇ ὄντων, ἵνα ἤρεμον καὶ ἡσύχιον βίον διάγωμεν ἐν πάσῃ εὐσεβείᾳ καὶ σεμνότητι.

4 Mt 5:44: Ἐγὼ δὲ λέγω ὑμῖν, ἀγαπᾶτε τοὺς ἐχθροὺς ὑμῶν καὶ προσεύχεσθε ὑπὲρ τῶν διωκόντων ὑμᾶς.

Clement of Rome

The first text that we come across after those two scripture passages is of great interest. It comes to us from the most venerable Christian antiquity, since, dating from around the year 96, it is scarcely more recent than some of the New Testament texts. But more than that, it provides the actual text of a long prayer of thanksgiving and supplication. We are speaking, of course, of the 'great prayer' from the letter of Clement of Rome to the Corinthians.[5]

Undoubtedly this passage provides us with an example of early Christian prayer, but the context does not give us any indication as to its use. Most experts agree however that here we are in the presence, if not of a liturgical prayer itself, at least of a prayer strongly influenced by liturgical usage in the early Roman community.[6] They also like to identify Jewish expressions and themes and to see it as a Christianisation of the synagogal prayer. Indeed they frequently compare it to the *šemonèh — 'èśréh* or the prayer of the Eighteen Benedictions.[7]

---

5 Clement of Rome, *Letter to the Corinthians*, 59, 2–61, 3, ed. F. X. Funk, (1901), or Jaubert (SC 167), 194–201. Eng. tr. Johnson (2009), vol. 1, 44.

6 The study recently dedicated to this letter by O. Knoch (1964), (with extensive bibliography), deals with our letter on pages 56–63. The author points out that the spirit of this passage differs from the rest of the letter in its more mystical character and in a vocabulary taken from the Hellenistic synagogue.

Here is what S. Bäumer (1905), 432, wrote about this 'great prayer': 'What we know about this prayer with any certainty is that it can, perhaps, be considered as a more or less textual repetition of a liturgical prayer, whose precise place in the liturgy is known with little exactitude. In any case, it is one of the primitive formulas, if not the primitive formula, that serves as the basis for the προσφώνησις ὑπὲρ τῶν πιστῶν of the Apostolic Constitutions'.

L. Duchesne (1925), 51, saw in this text 'a piece with obvious liturgical character'. 'One cannot claim without doubt the reproduction of a consecrated formula, but it is a good example of the style of the Solemn Prayer', he writes.

T. Schermann (1915), vol. 2, 452, went as far as suggesting that this letter was read at the synagogue and that the 'great prayer' occupied the place of the Universal Prayer, after the reading. This theory was taken up again by R. Knopf (1920), 138, after he had already proposed a similar although less precise idea, in the commentary accompanying the edition of the letter published in 1899 (*Der erste Clemensbrief untersucht und herausgegeben*, TU 20, 1, Leipzig, 1899, 188). Similarly, L. Clerici (1966), 125, seeks to find there an echo of an intercessory prayer used in the Church of Rome.

7 For comparison with our passage see W. Osterley (1925), 125–147. A. Baumstark (1958), 74, note 4. considers that 'long quotations of the most primitive Roman formulary of this venerable prayer can be found in chapters 59–61'. He also links the prayer of intercession of Christian worship with the synagogal rite. (see p. 45).

C. Bouman, *Communis oratio*, (1959), 10, speaks of our prayer as a 'Christianised tephillāh'. As we have noted, this author strongly insists on Jewish sources for the *oratio fidelium*. In the introduction to her recent publication, Annie Jaubert (1971), 40, believes that 'it is not possible to assign a precise literary origin to these twists and turns. Written and transmitted in a living and moving environment, they reveal only their Jewish roots. One should not be surprised, then, to discover formularies related to the synagogal prayer of the Eighteen Benedictions'.

Truth to tell, these indications do not allow us to draw very much from it for our purpose, since we cannot pinpoint this prayer with any accuracy in the structure of a liturgical celebration. We will simply take note of the numerous comparisons indicated by Funk between this text and subsequent liturgies, which seem to have drawn on them. In particular we cite the expressions αἰτησόμεθα ἐκτενῆ τὴν δέησιν καὶ ἱκεσίαν ποιούμενοι, ὅπως ...[8] and ἀξιοῦμέν σε, δέσποτα...[9] which can be found in numerous Eastern litanies; and of course, we note the series of intentions.[10]

In summary, this prayer, influenced in both its themes and formulation by the Hellenistic synagogue, provides evidence for us that pleas were made for the needs of all people, especially civil authorities;[11] Whatever its exact function, it can be considered as a link between 1Tim 2:1–2 and Justin Martyr's descriptions of the Eucharist.

The Didache

Ought we to mention the Didache here? A recent book[12] has sought to find in it the source of the liturgical prayer of intercession. Despite the fact that the thesis may be somewhat contrived, the study does contain some interesting elements. Let us begin by citing the text in question:

T 3 10, 5: Lord, remember your Church; deliver it from all evil and perfect it in your love. Gather this sanctified Church from the four winds into the kingdom you have prepared for it. For to you belong the power and the glory forever.[13]

Clerici notes (p. 48 ff.) that here is found for the first time the famous 'remember' (μνήσθητι), the typical formulary of all of the commemorations of subsequent liturgies. He points out the biblical significance of this. This cry is not merely, 'Do not forget us'; it evokes much more than a simple reminder or memory. It provokes God to act, to intervene in history, in other words, to reveal Godself. This formula was common in Jewish prayer;[14] the Christian liturgy thus assumes

---

8 Clement, *First Epistle to the Corinthians*, 59, 2: 'We request with continual prayer and supplication, that...'.

9 Clement, *First Epistle to the Corinthians*, 59, 4: 'We ask you, O Lord...'.

10 Clement, *First Epistle to the Corinthians*, 59, 4–60.4.

11 Concerning this see Mikat (1973), 455–471.

12 L. Clerici, *Einsammlung der Zerstretuen*, (LQF 44) Munster, 1966.

13 Didache 10, 5, ed. F. X. Funk (1901), 24: Μνήσθητι, κύριε, τῆς ἐκκλησίας σου τοῦ ῥύσασθαι αὐτὴν ἀπὸ παντὸς πονηροῦ καὶ τελειῶσαι αὐτὴν ἐν τῇ ἀγάπῃ σου, καὶ σύναξον αὐτὴν ἀπὸ τῶν τεσσάρων ἀνέμων, τὴν ἁγιασθεῖσαν, εἰς τὴν σὴν βασιλείαν, ἣν ἡτοίμασας αὐτῇ· ὅτι σοῦ ἐστιν ἡ δύναμις καὶ ἡ δόξα εἰς τοὺς αἰῶνας. Eng. tr. Johnson (2009), vol. 1, 38.

14 There are 37 examples in the Old Testament of μνήσθητι used in a prayer addressed either to God or to a human person, of which eight occur in the Psalms, where they are always addressed to God.

in its turn all the heritage of the Old Testament. It reveals its continuity with the Jewish liturgy, and Christianises it at the same time by transforming a nationalistic hope into an eschatological one. In the final part of his book, the author studies the traces of this prayer for the Church in the intercessions in the anaphoras of later liturgies.

This fine text cannot be used as evidence of the existence of a Universal Prayer in the *Didache*. It is part of a literary group which, despite the difficulties of interpretation, directs us towards intercessions within anaphoras rather than towards a Prayer of the Faithful.[15] Let us think of it, beyond an intercession for the Church, as the first usage of μνήσθητι and the semantic richness it contains.

Polycarp of Smyrna (*c.* 85–*c.* 170)

The following are the recommendations that Polycarp, bishop of Smyrna, addressed to the Philippians (between 110 and 135):

T 4 12, 3: Pray for all the saints. Pray also for the emperors, for authorities and princes, and for those who persecute you and hate you, and for the enemies of the cross; thus the fruit that you bear will be visible to all, and you will be perfect in him.[16]

These words reflect the concern of the Church to pray for different classes of people. This is one of the many lists of intentions that we will come across throughout our exploration. Note the reference to 1Tim 2:1–2, the classic text that recommends praying for kings and those in positions of authority, just as at Mt 5:44–45. The context does not provide us with any additional information.

This universal dimension of prayer is found in the *Martyrdom of Polycarp* (*c.* 170):

T 5 5, 1: night and day he used to pray for all people and for churches all over the world, as was his custom.[17]

T 6 8, 1:When he had finally ceased his prayer, in which he recalled all those that he had ever met, big and small, famous or obscure, and all the catholic Church spread throughout the world, it was time to leave, and they put him on a donkey and led him into the town…[18]

15 See the commentary of Audet (1958), 372–433.

16 Polycarp, *Epistle to the Philippians*, 12, 3, ed. and tr. Camelot (SC 10), 220–21. Original text (the only remaining translation of this passage is in Latin): *Pro omnibus sanctis orate. Orate etiam pro regibus et potestatibus et principibus atque pro persequentibus et odientibus vos et pro inimicis crucis, ut fructus vester manifestus sit in omnibus, ut sitis in illo perfecti.*

We note the similar expressions in the two texts:

- προσευχόμενος περὶ πάντων — μνημονεύσας ἁπάντων
- τῶν κατὰ τὴν οἰκουμένην ἐκκλησιῶν — τῆς κατὰ τὴν οἰκουμένην καθολικῆς ἐκκλησίας

However, nothing tells us that these formularies were used in worship and in fact the reference is expressly to personal prayer. In this regard, though, let us note once and for all that from a methodological point of view we refuse to exclude from this patristic record of the *oratio fidelium* any testimony of personal prayer, for this can certainly reflect liturgical prayer and incorporate the formularies of public prayer. The value of this remark seems to us to be corroborated by the fact that we are always in the presence of literary texts that are not necessarily literally faithful to the prayer of the person they honour, but were able to shape the prayer in a liturgical mould. Besides, the earliest writers were unaware of the modern distinction between liturgical and non-liturgical prayer; even the idea of 'liturgical formularies' remained imprecise.

Aristides

As evidence of the ancient *oratio fidelium*, von der Goltz[19] cites a passage from the *Apology* of Aristides, the Athenian philosopher of the first part of the second century. In chapter 16 we read that it is thanks to the prayer of Christians that the world subsists, and in chapter 17 Aristides says Christians pray for their own conversion.[20]

It is not on such testimony that we would want to base our conclusions.

Justin (*c.* 165)

The most important source for this chapter is Justin Martyr. He is the first to affirm for us the existence of the *oratio fidelium* in giving us a description of the liturgy. Here is what he writes toward the middle of the 2nd century:

---

17 Martyrdom of Polycarp, 5, 1: … νύκτα καὶ ἡμέραν οὐδὲν ἕτερον ποιῶν ἢ προσευχόμενος περὶ πάντων καὶ τῶν κατὰ τὴν οἰκουμένην ἐκκλησιῶν, ὅπερ ἦν σύνηθες αὐτῷ. ed. and tr. Camelot (SC 10), 248–49. Eng. tr. based on Lake (1912), 299.

18 Martyrdom of Polycarp, 8, 1: Ἐπεὶ δέ ποτε κατέπαυσεν τὴν προσευχήν, μνημονεύσας ἁπάντων καὶ τῶν πώποτε συμβεβηκότων αὐτῷ, μικρῶν τε καὶ μεγάλων, ἐνδόξων τε καὶ ἀδόξων, καὶ πάσης τῆς κατὰ τὴν οἰκουμένην καθολικῆς ἐκκλησίας, τῆς ὥρας ἐλθούσης τοῦ ἐξιέναι, ὄνῳ καθίσαντες αὐτὸν ἤγαγον εἰς τὴν πόλιν, … ed. and tr. Camelot (SC 10), 252–53.

19 von der Goltz (1901), 333.

20 Aristides, *Apology*, 16–17, ed. Hennecke (1893), 41–42.

T 7 First Apology, 65, 1–3: But after we have washed the one who has believed and has assented to our teaching, we bring him to where those who are called brethren have assembled. In this way we may offer prayer in common both for ourselves and for those who have received illumination, and for people everywhere, doing so with all our hearts so that we may be deemed worthy, now that we have learnt the truth, and by our works found to be good citizens and keepers of the commandments. In this way we may attain everlasting salvation. When the prayers have concluded, we greet one another with a kiss. Then, bread and cup containing water and wine are brought to him who presides over the assembly.[21]

And again:

T 8 First Apology, 67, 3–5: the day that we call Sunday, all who live in the cities or the country gather together in the one place; the memoirs of the apostles and the writings of the prophets are read for as long as time allows. When the reader has finished, the one who is presiding gives a discourse to instruct and encourage the imitation of these fine teachings. Next, we all stand and pray aloud together. Then, as I have already said, once the prayer is finished, the bread is brought forward…[22]

This time, we are on solid ground: after the readings, the Christians stand for common prayers. Three intentions are nominated: for ourselves, for the baptised (which means for a current need) and for everyone; these petitions are introduced by the ὑπέρ characteristic of the diaconal litanies of the East.[23] Next, the gifts are brought forward. Note that in both these passages Justin Martyr uses the same terms κοινὰς εὐχάς and κοινῇ … εὐχάς. However, we can't make too much of this parallel, for in 67, 5 he uses εὐχή to refer to the Eucharistic prayer, an ambiguity of vocabulary that we find through the long history of the Universal Prayer.[24] Given the parallelism between T 8 and T 7 (in which baptism seems to replace the function of the readings of T 8) one can clearly say that here,

---

21 Justin Martyr, *First Apology* 65, 1–3, ed. and tr. Pautigny, 139. Here is the principal passage in Greek: κοινὰς εὐχὰς ποιησόμενοι ὑπέρ. Eng. tr. Johnson (2009), vol. 1, 67, with minor amendments by J. O'Brien.

22 First Apology, 67, 3–5, ed. and tr. Pautigny, 142: ἔπειτα ἀνιστάμεθα κοινῇ πάντες καὶ εὐχὰς πέμπομεν. It would be more exact to translate: 'then we all stand up together and pray aloud'.

23 For example, that of the Liturgy of St James, in Br, 36–37.

24 Do the terms κοιναὶ εὐχαί form a technical expression to describe the Universal Prayer? Lampe's dictionary indicates that this is but one example of the phrase, but it is particularly interesting for our purposes. It occurs in a passage of John Chrysostom: 'That is why, in the mysteries, we exchange the kiss of peace with one another, so that, many, we become one; and we offer common prayers for the non-initiated, beseeching for the sick, for the fruits of the universe, for the land and for the sea. Do you know the power of love?' In Greek, the principal passage is the following: καὶ ἐπὶ τῶν ἀμυήτων κοινὰς ποιούμεθα τὰς εὐχάς, λιτανεύοντες ὑπὲρ νοσούντων. καὶ τῶν καρπῶν τῆς οἰκουμένης, καὶ γῆς καὶ θαλάττης. Homily 78, 4 on John, PG 59, 426.

together with the kiss of peace, the prayers form the beginning of the Liturgy of the Eucharist.

Moreover, T 7 seems to be inspired by 1 Tim 2:1–4, which, after recommending prayers, continues: 'This is what is right and pleasing to God our Saviour, who desires all people to be saved, and to come to the knowledge of the truth'. The community to whom Justin is witnessing wants to respond to this apostolic recommendation and arrive, through the prayers, at knowledge of the truth and eternal salvation. Even though there is not a literal quotation, the theme is the same.

In the *Dialogue with Trypho*, Justin attests that Christians in fact pray for all people. To the false Christians he writes:

T 9 *First Dialogue* 35, 8: 'This is why we pray for you and for all those who are our enemies, in order that, changing your mind and agreeing with us, you may not blaspheme ... Jesus Christ'.[25]

And to the Jews:

T 10 *Second Dialogue* 96, 3: And beyond all that, we pray for you so that Christ may have mercy on you.[26]

And again to the Jews:

T 11 *Second Dialogue* 133, 6: In addition.to all this, we pray for you and for all people without exception, as our Christ and Lord has taught us to do, since he commanded us to pray even for our enemies, to love those who hate us and to bless those who curse us.[27]

And finally to public authorities:

T 12 *First Apology* 17, 3: We adore God alone, but in other things we gladly obey you, recognizing you as masters and leaders of people, and praying to God for you that with your kingly power you might also exercise wisdom and reason.[28]

---

25 *Dialogue with Trypho* 1, 35, 8, ed. and tr. Archambault (1909), vol. 1, 160–61: Διὸ καὶ ὑπὲρ ὑμῶν καὶ ὑπὲρ τῶν ἄλλων ἁπάντων ἀνθρώπων τῶν ἐχθραινόντων ἡμῖν εὐχόμεθα, ἵνα μεταγνόντες σὺν ἡμῖν μὴ βλασφημῆτε ... χριστὸν Ἰησοῦν.

26 *Dialogue with Trypho* 2, 96, 3, ed. and tr. Archambault (1909), vol. 2, 106–07: καὶ πρὸς τούτοις πᾶσιν εὐχόμεθα ὑπὲρ ὑμῶν, ἵνα ἐλεηθῆτε ὑπὸ τοῦ Χριστοῦ.

27 *Dialogue with Trypho* 2, 133, 6, ed. and tr. Archambault (1909), vol. 2, 278–281: πάντων ἡμῶν εὐχομένων ὑπὲρ ὑμῶν καὶ ὑπὲρ πάντων ἁπλῶς ἀνθρώπων, ὡς ὑπὸ τοῦ Χριστοῦ ἡμῶν καὶ κυρίου ποιεῖν ἐδιδάχθημεν, παραγγείλαντος ἡμῖν εὔχεσθαι καὶ ὑπὲρ τῶν ἐχθρῶν καὶ ἀγαπᾶν τοὺς μισοῦντας, καὶ εὐλογεῖν τοὺς καταρωμένους.

Here we see the implementation of the New Testament recommendations.

In short, Justin is the first ecclesiastical writer who provides us with certainty of the existence of the *oratio fidelium*, placed between the readings and the carrying forward of the gifts. In it prayers are offered for Christians, for all people and their concrete needs, and no doubt, as random extracts from his writings attest, for false Christians, for the Jews, for enemies and for civil authorities.

Athenagoras

Around 177, the Athenian Christian philosopher Athenagoras wrote an Apology entitled *Supplication for the Christians* to Marcus Aurelius and his son Commodus. Here is its conclusion:

T 13 Indeed, who have more right to obtain what they ask for than those who like us pray for your authority, so that you might receive the empire by succession — as is perfectly just — son from father; and that your power might achieve increase and addition, all men being subject to your authority? That is to our advantage too, so that we may lead a calm and peaceful life, and may ourselves carry out willingly everything commanded of us.[29]

The final allusion to 1 Tim2:1–2 is even clearer than with Polycarp (T 4), since the expression 'so that we may lead a calm and peaceful life' is a literal quotation. However, Athanagoras does not use the preposition ὑπέρ, which is found in St Paul and which will soon be characteristic of all prayer intentions, but περί, used also in the New Testament with the same meaning. Are we here in the presence of an allusion to the Universal Prayer? It is rather difficult to establish. What is certain is that the community that Athenagoras frequents, faithful to the prescriptions of the Apostle, has the custom of praying for the emperor. We can even presume that this prayer extended to others besides the emperor, but since this work was addressed to Augustus and his son, there was no need to mention them. We note that neither Ubaldi nor Bardy give any thought in the presentation of this text to the Universal Prayer, but both refer to other passages of the Fathers concerning prayer for the emperor.

---

28 *First Apology* 17, 3, ed. and tr. Pautigny, 36–37: Ὅθεν θεὸν μὲν μόνον προσκυνοῦμεν, ὑμῖν δὲ πρὸς τὰ ἄλλα χαίροντες ὑπηρετοῦμεν, βασιλεῖς καὶ ἄρχοντας ἀνθρώπων ὁμολογοῦντες καὶ εὐχόμενοι μετὰ τῆς βασιλικῆς δυνάμεως καὶ σώφρονα τὸν λογισμὸν ἔχοντας ὑμᾶς εὑρεθῆναι.

29 *Supplication for the Christians*, 37, tr. Bardy (SC 3), 170: Τίνες γὰρ καὶ δικαιότεροι ὧν δέονται τυχεῖν ἢ οἵτινες περὶ μὲν τῆς ἀρχῆς τῆς ὑμετέρας εὐχόμεθα, ἵνα παῖς μὲν παρὰ πατρὸς κατὰ τὸ δικαιότατον διαδέχησθε τὴν βασιλείαν, αὔξην δὲ καὶ ἐπίδοσιν καὶ ἡ ἀρχὴ ὑμῶν, πάντων ὑποχειρίων γιγνομένων, λαμβάνῃ; τοῦτο δ'ἐστὶ καὶ πρὸς ἡμῶν, ὅπως ἤρεμον καὶ ἡσύχιον βίον διάγοιμεν, αὐτοὶ δέ πάντα τὰ κεκελευσμένα προθύμως ὑπηρετοῖμεν. ed. Ubaldi (1933), 166–67.

Among the texts frequently cited by authors and fitting into this section is a passage from the *Martyrdom of Apollonius*, a noble Roman who died around 183–185.[30] This text certainly speaks of prayer, but it would be a mistake to pretend that it is describing the Prayer of the Faithful.

Conclusion

What conclusion can be drawn from this first section? Thanks to Justin, we are certain that at least in Rome around 150 the *oratio fidelium* existed. Does it have the long and fairly free form that Clement speaks of around years earlier? We simply don't know. What we do know is that Christians obeyed the prescriptions of 1 Tim 2:1–2, to which three of our texts (T 4, T 7, T 13) allude, and that they prayed not only for the Church (T 3, T 5, T 6) and for themselves (T 4 and T 7), but also for the emperors and the authorities (T 4, T 12, T 13), for the Jews (T 10 and T 11), for false Christians (T 9), and even for their enemies and persecutors, as Christ asked (Mt 5:44–45, cited by T 4); in short, for all people (T 5, T 6 and T 7).

But do all these petitions originate from the Prayer of the Faithful? There is no convincing evidence. It is certain that from its origins the Church has known prayers of petition, even if we are not sure that these formed from the beginning what is called the *oratio fidelium* to which Justin attests.

30 *Martyrdom of Apollonius*, 6 and 8, ed. Klette (1897), 96 and 98.

Section Two

The Church of Africa

We will begin by examining the texts of the African authors for the simple reason that they are the first in the West to speak of our prayer, following those we have called 'the first witnesses'.

We will consider in order the works of Tertullian, Cyprian, Arnobius, Marius Victorinus and Augustine.[1]

Tertullian (*c.* 160–† after 220)

No text of Tertullian[2] speaks directly of the *oratio fidelium*; even less does he actually use the phrase. However, putting together the clues, we are convinced that at that time, the Church of Carthage knew the Universal Prayer. Our argument rests on two principal points: the way in which Tertullian describes the unfolding of the liturgical celebration, and the series of prayer intentions that it included.

1. The Structure of the Celebration

There are three passages for our consideration:

T 1 *Apology* 39, 2–5: Coimus in coetum et congregationem facimus, ut ad Deum quasi manu facta precationibus ambiamus. Haec vis Deo grata est. Oramus etiam
pro ministeriis eorum ac potestatibus,
pro statu saeculi,
pro rerum quiete,
pro mora finis.
Coimus ad litterarum divinarum commemorationem,
Ibidem etiam exhortationes, castigationes et censura divina
Praesident probati Quique viri[3]

---

1 The African liturgy has been the subject of several comprehensive studies. We refer to: F. Probst, *Liturgie der drei ersten christlichen Jahrhunderte*, Tübingen, 1879, and *Liturgie des vierten Jahrhunderts und deren Reform*, Munster, 1893, 272–307, works that seem to have served as sources for many succeeding writers; F. Cabrol, *Afrique (Liturgie anténicéenne d l')*, DACL, 1, 591–619 and 620–657; W. C. Bishop, *The African Rite*, JTS, vol. 13 (1912), 250–277, which from p. 270 onwards cites very important texts; A. Fortescue, *La messe*, Paris, 1921, 51–63.

2 An in-depth study of the liturgy as reflected in the writings of Tertullian has been made by E. Dekkers, *Tertullianus en de geschiedenis der liturgie*, Brussels-Amsterdam, 1947.

T 2 *De praescriptione haereticorum*, 41, 2: Inprimis quis catechumenus, quis fidelis incertum est, pariter adeunt, pariter audiunt, pariter orant.[4]

T 3 *De Anima*, 9, 4: Est hodie soror apud nos revelationum charismata sortita, quas in ecclesia inter dominica sollemnia per ecstasin in spiritu patitur. ... Iamvero prout Scripturae leguntur aut psalmi canuntur aut allocutiones proferuntur aut petitiones delegantur, ita inde materiae visionibus subministrantur.[5]

Although this dates from the Montanist period, this last text appears to us to be decisive. Whether *dominica sollemnia* describes a complete Eucharist or not,[6] it is only with great difficulty that the expression *petitiones delegantur* can be understood to refer to the great Eucharistic Prayer. As this is a fairly accurate description we have no fear in recognizing it as the *oratio fidelium*.

The *pariter orant* of *De Praescriptione* (T 2) may possibly refer to the anaphora. Considering the expressions that precede it, we would be open to including it in a wider context that incorporates the Universal Prayer and the Eucharistic Prayer. We note that mention of catechumens and faithful assists us in identifying the 'prayer' that they are offering together (*oratio fidelium* or Eucharistic prayer), since in the Great Church the catechumens were sent out just before the Prayer of the Faithful. Their participation in this latter, even in the assemblies of the heretics, would have been as unusual as their presence during the Anaphora.

Fr Dekkers sees in the passage from the *Apologeticum* (T 1) a detailed description of the synaxe,[7] which would have had the following structure: Common Prayer, reading from Scripture, exhortations and reprimands for the community,

---

3 *Apology*, 39, 2–5 (PL 1, 532; CC 1, 150) (written late 197): 'We gather as one body and congregation so that we might wrestle with God in our prayers, a violence pleasing to him. We pray also for emperors, for their ministers and for those in power, for the state of the world, for peace, and for the end to be delayed. We meet together to read the sacred scriptures. Also exhortations, reprimands and holy censure takes place there. Presiding over us are the elders who have been proven' Eng.tr. Johnson (2009), vol. 1, 117.

4 *De praescriptione haereticorum*, 41, 2 (PL 2, 68; CC 1, 221) (written *c.* 200): 'To begin with, it is not certain who is a catechumen or who is a member of the faithful; both approach; both listen, both pray'. Eng.tr. Johnson (2009), vol. 1, 118.

5 *De anima*, 9, 4 (PL 2, 700–701; CC 2, 792) (Written *c.* 210–211): 'At present we have amongst us a sister who has been allotted various gifts of revelation. These she experiences in the Spirit during the Sunday solemnities in the church, by falling into ecstasy. Whether it be during the reading of the Scriptures, during the chanting of psalms, while sermons are being given, or while petitions are being made, all these are occasions when she experiences visions'. Eng.tr. Johnson (2009), vol. 1, 141.

6 Cf. Dölger (1940), vol. 6, 108–117. Based on later literature, notably the *Acta Sancti Saturni* (*c.* 300), the author shows that *dominicum* does not have the sense of the current term 'dominical', but is the equivalent of the genitive *Domini*. More precisely, the substantive *dominicum*, just like *dominica sollemnia*, describes the Eucharistic celebration.

Dekkers (1954, CC 1), 46 follows Dölger and notes that if the Eucharist is not explicitly mentioned by means of a specific expression, alongside the readings, psalms, preaching and prayers, it is because the anaphora as such does not offer matter on the subject and therefore had no reason to be mentioned in this context. We note that Dölger's argument is based on much later texts.

7 E. Dekkers, (1954, CC 1), 23–24.

and Collect, all under the direction of the *seniores probati*. It seems to us that this interpretation does not take sufficient account of the literary genre of the *Apologeticum*. This work is entirely a response to objections by detractors of Christianity. It does not pretend to give Christians a detailed description of the liturgy, but rather refutes arguments and demonstrates that Christian worship includes many good things, notably prayer for the emperor. The first sentence of no. 2 describes, it seems to us, the general prayer of worship; the second sentence has in mind the Prayer of the Faithful that this worship entails. But in our view the different paragraphs of chapter 39 do not describe a chronological unfolding of the celebration. In other words, until proven otherwise, we do not believe that the liturgy of Carthage began with a prayer of intercession: this text offers too fragile a basis to build such a hypothesis.

We might add that sometimes the following text is cited as providing a trace of the Prayer of the Faithful:

T 4 *De Oratione*, 18, 1: Alia iam consuetudo invaluit: ieiunantes habita oratione cum fratribus subtrahunt osculum pacis, quod est signaculum orationis ... Quae oratio cum divortio sancti osculi integra?[8]

For N. M. Denis-Boulet, for example, 'it is most probably referring to the *oratio fidelium*',[9] followed, in the time of Tertullian, by the kiss of peace, which preceded the Canon, as per Justin (Section One, T 7), the Apostolic Tradition[10] and in the East. But is this interpretation valid?

The context clearly shows us that it is a question of public prayer: *habita oratione cum fratribus*; and further on Tertullian accuses this custom of being contradictory to the Lord's teaching to fast in secret. If you have reason to flout this commandment, he continues, do so in your home, although even there it is not possible to hide entirely your ascetic practice. Whenever it is possible, keep these practices secret and remember the precept: in this way you honour the rule in public and the custom in the home.

You might think that Tertullian here alludes to worship and even precisely to the Prayer of the Faithful followed by the Kiss of Peace. Possibly, but due to lack of precise liturgical indications in the context we would not dare to claim that.

2. The Series of Prayer Intentions

Here we have to distinguish between apologetic writings and doctrinal or ascetical treatises.

---

8 *De Oratione*, 18, 1 (PL 1, 1280–1; CC 1, 267): 'Another custom has developed, namely, that at the end of the prayer those who are fasting refrain from the kiss of peace, which is the seal of prayer. ... Is any prayer complete when separated from the holy kiss?' Eng.tr. Johnson (2009), vol. 1, 133.

9 N. M. Denis-Boulet, in Martimort(1965), 435.

10 Botte (1963), 54–55.

In *Apologeticum* and *Ad Scapulam* Tertullian continually returns to the same argument: Christian prayer for the emperor is superior because it is addressed not to impotent idols but to the true God who is capable of fulfilling it, and is master even of the emperor. There is no other purpose here than to pray for the good of the state and its leader — which is what the literary genre calls for — but that does not exclude the possibility that Christians also prayed for the Church and its members, as is attested in other works of his. Let us check out some of these passages:

T 5 *Apology*, 30, 1 and 4:
1. Nos enim pro salute imperatorum Deum invocamus aeternum, Deum verum, Deum vivum, quem et ipsi imperatores propitium sibi praeter ceteros malunt.
4. ... precantes sumus semper pro omnibus imperatoribus,
vitam illis prolixam,
imperium securum,
domum totam,
exercitus fortes,
senatum fidelem,
populum probum,
orbem quietum,
quaecumque hominis et Caesaris vota sunt.[11]

T 6 *Apology*, 39, 2: Oramus etiam
pro imperatoribus,
pro ministeriis eorum ac potestatibus,
pro statu saeculi,
pro rerum quiete,
pro morta finis (= T 1)

The passages generally quoted from *Ad Scapulum* (2, 6–9) have, according to us, only a very weak link with the *oratio fidelium* and vouchsafe only that Christians pray for the emperor.

In the dogmatic or ascetic treatises written for Christians, Tertullian supplies us with more detailed texts. In addition to the passages already cited, there is an extract from *De Oratione*:

11 *Apology* 30, 1 and 4 (PL 1, 504; CC 1, 141): 'We pray for the safety of our emperors to the eternal God, to the true and living God, whose favour beyond that of all others they should prefer'. 4 'We pray unceasingly for all our rulers. We pray that they may have long life, that the empire might be secure, that the imperial household be safe, that armies be brave, that the senate be faithful, that the people be righteous, that the world be at peace, and for whatever the people and Caesar desire'. Eng.tr. Johnson (2009), vol. 1, 117. We note that in the following chapter of his book, Tertullian gives the grounds for these petitions: 'It is a precept for us ... to pray to God for our enemies and to seek the good of our persecutors ... But [Scripture] also explicitly and openly says, "Pray for kings and princes and authorities, so that you can live in harmony"'. Here we recognise the allusion to Mt 5:43–43 and 1 Tim 2:2.

T 7 *De Oratione*, 29, 2: Sed et retro oratio plagas irrogabat, fundebat hostium exercitus, imbrium utilia prohibebat. Nunc vero oratio iustitiae omnem iram Dei avertit, pro inimicis excubat, pro persequentibus supplicat. Mirum si aquas caelestes extorquere novit, quae potuit et ignes impetrare? Sola est oratio quae Deum vincit; sed Christus eam nihil mali voluit operari, omnem illi virtutem de bono contulit. Itaque nihil novit nisi
defunctorum animas de ipso mortis itinere revocare,
debiles reformare,
aegros remediare,
daemoniacos expiare,
claustra carceris aperire,
vincula innocentium solvere.
Eadem diluit delicta,
temptationes repellit,
persecutiones extinguit,
pusillanimos consolatur,
magnanimos oblectat,
peregrinantes deducit,
fluctus mitigat,
latrones obstupefacit,
alit pauperes,
regit divites,
lapsos erigit,
cadentes suspendit
stantes continet.[12]

Such a text, which already makes us think of later litanies,[13] describes the effects of prayer rather than the petitions themselves; but the two things are not so different.

12 *De Oratione*, 29, 2 (PL 1, 1303–4; CC 1, 274): 'But already in former times prayer brought on disasters, scattered enemy armies, prevented beneficial rain from falling. Now, however, righteous prayer turns aside the entire wrath of God, mounts a watch for enemies, makes supplication for persecutors. Is it surprising that it manages to obtain rain from the skies, since once it was able to draw down fire from them? It is prayer alone that conquers God. But Christ willed that it would cause nothing of evil: he has conferred upon it all his power for good. It knows nothing apart from calling the souls of the dead back from the path of death, straightening the crippled, healing the sick, releasing those possessed, opening the gates of prisons, unbinding the chains of the innocent. It also diminishes faults, repels temptations, extinguishes persecutions, consoles the weak of heart, delights the magnanimous, leads back travellers, soothes the waves, astounds robbers, feeds the poor, governs the rich, raises up those who have fallen, supports those falling, confirms those who stand firm'. Tr.J.O'Brien.

13 Diercks (1947), 288, compares this text with the Solemn Prayers, notably with the fifth petition. He cites F. Probst (1870), 195, who reckons that Tertullian does not provide an arbitrary list here, but 'that his enumeration of prayer petitions and their effects is based on liturgical prayer'. ('*daß seiner Aufzählung der Gebetsobjekte und Gebetswirkungen das liturgische Gebet zu Grunde liegt*') We also note that Novatian cites among the prayer intentions the *lapsi* and the *stantes*, cf. infra, p. 80.

3. Conclusion

These lists, the expressions *oramus pro, precantes pro* from the *Apologeticum*, and the indications in the descriptions of the liturgy that put the Prayer of the Faithful in its traditional place, compel us to conclude that it is probable that the Church of Carthage at the end of the 2nd and beginning of the 3rd centuries was familiar with an *oratio fidelium*.

Even so, a survey of the vocabulary does not reveal any consistency. Only twice do we find the expression *pro salute imperatoris* (T 5 and *Ad Scapulam* 2, 9), and twice also a petition for peace (*orbem quietum* T 5, *pro rerum quiete* T 6). If *orare pro* is frequent, then *precari pro* (T 5) and *supplicare pro* (T 7) are equally so.

In short, the vocabulary used does not lead us to assume the existence of fixed formularies, which would appear to be implausible for the period. Only a comparison with later writers, especially Cyprian, would be likely to tell us more.

Cyprian of Carthage (200/210-† 258)

Cyprian's writings allow us to judge whether or not the Church of Carthage was familiar with the Universal Prayer in the mid-third century. The fact appears less clear to us than for Tertullian, although numerous authors cite as proof of its existence the famous phrase: 'Publica est nobis et communis oratio'. *Communis oratio* must 'evidently' mean the *oratio fidelium*! C. A. Bouman made this the title of the inaugural lecture he devoted to the topic following his appointment as professor at the University of Nijmigen in 1959.[14] The Constitution *De sacra liturgia* of the Second Vatican Council reinstated the custom of the Prayer of the Faithful but described it as *oratio communis seu fidelium*.[15] Even a superficial glance at the context clearly shows that this citation is not *ad rem*! The title alone of the passage from which the sentence is taken — *De dominica oratione* — should be enough to alert us to this. Here is the passage:

T 1 Ante omnia pacis doctor adque unitatis magister singillatim noluit et privatim precem fieri, ut quis cum precatur pro se tantum precetur. Non dicimus: Pater meus, qui es in caelis nec: Panem meum da mihi hodie, nec dimitti sibi tantum unusquisque debitum postulat aut in temptationem non inducatur adque a malo liberetur pro se solo rogat. Publica est nobis et communis oratio, et quando oramus, non pro uno sed pro populo toto oramus, quia totus populus unum sumus.[16]

---

14 Bouman (1959).

15 Constitution, *De sacra liturgia*, n. 53.

16 Cyprian, *De dominica oratione*, 8, CSEL 3, 1, 271; Eng. tr. Bindly (1904), 32–33: 'Before all things the Teacher of Peace, Master of unity is unwilling for prayer to be made singly and individually, teaching

Clearly, this passage is dealing with the Our Father; more broadly, it describes a characteristic of Christian prayer which is by nature public and communitarian. But we cannot therefore translate this 'public prayer' as 'Common Prayer' as many seem to do.

Therefore let us review the different texts cited by authors as evidence of the *oratio fidelium*, and let us include several others as well, as we try to determine the question of its existence.[17] In the first instance we will examine the texts that include a series of intentions (as we did with Tertullian). Then we will attempt to discover the structure of the celebration that the bishop of Carthage is describing for us. Next we will establish the existence of diptychs, and finally we will examine the meaning of the expression *in mente habere*.

1.The Lists of Intentions

1 In his treatise *Ad Demetrianum* (252), Cyprian explains to this pagan that Christians live in the hope of the Kingdom, but nevertheless:

T 2 20: 'Et tamen pro arcendis hostibus
et imbribus impetrandis
et vel auferendis vel termperandis adversis rogamus semper et preces fundimus et pro pace ac salute vestra, propitiantes et placantes Deum; diebus ac noctibus iugiter adque instanter oramus'.[18]

2 Letter 11, written by Cyprian around 250 to his brother priests and deacons, is entirely focused on prayer. Here is its conclusion

T 3 *Epistola* 11, 8: 'Nos tantum sine cessatione poscendi et cum fide accipiendi simplices et unianimes Dominum deprecemur, cum gemitu pariter et fletu

---

that he who prays is not to pray for himself alone. For we do not say, *My Father who art in heaven*, nor *Give me this day my bread*, nor does each one ask that his debt only be remitted, nor does he request for himself alone that he may not be led into temptation and may be delivered from the evil one. Prayer with us is public and common; and when we pray, we do not pray for one but for the whole people, because we, the whole people, are one'.

17 To our knowledge, the most detailed work done on this subject is the (unedited) doctoral thesis presented at the Faculty of Theology of the University of Louvain in October 1967 by Abbot B. Renaud, under the title, *Eucharistie et culte eucharistique selon Saint Cyprien*. In Chapter 4 of this work, 'The African Mass in the 3rd century', the second section is dedicated to 'The Prayer of the Faithful' (180 ff.). This study, which we have been able to consult through the generous authorization of the author, has provided us more than one piece of information. It seems to us a careful study. See also Saxer (1969), 211–13.

18 Cyprian, *Ad Demetrianum*, 20, (CSEL 3.1), 365: 'However, we always ask for triumph over our enemies and for rain, or for the diminishment or removal of hostile elements; honouring and placating God, we pour out our prayers for peace and for your health; day and night, continually and insistently we pray'. Tr.J.O'Brien.

deprecantes, sicut deprecari oportet eos qui sint positi inter plangentium ruinas et timentium reliquias, inter numerosam languentium stragem et exiguam stantium firmitatem.
Rogemus pacem maturius reddi,
cito latebris nostris et periculis subveniri,
inpleri quae famulis suis Dominus dignatur ostendere,
redintegrationem ecclesiae suae,
securitatem salutis nostrae,
post pluvias serenitatem,
post tenebras lucem,
post procellas et turbines placidam lenitatem,
pia paternae dilectionis auxilia,
divinae maiestatis solita magnalia,
quibus et persequentium blasphemia retundatur,
et lapsorum paenitentia reformetur
et fortis et stabilis perseverantium fiducia glorietur'.[19]

3 In his long *Epistola* 59, sent around 251 to Cornelius, the bishop of Carthage speaks of persecutions. In a totally non-liturgical context, he writes:

T 4 *Epistola* 59, 18, 'Oramus ac deprecamur Deum quem provocare illi et exacerbare non desinunt,
ut eorum corda mitescant,
ut furore deposito ad sanitatem mentis redeant,
ut pectora operta delictorum tenebris paenitentiae lumen agnoscant et magis petant fundi pro se preces adque orationes antistitis quam ipsi fundant sanguinem sacerdotis'.[20]

19 Cyprian, *Epistola 11*, 8 (PL 4, 245), ed. Bayard vol. 1, 32–33; Eng. tr. Donna, (FC 51), 34: 'Let us pray to the Lord alone without ceasing to ask and, with faith in receiving, straightforward and of one mind, entreating with both groaning and weeping, as those who are placed between the ruins of the moaning and the remains of the fearful, between the manifold destruction of the fallen and the paltry strength of the standing, ought to pray. Let us ask for peace to be restored sooner, to be succoured quickly in our hiding places and dangers, for what the Lord deigns to manifest to his servants to be fulfilled: the restoration of his Church, the security of our salvation, serenity after the rains, light after darkness, peaceful calm after storms and dangers; blessed aids of his fatherly love, the accustomed grandeurs of his divine majesty, by which the blasphemy of the persecutors may be beaten back and the penance of the lapsed may be accomplished, and the strong and stable faith of the persevering may glory'.

20 Cyprian, *Epistola* 59, 18, 3, ed. Bayard, vol. 2, 188; Eng tr. Donna (FC 51), 191: 'We pray and we entreat God, whom those men do not cease to provoke and exasperate, that they may soften their hearts, that they may return to health of mind when this madness has been put aside, that their hearts, filled with the darkness of sin, may recognise the light of repentence, and that they may rather seek that the intercessions and prayers of the bishop be poured for themselves than that they themselves shed the blood of the bishop'.

4 Letter 76 is addressed around 257 to a group of faithful, deacons and bishops who are captives in a mine. To these 'confessors' he writes:

T 5 *Epistola 76, 7, 3*: 'Plane quia nunc vobis in precibus efficacior sermo est et ad inpetrandum quod in pressuris petitur facilior oratio est, petite inpensius et rogate
ut confessionem omnium nostrum dignatio divina consummet,
ut de istis tenebris et laqueis mundi nos quoque vobiscum integros et gloriosos Deus liberet,
ut qui hic caritatis et pacis vinculo copulati contra hereticorum iniurias et pressuras gentilium simul stetimus partier in regnis caelestibus gaudeamus'.[21]

5 The *Acta proconsularia Cypriani*, written shortly after his death, echo a prayer of the saint on the way to martyrdom:

T 6 1: 'Cyprianus episcopus dixit: ... huic Deo nos christiani deservimus: hunc deprecamurdiebus ac noctibus
pro nobis
et pro omnibus hominibus
et pro incolumitate ipsorum imperatorum'.[22]

Finally we note that we cannot accept Chapter 17 of *De oratione dominica* as witnessing to a prayer intention. Since chapter 14 Cyprian has been explaining the petition: 'may your will be done on earth as it is in heaven'. In chapter 16 he identifies earth and body, heaven and soul; the prayer consists in asking that harmony be realised between these two parts of our being. But in chapter 17 he proposes a new interpretation:

T 7 17: 'Potest et sic intelligi, fratres dilectissimi, ut quoniam mandat et monet Dominus etiam inimicos diligere et pro his quoque qui nos persecuntur orare, petamus et pro illis qui adhuc terra sunt et necdum caelestes esse coeperunt, ut et circa illos voluntas Dei fiat ... merito et nos ... Christo monente oramus et petimus, ut precem pro omnium salute faciamus'[23]

---

21 *Epistola 76*, 7, 3, ed. Bayard, vol. 2, 314–15; Eng. tr. Donna, (FC 51), 318: 'Because now your speech is clearly more efficacious in prayers, and supplication is quicker to obtain what is sought for in persecutions, seek more eagerly and ask that the divine condescension may perfect the confession of us all, that, from this darkness and from the deceits of the world God may free us, safe and glorious also with you, and that we who here bound by the bond of love and peace have stood firm against the injuries of the heretics and the persecutions of the Gentiles may, likewise, rejoice together in the heavenly kingdom'.

22 *Acta proconsularia Cypriani*, 1, CSEL 3, 3, cx: 'The Bishop Cyprian said: ... It is this God that we Christians serve, it is he to whom we pray day and night for ourselves, for all humankind, and for the safety of the emperors themselves'. Tr.J.O'Brien.

F. Probst[24] sees here an allusion to the prayer of intercession; M. Reveillaud[25] agrees. B. Renaud considers that at first sight the *oratio fidelium* and the Canon are the two moments that can claim with greatest probability the prayer 'for the salvation of all'; but the connection with the text from *De bono patientiae*, 16: 'ut pro adversariis et persecutoribus precem facias' allows him 'to conclude with high probability that *De oratione* 17 makes a conscious allusion to a petition of common prayer: "for the salvation of all"'.[26]

But it seems to us that the context clearly shows, as the translation by Réveillaud elsewhere indicates, that Cyprian does not quote a prayer intention here. The *ut precem pro omnium salute faciamus* reveals the content of the third petition of the Our Father according to the new interpretation that Cyprian proposes in this paragraph. This passage therefore cannot be included in our survey.

What can we draw from these preceding five texts? Honestly, not very much, at least at first glance. We do not find a common scheme or a similar vocabulary. Certainly, we find the expression *preces fundere* in both T 2 and T 4; *diebus ac noctibus* appears in T 2 and T 6; three times we read the verb *deprecari* (T 3, T 4 and T 6); similarly three times we meet the term *pax* (T 2, T 3 and T 5); and rain (*imber* T 2; *pluvia* T 3) is mentioned twice, in a figurative sense in T 3.

But what does this prove? In a series of prayer intentions, one can expect *a priori* to meet the term *pax*, especially if it dates from a period of persecution; and if it is known to originate in a hot and dry country, it is not surprising to find a petition for rain.

We can scarcely see here anything more than the concern of Christians to pray for their brothers experiencing difficulties (T 3, T 4 and T 5) and to take care of the needs of all people (T 2 and T 6) according to the direction of 1 Tim 2:1–2 (to which T 6 is also quite close). But is this concern translated liturgically into an *oratio fidelium*? Rather, it seems that Cyprian is guided by literary style.

However we must note that the bishop of Carthage has been able to put to good use in the liturgical celebration the same procedure that he used in writing his letters. Let us remember that we are dealing for the most part with an 'improvised' liturgy. If a Prayer of the Faithful existed, no doubt Cyprian would build it in the same way as the lists of intentions found in his letters.

Can we push the argument even further, looking at it another way, and suggesting that if we read these series of intentions in his letters, it is because it is

---

23 Cyprian, *De dominica oratione*, 17, ed. and tr. M. Reveillaud, 102–03; Bindley (1904), 45–46: 'It is to be understood, dearly beloved brothers, that since the Lord commanded and admonished us to love even our enemies and to pray likewise for those who persecute us, we pray also for those who are still on earth and have not yet begun to be heavenly, so that even in respect of these God's will might be done … According to Christ's admonition to make intercession for the salvation of all'.

24 Probst (1870), 222 ff.

25 Reveillaud (1964), 184.

26 Renaud (Unpublished doctoral thesis, 1967), 184.

only natural that he will adopt the form of the Universal Prayer that he presided over in worship? In order to answer this question, let us examine another series of texts.[27]

2. Structure of the Celebration

While Tertullian's writings provided us with more or less precise descriptions of the unfolding of the liturgical celebration, we find nothing similar in Cyprian. Nowhere does he give a clear indication of the place of the *oratio fidelium*, if indeed it existed.

All the same, we will make mention of an hypothesis that has come to mind in reading and rereading these texts in order to extract from them anything of substance. We consider it highly unlikely, but we will present it anyway; it would not be the first time that criticism of a poorly-founded hypothesis enabled the advancement of knowledge.

In his (synodal) letter to Pope Lucius (253), Cyprian writes that he and his brothers not only send this letter to express their joy, but

T 8 *Epistola 61*, 4, 2: 'hic quoque in sacrificiis adque in orationibus nostris non cessantes Deo patri et Christo filio eius Domino nostro gratias agere et orare pariter ac petere ut qui perfectus est adque perficiens custodiat et perficiat in vobis confessionis vestrae gloriosam coronam'.[28]

Putting the central passage of this text into two columns results in the following:

in sacrificiis	in orationibus nostris
Deo patri	Christo Filio eius Domino nostro
gratias agere	orare pariter ac petere
qui perfectus est	perficiens
custodiat	perficiat

27 F. Cabrol et H. Leclercq, *Relliquiae liturgicae vetustissimae*, vol. 1, Paris, 1900–1902, 175, n. 1894, discover in a passage from Cyprian an expression which might well be a liturgical formula. Here is the text: 'Rogamus vos ut pro vobis Dominum rogare possimus, preces ipsas ad vos prius vertimus quibus *Deum pro vobis ut misereatur oramus*', *De lapsis*, 32, ed. G. Hartel, (CSEL 3, 1) 261.
We quote this from memory; we have found no evidence to justify this assertion.

28 Cyprian, *Epistola 61*, 4, 2, ed. Bayard, vol. 2, 196; Eng. tr. Donna (FC 51), 199: 'here also in our sacrifices and in our prayers not ceasing to give thanks to God the Father and to Christ, his Son and our Lord, and likewise to pray and to beseech that he, who has brought this about and is perfecting it, may guard you doing his work and accomplish in you the glorious crown of your confession'.

Could one conclude that in Cyprian's mind the sacrifice of thanks is addressed to the Father and the prayer to Christ? This seems to be confirmed by his Letter 65, addressed around 251 to the Church of Assuras:

T 9a *Epistola* 65, 4, 2: 'quomodo se putat posse agere pro Dei sacerdote qui obtemperavit et servivit diaboli sacerdotibus, aut quomodo putat manum suam transferri posse ad Dei sacrificium et precem Domini quae captiva fuerit sacrilegio et crimini'[29]

And similarly, in paragraph 5 of Letter 11, of which we have already read an excerpt (T 3), which deals with Christ, who also prayed several times for his disciples:

T 10 *Epistola* 11, 5, 2: Quod si pro nobis ac pro delictis nostris ille (Christus) et laborat et vigilat et precatur, quando nos magis insistere precibus et orare et primo ipsum Dominum rogare, tunc deinde per ipsum Deo patri satisfacere debemus![30]

If the opposition thus introduced between the sacrifice offered to the Father and the prayer addressed to the Son is pertinent, then one could think that *in sacrificiis* (T 8), *sacrificium* (T 9a), and *Deo patri satisfacere* (T 10) refer to the Eucharist, while the terms *in orationibus nostris* (T 8), *precem Domini* (T 9a) and *Dominum rogare* (T 10) refer to the Universal Prayer. This, in fact, is traditionally associated with Christ — just think about the response *Kyrie eleison* (even though this does not appear, even in the East, until the end of the 4th century).

The objection can be made that in T 9a Cyprian cites sacrifice first and then speaks of the prayers, and this does not accord with the normal order. But there is nothing here to say that the author is following the order of the celebration; it could also be that he is simply mentioning the most important element first. Since the pairing *sacrificium* — *oratio* that we find in T 8 recurs several times under the pen of the holy martyr, can we at least admit the equivalence of the terms *oratio*, *prex* and *preces*. Here are the texts:

---

29 Cyprian, *Epistola* 65, 4, 2, ed. Bayard, vol. 2, 218; Eng. tr., Donna (FC 51), 220–21: 'How does he think he who has obeyed and served the priests of the devil can act as a bishop of God or how does he think that his hand, which was captive to sacrilege and crime, can be transferred to the sacrifice of God and the prayer of the Lord?' B. Renaud, [Doctoral thesis, p. 181], rejects what, in his eyes, describes 'the priestly prayer of sacrifice'. See also p. 207.

30 Cyprian, *Epistola* 11, 5, 2, ed. Bayard, vol. 1, 31; Eng. tr. Donna (FC 51), 32: 'But if he (Christ) also labours and watches and prays for us and for our sins, how much more ought we to be insistent in prayers; and to pray and, first, to ask the Lord himself, then, finally, through him, to make satisfaction to God the Father!'

a) Letter 37, written *c.* 250 and addressed to a number of imprisoned confessors:

T 11 *Epistola* 37, 1, 2: 'Et nos quidem vestri diebus ac noctibus memores, et quando **in sacrificiis precem** cum pluribus facimus et cum in secessu privatis precibus oramus, coronis ac laudibus vestris plenam Domini faventiam postulamus'.[31]

The text places private prayer in opposition to public prayer, described by *in sacrificiis*; certainly this expression can refer uniquely to the anaphora, but the content of the prayer that Cyprien formulates for these confessors does not seem to correspond to the anaphoric intercessions. The text would be clearer if *in sacrificiis* were to refer to the entire Mass. But does the term *prex* then describe the Universal Prayer?

b) Letter 65, from which we have already cited the central passage above (T 9a):

T 9b *Epistola* 65, 2, 1–2: 'Cum ergo haec tormenta, haec supplicia in die iudicii Dominus comminetur his qui diabolo obtemperant et idolis sacrificant, quomodo se putat posse agere pro Dei sacerdote qui obtemperavit et servivit diaboli sacerdotibus, aut quomodo putat manum suam transferri posse ad Dei **sacrificium et precem** Domini quae captiva fuerit sacrilegio et crimini, quando in Scripturis divinis Deus ad sacrificium prohibeat accedere sacerdotes etiam in leviore crimine constitutos et in Levitico dicat: "Homo in quo fuerit vitium et macula non accedet offerre dona Deo" (Lev 21:17). Item in Exodo: "Et sacerdotes qui accedunt ad Dominum Deum sanctificentur, ne forte derelinquat illos Dominus" (Ex 19:22), et iterum: "Et qui accedunt ministrare ad altare Sancti, non adducent in se delictum ne moriantur" (Ex 19:31). Qui ergo gravia delicta in se adduxerunt, id est qui idolis sacrificando sacrilege sacrificia fecerunt, sacerdotium Dei sibi vindicare non possunt, ne ullam in conspectu eius precem pro fratribus facere, quando in Evangelio scriptum sit: "Deus peccatorem non audit, sed qui Deum coluerit et voluntatem ipsius fecerit, illum audit"' (Jn 9:31).[32]

---

31 Cyprian, *Epistola* 37, 1, 2, ed. Bayard, vol. 1, 92–93, Eng. tr., Donna (FC 51), 94: And we, indeed, mindful of you both day and night, both when we offer prayer in the Sacrifices with many and when we petition apart in private prayers we make to him at home, beg the full favour of the Lord for your crowns and praises.

32 Cyprian, *Epistola* 65 2, 1–2, ed. Bayard, vol. 2, 218; Eng. tr., Donna (FC 51) 220–21: Since, therefore, the Lord threatens these torments, these punishments in the day of judgment, to those who obey the devil and sacrifice to idols, how does he think that he who has obeyed and served the priests of the devil can act as a bishop of God or how does he think that his hand, which was captive to sacrilege and to crime, can be transferred to the sacrifice of God and the prayer of the Lord, when in the divine Scriptures God prohibits from approaching the sacrifice priests found even in slighter crime? And in Leviticus, he says: 'The man who has a defect and stains shall not come forward to offer up gifts to God?' (Lev 21:17) Likewise in Exodus: 'The priests, too, who approach the Lord God must be sanctified lest perhaps the Lord abandon them' (Ex 19:22). And again: 'And those who approach the altar of the Holy One to minister will not bring sin upon themselves, lest they die' (Ex 28:43). They,

Here too we believe we can distinguish between *sacrificium* and *prex*, in the first instance based on the genitives that qualify them, as we have noted above. Secondly, the three quotations from the Old Testament apply to the anaphora (*ad sacrifium prohibeat accedere; offerre dona Deo; ministrare ad altare Sancti*) and so illustrate the term *sacrificium*, while the quotation from John indicates the conditions upon which God listens to prayer and is so linked precisely with the term *prex*. Could we see in this the *oratio fidelium*?

c) Letter 67, from the synod of 254, might well contradict the preceding conclusions:

T 12 *Epistola 67, 2, 2*: 'non nisi immaculatos et integros antistites eligere debemus, qui sancte et digne **sacrificia** Deo offerentes audiri **in precibus** possint quas faciunt pro plebis dominicae incolumitate, cum scriptum sit: "Deus peccatorem non audit, sed qui Deum coluerit et voluntatem eius fecerit, illum audit" (Jn 9:4). Propter quod plena diligentia et exploratione sincera eos oportet ad sacerdotium Dei deligi quos a Deo constet audiri'.[33]

The grammatical subordination of *digne sacrificia Deo offerentes* to *audiri in precibus possint* seems to indicate that it is a matter of one and the same action; it is the offering of sacrifice that is considered in its entirety as the prayer to which God must listen. In other words, *in precibus* here describes the anaphora or even more broadly the whole Mass.

At a pinch one could imagine that *sacrificia Deo offerentes* characterises the overall celebration, and *in precibus* refers to the Universal Prayer in particular. But the context makes us lean in favour of the two expressions being equivalent.

d) The expression *in sacrificiis et precibus* is found in Letter 62 (T 16), but the text is too clearly referring to diptychs to be considered here.

Could not an in-depth study of Cyprian's vocabulary clear up these matters? The conclusions reached by B. Renaud[34] do little to confirm the distinction that we would suggest here between *sacrificium* and *prex-preces*. According to him, *sacrificium, oblation,* and *dominicum* refer to the Mass in its entirety; *prex* refers above all to the anaphora (he provides 6 certain texts to support this conclusion),

---

therefore, who have brought grave sins upon themselves, that is, who have offered sacrilegious sacrifices by sacrificing to idols, cannot claim the priesthood of God for themselves, nor can they offer any prayer for the brethren in his sight since it is written in the Gospel, 'God does not hear the sinner; but if anyone has worshipped God, and done his will, him he hears' (Jn 9:31).

33 Cyprian, *Epistola 67, 2, 2*, ed. Bayard, vol. 2, 229; tr. Donna (FC 51), 223: 'we ought to choose none but spotless and upright priests who, offering sacrifices holily and worthily to God, may be able to be heard in the prayers which they offer for the safety of the people of the Lord since it is written, "God does not hear the sinner, but if anyone is a worshipper of God and does his will, him he hears"' (Jn 9:4). Because of this, it is necessary, with full diligence and sincere examination, that they be chosen for the priesthood of God who, it is certain, may be heard by God'.

34 Renaud, (Unpublished doctoral thesis, 1967), 195–96.

while the plural *preces* corresponds above all to the 'prayers of the Canon'. He recognises nevertheless that neither the plural *preces* nor the singular *prex* are reserved exclusively to this usage; in T 1, for example, *prex* refers above all else to the Our Father.

In our opinion, as we have already noted on p. 35, Cyprian's vocabulary was not fixed. These terms were not yet sufficiently established in a technical sense to allow us to decide one way or another in a doubtful case.

In conclusion to this second paragraph, it seems to us that we cannot draw any certainty from the texts we have read. As we said from the outset, we have only provided these quotations in order to extract as much information as possible, because in the end, we rarely find what we are looking for. However, our hypothesis seems rather weak to us. We have no precise description of the unfolding of the celebration, which means that we cannot locate the Universal Prayer in it. If the Church of Carthage was indeed familiar with it in the middle of the third century, we have so far had no decisive evidence. Let us see if another track could prove more profitable.

3. Diptychs

We are familiar with these. In secular usage diptychs were comprised of two small wings folded on each other by means of a hinge; the inside was covered with wax on which annotations were written. Diptychs served as a kind of note-book. In the liturgy they were used to write the names of the living or the dead who were to be recommended to God in prayer. From there, the term 'diptych' came to mean the actual reading of the names.[35]

Cyprian seems to provide evidence of them in a number of texts that we will read in conjunction with each other.

1 Letter 1 was written *c.* 249 to priests, deacons and the people of Furni. It is about Victor who, on his death, appointed the priest Geminius Faustinius as tutor for his children; but a recent Council has defended the choice of a tutor or curator from among the clergy.

T 13 *Epistola 1, 2, 1–2*: 'Quod episcopi antecessores nostri religiose considerantes et salubriter providentes censuerunt ne quis frater excedens ad tutelam vel curam clericum nominaret, ac si quis fecisset, non offerretur pro eo nec sacrificium pro dormitione eius celebraretur (vel: non offerretur pro eo sacrificium nec pro dormitione eius celebraretur). Neque enim apud altare Dei meretur nominari in sacerdotum prece qui ab altari sacerdotes et ministros voluit avocari. Et ideo Victor cum contra formam nuper in concilio a sacerdotibus datam Geminium Faustum presbyterum ausus sit tutorem constituere, non est quod pro dormitione

35 On this topic see the article by F. Cabrol, 'Diptyques (Liturgie)' in DACL, vol. 4, 1045–94. For the African liturgy in particular, see W. C. Bishop (1912), 257–59; also Renaud (Unpublished doctoral thesis, 1967), 213–17.

eius apud vos fiat oblatio, aut deprecatio aliqua nomine eius in ecclesia frequentetur, ut sacerdotum decretum religiose et necessarie factum servetur a nobis, simul et ceteris fratribus detur exemplum, ne quis sacerdotes et ministros Dei altari eius et ecclesiae vacantes ad saecularem molestiam devocet'.[36]

The expressions *non offerretur pro eo, nec pro dormitione eius, apud altare Dei meretur nominari in sacerdotum prece*, and *deprecatio aliqua nomine eius*, point us in this context, it seems, towards the diptychs, and more precisely toward the reading of the names of the deceased. Mention of the altar and the offering, as well as the whole context, precludes us from thinking in this case of an *oratio fidelium*. But this is not the only text on which we can lean; let us examine some others.

2 In Letter 16, which he wrote *c.* 350 to his brother priests and deacons, Cyprian deals with the *lapsi* and is offended that

T 14 *Epistola 16*, 2, 3: 'nunc crudo tempore persecutione adhuc perseverante, nondum restituta ecclesiae ipsius pace, ad communicationem admittuntur et offertur nomine eorum, et nondum paenitentia acta, nondum exomologesi facta, nondum manu eis ab episcopo et clero inposita, eucharistia illis datur'.[37]

Offertur nomine eorum most likely points to the existence of diptychs which, if need be, concerned the living, and in particular, the *lapsi*.

Similarly, in Letter 15:

T 15 *Epistola 15*, 1, 2: 'ante actam paentitentiam, ante exomologesim gravissimi adque extremi delicti factam, ante manum ab episcopo et clero in paenitentiam inpositam, offerre pro illis et eucharistiam dare id est sanctum Domini corpus profanare audeant'....[38]

---

36 Cyprian, *Epistola 1*, 2, ed. Bayard, vol. 1, 3; Eng. tr. Donna (FC 51), 4: 'The bishops, our predecessors, conscientiously considering this and wisely providing, decreed that no dying brother should name a cleric for guardianship or for trusteeship and, if anyone had done this, prayers should not be offered for him and the Sacrifice should not be celebrated for the repose of his soul. For he who has wished bishops and priests to be distracted from the altar does not deserve to be named at the altar of God in the prayer of the bishops. And therefore, since Victor, contrary to the decree recently promulgated by the bishops in council, has dared to appoint Geminius Faustinus, a priest, as tutor, the Holy Sacrifice is not to be offered among you for his repose, nor is any prayer to be repeated in his name in the Church, so that the decree of the bishops may be conscientiously and exactly observed by us and that, at the same time, an example may be given to the rest of the brethren lest anyone call away to secular pursuits bishops and ministers of God devoted to his altar and Church'.

37 Cyprian, *Epistola 16*, 2, 3, ed. Bayard, vol. 1, 47; Eng. tr. Donna, (Fc 51), 47–48: 'now in an unpropitious time with a persecution still raging, with the peace of the Church itself not yet restored, they are admitted to Communion and there is an offering in their name. And, although penance has not yet been performed, confession has not yet been made, hands have not yet been imposed upon them by bishop and clergy, the Eucharist is given to them'.

Given the similarity of the context, it is justifiable to understand *offerre pro illis* (T 15) in the same sense as *offertur nomine eorum* (T 14). The same could be said of the following:

> *Epistola 16*, 3, 2: 'communicent cum lapsis et offerant et eucharistiam tradant'.
> *Epistola 17*, 2, 1: 'cum lapsis communicare … et offerre pro illis et eucharistiam dare'.
> *Epistola 34*, 1: 'communicando cum lapsis et offerendo oblationes eorum'.

As B. Renaud notes, if there is any mention of names here, it must take place during the sacrifice itself.[39]

3 Letter 62, written *c.* 253 to some Numidian bishops, provides us with the most convincing argument for asserting the existence of diptychs. The bishop of Carthage sends a sum of money to his colleagues, together with the names of the donors.

T 16 *Epistola 62*, 4, 2: 'Ut autem fratres nostros ac sorores … in mente habeatis orationibus vestris et eis vicem boni operis in sacrificiis et precibus repraesentetis, subdidi nomina singulorum. Sed et collegarum quoque et sacerdotum nostrorum … nomina addidi …, quorum omnium secundum quod fides et caritas exigit in orationibus et precibus vestris meminisse debetis'.[40]

The mention of *nomina* seems to us clearly to indicate diptychs.[41]

In short, these different passages win us over and convince us of the existence of diptychs for both the living (T 14, T 15 and T 16) and for the dead (T 13) in the Mass in the Church of Carthage in the middle of the third century.

---

38 Cyprian, *Epistola 15*, 1, 2, ed. Bayard, vol. 1, 43; Eng. tr. Donna (FC 51), 44: 'before the confession of a very serious and low crime has been made, before hands have been imposed by bishop and priest in penance, they dare to offer the Holy Sacrifice for them and to give them the Eucharist, that is, to profane the sacred body of the Lord'.

39 And not before the Canon, as proposed, without proof, by W. C. Bishop (1912), 259.

40 Cyprian, *Epistola 62*, 4, 2, ed. Bayard, vol. 2, 199; Eng. tr. Donna (FC 51), 202: 'But that you may have in mind in your prayers our brethren and sisters … and that you, in return, may intercede for them in the sacrifices and prayers of good work, I have supplied the names of each. And I have also added the names of our colleagues and of our bishops … You ought to remember in your prayers and orations all of these according to what faith and charity demand'.

41 B. Renaud also cites other texts (see 213–14): *Epistola 12*, 2, 1: 'Denique et dies eorum quibus excedunt adnotate, ut commemorationes eorum inter memorias martyrum celebrare possimus…; et celebrentur hic a nobis oblationes et sacrificial ob commemorations eorum'.
Epistola 39, 3, 1: 'Sacrificia pro eis semper, ut meministis, offerrimus, quotiens martyrum passiones et dies anniversaria commemoratione celebramus'.
But is there not a certain subtle shift here? These two texts are speaking of the Eucharist celebrated on the anniversary of martyrs: is this the same thing as offering it for the salvation of the *lapsi*? Were not both the names of the martyrs in whose honour the sacrifice was offered, and those of the living for whom the Eucharist was celebrated, read from the diptychs?

4. The Expression 'in mente habere'

We have just read this expression in Letter 62 (T 16). The sense is clear, and the idea appears regularly in Cyprian's work. We meet it, for example, in Letter 37, from which we have already quoted (T 11):

T 17 *Epistola* 37, 4, 1: 'Nunc est, fratres beatissimi, ut memores mei sitis, ut inter magnas adque divinas cogitationes vestras nos quoque animo ac mente volvatis, simque in precibus et orationibus vestris'[42]

The turn of phrase *in mente habere* is classic; Forcellini's Lexicon points out that the term *mens* also refers to the memory, and cites several examples of *in mente(m) venire* from Cicero, and points out that *in mente habere* is a common prayer expression in the Christian *tituli*.

It is biblical as well, with the Vulgate offering four examples;[43] but what is even more interesting to us, it already features in the ancient Latin versions of Scripture,[44] and therefore certainly pre-dates St Jerome (347?-420).

The expression is found in Letter 78, sent to Cyprian towards the end of his life by Lucius and his brothers:

T 18 *Epistola* 78, 2, 2: 'Hoc totum fiet, dilectissime, si nos orationibus tuis **in mente habueris**, quod te facere confido, sicut et nos utique facimus'.[45]

Similarly, in Letter 79, addressed to Cyprian around 257, in which confessors held in the mine thank him for his encouragement.

T 19 *Epistola* 79, 1, 2: 'petentes de animi tui candore ut nos adsiduis orationibus tuis **in mentem habere** digneris ut confessionem vestram et nostrum quam Dominus in nobis conferre dignatus est suppleat'.[46]

---

42 Cyprian, *Epistola* 37, 4, 2, ed. Bayard, vol. 1, 95; Eng. tr. Donna (FC 51), 96: 'Now it is fitting, most blessed brethren, for you to remember me so that, among your great and divine thoughts, you may also think of me in your heart and mind, and I may be in your prayers and your prayers'.

43 Tob 4:6; Ps 76:6; 2 Mac 15:8; Rev 3:3.

44 e.g. Tob 4:6: 'Et omnibus diebus tuis, fili, Deum tuum in mente habe'. Cf. Blanchini, (1740), cccliii (MS Vatic.Tegin.7, 9th c.). In addition to this text, which it omits, the Thesaurus (vol. 8, 724, 1.32–55) cites 8 examples.

45 Cyprian, *Epistola* 78, 2, 2, ed. Bayard, vol. 2, 318; Eng. tr. Donna, (FC 51), 322: 'This will all be accomplished, dearly beloved, if you if you keep us in mind in your prayers; this I trust you do, just as we certainly do'.

46 Cyprian, *Epistola* 79, 1, 2, ed. Bayard, vol. 2, 319; tr. Donna (FC 51), 323: 'seeking from the brightness of your spirit that you may deign to keep us in mind with your constant prayers that the Lord may make good your confession and ours which he has deigned to confer upon us'.

It is used, too, by the author of the Acts of Fructuosus, bishop of Tarragon, who died on January 21, 259, while he was on the way to martyrdom,

T 20 'accessit ad eum commilito frater noster, nomine Felix et apprehendit dexteram eius, rogans ut sui memor esset. Cui sanctus Fructuosus, cunctis audientibus, clara voce respondit: **In mente me habere** necesse est Ecclesiam catholica, ab Oriente usque in Occidentem diffusam'.[47]

These Acts have recourse to the protocol of the proconsular archives and so their authenticity is well-founded. They appear to date from the 3rd century or the beginning of the 4th century, since they are poetically reproduced in one of Prudentius' hymns (*Peri Stephanon*, 6, from the beginning of the 5th century), and quoted in one of Augustine's sermons as if the Church in Africa read them in public in his era.[48]

This is what P. Allard says about it: 'There is nothing to prevent them from being regarded as contemporaneous with the facts they tell. Everything breathes the scent of ancient times. The simplicity, the gravity of the language, certain expressions — such as *fraternitas* to describe Christians, *in mente habere* to mean "remember" — indicate the third century in preference to any other; one feels transported to the time when Cyprian was writing, when the ancient pilgrims inscribed the first illustrations on the walls of the papal crypt in the catacomb of St Callistus.'[49]

A large number of inscriptions using the phrase in question have been gathered together by E. Diehl.[50] Here are several examples:

2323 Paule, Petre, in mente habete Sozomenum et tu qui legit (catacomb of St Callistus)

---

47 Felix, our brother and companion in arms, came to him, grasped his right hand, asking that he remember him. All listened to Saint Fructuosus answer him aloud: 'I must remember the Catholic Church that has spread from the East to the West'. *Acta Fructuosi*, 3, ed. T. Ruinart, *Acta Martyrum*, Ratisbonne, 1859, 266; or *Acta Sanctorum* January II, 704. We read here the expression 'the Church spread from the East to the West'; more frequently we come across the formula, 'Ecclesia ab Oriente usqe in Occidentem diffusa' that authors generally compare to the analogous phrase in the Roman Canon: 'pro Ecclesia tua ... toto orbe terrarium', thereby aligning it with the intercessions of the anaphora. Cf. Botte (1953), 33, and above all, Eizenhöfer (1966), which, in numbers 261–298 quotes numerous examples of intercession for the Church where this formula is used. No. 266 is none other than the first intercession of the litany *Divinae pacis* that we will study extensively in Part 2 of this work, and no. 284 quotes the first of the Solemn Prayers of Good Friday; the anaphoric origin of the expression cannot therefore be taken for granted.

48 Augustine, *Sermo 273* (PL 38, 1247 ff.). St Augustine uses the expression also on his own account in *Sermo 173*: 'Quando celebriamus dies fratrum defunctorum, in mente habere debemus, et quid sperandum et quid timendum sit'. (PL 38, 937).

49 Allard (1924), 105–06, note 5.

50 Diehl (1961), vol. 1, 452 ff., nos. 2323–31.

2324d sante Suste, in mente habeas in horationes Aureliu Repentinu! (catacomb of St Callistus)

2329 Marine, in mentem nos habeto duobus (catacomb of Priscilla)

2330 Martyres sancti, in mente havite Maria! (Aquileia)

We might wonder what link exists between all this and the *oratio fidelium*. It is W. C. Bishop who establishes it, in his article on the African Rite,[51] by quoting a prayer from the Hispanic liturgy where the expression *in mente habere* is to be found:

T 21 'Dicat sacerdos elevando manus
Oremus
Agyos, Agyos, Agyos. Domine Deus Rex eterne tibi laudes et gratias.
Ecclesiam sanctam catholicam in orationibus **in mente habeamus** ut eam Dominus fide et spe et charitate propicius ampliare dignetur. Omnes lapsos captivos infirmos atque peregrinos **in mente habeamus** ut eos Dominus propicius [respicere] redimere sanare et confortare dignetur.
Repondeat Chorus: Presta eterne omnipotens Deus'.[52]

In the footnotes of his edition, Lesley makes the link with the Acts of Fructuosus; and W. C. Bishop considers that here we are faced with traces of an ancient litany (including mention of the *lapsi* and the *captivi*) that utilise the expressions *in mente habere* and *ab Oriente usque ad Occidentem diffusa*, litanies whose inscriptions cited above offer us an echo of it, as do certain passages from Cyprian and even Augustine. It appears as if the Christians of the period, imbued with these formulas that they would have heard frequently in the liturgy, have used them spontaneously when they came to engrave their prayers to the saints on the walls of the catacombs, or when responding with a prayer of intercession on the way to martyrdom. This litany must have had a wide geographic range since traces of it are found in Africa (Cyprian, Augustine), Spain (Acts of Fructuosus), and Italy (Aquileia, Rome). This hypothesis is taken up again by A. Fortescue[53] and M. Righetti.[54]

What are we to make of this? It appears certain that *in mente habere* has been used in the liturgy, given its frequency, the context of prayer in which it is always found, and its presence in the Hispanic liturgy. There are numerous

51 W. C. Bishop (1912), 254 ff.

52 *Missale mixtum*, ed. Lesley, PL 85, 113ff or 540 ff.: this passage will be studied in Part 2, in the appendix to Section 4, in connection with the *oratio fidelium* in Spain. Cf. also M. Ramos, *Oratio admonitionis*, (1964), 71 ff.; his footnote 46 (p. 72) deals with the expression *in mente habere*.

53 Fortescue (1912) 60–61.

54 Righetti (1956), vol. 3, 301–02; it seems that, on his own initiative, he introduces into the Hispanic text the intervention of a deacon.

other parallels, such as the *Memento* in the Roman liturgy or the Μνήσθητι in the Byzantine liturgy.[55]

But is it necessarily in the course of the Universal Prayer? Here we touch again on one of the major difficulties of this research: the imprecise nature of the texts. The absence within them of any detailed descriptions of the celebration makes any decision presumptuous. In any case, none of the texts that we study in Part 2 uses the phrases *in mente habere* or *Ecclesia ab Oriente usque ad Occidentem diffusa,* at least not literally.

B. Renaud is right when he affirms that 'he cannot see anything that justifies placing [the expression *in mente habere*] in the Prayer of the Faithful rather than during the reading of the diptychs, for example'.[56] Indeed, in as much as T 16 speaks of diptychs and the priestly intercession in the sacrifice, and T 18 and T 19 or the inscriptions always mention the names of people who must be remembered, we are inclined to think that *in mente habere* introduced the dyptichs in the same way that the *Memento* introduced the Roman Canon, rather than serving as part of the Universal Prayer.

On the other hand, the passage from the Acts of Fructuosus (T 20), closest to the Hispanic prayer cited by Bishop (T 21) is able to direct us toward the *oratio fidelium,* since here the object of remembering is the universal Church. Moreover, it is well known that at that time there were many parallels between Africa and Spain. The experts have noted that the ancient Christian monuments in Spain were influenced by 'African' art. The liturgy of North Africa would have been Romanised only during Augustine's time.[57]

Conclusions

It is time to take stock. Let us begin with what is clearest: the dyptichs. Until proven otherwise, the texts that we have put forward convince us of the existence of lists of names, both of the living and the dead, read during the Eucharistic celebration in the Church of Africa during Cyprian's time.

As for the *oratio fidelium* we have to admit that the harvest is not abundant! Despite the statements of many authors, no text of the bishop martyr enables us to put our finger on it. Nor does it provide us with a description of the unfolding of the Mass that would reveal for us the existence and place of a possible Universal Prayer. Neither the lists of prayers, found at random places in his writings, nor the expression *in mente habere,* taken in isolation, constitute sufficient evidence for us to conclude with any certainty the presence of our prayer. Finally, the lexicographical study does not reveal to us any determined and binding relationship.

55 *Missale Romanum, Canon Missae,* Byzantine Rite, anaphoras of St Basil and St John Chrysostom, intercessions after the epiclesis. See Brightman (1896).
56 Renaud, (Unpublished doctoral thesis, 1967) 188.
57 Cf. Pinell, 'Liturgia hispanica' in DHEE, vol. 2, 1303–20.

Very often, the reading of these texts has left us perplexed, and on many occasions we were left wondering exactly what Cyprian meant by 'prayer' in this or that passage.

Nevertheless, as was the case with Tertullian, we have to pay careful attention to the convergence of clues while maintaining the strictest accuracy. We cannot deny the presence of lists of intentions in the martyr's writings, nor the frequent mention of the Church's concern to take on, in prayer, all people and their needs, following the admonition of the Letter to Timothy.

In addition, we have shown that fifty years later, in the time of Tertullian, the Church of Africa was probably familiar with the Prayer of the Faithful, and since no text gives any indication that it was suppressed, it is reasonable to suggest that the community of Carthage must also have known it. And so we can interpret the texts with a positive bias, without appealing solely to them.

Taking all the arguments together we can conclude, until any proof to the contrary, that the Church of Cathage in the middle of the third century would have been familiar with the *oratio fidelium*.

What liturgical form did it take? Was it a diaconal litany or did it take the form of the Roman *orationes sollemnes*? We do not know, except that on no occasion is there any allusion to a deacon in connection with this prayer.

As for its content, several passages provide some clue. In T 2 the prayer seeks to remove enemies and difficulties, and begs for the coming of rains and the salvation of the pagans. T 3 prays for peace and, in various ways, the restoration of the Church, the repentance of the *lapsi* and the perseverance of the *stantes*. In T 6 Cyprian notes that Christians pray for themselves, for all people and even for the emperors. Putting it into some order we can say that the following were prayed for:

- the Church, for its restoration in these troubled times of persecution (T 3, T 4 and T 5), and notably for the *lapsi* and the *stantes* (T 3 and T 4);
- for various categories of people:
  Christians themselves (T 6 and T 12),
  all people (T 6),
  the emperors (T 6),
- for peace (T 2 and T 3)
- for concrete needs such as rain (T 2)

Remarkably, as A. Fortecue has also noted,[58] these same intentions are found in Tertullian: prayer for the emperor and civil needs are found in the

58 Fortescue (1912), 42, affirms the existence of 'public prayers in Cyprian's time and details the intentions (the same, he says, as Tertullian and in the ancient liturgical texts):

- the Church and its unity, with reference to *De dominica oratione*, 8 and 17 (T 1 and T 7, which deal not with the universal prayer but with the Our Father);
- the pope, according to Letter 61 to Pope Lucius, § 4 (T 8);
- the other bishops, the priests, the confessors in prison;

Apologeticum 30, 1 and 4, and 39, 2, while *De Oratione* 29, 2 mentions pleas for persecutors, the *lapsi* and the *stantes*, as well as for favourable natural elements. But study of Tertullian's texts do not lead us to assume the existence of forms of the *oratio fidelium*; And let's face it, Cyprian does not furnish us with any more clues in favour of this hypothesis. In our opinion, the similarity of the petitions can be explained without the intermediary of a text; we are, quite simply, in the presence of the most normal intentions of any Christian community.

We will conclude by quoting a remark of B. Renaud. 'As much as it is legitimate and useful to look for traces of the ancient *oratio fidelium*, it seems illusory to want to make of these traces a particular form of it in early prayer ... it would have been unthinkable to offer thanks and praise to God without at the same time beseeching him for the Church, for Christians in difficulty, and for all people. All prayer was at the same time intercession'.[59]

Arnobius

At the turn of the third and fourth centuries the rhetorician Arnobius left us a quite interesting testimony. He posed the following question to the pagans:

> *Adversus Nationes* 4, 36: 'Nam nostra quidem scripta cur ignibus meruerunt dari?
> cur immaniter conventicula dirui, in quibus
> summus oratur deus
> pax cunctis et venia postulator magistratibus
> exercitibus
> regibus
> familiaribus
> inimicis
> adhuc vitam degentibis
> et resolutis corporum vinctione,
>
> in quibus aliud auditur nihil
> nisi quod humanos faciat,
> nisi quod mites
> verecundos

- benefactors, as in Letter 62, 4, 2 (T 16).

The author neglects certain petitions of which Cyprian has spoken explicitly, e.g. rain, the emperor, protection against enemies (T 2). But it goes without saying that there cannot be an exhaustive list; we must cast aside the dream of reconstructing the form used by the Church of Carthage in the third century, first of all because the variety of intentions provided by Cyprian invites us to believe that they were praying for real but ever-changing needs, and secondly, because even if the prayer was based on a particular outline, it is utopian to want to restore if from the fragments of information that we have.

59 Renaud (Unpublished doctoral thesis, 1967), 189.

pudicos
castos
familiaris communicatores rei
et cum omnibus vobis solidae germanitatis necessitudine copulatos'.[60]

Here is testimony of the concern of the Church to pray for all people. We have already encountered this type of apologetic text where Christians affirm their civic and humanistic concerns (*nisi quod humanos faciat*). No, they say, religion is not an evil to be fought against; it actually serves the good of society since the Church prays for all categories of citizens and thus creates a strong sense of brotherhood amongst everyone (*solida germanitas*).

But are we here in the presence of an *oratio fidelium*? The fact that there is no prayer for the Church or her ministers ought not move us to give a negative response to this question, for what is involved here is just the usefulness of the Church for civil society. However, it is better to recognise that it is not possible to give a confident answer. What is certain is that, in one way or another, the Church prays for the intentions of the entire human race.

Marius Victorinus (*c.* 280–363)

A more decisive judgement can be made on a text sometimes quoted by various authors: the commentary of Marius Victorinus on the epistle to the Ephesians.[61] When, in Eph 6:19, Paul asks them to pray also for him, the author explains that superiors ought to pray for their subordinates, and subordinates for their masters. But the complete absence of any indication of a liturgical order does not allow to consider this passage as a witness to the Universal Prayer.

Augustine (354–430)

Now we come to Augustine, the giant whose personality completely dominated African Christianity. Here the ground becomes less slippery, the allusions to the Universal Prayer more precise and the vocabulary somewhat more fixed. After

---

60 Arnobius, *Adversus Nationes*, 4, 36, (CSEL, 4), 171: 'Why indeed have our writings deserved to be put to the flames, and the churches savagely destroyed, where we pray to the supreme God, where peace and forgiveness are sought for all: magistrates, armies, kings, friends, enemies, those who still live and those who are freed from the bond of the flesh; where we hear nothing other than what makes people humane, what makes them sweet, decent, modest, chaste, what pushes them to share a friendly thing and binds them to all of you by the bonds of a steadfast brotherhood?' Tr.J.O'Brien.

61 PL 8, 1293.

establishing the existence of our prayer, we will indicate the title that it bore, and we will attempt to reveal the form and describe its content.[62]

1. The Existence of the Oratio Fidelium

All the texts that we will read in the course of this section on Augustine convince us without too much difficulty that the liturgy celebrated by the Bishop of Hippo included, in addition to the diptychs,[63] the Universal Prayer. In order to persuade the reader, we will present three categories of texts: one furnishing the lists of intentions, another the descriptions of the Mass, the final one confirming for us the previous quotations by means of apologetic argument.

a) *Lists of intentions*

It is the long letter of 217 to Vital, tainted by semi-Pelagianism, that provides for us the best examples:

T 1 *Epistola* 217, 2: 'quando audis sacerdotem dei ad altar (dei) exhortantem populum dei orare
pro incredulis, ut eos deus convertat ad fidem,
et pro catechumenis, ut eis desiderium regenerationis inspiret,
et pro fidelibus, ut in eo, quod esse coeperunt, eius munere perseverent,
subsanna pias voces...'[64]

T 2 *Epistola* 217, 26: Numquid et orare prohibebis ecclesiam
pro infidelibus, ut sint fideles,
pro his, qui nolunt credere, ut velint credere,
pro his, qui ab eius lege doctrinaque dissentiunt, ut legi eius doctrinaeque consentiant...?

Numquid, ubi audieris sacerdotem dei ad eius altare populum hortantem ad deum orandum vel ipsum clara voce orantem, ut incredulas gentes ad fidem suam venire compellat, non respondebis: 'Amen'?[65]

---

62 Apart from the works cited at the beginning of this section, see also the indepth study by Roetzer (1930).

63 Concerning the diptychs, see the texts collected by W. C. Bishop (1912), 272–74, and his comments, 257 ff.

64 Augustine, *Epistola* 217, 2, (PL 33), 978; (CSEL 57), 404; tr. Parsons, (FC 32), 76: 'When you hear the priest of God at the altar exhorting the people of God to pray for unbelievers so that God may convert them to faith, and for catechumens, that he will inspire their desire for rebirth, and for the faithful, so that by his grace they may persevere in what they have begun to be, do you make fun of these pious words?'

65 Augustine, *Epistola* 217, 26, (PL 33), 987–88; (CSEL 57), 421–22; tr. Parsons (FC 32), 93: 'But surely you will not forbid the Church to pray for unbelievers that they may be believers, for those who refuse to believe, so that they may willingly believe; for those who are at variance with God's law and doctrine that they may submit to his law and doctrine ...? When you hear the priest of God at his

This is the first time that we come across such well-constructed petitions (*orare pro … ut…*). For the moment let us just note the parallelism of these two texts (*audis sacerdotem ad altar (ex)hortantem populum orare pro … ut…*) and the clear intentions that they express.

b) *Structure of the Mass*

Towards 410 Paulinus of Nola wrote to St Augustine, asking several questions, notably with regard to the passage of 1 Tim 2:1. 'Please explain', he asked, 'the difference between the diverse terms (requests, prayers, thanksgiving) when everything there seems to apply to the duty of praying'.[66]

Augustine's response comprises a veritable exercise in philology. He notes the differences between manuscripts and the difficulties associated with interpretation, and finally he gives his exegesis:

T 3 *Epistola 149*, 16: 'Sed eligo in his verbis hoc intelligere, quod omnis vel paene omnis frequentat ecclesia, ut **precationes** accipiamus dictas, quas facimus in celebratione sacramentorum antequam illud, quod est in domini mensa, incipiate benedici;

orationes, cum benedicitur et sanctificatur et ad distribuendum comminuitur, quam totam petitionem fere omnis ecclesia dominica oratione concludit.

interpellationes autem sive, ut vestry codices habent, postulationes fiunt, cum populus benedicitur; …

Quibus peractis et participato tanto sacramento **gratiarum actio** cuncta concludit, quam in his etiam verbis ultimam commendavit apostolus'.[67]

Whatever the value of his exegesis might be, the African bishop here presents for us the unfolding of a Eucharistic celebration, where we can easily recognise in *precationes* the Universal Prayer; in *orationes* the Canon; in *interpellationes* the blessing, at the same place as in the Gallican liturgy, and in the *gratiarum actio*, it goes without saying, the final thanksgiving.

---

altar, exhorting the people to pray to God, or himself praying in a loud voice, that he would compel the unbelieving nations to come to his faith, will you not answer, "Amen"?'

66 Paulinus of Nola, *Epistola 121*, 10 (PL 33), 465; (CSEL 34/2), 731.

67 Augustine, *Epistola 149*, 16, (PL 33), 646–47; (CSEL 44), 362–63); tr. Parsons (FC 20), 250 and 251: 'I prefer to understand by these words what the entire or nearly all the entire Church observes: that we take as supplications [*precationes*] those prayers which are said in celebrating the Mysteries, before we begin to consecrate what lies on the table of the Lord; prayers [*orationes*] are said when it is blessed and sanctified and broken for distribution; and the whole Church, for the most part, closes this complete petition with the Lord's Prayer … Intercessions [*interpellationes*], however, or, or as your texts have it, requests [*postulationes*], are offered while the blessing is being given to the people; … When this is completed and all have received the holy Sacrament, the whole is ended by thanksgiving, and this last is the very term called to our notice by the Apostle'.

This interpretation is confirmed for us in his Sermon 227, which is a catechesis of the Mass for Easter day:

T 4 *Sermo 227*: 'Tenetis sacramenta ordine suo. Primo post orationem, admonemini sursum cor habere ... respondetis, Habemus ad Dominum ... Deinde post sanctificationem sacrificii Dei ... dicimus orationem dominicam'.[68]

W. C. Bishop sees in this prayer a *post nomina*,[69] such as occurs at this point in the liturgies of Gaul and Spain; but only his thesis on the similarity between African and Hispanic liturgies can explain this position; none of the African texts that he cites for the diptychs allows them to be placed before the beginning of the Canon and be followed by an *oratio post nomina.* As W. Roetzer assures us that there is no mention in Augustine of a prayer over the offerings,[70] it is reasonable to see in T 4 an allusion to the *oratio fidelium.*[71]

c) *The 'liturgical argument'*

If we are not already convinced, then we certainly will be after examining a variety of anti-Pelagian polemical texts. One of the strongest arguments by which Augustine opposes his adversaries is that their doctrine is contrary to the practice of the Church, and in particular its prayers. If the faithful implore God for faith, this is surely a proof that grace is necessary to act faithfully.[72] K. Federer has carefully analysed this reasoning, which occurs frequently in Augustine and, taken up by Prosper of Aquitaine, emerged as the classic adage *legem credenda statuat lex supplicandi*;[73] Federer names this 'the liturgical argument', just as theologians are

68 Augustine, *Sermo 227*, (PL 38), 1100–01; (SC 116), 238–240: 'You have the sacraments in their order. First, after the prayer, you are urged to lift up your hearts, ... you respond "We have lifted them up to the Lord" ... then after the consecration of the sacrifice of God ... we say the Lord's Prayer'. Tr.J.O'Brien.

69 W. C. Bishop (1912), 259.

70 Roetzer (1930), 117.

71 It is not necessary, in our opinion, to retain this passage of sermon 49, 8, even though it is frequently cited, even by Roetzer (p. 113): 'Ecce post sermonem fit missa catechuminis. Manebunt fideles. Venietur ad locum orationis'. For Augustine continues on immediately after, 'Scitis quo accessuri sumus. Quid prius deo dicturi sumus? Dimitte nobis debita nostra, sicut et nos dimittimus debitoribus nostris'. (PL 38), 324; (CC 41), 620).

Neither the preceding not the following contexts indicate that the term *oratio* refers here to the *oratio fidelium*; only the succession of terms *sermo-missa-oratio* makes us prick up our ears. But when the author specifies this prayer, he cites a line from the Our Father! And since in no way could anyone suppose that the Our Father was prayed before the Canon (see T 3), this passage is not *ad rem.* Moreover, Augustine does not speak of the rest of the Mass throughout the whole of this sermon; these few lines are in the manner of an *excursus.* Once again it seems that a number of authors who cite this passage have not taken into account the context.

72 On this anti-Pelagian context of prayer see C. Kannengiesser, '*Enarratio in psalmum CXVII*: Science de la révélation et progrès spirituel' in *Recherches augustiniennes*, vol. 2, Paris, 1962, 359–381, particularly 376–77.

73 Federer, (1950), in particular 19–41. On the adage, see Schmidt (1960), 130–39.

accustomed to speak of the 'biblical' argument or the argument 'of tradition'. Here are some examples:

T 5 *De Haeresibus* 88. With regard to the Pelagians, Augustine wrote:
'Destruunt etiam orationes, quas facit Ecclesia,
sive pro infidelibus et doctrinae Dei resistentibus, ut convertantur ad Deum;
sive pro fidelibus, ut augeatur in eis fides, et perseverant in ea'.[74]

T 6 *De dono perseverantiae,* 15: 'A quo enim, nisi ab illo accipimus (haec beneficia), a quo iussum est ut petamus? Prorsus in hac re non operosas disputationes exspectat Ecclesia, sed attendat cottidianas orationes suas. Orat ut increduli credant. Deus ergo converit ad fidem. Orat ut credentes perseverant. Deus ergo donat perseverentiam usque in finem'.[75]

There is also the whole of Letter 217 that ought to be cited here; it is entirely constructed on the liturgical argument. For example, here is what Augustine replied to Vital, the recipient of his letter, who contended that the beginning of faith depended on the individual person's action:

T 7 *Epistola* 217, 1–2: 'Quae si dicis, profecto nostris orationibus contra dicis. Dic ergo apertissime nos pro his, quibus evangelium praedicamus, non debere orare, ut credant, sed eis tantum modo praedicare. Exerce contra orationes ecclesiae disputationes tuas et, quando audis sacerdotem dei altare…' (then follows T 1)[76]

And further on:

T 8 *Epistola* 217, 27: 'Sed ideo Deus per orationes credentium nondum credentes credere facti, ut ostendat, quia ipse facit; nemo est enim tam inperitus, tam carnalis, tam tardus ingenio, qui non videat deum facere, quod rogari se praecipit ut faciat'.[77]

---

74 Augustine, *De Haeresibus* 88, (PL 42), 48; tr. Müller (1956), 123–25: 'They deny the efficacy of the prayers which the Church offers up, either for infidels and those who resist the teaching of God that they might be converted to God, or for the faithful that faith might be increased in them and that they might persevere in it'.

75 *De dono perseverantiae,* 15, (PL 45, 1002); tr. Schaff, (NPNF vol. 1), 5: 'For from whom do we receive but from Him from whom it is right for us to ask? Truly in this matter let not the Church look for laborious disputations, but consider its own daily prayers. It prays that the unbelieving may believe; therefore God converts to the faith. It prays that believers may persevere; therefore God gives perseverance to the end'. See also nos. 60 and 63 cited in the appendix of K. Federer (1950), 129.

76 Augustine, *Epistola* 217, 1–2, (PL 33), 978; (CSEL 57), 404; tr. Parsons (FC 32), 75–76: 'If you say this, you surely contradict our prayers. Say openly, then, that we ought not to pray that those to whom we preach the Gospel may believe, but we ought only to preach to them. Use your arguments against the prayers of the Church, and when you hear the priest of God at the altar (T 1 follows).

77 Augustine, *Epistola* 217, 27, (PL 33), 988; (CSEL 57), 423; tr. Parsons, (FC 32), 94: God, too, through the prayers of believers, makes those believe who do not yet believe, in order to show that it

Let us sum up by citing the Doctor himself:

T 9 'Ipsa igitur oratio clarissima est gratiae testificatio'.[78]

And this prayer, in our opinion, is not just any prayer; it is indeed the *oratio fidelium*, given the way it is described, the vocabulary used and the intentions that are set out in it. Let us look at it in a little more detail.

2. Its Name

In Letter 149 (T 3) Augustine comments extensively on the order given in 1 Tim 2:1–2; the Prayer of the Faithful is designated by the term *precationes*, while *orationes* refers to the Eucharistic Prayer. In our opinion, however, we do not consider that *precationes* was the technical term for our prayer, for this term is not found in any of the texts that we have read so far.[79] On the other hand, *oratio* occurs frequently, and is often qualified by a possessive or a genitive, so much so that we are very close to the tradition expression *oratio fidelium* Here are the texts:

T 10 *Epistola 217*, 1: 'quae si dicis, profecto **nostris orationibus** contra dicis' (cf. T 7)

T 11 *Epistola 217*, 2: 'exerce contra **orationes Ecclesiae** disputationes tuas'

T 12 *Epistola 217*, 8: 'iussioni Domini et **orationibus Ecclesiae** contra dicis'

T 13 *Epistola 217*, 13: 'ut quosdam non credentes ad fidem suam **orationes credentium** pro eis exaudiendo convertat'

T 14 *Epistola 217*, 27: 'sed ideo Deus per **orationes credentium** nondum credentes credere facit' (cf. T 8)

T 15 *Epistola 217*, 29: 'de **orationibus** autem iam **fidelium,** quas et pro se et pro aliis fidelibus faciunt, ut...'

T 16 *Epistola 179*, 4: 'non solum contradicitur **orationibus nostris,** quibus a Domino petimus quicquid sanctos, petisse legimus...' (PL 33), 775; (CSEL 44), 693

T 17 *Sermo 227*: 'Primo post **orationem**, admonemini cor sursum habere' (cf. T 4)

---

is he who does it; for there is no-one so unlearned, so carnal, and so slow of wit not to see that God does what he commands us to ask him to do'.

78 Augustine, *Epistola 177*, 4 (P 33), 766; (CSEL 44), 673; tr. Parsons, (FC 39), 97: 'Thus it is prayer itself that is the clearest testimony of grace'.

79 It seems that in Letter 149 Augustine, urged on by Paulinus of Nola, wanted to find a definitive meaning to assign to the four terms cited in 1 Tim 2, and managed to distinguish four types of prayer within the Eucharistic celebration; but this philological exercise causes him to depart from his usual terminology. However, we find *precantes* again in T 26.

T 18 *De Haeresibus*, 88: 'Destruunt etiam **orationes, quas facit Ecclesia**, sive pro infidelibus' (cf. T 5)

T 19 *De dono perseverantiae*, 15: 'sed attendat (Ecclessia) cottidianas **orationes suas**' (cf. T 6)

T 20 *De dono perseverantiae* 63: 'ut magis intuerentur **orationes suas**, quas semper habuit et habebit **Ecclesia**'.

And though they are not *ad rem*, let us add the following texts for the benefit of comparison:

T 21 *Epistola* 55, 34: '...cum legitur aut disputatur aut antistites clara voce deprecantur aut **communis oratio** voce diaconi indicitur?' (PL 33), 221; (CSEL 34/2), 209

T 22 *Epistola 149*, 16: '**orationes**, cum benedicitur et sanctificatur et ad distribuendum comminuitur' (cf. T 3)

T 23 *Sermo* 49: 'Ecce post sermonem fit missa catechuminis. Manebunt fideles. Venietur ad locum **orationis**. Scitis quo accessuri sumus. Quid prius deo dicturi sumus? Dimitte nobis debita nostra' (cf. note 71, p. 49)

Now let us classify the terms we have just read:

- *orationes Ecclesia* is found twice (T 11 and T 12); with this we can also include:

T 18 'orationes quas facit Ecclesia'

T 19 'attendat (Ecclesia) cottidianas orationes suas'

T 20 'ut magis intuerentur orationes suas, quas semper habuit et habebit Ecclesia'.
- *orationes credentium*: twice (T 13 and T 14)
- *orationes fidelium*; once (T 15)[80]
- *orationes nostrae*: twice (T 10 and T 16)
- *oratio*: 3 times (T 17), T 22 and T 23)
- *communis oratio*: once (T 21).

80 Augustine does not use the singular *oratio fidelium* to designate the Universal Prayer. The only example of this expression that we have found refers to the Our Father, called 'prayer of the faithful' because the non-baptised cannot recite it: 'De cotidianis autem brevibus levibusque peccatis, sine quibus haec vita non ducitur, cotidiana **oratio fidelium** satisfacit. Eorum est enim dicere: "Pater noster, qui es in caelis, qui iam patri tali regenerati sunt ex aqua et spiritu"', (*Enchiridion* 71, ed. Scheel, 45; (PL 40), 265. See in the same sense *Sermo 181*, 7 (PL 38), 982 and *Enarratione in psalmos 142*, 6 (CC 40), 2065; (PL 37), 1849.

But note, *oratio* on its own signifies the Universal Prayer only in T 17,[81] and *communis oratio* (T 21) could well refer to the Our Father.[82] This leaves only the four first terms. Since the Church is the assembly of believers, they are remarkably close to each other in meaning, in fact, they are synonymous. But none of them stands out as the technical term. Even if the terminology is precise it is not yet fixed, and *oratio* on its own designates not only the Universal Prayer but also the Canon or the Lord's Prayer. It is therefore not enough to meet *oratio* in a text to assume that we are talking about the Prayer of the Faithful.

Moreover, other terms are still being used for the latter: *precationes* in T 3, and *preces* in Letter 217, 3:

T 24 'Quod si de precibus Ecclesiae ... parum putas esse quod dixi, aude maiora'.[83]

In short, where the Universal Prayer does not have a specific designation in the writings of Augustine it is most frequently described by the expressions *orationes Ecclesiae, orationes credentium* or *orationes fidelium*.

3. Its Liturgical Form

The excerpts we have read so far have clearly shown what the form of the Universal Prayer could have been in the African liturgy at the beginning of the fifth century. A minister would pray for a particular category of people, that God might grant them such and such a favour (*orare pro ... ut...*) and the people would respond, 'Amen'.[84] In other words, an intention was proposed (*orare pro*), followed by a plea (*ut*), the whole thing being concluded with the response *Amen*. We will determine the content in the next section of this work. Before that, however, it is necessary to consider two difficult problems: Was a deacon involved? Was there a general introduction to this prayer?

---

81 In T 22, *orationes* indicates the Eucharistic Prayer (cf. T 3); in T 23 it acts as the Our Father (cf. note 71, p. 59).

82 Cf. section III, a) The minister.

83 Sometimes *preces* also indicates the Canon, as in Sermon 229 (= Denis 6): 'Et inde iam quae aguntur in precibus sanctis quas audituri estis, ut accedente verbo fiat corpus et sanguis Christi'. ed. Morin (1930), 31.

84 Cfr.T 2. As a witness to the response 'Amen', the following text is also cited, but to us it seems less clear: *De dono perseverantiae*, 63: 'Aut quis sacerdotem super fideles Dominum invocantem, si quando dixit: "Da illis, Domine, in te perseverare usque in finem", non solum voce ausus est, sed saltem cogitatione reprehendere ac non potius super eius talem benedictionem, et corde credente et ore confitente respondit; Amen' (PL 45), 1031.The terms *sacerdotem super fideles Dominum invocantem* and *benedictionem* make us think less of a prayer than a blessing.

a) The Minister

We can assume that a minister led the prayer, but which minister was it? A priest or a deacon? One text seems to reserve this role to the latter; in his *Letter* 55 Augustine speaks of the psalms, which many of the African Christians were keen to sing, so much so that the Donatists reproached them, and the Pastor said:

T 25 *Epistola* 55, 34: 'quando autem non est tempus, cum in ecclesia fratres congregantur, sancta cantandi, nisi cum legitur aut disputatur aut antistites clara voce deprecantur aut communis oratio voce diaconi indicitur?'[85]

Fr. Gy suggests a first interpretation for us, whereby we do not read this text as a description of different moments of the celebration, but see it as a list of the liturgical actions during which it is not appropriate to sing: during the readings, the homily, the public prayer of the priest, and the 'common prayer', understood in the sense of the collective prayer of the whole assembly, including, therefore, the Universal Prayer.

Undoubtedly, this is the simplest interpretation. However, it does not solve the problem of the deacon, which was precisely the topic of this paragraph.

Customary Interpretation

The majority of liturgists have sought a more precise description, especially with regard to the *oratio fidelium*. Probst concludes that 'the *oratio pro fidelibus* was announced (*angesagt*) as a common prayer by the deacon, and that it was prayed by the priest'.[86] Boumann considers it to have been introduced by a diaconal invitatory.[87] According to Willis, the deacon announced the prayer and even gave the intentions, but it was said by the priest or the bishop.[88] Roetzer agrees with Connolly, whose article, in my opinion, enjoyed too great a success.[89] This author is quite sure that the prayers in question in T 1 and T 2 are the same as those named by Augustine in T 25 as *communis oratio* and that the intentions and the requests were announced by the bishop or the priest. But what, then, was the role of the deacon? How are we to understand the expression: 'communis oratio voce diaconi indicitur' (T 25)? Connolly thinks the deacon would give an order in the

---

85 *Epistola* 55, 34 (PL 33), 221: (CSEL 34/2), 209: 'But, is not any time appropriate for singing sacred hymns when the brothers are gathered in the church, except when there is reading or discussion or praying aloud by the bishop, or prayer in common prayer, led by the voice of the deacon?' Tr. Parsons (FC 1), 290.

86 Probst (1893), 281.

87 Bouman (1959), 16.

88 Willis (1964), 7.

89 Connolly (1920), 219–232. This is taken up again by Kennedy (1963), 28.

same manner as the *Flectamus genua* of the Solemn Intercessions of Good Friday in the Roman Rite. He bases his argument on two points.

First, the verb *indicere*, would, of itself, provide only a weak basis for this — it would not be used to describe the diaconal role in an Eastern liturgy. But Caesarius of Arles uses the same verb to designate specifically the *Flectamus genua* of the deacon.[90] And so Connolly concludes: when one compares the passages of Augustine and considers them in in relation to those of the *Auctoritates* and to *De vocatione omnium gentium*,[91] there is scarcely any doubt that in Africa too, at the beginning of the fifth century, the practice of reciting a series of prayers 'for all species and conditions' was already established, and that these prayers (both in their content and in the manner of pronouncing them) was exactly analogous to the Roman *Orationes sollemnes*. Of course, he adds, we need not assume that these African prayers were identical in their literalness or in the series of intentions to the Roman prayers, but there was obviously considerable agreement, and a real historical link must have existed between these two expressions of prayer.[92]

This reasoning leaves us perplexed. If it is indeed well established that Caesarius of Arles (470/71–543) was familiar with Augustine's works, what allows us to interpret his writings in the light of those of a devotee who lived a century later in another ecclesiastical province? No textual relationship can be established between the writings of Augustine and the Roman *Orationes Sollemnes* of Good Friday. The connections that *can* be made are not convincing: the term *convertere* appears in the 9th invitatory, *regeneratio* in the 5th (concerning catechumens), and *perseverare* in the first oration, but these terms are too common to prove any dependency. Moreover, neither the verb *credere*, so frequent in Augustine, nor the terms *infideles* or *increduli*, are found in the *Orationes Sollemnes*. No grouping of words appears simultaneously in either form, and the themes evoked by Augustine are far from exhausting those of the *Orationes Sollemnes* that also pray for the Church, the Pope, the different ecclesiastical orders, for concrete needs, and for the Jews. Finally, there is no trace found in the work of the Bishop of Hippo of a *Flectamus genua*. This lack does not, of itself, constitute an argument, since the Gallican tradition of the *Orationes Sollemnes* ignores this admonition (cf. the critical edition, the tenth section).

One cannot therefore honestly rely solely on the use of the verb *indicere* by Augustine and Caesarius to conclude that if the latter employs it in relation to the

---

90 Caesarius of Arles, *Sermo* 77: 'Rogo ... ut quotienscumque iuxta altarium a clericis oratur, aut oratio diacono clamante indicitur, non solum corda sed etiam corpora fideliter inclinetis. Nam dum frequenter, sicut oportet, et diligenter adtendo, diacono clamante FLECTAMUS GENUA maximam partem populi velut columnas erectas stare conspicio'. (PL 39), 2285; (CC 103), 319.

Sermo 76: 'Supplico ... ut quotienscumque oratio indicitur, qui forte pro aliqua infirmitate non potest genua flectere, vel dorsum curvare et cervicem humiliare non differat'. (PL 39), 2284; (CC 103), 316.

91 For works of Prosper of Aquitaine, which, in certain passages, paraphrase the Roman *Orationes sollemnes*, see Section 3 of this chapter.

92 Connolly (1920), 225.

Orationes Sollemnes, the former must have equally known and used them in the African liturgy. All the more since it is not certain that the passages in Caesarius describe the *Orationes Sollemnes*! Their context seems to evoke the Eucharistic celebration, yes; but nowhere do these two sermons specify at what time this prayer — for which one must genuflect — takes place. The words 'humiliter supplicantes et pro se et pro aliis'[93] do not shed much light on the content of the prayer. Both sermons do, however, seem to place this prayer after a psalm.[94]

Of itself, the expression *Flectamus genua* indicates a penitential prayer, but not automatically the *Orationes Sollemnes*. The Gallican tradition, which does not prescribe a genuflection, shows us that the two things are not necessarily connected. And the placing of this prayer after a psalm makes us think of the information given to us by Cassian — even though he is referring to the Office — who informs us that in Gaul as well as in Egypt, at the end of a psalm the monks genuflect and even make a prostration. This same practice is recorded by Isidor of Seville and Fructuosus of Braga.[95]

In short, if it is not even clear that the texts of Caesarius use the verb *indicere* to introduce the diaconal invitation, *Flectamus genua*, in reference to the *Orationes Sollemnes*, how could the presence of these in the African liturgy be deduced from Augustine's use of the verb *indicere*?

Moreover, the role of the deacon in the liturgical action seems greatly reduced in Africa; the Bishop of Hippo scarcely mentions it.[96] In addition, it is not clear where a *Flectamus genua* could be integrated into the literary form used (*orare pro ... ut ... Amen*).

But above all, this interpretation by Connolly seems not to respect the text of *Epistola* 55 (T 25) which it is supposed to be explaining. Let us remember that Augustine cites the moments of the Mass during which it is not appropriate to sing the psalms: 'cum legitur aut disputatur aut antistites clara voce deprecantur aut communis oratio voce diaconi indicitur'. The first verb does not pose any problem; the second indicates the homily, which Augustine also calls *disputatio*.[97] But what does the end of the sentence mean? All the authors that we have cited seem so blinded by the expression *communis oratio* that they immediately identify

93 Caesarius of Arles, *Sermo* 77, 6; (CC 103), 322.

94 Caesarius of Arles, *Sermo* 76, 1: 'Quid tibi prodest quod fideliter psallis, si posteaquam psallere desinis, deo supplicare nolueris? Et ideo unusquisque, quando psallere cessaverit, cum omni humilitate oret et supplicet domino; ut quod verbis protulit ex ore, deo auxiliante implere mereatur in opere'. (CC 103), 316.

95 John Cassian, *De institutis coenobiorum*, 2, 7, (PL 49), 91; (SC 109), 71. Isidore of Seville, *Regula monachorum*, 6, 1, (PL 83), 875–76. Fructuosus of Braga, *Regula monachorum*, 3, (PL 87), 1101. On this matter refer to the article by Leclercq, 'Genuflection' in DACL 6/1, 1017–21.

96 The tables of the Mauristes provide only six references for the term *diaconus* (PL 46), 237.

97 Cf. Roetzer (1930), 109.

with the *oratio fidelium*.[98] But what is meant by *aut antistites clara voce deprecantur*? [99] Since at no time does the Bishop of Hippo ever speak of an *oratio post sermonem* positioned between the preaching and the *oratio fidelium*, the only thing one can see in this *deprecatio* of the priests is the Universal Prayer itself; the third and fourth phrases of the sentence would therefore be synonymous.

To this we can make three objections. First, the three repetitions of *aut* seem to preclude that any elements of this clause are synonymous. Secondly, and most importantly, St Augustine, in quoting the moments of the celebration when the faithful may not sing, has sought to paint a picture of the whole sequence of the Mass, without being exhaustive. Following the usual interpretation he would have stopped after the *oratio fidelium* without mentioning the Liturgy of the Eucharist. Finally, we do not see any advantage in the pastor using synonymous expressions if his intention was to indicate to his people different moments of the liturgy; it would only have resulted in confusing them.

A Personal Hypothesis

How, then, should this text be understood? It seems simpler to us to let ourselves be led by the obvious meaning that these expressions can take on in the unfolding of the Mass: one sings neither when one reads, nor when one preaches, nor when the priests pray aloud, nor when the common prayer is announced by the voice of the deacon. It is also justifiable to understand by 'prayer of the priests' the Canon of the Mass and by 'the common prayer' the Our Father.

Immediately the objection leaps out at us: in this case, Augustine is incomplete since he makes no mention of the Prayer of the Faithful! Our reply is that, on balance, it is not a matter of him affirming the current description, according to which he omits entirely the Eucharistic Prayer and the Our Father. Augustine is not a person for exact precision, and the context of his letter does not lead us to expect that he will be exhaustive in this case.

But let us continue our hypothesis further by considering the third element of the sentence first. *Deprecari* does not appear in any passage dealing with the *oratio fidelium*. In Letter 217 (T 1 and T 2), which is more developed on this point, we read that the priest (*sacerdos*) exhorts (*exhortare* the first time, *hortare* the second) the people to pray (*orare*) or that he prays himself. As for *communis oratio*, if the expression immediately evokes the Universal Prayer for modern liturgists, the same cannot be certain in times past. Nowhere does Augustine make use of this phrase when speaking about the *oratio fidelium*, not even in his long Letter 217. Moreover, let us remember that for St Cyprian the *communis oratio* was the Lord's

98 In addition to the authors cited on p. 64, see Jungmann (1962), vol. 1, 614, footnote 5: 'Der Ausdruck *communis oratio* für das in Rede stehende Gebet steht fest bei Augustinus, Ep. 55, 34'. ("The expression *communis oratio* for the prayer in question is fixed in Augustine, *Epistola* 55, 34').

99 The variant *antistes … deprecatur* of manuscript m does not seem able to enlighten us.

Prayer;[100] while we know that *De dominica oratione* was for Augustine a bedside book.[101] Finally, any text from Augustine concerning the Universal Prayer makes no allusion to a deacon.

But we cannot just reject the current interpretation of Letter 55, 34; we must show that ours better reflects the text. One point has already been made: our hypothesis better frames the context by describing the overall celebration. No one will deny that *antistites clara voce deprecantur* can just as easily apply to the Canon. And the ending? If we assume that *communis oratio* describes the Lord's Prayer, then the problem raised by 'voce diaconi indicitur' resurfaces: is the deacon announcing the Our Father? The liturgical books are silent on this point. One can recall, however, that before Gregory the Great the Lord's prayer did not follow immediately after the anaphora: the two were separated by the fraction rite.[102] It is possible that the *Oremus* that nowadays introduces the Our Father was required for this interpolated rite. Once the fraction was concluded there would have been need to call people back to attention. It may be that already at Augustine's time prayers were included in the fraction rite,[103] prayers that the Ambrosian rite has preserved.[104] In short, we find ourselves confronting a rather complex rite, and we cannot rule out that the deacon may have intervened to announce the Lord's Prayer to the people.

Undoubtedly the existence of this diaconal invitation to the Our Father cannot be taken as a certainty. However, our interpretation of Letter 55 seems sufficiently coherent to be able to form a valid hypothesis. If critics were to deny its merits and stand by the usual explanation of this passage, then we would have to accept the intervention of the deacon during the *oratio fidelium*. For reasons set out above, then, we are not able to follow Connolly in thinking that the deacon invited the assembly to pray by using the formula *Flectamus genua*. 'Communis oratio voce diaconi indicitur' would, in our opinion, simply mean that the deacon invites people to prayer before the priest formulates the intentions. Let us leave this question on hold for a moment. We will come back to it soon, perhaps better armed, after examining another problem.

b) Meaning of the Formula 'Conversi ad Dominum'

What, then is the meaning of the formula *Conversi ad Dominum* that is found at the end of a number of Augustine's sermons? The formula alludes to turning to

---

100 Cf. above, pp. 38–39.

101 Only in Letter 217 does Augustine cite twice from the text of *De dominica oratione* (nos. 6 and 26); in n. 2 he twice alludes to it; in n. 22 he refers to *De mortalite*.

102 This ordinance is specifically attested to by Augustine, cf. Roetzer (1930), 128. The fraction rite still precedes the Our Father in all the Eastern rites except the Byzantine, Armenian and Maronite (which have all been influenced by the Roman rite); similarly in Spain and Gaul.

103 This is the opinion of Roetzer (p. 128), based on Letter 149, 16: '*orationes, cum benedicitur et sanctificatur et ad distribuendeum comminuitur*' (cf. T 3).

104 *Missale ambrosianum*, ed. Ratti and Magistretti (1913), 245.

the east, which was required for prayer,[105] but this expression is often followed by a prayer whose meaning is disputed.[106] We find

2 times — *Conversi*, etc.[107]
59 times — *Conversi ad Dominum*[108]
5 times the following formula is used:

T 26 Conversi ad Dominum Deum Patrem omnipotentem puro corde ei, quantum potest parvitas nostra, maximas atque veras (uberes) gratias agamus; precantes toto animo singularem mansuetudinem eius, ut preces nostras in beneplacito suo exaudire dignetur; inimicum a nostris actibus et cogitationibus sua virtute expellat, nobis multiplicet fidem, gubernet mentem, spiritales cogitationes concedat, et ad beatitudinem suam perducat. Per Iesum Christum filium eius, Amen.[109]

Twice as follows:

T 27 Conversi ad Dominum, ipsum deprecemur pro nobis et pro omni plebe sua nobiscum in atriis domus suae, quam custodire protegereque dignetur per Iesum Christum Filium eius (unicum) Dominum nostrum, qui cum eo vivit et regnat in saecula saeculorum. Amen.[110]

Once the following form is used:

T 28 Conversi ad Dominum, gratias agamus ei qui vivit et regnat in saecula saeculorum.[111]

---

105 It is not our intention or purpose to consider this question, for which the classis work is Dölger (1920); for recent biography see Vogel (1964), 3–37.

106 The listing is given in Dölger (1920), 255, which cites all the places where our formula is found. To this must be added the sermons edited by Morin (1930), (refer to tables on 794).

107 e.g. *Sermo 1* (PL 38), 26.

108 e.g. *Sermo 26* (PL 38), 178.

109 e.g. *Sermo 34* (PL 38), 213: 'Turn to the Lord God, Father almighty, with a pure heart and, as much as our smallness will allow, let us give thanks, greatly and sincerely, begging his clemency with all our soul, so that in his good will he deigns to answer our prayers; that by his power he might drive out anything hostile to our actions and thoughts, that he might increase faith in us, that he might direct our mind, that he might grant us spiritual thoughts and leads us to his happiness. Through his Son Jesus Christ. Amen'. Tr.J.O'Brien. This text also figures at the end of his *Ennarationes in psalmos* (PL 37), 1966; (CC 40), 2196. The doxology is sometimes more extended.

110 *Sermo 100* (PL 38), 605 and *Sermo 362* (PL 39), 1634: 'Turn to the Lord, pray to him for us and for all his people who stand with us in his house; that he may deign to watch over it and protect it through Jesus Christ his (only) Son, our Lord, who lives and reigns with him for ever and ever. Amen'.

111 *Sermo 141* (PL 38), 778, according to the majority of manuscripts. 'Turn to the Lord, let us give thanks to him, who lives and reigns for ever and ever'.

In the ending of the *Sermo Denis II* we read the following:

T 29 Conversi ad Dominum *et oratio*: Virtus misericordiae eius confirmet in veritate sua cor nostrum, confirmet et tranquillet animas nostras; abundet super nos gratia eius, et misereatur nostri, et auferet scandala a nobis, et ab ecclesia sua, et ab omnibus carissimis nostris, faciatque nos placere sibi virtute sua et abundantia misericoridae suae super nos in aeternum. Per Iesum Christum filium suum dominum nostrum, qui cum eo vivit et regnat et cum Spiritu sancto in saecula saeculorum. Amen.[112]

And finally this anti-Pelagian passage, the only one which does not conclude a sermon; nevertheless, it is a good example of the 'liturgical argument':

T 29a Benedictiones, fratres mei, benedictiones nostras, quas super vos facimus, evacuant, exinaniunt, elidunt. Auditis me, credo, fratres mei, quando dico,
Conversi ad Dominum benedicamus nomen eius, det nobis
perseverare in mandatis suis,
ambulare in via recta eruditionis suae,
placere illi in omni opera bono,
et caetera talia.
Prorsus, inquiunt, hoc totum in potestate nostra est constitutum…
Defendamus et nos, et vos; ne et nos sine causa benedicamus, et vos sine causa Amen subscribatis.[113]

What, then, is the function of these *Conversi*? W. C. Bishop considers them, without hesitation, as introductions to the *oratio fidelium*.[114] So too do F. J. Dölger — although he is concerned, it is true, more with the problem of orientation

---

112 *Sermo Denis II*, ed. Morin (1930), 17. 'Turn to the Lord', and the prayer: 'May the power of his mercy strengthen our hearts in his truth, may it strengthen and soothe our souls, may his grace abound in us, and may he take pity on us and remove scandals far from us and from his Church and all those dear to us; may his power and the abundance of his mercy make us able to please him for ever. Through Jesus Christ, his Son, our Lord who lives and reigns with him and with the Holy Spirit for ever and ever. Amen'. Tr.J.O'Brien.

113 Fragment 3 against Pelagius (PL 39), 1721: 'May the blessings, my brothers, our blessings which we make over you, strike them down, wipe them out, overcome them. You hear me, I believe, brothers, when I say, Turn to the Lord and let us bless his name, and he will grant us to persevere in his commandments, to walk on the right path of his teaching, to please him in every good work, etc. But assuredly, they say, all that is in our power … Let us defend ourselves, both of us, so that it is not without reason that we might bless nor that you might give assent with your Amen'. Cited by Gamber (1966), 107–08. Based on this passage he understands the *Conversi* to be the 'blessings' that come between the homily and the sending out of the catechumens. His article, (1972), 49–64, deals only with the question of orientation. Probst (1893), 304, followed by Roetzer (1930), 132 sees in them a blessing before Communion, as in the Gallican rite. W. C. Bishop similarly accepts the existence of such a blessing, on the basis of Letters 149 (T 3) and 179 (PL 33), 775; (CSEL 44), 693. For our part, we do not see what prevents us from interpreting this text in the same way as the previous ones.

114 W. C. Bishop (1912), 260 and 271.

than the question we are facing[115] — C. Vogel[116] and more clearly J. Jungmann.[117] W. Roetzer shows himself to be more circumspect and does not even raise the problem.[118]

A Prayer after the Sermon?

On the other hand, G. Dix,[119] followed by C. A. Bouman,[120] regard it as a 'prayer after the sermon' such as is found in the Euchology of Serapion,[121] in the Egyptian liturgy of St Cyril and in the Ethiopian liturgy.[122] What are we to make of it?

In fact, these three formularies do include a prayer after the Sermon;[123] but their content is quite different from that of the Augustinian formularies. These are addressed to the people; after the homily comes the invitation to give thanks (T 26, T 28 and T 29) and to pray for different intentions (apart from T 28). The best-constructed form is evident in T 26: 'Conversi ad Dominum ... ei ... gratias agamus, precantes ... ut preces nostras exaudire dignetur' followed by the concrete requests. But what do we find in the texts cited as parallels by G. Dix? The prayer from the Egyptian and Ethiopian liturgies is a collection of short intercessions, introduced by μνήσθητι, dealing with things as well as persons. This has nothing in common with the *Conversi*. The prayer of Serapion comes closer to it, but it is addressed to God and not to the people; it is a true prayer that begins by setting out the divine attributes and moves on to the requests in the usual style. The formulas that commence with *Conversi* are, strictly speaking, not prayers. They are addressed to the people and exhort them to pray, and are therefore come under the category of 'invitation'.

In short, it is not enough to consider texts found in other liturgical families that occur in the same place as ours as parallel to ours and to explain the one in terms of the other Their content too must be analogous. Until proven otherwise, we do not believe that we can give these *Conversi* the hypothetic title of 'prayer after the sermon'.[124]

115 Dölger (1920), 256 puts the two following elements in apposition: 'das *Conversi ad Dominum*, die Aufforderung zum Gemeindegebet am Predigtschluβ' (The *Conversi* and the invitation to congregational prayer at the sermon.).
116 Vogel (1964), 12.
117 Jungmann (1962), vol. 1, 614–15.
118 Roetzer (1930), 89 and 245.
119 Dix (1945), 472–73.
120 Bouman (1959), 13.
121 *Didascalia et Constitutiones apostolorum*, ed. Funk (1905), vol. 2, 160.
122 Brightman (1896), 157 and 220 respectively.
123 Truth to tell, only the Euchologion of Serapion contains a prayer after the sermon: μετὰ τὸ ἀναστῆναι ἀπὸ τῆς ὁμιλίας εὐχή. The two other texts are prayers accompanying the Gospel.
124 An *oratio post evangelium* is found in several of the liturgical books, notably in the *Benevento Missal* (cf. Dold (1934), xxx–xxxiii). We do not believe that this can throw light on our problem.

The Opinion of Ramos

What, then, is the purpose of these texts introduced by *Conversi*? We think that they will be better understood with the help of another comparison, this time the Spanish liturgy. Recently, M. Ramos devoted an entire book[125] to the *missa*, the first of ten variable prayers in the Hispanic liturgy which follow the Offertory chant. These are followed by an *alia* (*oratio*), then the diptyques, the prayers *post nomina* and *ad pacem*, and finally by the Preface.

According to this Spanish Jesuit, the *missa* was sometimes an invitation to prayer by the priest to the faithful. It was followed by a form of the *oratio fidelium* of which traces can still be found in the *Ecclesiam sanctam catholicam* … used in the Ordinary of the Mass in the *Missale Mixtum* of Cardinal Ximenez de Cisneros.[126] *The oratio admonitionis* serves as a transition between the homily and the Prayer of the Faithful on those occasions when the preacher preferred to conclude his sermon with a prayer. This is the origin of the deviations that this prayer underwent.

Ramos allows himself to suggest — and it is here that our problems coincide — that the prototype of this *missa* may well have been found in Africa, and more particularly, in the *Conversi ad Dominum* formulas. Indeed, the structure of these *missae* is very close to that of the Augustinian formularies. Here are some examples:

- Deum, qui …, fratres carissimi, suppliciter exoremus: ut … det … donet … ut nobis proficiat ad salutem.[127]
- Deum qui …, tota poscamus dilectissimi fratres mentis intentione, ut concedat … ut … ut … celestium Sacramentorum participium consequi mereamur.[128]
- Deum Regem omnipotentem … fratres karissimi, oratione poscamus: ut preces nostras … suscipiat. Nos … liberos paradysi reddat et celo. Ipse presta.[129]

Ramos is careful not to declare a possible dependence of the *missae* on the *Conversi*, but nevertheless judges that it would not be far from the truth to see the origin of these two formulas in the transition from preaching to the Universal Prayer.

We note that the Gallican liturgical tradition presents the same prayer schema: the invitatory is called *praefatio* and the prayer *collectio* or *collectio sequitur.* More

125 Ramos (1964). 'Oratio admonitionis' is a more adequate term to describe the 'missa'.

126 *Missale Mixtum*, (PL 85), 114 and 540. Here is the text: 'Ecclesiam sanctam catholicam in orationibus in mente habeamus: ut eam Dominus fide et spe et charitate propicius ampliare dignetur. Omnes lapsos captivos infirmos atque peregrinos in mente habeamus: ut eos Dominus propicius redimere sanare et confortare dignetur'. Response: 'Presta eterne omnipotens Deus'. We have already cited this text when we studied the formula in mente habere of Cyprian, p. 50. Speak of it again in Part 2, p. 290.

127 *Liber mozarabicus sacramentorum*, ed. Ferotin (1912), 478, n. 1033; or PL 85, 960.

128 *Liber mozarabicus sacramentorum*, ed. Ferotin (1912), 79, n. 173; or PL 85, 220.

129 *Liber mozarabicus sacramentorum*, ed. Ferotin (1912), 175–76, n. 381; or PL 85, 331.

study is needed here.[130] Thus we find ourselves confronted by a construction particular to Spain; Africa may have known it as well.

This hypothesis of Ramos seems to us able to be retained. It is more satisfactory than that which saw the *Conversi* as a 'prayer after the sermon', since it is in fact an invitatory and not an oration. It also has the advantage of providing a valid explanation of the presence of these expressions at the end of Augustine's sermons, making of them a transition between preaching and the Prayer of the Faithful. In this it stands with the majority of liturgists, as we have seen above.

Formulary of the Universal Prayer?

Another theory would be that *Conversi* and the formulas that follow constitute the actual text of the Universal Prayer, perhaps from the days before it was well-developed. This opinion can be based on the fact that four out of five formulas include a conclusion, and so could scarcely act as an introduction to something else, but these conclusions may have been added over time, as is the case with so many other invitatories, especially since these formulas end the sermon. Another, more solid, argument might be that four out of five texts include petitions, and so there is no expectation that other invitatories will follow. On the contrary, the impression is that we are dealing with a complete unit.

We can now resume our discussion on the role of the deacon. In the event that Letter 55, 34 (T 25) obliges us to admit a diaconal intervention during the Prayer of the Faithful — of which we are not persuaded — it seems to us that the expression would apply very well to the announcement by the deacon of the monition introduced by the *Conversi ad Dominum*.

The first thing to say is that Augustine never tells us that this monition was made by the deacon. On the contrary, everything points to the priest using it to conclude his homily.

Next, how can we harmonise this supposition with the passages of Letter 217: 'quando audis sacerdotem dei ad altare (dei) exhortantem populum dei orare pro…' (T 1) and 'ubi audieris sacerdotem dei ad eius altare populum hortantem ad deum orandum vel ipsum clara voce orantem…' (T 2)? What could better correspond to this exhortation by the priest than the invitatory introduced by *Conversi*? Once again the role of the deacon appears very problematic.

130 Cf. this title in *Missale Gothicam*, ed. Mohlberg, n. 66–67, 449–400; *Messes de Mone*, ed. Mohlberg, n. 24–25, 70–71. All the Gallican texts of interest to our topic are systematically listed by Ramos (1964), 165 ff. Duchesne (1925), 110–11 had already indicated the existence of this euchological structure (which he called 'collective prayer') with a *praefatio* followed by an *oratio*. As an example of this he gave the invitatory followed by the *collectio* in the Gallican rite, and from Rome the *Orationes sollemnes*, as well as the *Oremus* that precedes the prayers (1925), 110–13. Dix (1945), 489, adds the Spanish *missa* and *alia*. But Mgr Duchesne indicates that between the monition and the prayer there is only the silent prayer of the assembly. For our part, we believe that these two elements may have framed an intercessory prayer.

c) Conclusion

Let us summarise what we have so far. We are not at all certain that Letter 55, 34 (T 25) is dealing with the *oratio fidelium*. If we did accept that premise, then the unfolding of the prayer of the faithful could be reconstituted as follows: At the end of the sermon Augustine invited the assembly to turn towards the east with the words *Conversi ad Dominum*. This would be followed by an invitatory, whose text has been preserved for us (T 26 — T 29a). Then he would probably have spoken some other petitions, cast in the form *orare pro ... ut ...*, to which the people responded each time, *Amen*.

If, however, it turns out that Letter 55, 34 applies to the Universal Prayer, we would suggest attributing to the deacon the monition introduced by *Conversi*.

In Spain the priest concluded the whole thing with a prayer (*alia*), but we do not find any trace of it in the works of the Bishop of Hippo. Finally, we note that in no way does it resemble a diaconal litany as is found in the Eastern rites.

4. Its Content

Let us cite, first of all, these interesting texts:

T 30 *Epistola* 217, 2: 'Dic ergo apertissime nos pro his, quibus evangelium praedicamus, non debere orare ut credant' (T 7)

T 31 *Epistola* 217, 2: 'orare
pro incredulis, ut eos deus convertat ad fidem,
et pro catechumenis, ut eis desiderium regenerationis inspiret,
et pro fidelibus, ut in eo, quod esse coeperunt, eius munere perseverent' (T 1)

T 32 *Epistola* 217, 2: 'deum pro infidelibus, ut eos fideles faciat, non rogare'.

T 33 *Epistola* 217, 5: 'orare, ut deus ad fidem suam infidelium corda converteret, et conversis proficientem perseverentiam eiusdem suae gratiae largitate donaret'

T 34 *Epistola* 217, 13: 'Non enim hoc oramus pro infidelibus ut fiat eorum natura ... sed oramus, ut voluntas corrigatur, doctrinae consentiatur, natura sanetur'

T 35 *Epistola* 217, 14: 'ut perseverent in eo, quod esse coeperunt, etiam pro se ipsis orant fideles'

T 36 *Epistola* 217, 16: 'scimus pro eis, qui nolunt credere, nos, qui iam credimus, recta fide agere, cum deum oramus, ut velint'

T 37 *Epistola* 217, 26: 'numquid et orare prohibebis ecclesiam
pro infidelibus, ut sint fideles,
pro his, qui nolunt credere, ut velint credere,
pro his, qui ab eius lege doctrinaque dissentiunt, ut legi eius doctrinaeque consentiant...' (T 2)

T 38 *Epistola* 217, 26: 'sacerdotem ... orantem ut incredulas gentes ad fidem suam venire compellat'

T 39 *Epistola* 217, 29: 'de orationibus autem iam fidelium, quas et pro se et pro aliis fidelibus faciunt, ut proficiant in eo, quod esse coeperunt'

T 40 *Epistola* 217, 29: 'pro infidelibus deum rogari, ut credant'

T 41 *Epistola* 217, 30: 'orandum esse, ut, qui nolunt credere, velint credere'

T 42 *Epistola* 217, 30: 'orare nos deum pro nolentibus credere, ut velint credere, et pro eis, qui adversantur et contradicunt legi eius atque doctrinae ut ei cedant eamque sectentur'

T 43 *De dono perseverantiae,* 15: 'Orat (Ecclesia) ut increduli credant … Orat ut credentes perseverent' (T 6)

T 44 *De dono perseverantiae,* 63: 'Quando enim non oratum est in Ecclesia pro infidelibus atque inimicis eius ut crederent?'

T 45 *De Haeresibus,* 88: 'Destruunt etiam orationes, quas facit Ecclesia sive pro infidelibus et doctrinae Dei resistentibus, ut convertantur
ad Deum
sive pro fidelibus, ut augeatur in eis fides, et perseverant in ea' (T 5)

T 46 *Contra Maximinum,* 1: 'cum scias nobis esse praeceptum orare pro regibus, ut in agnitionem veniant veritatis' (1 Tim 11:4)

T 47 *De civitate Dei* 22, 24, 1: 'Nunc enim propterea pro eis orat, quos in genere humano habet inimicos, quia tempus est paenitentiae fructuosae'.

Let us classify this information, distinguishing between the beneficiaries and the aim of the petition.

a). The Beneficiaries

Augustine names five groups of people for whom the Church prays:

1 unbelievers or heretics:
 – 'pro infidelibus': 6 times (T 32, T 34, T 37, T 40, T 44, T 45)
 'ut deus … infidelium corda converteret' (T 33)
 – 'pro incredulis' (T 31)
 'ut incredulas gentes … compellat' (T 38)
 'ut increduli credant' (T 43)
 – 'pro eis qui nolunt credere': 4 times (T 36, T 37, T 41, T 42)
 – 'pro his quibus evangelium praedicamus' (T 30)
 – 'pro his qui ab eius lege doctrinaque dissentiunt' (T 37)
 – 'pro eis qui adversantur et contradicunt legi eius atque doctrinae' (T 42)
2 believers:
 – 'pro fidelibus': 4 times (T 31, T 35, T 39, T 45)
 – 'pro conversis' (T 33)
3 catechumens (T 31)
4 kings (T 46)
5 enemies: 2 times (T 44 and T 47)

Note that this series only includes people; no reference is made to a prayer for peace or for good weather. W. Roetzer, on the basis of T 31, indicates only three beneficiaries: unbelievers, the faithful and catechumens.[131] We ourselves have cited five, but we do not claim that the Christians of Hippo never prayed for other intentions. All these texts are occasional; nowhere did the bishop take the trouble to copy his *Ordo Missae* for the benefit of posterity. The fragments that remain only serve to remind us of the fragmentary state of the documentation.

b). The Aim of the Prayer

1 With regard to unbelievers, what does it ask?
  'ut credant' (that they might believe): 4 times (T 30, T 40, T 43, T 44)
  'ut velint credere' (that they might wish to believe): 4 times (T 36, T 37, T 41, T 42)
  'ut eos Deus convertat ad fidem' (that God might convert them to faith): 1 time (T 31)
  'ut Deus ad fidem suam infidelium corda converteret' (that God will convert the heart of the unbelievers to his faith): 1 time (T 33)
  'ut incredulas gentes ad fidem suam venire compellat' (that he might impel unbelieving people to come to his faith): 1 time (T 38)
  'ut convertantur ad Deum' (that they might be converted to God): 1 time (T 45)
  'ut eos fideles faciat' (that he might make them faithful): 1 time (T 32)
  'ut sint fideles' (that they might be faithful): 1 time (T 37)
  'ut voluntas corrigatur, doctrinae consentiatur, natura sanetur' (that the will might be corrected, doctrine assented to, nature healed): 1 time (T 34).
2 For the faithful:
  'ut in eo quod esse coeperunt perseverent' (that they might persevere in what they began to be): 2 times (T 31, T 35)
  'ut in eo quod esse coeperunt proficiant' (that they might progress in what they began to be): 1 time (T 39)
  'ut conversis proficientem perseverantiam eiusdem suae gratiae largitate donaret' (that by the bounty of his grace he might give to the converted to progress in perseverance) (T 33)
  'ut credentes perseverent' (that believers might persevere) (T 43)
  'ut augeatur in eis fides, et perseverent in ea' (that faith might grow in them and they might persevere in it) (T 45)
3 For catechumens:
  'ut eis desiderium regenerationis inspiret' (that they might be inspired with a desire for regeneration [baptism]) (T 31)
4 For kings:

131 Roetzer (1930), 114–15.

'ut in agnitionem veniant veritatis' (that they might come to knowledge of the truth) (T 46)

5 For enemies:
'ut crederent' (that they might believe) (T 44)

It is striking to note the convergence of all these petitions. They are always prayed with a view to a truly Christian reality, namely, the faith. They ask that non-Christians and even their enemies might be converted, and that the faithful might persevere. The prayer for catechumens, even though it has a specific aim, follows the same line, as does the prayer for kings, being a reprise of 1 Tim 2:1–2.

For the first time we are faced with a fairly unified vocabulary. Even though the overwhelming majority of these texts (72%) are taken from Letter 217, where the Pelagian controversy undoubtedly had an influence, and therefore have less probative value than if they were found in different works, we think we can put our finger on certain liturgical formulas. The verbs *credere* (which occurs 9 times), *convertere* (4 times), *perseverare* (4 times), *proficere* (twice), along with the substantive *fides* (5 times) were to become part of the customary vocabulary of the Universal Prayer, and without much risk of being mistaken, we can say that the expression 'ut in eo quod esse coeperunt perseverant (proficiant)' has a similar provenance.[132] This is probably not enough to maintain that the Church in Africa used a fixed form. While the actual composition of the prayer was left in the hands of liturgists, there were nevertheless dominant themes: the conversion and the faith of unbelievers and enemies, the perseverance of Christians. Without this structure and these theme it is not possible to understand the liturgical argument.

Summary

The lists of prayer-intentions as well as the descriptions of the Mass that are found in the writings of the African bishop convince us that the African liturgy at the beginning of the 5th century included an *oratio fidelium*. This conviction is reinforced by the liturgical argument that Augustine employs during the Pelagian controversy: grace is necessary for faith since Christians ask for it in prayer. Read here: the Universal Prayer.

No technical term was yet attached to this prayer. Three expressions were in use: *orationes Ecclesiae, orationes fidelium, orationes credentium*. It was carried out in the following way: after the homily, the priest (most probably, or perhaps the deacon) invited the faithful to turn to the east with the words *Conversi ad Dominum*, and then prayed the invitatory; then the priest announced several petitions to which the assembly responded *Amen*.

132 The theme of perseverance in the faith occurs frequently in Augustine, who devoted an entire work, *De dono perseverantiae*, to it.

The content of these petitions was not linked to any fixed formula. We recognise in them, however, major themes: unbelievers, the faithful, catechumens, the civil authorities, and enemies. For Christians, the petition was for perseverance; for the others it was the gift of faith.

Conclusions from the Second Section

Let us take stock of what we have learnt so far. Agreement among various indicators noted in the works of Tertullian makes us consider feasible the existence of a Universal Prayer in the liturgy of Carthage at the turn of the 2nd and 3rd centuries. Fifty years later, Cyprian gives us no direct indication about the *oratio fidelium*, but an analysis of his writings nevertheless convinces us of its continuance. While these two authors do give some indication of the content of the prayer, their information is not precise enough for us to know the liturgical form.

The evidence from Arnobius and Marius Victorinus is of little use to us.

With Augustine, the information is more precise. It is beyond doubt that the Bishop of Hippo was familiar with the Universal Prayer. After the homily he would invite the assembly to turn to the east with the formula *Conversi ad Dominum*, followed by an invitatory. They would pray especially that the faithful would persevere in the faith and that unbelievers would be converted to it; all would respond *Amen*. This practice also served as a means for the African Doctor to prove to the Pelagians that faith is a gift from God.

In this 5th century the vocabulary is already becoming more stable, but not enough to suggest the existence of fixed formulas.

Section Three

The Church of Rome

Hippolytus († 235)

The first text that we will examine in this section is taken from the celebrated *Apostolic Tradition* until recently attributed to Hippolytus. It dates from around the year 215 and is understood to be ecclesiastical regulations written by a Roman priest, although what corresponds in his work to practice in the Church of Rome and what is personal to him is not able to be clearly distinguished. As with Justin almost a century earlier (Section One, T 7), the author describes for us a Baptism followed by a Eucharist:

T 1 *Apostolic Tradition*, 21: 'And having signed him [the newly-baptised] on the forehead, he [the bishop] will give him a kiss and say: The Lord be with you. And he who has been signed shall say: And with your spirit. He [the bishop] will do so with each one.

And then they shall pray together with all the people: they do not pray with the faithful until they have carried out all these things. And when they have prayed, they shall give the kiss of peace.

And then the offering shall be presented'[1]

This description corresponds exactly to that of St Justin. However, since this baptism is not preceded by a Liturgy of the Word, can we therefore speak of an *oratio fidelium* in the strict sense?

Justin's description of a Baptism in chapter 65 of his *First Apology* was followed at chapter 67 by the description of a Eucharist including the Liturgy of the Word and the Universal Prayer, each of these two passages shedding light on the other. This author, by contrast, never describes for us the order of a normal Mass. During the ordination of the bishop he mentions neither the readings nor the Prayer of the Faithful; the prayer of episcopal consecration is followed immediately by the kiss of peace and the presentation of the gifts.

Also, the text we have just quoted can be used as an argument in favour of the existence of the *oratio fidelium* proper only if it we accept that it must be read alongside what Justin taught us, which is to say that baptism took the place of the

---

1 Hippolytus, *Apostolic Tradition*, 21, ed. Cuming (1976), 20–21.

Liturgy of the Word, after which the action passed to the Universal Prayer, the kiss of peace and the bringing forward of the gifts.

Note that 'Hippolytus' makes of this Prayer of the **Faithful** a rite that is proper to them; we can understand this passage when we are aware that several liturgies included a prayer of the catechumens and their dismissal before the Prayer of the Faithful.[2]

The *Apostolic Tradition* teaches us nothing about the content of the prayer.

Novatian

The second text is a letter of Novatian, a Roman priest who lived in the mid-3rd century. It is classified among the correspondence of St Cyprian and bears the number 30.[3] It is addressed to him, around 250, by the priests and deacons of Rome who speak to him of the *lapsi* and recommend severity with regard to them. While the context does not refer to the liturgy, they write:

T 2 *Epistola 30, 6, 1–2*: 'Uno igitur eodemque consilio, isdem precibus et fletibus, tam nos qui usque adhuc videmur temporis istius ruinas subterfugisse, quam illi qui in has temporis videntur clades incidisse, divinam maiestatem deprecantes pacem ecclesiastico nomini postulemus. Mutuis votis nos invicem foveamus, custodiamus, armemus.
Oremus pro lapsis ut erigantur,
oremus pro stantibus ut non ad ruinas usque temptentur,
oremus ut qui cecidisse referuntur delicti sui magnitudinem agnoscentes
intellegant non
momentaneam neque praeproperam desiderare medicinam.
Oremus ut effectus indulgentiae lapsorum subsequator paenitentiam,
ut intellecto suo crimine velint nobis interim praestare patientiam, nec adhuc fluctuantem turbent ecclesiae statum,
ne interiorem nobis persecutionem ipsi incendisse videantur et accedat ad criminum
cumulum quod etiam inquieti fuerunt'.[4]

---

2 Cf. for example, CAp, vol. 1, 478; Br, 3–4.

3 Clavis (CC), no. 72.

4 Cyprian, *Epistola 30, 6, 1–2*, (PL 3, 968; CSEL 3.2, 554); ed. Bayard, vol. 1, 75; Eng. tr. Donna (FC 51), 72–78: 'With the same counsel, with the same prayers and tears, let all of us, and those who, like us, seem to have so far escaped these destructions, and those who have fallen into these disastrous calamities, implore the divine majesty, and ask for peace for the Church and her people. In praying for each other let us help each other, watch over each other, arm one another. Let us pray for those who have fallen that they may be raised up; let us pray for those who are standing, that they may not succumb to trial; let us pray that those who have said to have fallen may acknowledge the greatness of their fault and will understand that it is not a short or hasty cure that is called for; let us pray that forgiveness granted to the *lapsi* will be effective, since it comes after penitence, so that,

This prayer appears to begin with a formula: *pro lapsis ut erigantur*; but it would be unrealistic to see in it a complete formulary of the Universal Prayer; apart from the *stantes* — mentioned once — the intentions concern only the *lapsi*. As with many passages from Cyprian, one can hypothesise that Novation is familiar with a prayer of intentions within the liturgy; writing at his desk, it is only natural that he is inspired by it and composes the intentions according to the specific subject of his letter.

Ambrosiaster

Here is how Ambrosiaster, who lived in Rome during the second half of the 4th century comments on 1 Tim 2:1–4:

T 3 'Haec regula ecclesiastica est tradita a magistro gentium, qua utuntur sacerdotes nostri, ut pro omnibus supplicant

deprecantes pro regibus huius saeculi, ut subiectas habeant gentes, ut in pace positi in tranquillitate mentis et quiete deo nostro servire possimus,

orantes etiam pro his, quibus sublimis potestas credita est (est credita), ut in iustitia et veritate gubernent rem publicam subpeditante rerum abundantia, ut amota perturbatione seditionis succedat laetitia — panis enim confirmat cor et vinum laetificat mentem -,

postulantes vero pro his qui in necessitate varia sunt, ut erepti (eruti) et liberati deum conlaudent incolomitatis auctorem,

referentes autem (quoque) gratiarum actiones pro his, quae nobis quotidie dei providentia praestantur ad vitam, ut in his omnibus pater conlaudetur deus, ex quo sunt omnia, et filius eius, per quem sunt omnia, ut sopitis omnibus, quae huic imperio infesta et inimica sunt, in affecta pietatis et castitatis deo servire possimus'.[5]

---

understanding well their guilt, they may consent in the meantime to show patience and not upset a Church that is still wavering; lest they may appear to inflame an internal persecution for us and bring their guilt to the extreme by showing themselves unable to remain quiet'.

5 Ambrosiaster, *In Epistolam B. Pauli ad Timotheum Primam*, ed. Vogels, (CSEL 81.3), 259–60; (PL 17), 466: 'It is the ecclesiastical rule, transmitted by the teacher of the Gentiles, which our priests follow when they make supplications for all people. They pray for the kings of this world, that the nations may be subject to them so that in peace we may serve our God with a tranquil spirit and at ease. They pray for those to whom supreme power is entrusted, that they might lead the State in justice and truth. Thus, with an abundance of goods and with the threat of danger removed, there can be joy; for bread strengthens the heart and wine makes the spirit rejoice. They also petition for those who find themselves in various needs, so that they might give praise to God, the author of their

The author states right away that this is a priestly formula; it is considered to be a tradition in the Church, transmitted by St Paul himself. The rest of the commentary provides no clue as to the place or function of such supplication. The author is guided by the four subjects of prayer included in 1 Tim as he briefly lays out the beneficiaries of the prayer. We cannot, therefore, rely on these four proposals as being the four petitions that comprise a formulary for the *oratio fidelium* at the end of the 4th century. V. L. Kennedy affirms, for his part, that this text is a witness to the Prayer of the Faithful in the 4th century.[6]

In recording and studying these patristic texts, this passage did not seem particularly important to us; we were inclined to follow V. L. Kennedy, although with a little more caution. However, after reading them again after studying the texts presented in Section Two, we believe that there are some similarities that are rather surprising. Could Ambrosiaster have provided a reflection of the ancient formulary of the Universal Prayer, just as happened with the *Orationes Sollemnes* in the works of Prosper of Aquitaine? First of all, let us set out the parallels.

1 *pro regibus huis saeculi* is found in almost identical form in one of the Hispanic formulas (*Hb* IX): *pro regibus saeculi hujus*. Note that this expression does not appear in the New Testament, which therefore cannot be its common source. It does, however, often employ the phrase 'reges terrae', which comes from Ps 2:2
2 *ut subiectas habeant gentes* recalls the fourth invitatory of the *Orationes sollemnes: ut … subditas illis faciat omnes barbaras nationes*. It can be compared to another Hispanic formula (*Ha* III a): *ut … barbaras gentes refrenet*. The expression is also found in the intercessions of the Anaphora of the Greek liturgy of St James (Br 55, 16–16, cited in the study of the *Orationes sollemnes*).
3 *in tranquillitate mentis et quiete*, together with *pro his quibis sublimis potestas est credita*, and (at the end of this excerpt) *in affectu pietatis et castitatis*, all come from 1 Tim 2:1–2, as Ambrosiaster made mention. Nevertheless, let us note that the litany *Dicamus omnes* from the Stowe Missal that we will study in Part 2 and which we date from the end of the fourth or beginning of the fifth century, prays *pro omnibus qui in sublimitate constituti sunt* (*Irl*[1] VI)!
4 *pro his qui in necessitate varia sunt* can be compared with *pro his qui variis necessitatibus detenti Paschae interesse non possunt* (*Hb* I) or with *pro his quos saeculi necessitas aut inquietudo detentat* (*Ha* IVa). This petition could very well summarise the prayers that the litanies make for widows, orphans travellers and other needy persons.

salvation. Finally, they give thanks for what God's providence offers us every day in order to live, so that in all things God the Father, 'from whom everything comes' (1 Cor 8:6) and his Son 'through whom all things exist' (ibid.), and that once what harms and fights against this state has disappeared, we might serve God with piety and purity of heart. Tr. J.O'Brien.

6 Kennedy (1963), 31.

What are we to make of this? These comparisons are striking; in our opinion their similarities are too strong to be put down to chance. The second example shows that Ambrosiaster was, without doubt, familiar with the invitatories of the *Orationes Sollemnes,* which would not have been impossible since they date from the late-third or early- fourth century (cf. Part Two of this work). The others tend to show that the author had a knowledge of one or more of the litanic formularies, which would provide a wonderful external proof of the dating that we are proposing: on the basis of internal criticism alone we will situate (in Part 2) the oldest litanic text (*Dicamus omnes* of the Stowe Missal) at the end of the fourth or beginning of the fifth century.

There is one appreciable difference, however. These litanies, as is the case with Ambrosiaster, certainly introduce the petitions with *pro,* but they never include the *ut* with its final proposal. Their origin must therefore be the invitatories of the *Orationes Sollemnes.*

At any rate, it is in our opinion beyond dispute that Ambrosiaster knew this common source that we find in all Latin litanies right up to the late Hispanic *orationes paschales.* T 3 must therefore be considered as evidence of the Universal Prayer. Thanks to him we have for the first time a concrete formulary, or at least a thematic, which is able to be traced in the liturgical books. Note that if it is indeed a litany, then the first sentence of T 3 seems to exclude the possibility of it being said by a deacon.

Siricius, Felix III and the Public Penitents

V. L. Kennedy cites, with as much confidence as for T 3, a reply of Pope Siricius (384–399) to Bishop Himerius of Tarragon in the year 385. Here is the passage:

T 4 *Epistola 1*: 'De quibus, qui jam suffugium non habent paentitendi, id duximus decernendum, ut sola intra ecclesiam fidelibus oratione jungantur, sacrae mysteriorum celebritati, quamvis non mereantur, intersint; a Dominicae autem mensae convivio segregentur'.[7]

H. Connolly, who introduces this passage in his work on the Universal Prayer, later cites — in connection with a text of Pope Felix III — canon 11 of the Council of Nicea, taken up by Siricius in the lines preceding those we have just read, but perhaps he was unaware that there he was touching on a canonical

7 Pope Siricius, *Epistola 1, 6*; (PL 13, 1137): 'With regard to these people who no longer have the option of being penitents, we have made the following discernment: that they unite with the faithful through prayer alone, that they attend the sacred celebration of the mysteries, even though they do not deserve it, but let them be kept away from eating at the table of the Lord'. Tr.J.O'Brien.

prescription evidenced by many Eastern texts from the fourth century. Before interpreting Siricius' response, we must take a brief excursion to the East to get a better understanding of where these formularies originated.

1. The Didascalia of the Apostles

In the section dedicated to the reconciliation of penitents, the Syrian author from the first half of the third century uses expressions that come close to those of Siricius:

T 4a 39, 5: 'Consider, therefore, as "pagan and publican" the one who has been convicted of evil deeds and lies. If he later promises to repent, [we will treat him] like the pagans. When they wanted to convert, they promised to enter into penitence and claimed to be believers, therefore we received them into the assembly so that they would hear the Word, but we did not commune with them until they became perfect by receiving the seal. Likewise, we do not commune with these until they show the fruits of their penitence. Let them enter if they want to hear the Word, so that they are not lost entirely; let them not, however, join in prayer, but go out. Thus, seeing that they do not participate in the Church, they will submit themselves and do penance for their past deeds and strive to be admitted into the Church for prayer. On the other hand, those who see them coming out like pagans and publicans, and who take note of this, will take fright and beware of sinning, so that the same thing doesn't happen to them, namely that, being convicted of sin and lies, they are excluded from the Church'.[8]

In the phrases, 'Do not commune with them' and 'do not let them have part in prayer', to which prayer is reference being made? In his notes, Funk indicates the Universal Prayer, but can he be certain? The context seems to contradict this claim; would the author have spoken in this way if he had only the Prayer of the Faithful in mind?

2. The Penitential Canons in Asia Minor during the 3rd and 4th Centuries

Asia Minor, and the discipline of canonical penance that developed there, especially in the 4th century, provides us with the greatest number of parallels in order to situate Pope Siricius' words. From St Gregory Thaurmaturgus, the Councils of Ancyra, Neocaesarea, Nicea and Antioch, as well as the canonical letters of Gregory of Nyssa and in particular those of his brother Basil, we are offered abundant documentation from which we will cite the texts that are the most interesting from our point of view.[9]

---

8 *Didascalia Apostolorum*, 2, 39, 5–6; ed. Funk (1905), vol. 1, 126–128.

9 In this regard, read the following:

A. Gregory Thaumaturgus (c. 218–270)

It is in his *Epistola canonica* that we come across the expression κοινωνεῖν τῶν εὐχῶν,[10] 'to be united in prayer' — to participate in prayers with someone — a formula whose precise meaning we fail to detect in this work. We also find the expression ἐκκηρύξαι τῶν εὐχῶν[11] (whom to denounce by prayer) or on the contrary τῆς εὐχῆς ἀξιῶσαι[12] (considered worthy of our prayer) and the context shows that it is dealing with penitents who were to be excluded from the prayer or prayers,[13] or who were to be admitted only progressively. But which prayer is it? That it is a public, liturgical prayer is not in dispute; but is it the Eucharistic Prayer or is it the Prayer of the Faithful? It is not possible to split them. Sometimes the impression is given that 'to be excluded from the prayers' indicates a kind of excommunication: the penitent no longer has the right to pray with the faithful, to participate in worship with them, one might even say to be in their company. The text from the *Didascalia* (T 4a) was explicit enough, comparing them to 'pagans and publicans'. Εὐχή seems not to describe any prayer in particular.

We must set aside c. 11 which is much more precise but generally considered to be inauthentic.[14] This describes the four classes of penitents, some of whom were outlined in the previous canons and of whom Basil will speak profusely:

T 5 - the προσκλαίοντες, or weepers, who stand outside the church and implore a prayer from the faithful who enter it;

- the ἀκροώμενοι, or auditors who, from the narthex, can listen to the readings and the preaching and are then sent away, not being worthy of [joining in] the prayer (μὴ ἀξιούσθω προσευχῆς);

- the ὑποπίπτοντες, or prostraters, who position themselves in the church and are sent away at the same time as the catechumens;[15]

J. Morin, *Commentarius historicus de disciplina in administratione sacramenti paenitentiae*, Venice, 1702, Book 6, especially chapters 1–18; F. X. Funk, 'Zur altchristlichen Bußdisciplin', and particularly 'Die Bußstationen im christlichen Altertum', in *Kirchengeschichtliche Abhandlungen und Untersuchengen*, vol. 1, Paderborn, 1897, 155–181 and 182–209 respectively; E. Schwarz, 'Bußstufen und Katechumenatsklassen' in *Schriften der wiss. Gesellschaft in Strasburg*, VII, 1911, 1–61, reprinted in *Gesammelte Schriften*, vol. 5, Berlin, 1963, 274–362; G. Rauschen, *Eucharistie und Bußsakrament*, Fribourg Br. 1910, 191–209; and J. Grotz, *Die Entwicklung des Bußstufenwesens in der vornicänischen Kirche*, Fribourg, 1955.

10 Gregory Thaumaturgus, *Epistola canonica*, c. 1; (PG 10, 1020–1).

11 Gregory Thaumaturgus, *Epistola canonica*, c. 5; (PG 10, 1037).

12 Gregory Thaumaturgus, *Epistola canonica*, c. 9; (PG 10, 1044).

13 There seems to be no difference between the singular and the plural. In all this canonical literature, εὐχή — εὐχαί, προσευχή — προσευχαί, δέησις — δέησεις are synonymous, since we find the same expressions using the various substantives interchangeably, sometimes in the singular, sometimes in the plural.

14 Gregory Thaumaturgus, *Epistola canonica*, c. 11; (PG 10, 1048); cf. Schwartz (reprinted 1963), 309, and Funk (1897), vol. 1, 182.

- the συνεστῶτες, those who remain standing, who could stand with the faithful (συνιστῆται τοῖς πιστοῖς) and not go out with the catechumens.

After completing these four stages the penitent ceases to be a penitent; he is δεκτός, received back into communion, and can participate in the sacraments (ἡ μέθεξις τῶν ἁγιασμάτων).

To clarify further the participation of each of these classes in the liturgy, let us now glean the information provided to us by other sources.

B. The Council of Ancyra (314)

This is the first Council that deals with the fate of the various categories of penitents, and it does so in several canons. It repeats the four categories that we have already met in c. 11 of Gregory Thaumaturgus. In c. 4 of the Council of Ancyra we read in regard to the συνεστῶτες the expression frequently found in subsequent canons and which will be taken up in the West by Pope Siricius: εὐχῆς δὲ μόνης κοινωνῆσαι.[16] The German theologian S. Binius, who comments on this passage in Mansi, explains that the penitents 'were admitted to public prayers, but not to the reception of the Body and Blood of Christ'. He affirms that εὐχῆς δὲ μόνης κοινωνεῖν means the same as χωρὶς προσφορᾶς κοινωνεῖν, which is found in the following canons, and he refers to Baronius who writes, Videlicet satis sufficere cum fidelibus orare, nec a precibus ut audientes excludi; id enim erat communicare absque oblatione'.[17] Can we clarify this opinion? C.16 prescribes that the συνεστῶτες 'κοινωνίας τυγχανέτωσαν τῆς εἰς τὰς προσευχάς', in other words they get the κοινωνία τῶν εὐχῶν.[18]

---

15 μετὰ τῶν κατηχουμένων ἐξέρχηται; Funk (1897), vol. 1, 204–09, wanted to support the notion that the ὑποπίπτοντες weren't dismissed, but that they assisted at the entire Eucharist in the same way as the συνεστῶτες. The difference between the two categories would have been that the former had to kneel while the latter could stand.

This explanation ignores the specific claims of this canon as well as c. 56 of Basil (μετὰ τῶν ἐν ὑποπτώσει … ἐξελεύσεται). It had already been rejected by Rauschen (1910), 198–99 (which also refers to Jülicher's rejection of this).

Brightman (1896), 524, argues that the expression means only that they were sent back after the dismissal of the catechumens, but fails to specify the respective order of the dismissals of the different classes.

16 Council of Ancyra, c. 4; Mansi 2, 515; Bruns (1839), 67.

17 'It is sufficient, evidently, to pray with the faithful, and nor should the hearers be excluded from the prayers; for that is to share without offering'. Cf. Mansi 2, 536–37. The commentary by Baronius can be found in *Annales ecclesiastici* for the year 314; ed. Theiner (1867), vol. 3, 605.

18 Council of Ancyra, c. 16, Bruns (1839), 69.

C. The Council of Nicea (325)

T 6 Following what we learned from Gregory Thaumaturgus and the Council of Ancyra, the canons of Nicea do not reveal much that is new. C.11 prescribes that Christians who denied the faith during the persecution of Licinius should remain three years in the ἀκρόασις, seven years in the ὑπόπτωσις; and finally δύο δὲ ἔτη χωρὶς προσφορᾶς κοινωνήσουσι τῷ λαῷ τῶν προσευχῶν,[19] they take part in the prayers with the people, apart from the oblation.

T 7 With regard to the dying, c. 13 makes reference to an ancient canon law which prescribes that they should not be deprived of viaticum. If the dying person, having been forgiven his sins and received Communion during the celebration of the sacrifice [of the Mass], then recovers, he may take his place among the living but is to be counted among those who commune only in prayer.[20] We need to be cautious in interpreting the terms used in these canons and not be too quick to ascribe to them a meaning that a Christian from the twentieth century might deem obvious. Κοινωνίας τυχών undoubtedly refers to sacramental communion, but also ecclesial communion into which the penitent is newly received again, or to be more precise, communion in the prayers to which reference is made shortly after. Similarly, προσφορᾶς μετασχών certainly does not signify any part taken by the penitent in the Offertory, nor probably even participation in the Eucharistic Prayer, since this man is dying and no longer has the strength to take part. In context, this term refers to sacramental communion, the viaticum which is the subject of the beginning of the text. The participation 'as a result of the sacrifice' can be explained in a similar manner, although he will be excluded from this if he does indeed manage to escape death, for he will only be able to participate in the prayer.[21] In other words, exceptional circumstances call for exceptional measures, but these must not set a precedent; if the penitent recovers, he will resume the normal course of his penitence without being able to take advantage of the favour granted to him at the point of death.

But as yet we are not in a position to determine just which 'prayer' it is in which he will be able to take part.

---

19 Council of Nicea, c. 11; Mansi 2, 674; Bruns (1839), 17; COD, 10. Liddell-Scott, vol. 1, 969 notes explicitly that κοινωνέω is constructed with the genitive for things and the dative for persons, in the sense of 'participating in something with someone'.

20 Council of Nicea, c. 13: Εἰ δὲ ἀπογνωσθεὶς καὶ κοινωνίας τυχὼν καὶ προσφορᾶς μετασχὼν πάλιν ἐν τοῖς ζῶσιν ἐξετασθείη, ἔστω μετὰ τῶν κοινωνούντων τῆς εὐχῆς μόνης. The text is not absolutely certain; several editions omit καὶ προσφορᾶς μετασχών.

21 That προσφορά can mean sacramental communion is clearly proven in the *Apostolic Constitutions* VIII, 13, 5: Καὶ ὁ μὲν ἐπίσκοπος διδότω τὴν προσφορὰν λέγων Σῶμα Χρστοῦ, καὶ ὁ δεχόμενος λεγέτω Ἀμήν. ed. Funk, vol. 1, 516–18; Brightman (1896), 25, 6–9.

D. St Basil (c. 330-379)

Letters 188, 199 and 217,[22] addressed to Amphilochius, bishop of Iconium, contain a series of 84 canons, several of which deal with the reconciliation of penitents.

T 8 C. 4. authorises polygamists, after their time as 'hearers' to be συνεστῶτες, but to 'be apart from the communion of the good',[23] an expression that flowed frequently from the pen of the bishop of Caesarea. Having shown the fruits of their penitence they could then rejoin 'the place of communion'.

Canons 22, 56 and 75 are more detailed.

a) C. 22 speaks of those who abduct women:

T 9 χρὴ τῷ πρώτῳ (ἔτει) ἐκβάλλεσθαι τῶν προσευχῶν καὶ προσκλαίειν αὐτοὺς τῇ θύρᾳ τῆς ἐκκλησίας,

τῷ δευτέρῳ δεχθῆναι εἰς ἀκρόασιν

τῷ τρίτῳ εἰς μετάνοιαν

τῷ τετάρτῳ εἰς σύστασιν μετὰ τοῦ λαοῦ ἀπεχομένους τῆς προσφορᾶς εἶτα αὐτοὺς ἐπιτρέπεσθαι τὴν κοινωνίαν τοῦ ἀγαθοῦ.[24]

For the third class of penitent Basil does not use the term ὑπόπτωσις, but rather μετάνοια, which could correspond to the description in 1.VIII of the *Apostolic Constitutions* where the final participants dismissed before the εὐχὴ τῶν πιστῶν are called οἱ ἐν μετανοίᾳ. Penitents of the fourth class are to remain with the people but refrain from the offering (προσφορά). Are we to assume that this last term refers to the Eucharistic Prayer or to sacramental communion as is the case with c. 13 from the Council of Nicea? The final clause of the sentence, which describes the completion of penance, seems to us to adopt this last theory: 'the communion of the good' can indeed refer to the second part of the Mass, but is better understood as sacramental communion. And the rather laconic c. 44 determines that the deaconess convicted of fornication δεκτή ἐστιν εἰς τὴν κοινωνίαν, εἰς δὲ τὴν

---

22 Basil of Caesarea, *Letter 188*, (PG 32), 663 ff; *Letter 199*, (PG 32, 715 ff); *Letter 217*, (PG 32, 793 ff.), ed. Courtonne (1961), vol. 2, from which we will quote.

23 C.4, (PG 32, 673); ed. Courtonne (1961), vol. 2, 125: τῆς δὲ κοινωνίας τοῦ ἀγαθοῦ ἀπέχεσθαι.

24 C.22, (PG 32), 724; ed. Courtonne (1961), vol. 2, 158: 'In the first year they must be sent away from the prayers and weep at the door of the church; in the second they are to be received into "hearing"; the third they dedicate to penance; in the fourth they may stand with the people, but not take part in the offering; then they will be allowed the communion of the good'.

προσφορὰν δεχθήσεται τῷ ἑβδόμῳ ἔτει;[25] Here κοινωνία seems to indicate inclusion in the prayers, and προσφορά the Eucharistic sacrifice; but προσφορά could also be understood in a more limited sense and actually refer to sacramental communion.

b) Canon 56 states that an intentional murderer will be for twenty years ἀκοινώνητος τοῖς ἁγιάσμασι, excommunicated from the holy things. This period will be carried out as follows:

T 10 Ἐν τέσσαρσιν ἔτεσι προσκλαίειν ὀφείλει ἔξω τῆς θύρας ἑστὼς τοῦ εὐκτηρίου οἴκου καὶ τῶν εἰσιόντων πιστῶν δεόμενος εὐχὴν ὑπὲρ αὐτοῦ ποιεῖσθαι ἐξαγορεύων τὴν ἰδίαν παρανομίαν.

Μετὰ δὲ τὰ τέσσαρα ἔτη εἰς τοὺς ἀκρωμένους δεχθήσεται καὶ ἐν πέντε ἔτεσι μετ' αὐτῶν ἐξελεύσεται.

Ἐν ἑπτὰ ἔτεσι μετὰ τῶν ἐν ὑποπτώσει προσευχόμενος ἐξελεύσεται.

Ἐν τέσσαρσι συστήσεται μόνον τοῖς πιστοῖς, προσφορᾶς δὲ οὐ μεταλήψεται.

Πληρωθέντων δὲ τούτων μεθέξει τῶν ἁγιασμάτων.[26]

Apart from the dismissal of the ὑποπίπτοντες,[27] this canon does not provide us with anything new. For the fourth class, the distinction between the σύστασις alone (μόνον) and the προσφορά is again emphasised, without the term εὐχή being used. Here we find ourselves dealing with technical terms whose meaning we cannot easily determine.

T 11 C. 57 reinforces the theory that the συνεστῶτες were excluded only from sacramental communion, when it describes the end of the time of penitence as follows: καὶ … εἰς ἅγια τὰ ἅγια δεχθήσεται.[28]

Indeed, ἅγια commonly refers to the Eucharistic species; and we must also remember the proclamation of the priest before Communion in many Eastern liturgies: τὰ ἅγια τοῖς ἁγίοις.[29]

---

25 C.44, (PG 32, 729), ed. Courtonne (1962), vol. 2, 162; 'she may be included in communion, but she is not to be included in the offering until the seventh year'.

26 C.56, (PG 32, 797), ed. Courtonne (1962), vol. 2, 210–11: 'For four years he must weep, remaining outside at the door of the house of prayer and beg the faithful who enter to pray for him as he confesses his own sin. After the four years he will be admitted among the "auditors", and for five years he will go out with them. For seven years he will pray with the "prostrated" and will remain with them. For four years he will only stand with the faithful, but will not take part in the offering. Once these penances have been completed he may participate in the holy things'.

27 Cf. footnote 15, p. 86.

28 C. 57, (PG 32, 797), ed. Courtonne (1961), vol. 2, 211: 'and he will be admitted to the holy things'.

29 From the *Apostolic Constitutions*, cf. Brightman (1896), 24, 20: 'Holy things for holy people'.

c) C. 75 is the last that gives any extended description of the four classes of penitents. There is no point in citing what Basil writes about the first three; with regard to the last group he writes:

T 12 εἰς τὴν τῶν πιστῶν εὐχὴν δεχθήτω χωρὶς προσφορᾶς, καὶ δύο ἔτη συστὰς εἰς τὴν εὐχὴν τοῖς πιστοῖς, οὕτω λοιπὸν καταξιούσθω τῆς τοῦ ἀγαθοῦ κοινωνίας.[30]

Following what we have read so far, this makes us regard the expression εἰς τὴν εὐχὴν τῶν πιστῶν with caution and not leap to the conclusion that it is the *oratio fidelium*.

E. St Gregory of Nyssa († 394)

In his *Epistola canonica* to Letoius, bishop of Melitene,[31] several canons treat the reconciliation of penitents, and continually employ the expressions with which we are now familiar. It will suffice to cite c. 2, which teaches us that, with regard to those who lapse by choice

T 13 Οὐδέποτε γὰρ μυστικῆς ἐπιτελουμένης εὐχῆς, μετὰ τοῦ λαοῦ προσκυνῆσαι τὸν θεὸν καταξιοῦται, ἀλλὰ καταμόνας μὲν εὔξεται· τῆς δὲ κοινωνίας τῶν ἁγιασμάτων καθόλου ἀλλότριος ἔσται· ἐν δὲ τῇ ὥρᾳ τῆς ἐξόδου αὐτοῦ, τότε τῆς τοῦ ἁγιάσματος μερίδος ἀξιωθήσεται.[32]

Because the prayer in question is here qualified by the word 'mystical' we are led to believe that in this instance we are dealing with the Eucharistic Prayer rather than the Universal Prayer.

Finally, c. 5 confirms the interpretation that we gave to c. 13 from the Council of Nicea with regard to viaticum. Indeed, it decides that

T 14 Εἰ δὲ μετασχὼν τοῦ ἁγιάσματος, πάλιν εἰς τὴν ζωὴν ἐπανέλθοι, ἀναμένειν τὸν τεταγμένον χρόνον ἐν ἐκείνῳ τῷ βαθμῷ γενόμενον, ἐν ᾧ ἦν πρὸ τῆς κατὰ ἀνάγκην αὐτῷ δοθείσης κοινωνίας.[33]

Here Ἁγίασμα clearly is referring to sacramental communion.

---

30 C. 75, (PG 32, 803), ed. Courtonne (1961), vol. 2, 214: 'let him be received to the prayer of the faithful apart from the oblation, and after standing with the faithful in prayer for two years, let him finally be judged worthy of the communion of the good'.

31 Gregory of Nyssa, *Epistola canonica*, (PG 45, 221 ff.).

32 C. 2, (PG 45, 225C): 'During the mystical prayer, he is in no way worthy of worshipping God with the people, but he must pray apart; he is to be entirely an outsider at the communion of the holy things; but at the hour of his death, only then will he be worthy of his share of the holy thing'.

33 C. 5, (PG 45), 232C-D: If he has partaken of the holy thing and then returns to life, he must continue, for the appointed time, at the stage he had reached when because of necessity he was granted communion'.

Summary

Let us summarise what we have learnt about each of the classes of penitent:

1. The προσκλαίοντες had to remain outside the church and beg the faithful who were going inside to pray for them. Funk thinks that it is not just a question of the faithful 'keeping them in mind' but of praying for them in the prayers of intercession,[34] even though 'prayer for those who are weeping' as such does not exist.
2. The ἀκροώμενοι can stand in the narthex, listen to the readings and the homily, then they are dismissed without even a prayer being prayed over them.
3. The ὑποπίπτοντες can take their place inside the church; after the Liturgy of the Word and the prayer over them, they are dismissed.
4. The συνεστῶτες assist at the Liturgy of the Word and can 'stand with the faithful'; they are worthy of 'the prayer', but not of the offering.

Our problem now is to decipher what precise meaning should be given to the famous term εὐχή. In our opinion there are only two possibilities: either εὐχὴ χωρὶς προσφορᾶς refers to the *oratio fidelium*, or it is describing the Eucharistic Prayer.[35]

1 First hypothesis: εὐχὴ χωρὶς προσφορᾶς = *oratio fidelium*

What, then, was the sequence of events within the celebration? After the homily, the 'auditors' were dismissed; the ὑποπίπτοντες were also prayed for and, in their turn, dismissed. Then came the Prayer of the Faithful properly so-called. (So far this corresponds well to the ritual found in the *Apostolic Constitutions* VIII, 6 ff.) The συνεστῶτες were allowed to participate in the Prayer of the Faithful as well, but only in this, according to the canons. Therefore, according to this first hypothesis, they must always be dismissed right after it, and the χωρὶς προσφορᾶς is to be understood as exclusion from the Eucharistic sacrifice.

If this is the case then Pope Siricius, who was not familiar with these rites of dismissal, would not have understood the technical meaning of the term εὐχή in the East, since by insisting that the penitents unite with the faithful by prayer alone, he is authorising them to participate in the sacred celebration of the mysteries (cf. T 4). He does this with some hesitation, however, for he adds: 'although they are not worthy of it'. This remark gives a clear indication of his wrong interpretation of the term εὐχή.

---

34 Funk (1897), vol. 1, 190.

35 Of course εὐχή can also describe a prayer other than those of the Mass — it could mean morning or evening prayer, for example. Some texts seem to understand it in this way, in particular c. 1 and c. 5 of Gregory Thaumaturgus, whom we have already cited. In general, however, these canons refer to the Mass rather than to worship taken as a whole, and so we believe justified in limiting the debate to two theories.

For εὐχή to be able to refer to the *oratio fidelium* and it alone, one thing remains to be shown: that the penitents of the fourth class were in fact dismissed after the Prayer of the Faithful. Are we in possession of the liturgical books that give clues of this rite? It would seem not. However the compiler of the *Apostolic Constitutions* and two other authors do perhaps leave some traces.

a For our first author we turn to the *Apostolic Constitutions.* Section 1 of Chapter 8 contains a dismissal after the Prayer of the Faithful and the Kiss of Peace, just before the Anaphora begins: 'No more catechumens, no more auditors, no more infidels, no more of those with unorthodox beliefs. Let those who prayed the first prayer come near...'[36] Unfortunately, it only speaks about the συνεστῶτες, and the meaning of this 'first prayer' is not clear. Previously in 10, 2, after the dismissal of the auditors, the catechumens, the energumens, the *competentes* and the penitents (οἱ ἐν μετανοίᾳ), the deacon denies access to the Prayer of the Faithful and the Eucharist to all those who have no right to it,[37] repeating, as if with a generic formula, the previous dismissals. Reading 12, 2 one has the impression of being faced with a doublet or repeat from 10, 2, made 'to be certain' before the Anaphora begins, and not with the dismissal of a new class of penitents (in this case the συνεστῶτες). Moreover, the editor of the *Apostolic Constitutions* who, through the particular literary device that he employs has, since the end of the homily given the role of speaker to Andrew (VIII, 6, 1). In 12, 1, he hands this over to James to begin the Anaphora, a process that reinforces the impression of a doublet. In short, this first clue is not on very solid ground.

b Our second text comes from John Chrysostom. In his third homily on the Letter to the Ephesians he writes:

T 15 In vain is the sacrifice offered each day, in vain do we stand before the altar: there is no one to participate. In speaking this way, I do not aim to force you to participate blindly, but seek that you make yourselves worthy of it. Are you not worthy of the sacrifice or of communion? If so, then neither are you worthy of the prayer. You hear the deacon stand and announce, 'Let those who are undertaking penitence leave!' All those who do not participate are undergoing penitence. If you are among the penitents you may not participate, for those who do not participate are in penitence. Why then, when the deacon says 'Depart, you who do not have the right to pray' do you have the effrontery to stay? You are not one of these, but one of those who *can* participate, and you don't care about it? You regard this as nothing?[38]

---

36 *Apostolic Constitutions* VIII, 12, 2; Funk (1905), 494; Brightman (1896), 13, 26: 'Μή τις τῶν κατηχουμένων, μή τις τῶν ἀκροωμένων, μή τις τῶν ἀπίστων, μή τις τῶν ἑτεροδόξων. Οἱ τὴν πρώτην εὐχήν εὐχόμενοι προσέλθετε'.

37 *Apostolic Constitutions* VIII, 10, 2; Funk (1905), 488; Brightman (1896), 9, 25; 'Μή τις τῶν μὴ δυναμένων προσελθέτω'.

Is there in this second proclamation of the deacon any trace of the dismissal of the συνεστῶτες? In his reconstruction of the Antiochian liturgy based on the early works of John Chrysostom, Brightman sees in these diaconal admonitions two distinct dismissals. He situates the first after the departure of the catechumens, energumens and penitents, just before the Prayer of the Faithful,[39] and the second after the Prayer of the Faithful and the Kiss of Peace, just before the Anaphora.[40] In a note he explains that, although 'the place of these proclamations is indeterminate, they are placed here by analogy with the *Apostolic Constitutions* VIII, 12, 2'.[41] Since this last ritual, as we have just seen, is not clear, then what is built on it cannot be clear either. Moreover, to verify our hypothesis the deacon would have to dismiss 'those who had the right to pray' at the time of the Universal Prayer, when he in fact excluded 'those who do not have the right to pray'.

F. Van de Paverd, a recent commentator on the works of John Chrysostom,[42] considers the text of the first diaconal admonition to be corrupted; it should probably read: ὅσοι ἐν μετανοίᾳ δεήθητε πάντες. According to him, the two admonitions allude to the same reality, namely the litany for the penitents, located before the Prayer of the Faithful, as in the *Apostolic Constitutions.*

The second clue, then, is not conclusive.[43]

c The third clue is more substantial and comes to us from a response of Timothy, bishop of Alexandria (381–385), to the question as to whether a cleric can pray in the presence of heretics. Timothy responds:

T 16 'In the divine Anaphora, the deacon announces before the kiss [of peace]: "Let the excommunicated depart"'.[44]

Brightman used this text in his reconstruction of the Egyptian liturgy based on the authors of the 4th and 5th centuries.[45] Its interest is its precise location: before the Kiss of Peace, which normally followed the Prayer of the Faithful in which

38 John Chrysostom, *In epistulam ad Ephesios commentarius: Homilia* 3, (PG 62, 29). In Greek, in the text normally used, the deacon says: Ὅσοι ἐν μετανοίᾳ, ἀπέλθετε (πάντες) ... Ἀπέλθετε, οἱ μὴ δυνάμενοι δεηθῆναι'.

39 Brightman (1896), Appendix C: 'The Liturgy of Antioch based on the writings of St John Chrysostom'. 470–81. See 472, 26.

40 Brightman (1896), Appendix C, 473, 21.

41 Brightman (1896), 478, n. 16.

42 Van de Paverd (1970), 187–97. We thank this author for having kindly photocopied the proofs of his work before they had been published.

43 With regard to this whole question, F. Van de Paverd considers (see pp. 192–96) that Antioch was unaware of the fourth class of penitents. In fact, the whole theology of John Chrysostom opposes the idea that people are present at the Eucharistic Prayer without participating in Communion.

44 Timothy of Alexandria, *Responsa canonica,* (PG 33), 1295 ff. See col. 1301C: 'Ἐν τῇ θείᾳ ἀναφορᾷ ὁ διάκονος προσφωνεῖ πρὸ τοῦ ἀσπασμοῦ· οἱ ἀκοινώνητοι, περιπατήσατε'.

45 Brightman (1896), Appendix J: 'The Liturgy based on the writings on the Egyptian Fathers', 504–09. See especially 504, 24 and 507, n. 10.

the συνεστῶτες would have participated before being dismissed by this diaconal admonition. However, two objections arise. In the first place, the canons that we have cited never used the adjective ἀκοινώνητος to refer exclusively to the fourth class of penitents; the term refers to the entire period of penitence.[46] This admonition of the deacon would therefore refer to the dismissal of *all* the penitents. The second question is more important: to what extent can one rely on a liturgical fact which, although contemporaneous, comes out of Alexandria, to explain a canonical prescription from Anatolia, especially since it is vouched for by a single text?

In conclusion, we must say that the probability of this first premise does not seem very great.

2 Second hypothesis: εὐχὴ χωρὶς προσφορᾶς = Eucharistic Prayer

Εὐχή can, perhaps, be understood in a broader sense, and refer to the entire second part of the Mass, especially the Eucharistic Prayer, while also encompassing the Prayer of the Faithful. *A priori*, one would expect juridical prescriptions to be more explicit and precise, but since giving a strict meaning to this resulted in a low probability, then we must bring into play a broader semantic field.

If εὐχή refers to the Eucharistic Prayer, then conceivably the συνεστῶτες who, according to the canonical formula can κοινωνεῖν τῆς εὐχῆς χωρὶς προσφορᾶς, attended the Anaphora but were not authorised to receive sacramental communion: it was precisely this that was their penance. Immediately the objection springs to mind: is it conceivable that at the beginning of the 4th century the official texts — or better still, the conciliar decisions — distinguished in this way between attendance at Mass and receiving Communion, preventing some people from receiving Communion at a Eucharist at which in all other respects they were asked to be present? This is a weighty objection, and yet it is exactly in this way that the texts make most sense.

a Firstly, in certain texts εὐχή clearly refers to the Eucharistic Prayer. This is the case with c. 2 from Gregory of Nyssa (T13) where εὐχή is qualified by μυστική and where there can be no doubt that any prayer other than the Anaphora is being described. Similarly, in c. 2 of the Council of Antioch (341), which we have not yet cited, but belongs in the same context:

T 17 'Let all those who enter the church of God and listen to the sacred Scriptures, but do not commune in prayer together with the people or who out of insolence (ἀταξία) stand apart from participation at the Eucharist, be excluded from the church'[47]

46 For example, canons 56–59 of Basil, ed. Courtonne (1961), vol. 2, 210–11.

If the prayer in question was the Prayer of the Faithful then we would not see the adjective ἀταξία. There would have been no-one to take part, since several categories of Christians were officially excluded.

b Next, the canons on not refusing viaticum to the dying, even if they are penitents, sheds light on the meaning of the term ἁγίασμα, which occurs frequently. It is clear that in speaking of viaticum the canons have in mind only sacramental communion, not only because they are dealing with the dying who obviously no longer have the physical strength to participate in the Mass, but above all because of the context of the canons. C. 13 of Nicea (T 7) speaks about it as προσφορᾶς μετασχών, c. 5 of Gregory of Nyssa (T 14) as μετασχὼν τοῦ ἁγιάσματος, and his c. 2 (T 13) as ἡ τοῦ ἁγιάσματος μερίς (where the preceding line described the state of the penitent as τῆς κοινωνίας τῶν ἁγιασμάτων … ἀλλότριος). Ἁγίασμα, then, clearly refers only to sacramental communion.[48]

c But the difference between σύστασις and full communion is explained in c. 56 of Basil (T 10) by μέθεξις τῶν ἁγιασμάτων and in c. 5 of Gregory of Nyssa (T 14) by μετουσία τοῦ ἁγιάσματος. In c. 61 of Basil, a thief punished for a year will be banned only from the κοινωνία τῶν ἁγιασμάτων. In all these three cases, one can clearly see that penitents can assist at Mass and that their punishment consists in not being able to receive Communion.

The way in which other canons describe the end of the period of penitence, and therefore what the σύστασις are lacking, makes good sense from this perspective.

- Several canons from the Council of Ancyra use the expression τὸ τέλειον:
  καὶ τότε ἐλθεῖν ἐπὶ τὸ τέλειον, Ancyra c. 4 and 6,
  ἵνα τὸ τέλειον … λάβωσι, Ancyra c. 5,
  ἵνα … τοῦ τελείου μετάσχωσιν, Ancyra c. 9,
  καὶ … τελείως δεχθήτωσαν, Ancyra, c. 8.
- Several times Basil uses the formula ἡ κοινωνία τοῦ ἀγαθοῦ to describe either what is forbidden to the συνεστῶτες (c. 4: T 8), or what awaits them after their period of penitence (c. 22: T 9; c. 75: T 12; c. 81).
- The most explicit canons are Basil's c. 57: εἰς τὰ ἅγια δεχθήσεται, which we spoke about earlier (T 11), and his c. 82: εἰς τὴν κοινωνίαν τοῦ σώματος τοῦ Χριστοῦ.

How else can these texts be understood other than an authorization to attend Mass but without receiving Communion? How are we to we understand the expression συνίσταται τοῖς πιστοῖς used in c. 11 of Gregory Thaumaturgus (T 5) and canons 56 (T 10), 75 (T 12), 77, 81 and 83 of Basil (who sometimes adds

---

47 Council of Antioch, c. 2, Mansi 2, 1305; Bruns (1839), 81: Πάντας … μὴ κοινωνοῦντας δὲ εὐχῆς ἅμα τῷ λαῷ … The same canon can be found in the *Canons of the Apostles*, c. 9, (Funk (1905) vol. 1, 566) and in the Second Council of Braga, c. 83 (PL 84, 586).

48 This is confirmed by Lampe (1961) in his article 'ἁγίασμα', 17, 3b.

εἰς τὴν εὐχὴν) as a an indication solely of the participation of the συνεστῶτες in the Universal Prayer, with the dismissal after it, when the dismissal is never mentioned, while it is explicitly mentioned for the ἀκροώμενοι and the ὑποπίπτοντες?

Beyond these arguments of internal criticism, it can also be recalled that Pope Siricius understood the text in this way. Enjoining the penitents to join the faithful in the one prayer, he authorized them to attend the celebration of the sacred mysteries, even though they were not worthy to do so; but he forbade them to approach the *convivium dominicae mensae* (T 4).

For those scandalized by this Eucharist without Communion, we must point out that the same discipline exists in the Church of Milan under Ambrose, where the penitent is excluded from Eucharistic Communion until he is asked to take part in the whole celebration.[49] Let us remember also that with St Augustine[50] and also in Gaul there was, after the Our Father and before Communion, a blessing of dismissal for those who were not receiving Communion; there too Christians assisted at Mass without sharing in Communion. In *De officiis septem graduum* from around the end of the 5th century, the exorcist is charged with 'dicere populo qui non communicat ut det locum'[51] and in the life of Saint Benedict, Gregory the Great tells the story of two scarcely committed nuns whom the saint had threatened to exclude from Communion. In regard to this story we are told of the proclamation of the deacon: 'Si quis non communicat, det locum'. This expression is paraphrased several lines further on: 'a diacono iuxta morem clamatus est, ut non communicantes ab ecclesia exirent'.[52] Apart from the evidence from St Ambrose and St Augustine, all these texts are at least a century later than the canons that we have analysed. Nevertheless they attest to a much looser link between Mass and Communion than is generally assumed. Let us note that these texts do not speak of any disaffection with Communion on the part of the faithful, but rather of a liturgical rite of dismissal before Communion.

By supporting the hypothesis of exclusion of the συνεστῶτες from Communion alone, we are merely echoing the opinion of many authorities. Ioannis Zonaras, Greek canonist of the 12th century, writes concerning c. 9 of Gregory Thaumaturgus: 'That is to say, they will remain with the faithful until the end

49 Cf. Gryson (1968), 280.

50 Cf. above, The Church in Africa, p. 58.

51 *De officiis septem graduum*, a short thesis reproduced in the Romano-Germanic Pontifical of the 10th century, ed. Vogel and Elze (1963), vol. 1, 12–13. Cf. Clavis n. 1222.

52 Gregory the Great, *Dialogues* II, 23; (PL 66), 178–80. Cited notably by Jungmann (1962), vol. 2, 424.

of the prayer, banned only from holy communion'.[53] This is also the opinion of J. Morin,[54] F. X. Funk,[55] F. E. Brightman,[56] E. Schwartz,[57] G. Rauschen,[58] J. Grotz,[59] P.-M. Gy,[60] and F. Van de Paverd.[61]

Conclusions

In the 4th century canonical literature of Asia Minor, we do not think that the expression κοινωνία τῆς εὐχῆς τῷ λαῷ χωρὶς προσφορᾶς, describing the fourth class of penitence, refers to the *oratio fidelium*. The texts, taken together, are much more understandable if we assume that the συνεστῶτες had the right to assist at the entire Mass, but could not receive Communion.

A beautiful dream thus vanishes before our very eyes: that of finding evidence of the Universal Prayer in the ancient canonical literature of the East, and in the first ecumenical Council itself.

3. The Letter of Pope Siricius to Himerius (385)[62]

And so, after having tried at length to determine the original meaning of these formulas, we are now in a position to more accurately interpret the prescriptions of Pope Siricius. First, let us recall the text:

T 4 'De his vero non incongrue dilectio tua apostolicam sedem credidit consulendam, qui acta paenitentia, tamquam canes ac sues ad vomitus pristinos et volutabra redeuntes ... De quibus, qui jam suffugium non habent paentitendi, id duximus decernendum, ut sola intra ecclesiam fidelibus oratione jungantur, sacrae mysteriorum celebritati, quamvis non mereantur, intersint; a Dominicae autem mensae convivio segregentur'[63]

---

53 Zonaras, Commentary reproduced in PG 10, 1047C.
54 J. Morin (1702), Book. VI, ch. 17, 3 and 6.
55 Funk (1897), vol. 1, 206.
56 Brightman (1896), 585: 'Consistents stood with the faithful throughout the liturgy'.
57 Schwartz (1911), 308–10.
58 Rauschen (1910), 190: 'während des ganzen Gottesdienstes'.
59 Grotz (1955), 4.
60 P.-M. Gy, in Martimort (1965), 588.
61 F. van de Paverd (1970), 194–95. We were pleased to note that this study, which is more precise (particularly with regard to geography) than ours, and to which we will now have to refer, arrives independently, and via a different path, at exactly the same result as we have.
62 On the penitential discipline in the East you may consult the following, as well as those already cited: B. Poschmann, *Die abendländische Kirchenbuße im Ausgang des christlichen Alterums*, Munich, 1928; J. A. Jungmann, *Die lateinischen Bußriten*, Innsbruck, 1932; E. Göller, *Papsttum und Bußgewalt in spätrömischer und frühmittelalterlicher Zeit*, Fribourg Br., 1933 (the most interesting). Also H. Leclercq, art. 'Pénitents (renvoi des)', DACL,, 14, 1, col, 251-8.

The beginning of this response to bishop Himerius is a quotation of c. 12 from the Council of Nicea. The conclusion plunges us into the context of the Eastern canons that we have just examined: the progressive admission of penitents to the Eucharist. Here, however, we no longer find the four classes that were described in the texts from Asia Minor. Siricius speaks of those who have at some time been enrolled for public penitence and therefore can no longer resort to this. The end of the text recalls for us c. 11 from Nicea (T 6), decreeing that the συνεστῶτες 'χωρὶς προσφορᾶς κοινωνήσουσι τῷ λαῷ τῶν προσευχῶν'; and *sola oratione* finds its parallel in c. 13 (T 7) μετὰ τῶν κοινωνούντων τῆς εὐχῆς μόνης, just as in c. 4 of the Council of Ancyra 'εὐχῆς δὲ μόνης κοινωνῆσαι'. To the extent that the Pope referred to these sources, it is clear that he interprets them according to the second of the methods we proposed, namely that εὐχὴ χωρὶς προσφορᾶς signifies the Eucharistic prayer without Communion. In the light of this Eastern canonical background, it is obvious that there is no question here of the *oratio fidelium*. However, as we cannot be sure that the pope has correctly understood these sources or that the liturgical reality in the West is the same as that in the East, let us analyse the text itself.

In presenting this passage as a vestige of the Universal Prayer, Connolly remains cautious. How did he explain it? It is possible, he wrote, that Siricius did not use *oratione* and *mysteriorum celebritati* as equivalent terms, but meant rather that the persons in question could take part in the Prayers of the Faithful and also be present for the rest of the Mass. This interpretation was suggested to him by a passage of Felix III that we cited earlier (T18). However, he added, if this is not accurate, then *fidelibus oratione iungantur* refers to the Mass as a whole, and can in no way serve as an illustration for the *orationes fidelium*.[64] Dom Capelle also thought that this text probably referred to the Universal Prayer.[65] Let us examine it.

Inside the church, that is to say, in the course of the liturgy, the penitents can be together with the faithful. According to us, in the context of the Roman liturgy, this term *fidelibus* is here implicitly in apposition to *catechumenis*. These penitents are not reduced to the rank of catechumens and can therefore assist at the Eucharistic part of the Mass — as is stated explicitly in the second clause of the sentence. But they are authorized to be together with them only for the prayer and not to participate at the table of the Lord. The opposition therefore lies between the first two clauses of the sentence and the third, namely between *sola* ... *oratione* and *convivio*. This opposition is underlined by the word *autem*. In

63 Siricius, *Epistola 1*, 6; (PL 13, 1137): It is fitting that in your charity you saw fit to consult the Apostolic See about those who, having fulfilled their penitence, like dogs and pigs who return to their former vomit and mud ... With regard to these people who no longer have the option of being penitents, we have made the following discernment: that they unite with the faithful through prayer alone, that they attend the sacred celebration of the mysteries, even though they do not deserve it, but let them be kept away from eating at the table of the Lord'.

64 Connolly (1920), 227.

65 Capelle, Tr. Lit. (1955), vol. 2, 143.

other words, the problem is more one of classification of the penitents among the different 'orders' of Christians than of their participation at the Eucharist; they rank among the faithful, without however enjoying the same rights.

If we understand Connolly's thought, he would cut the text not into two parts, but three:

- union (*iungantur*) with the Prayer of the Faithful;
- assistance (*intersint*) at the Eucharistic Prayer;
- separation (*segregentur*) from Communion.

The second clause would follow as a consequence of the words *fidelibus oratione* that occur in the first. If these penitents are able to take part in the Prayer of the Faithful, they can then assist at the Eucharist proper, since the Prayer of the Faithful is part of that.

This interpretation comes up against several objections. Principal among these is that *oratione*, reinforced by *sola*, is in the ablative case and not in the dative as the English liturgist seems to think. It is not a question of uniting *to* the Prayer of the Faithful, as he believes, and of wondering if this prayer is the *oratio fidelium* or the Canon, but of being united *to* the faithful *by* the prayer alone, not by overall participation. Moreover, even if the text included *orationi*, this term would have to have a depth of meaning such that the reader would recognise in it the Universal Prayer and, knowing its function in the liturgy, thus understand the second clause of the sentence as a consequence of the first. In other words, it is the term *oratio* that would have clarified matters for Himerius. On the contrary, we believe that the word *fidelibus* was the most evocative for him in this first clause: from the outset he was able to understand that the pope classified these penitents among the faithful.

In short, the authors in search of traces of the *oratio fidelium* seem to have been blinded by the closeness of the words *fidelibus oratione* before having properly analysed the text. Here we touch on one of the difficulties of this quest: by dint of looking for the smallest clues of the *oratio fidelium* we end up finding it everywhere.

Let us conclude resolutely. Neither the analysis of the text, nor knowledge of the sources he uses, leads us to read in Siricius' response to Himerius any evidence of the Prayer of the Faithful. Therefore we must remove this text from our project.

4. *The Decisions of the Roman Synod under Felix III (488)*

An important consequence of the above interpretation is that the texts of Felix III[66] ought also be understood in the same way. So let us examine them now,

66 Felix III was an anti-pope. There is another Pope Felix who reigned from 483 until 492, sometimes called Felix II and sometimes Felix III. See Leclercq, 'Pope', in DACL 13/1, 1118. We will respect current usage as well as the historical reality and call him Felix III.

even if it means returning to chronologically more ancient authors. They are to be found in Letter 7, the synodal letter send by the Council of Rome in 488 to all the bishops, that deals with the re-admission into the Church of Christians who have been re-baptised.[67] On the matter of the bishops, priests and deacons, the attitude of the pope is severe. We read:

T 18 'Sed quia idem Dominus atque salvator clementissimus est, et neminem vult perire, usque ad exitus sui diem, in paenitentia (si resipiscunt) jacere conveniet; nec orationi non modo fidelium, sed ne catechumenorum omnimodis interesse, quibus communio laica tantum in morte reddenda est. Quam rem diligentius explorare vel facere probatissimi sacerdotis cura debebit'.[68]

On the subject of other Christians, the Synod aligns itself with the decision made at Nicea:

T 19 'tribus annis inter audientes sint; septem autem annis subjaceant inter paenitentes manibus sacerdotum, duobus autem annis oblationes modis omnibus non sinantur offerre, sed tantummodo saecularibus (*here read* popularibus) in oratione socientur'.[69]

With regard to those penitents who, being in danger of death, have received Communion and then regained their health, the Synod agrees with the decision of the first ecumenical Council:

T 20 servemus in eo quod Nicaeni canones ordinaverunt, ut habeatur inter eos qui in oratione sola communicant, donec impleatur spatium temporis eidem praestitutum.[70]

Generally, only the first of these three extracts is cited. It has already been offered by Probst[71] as proof of the existence of an *oratio fidelium* and an *oratio catechumenorum* at Rome at the end of the 5th century. Connelly has highlighted the

67 We will not get involved here with the difficult problem of the organisation of the Order of Penitence in the West. In this regard see Göller (1933), Introduction and chapters 1–3.

68 Felix III, *Epistola* 7: (PL 58, 925–26): 'But because this same Lord and Saviour is infinitely merciful, and does not want the death of anyone, it is appropriate that (as long as they convert) they should rank among the penitents until the day of their death, and that they do not participate at all in the prayer, not only of the faithful, but even of the catechumens. The communion of the laity is to be returned to them only at death. It is up to the priest to check this and to ensure that it is carried out'.

69 'let them be for three years be *audientes*; then for seven years they are to submit with the penitents to the direction of the priests; then for two years they are not permitted in any way to offer the sacrifices, but may only join with the people in prayer'.

70 'Let us keep to what the canons of Nicea ordered: that they will be ranked among those who participate in prayer alone, until the period of time fixed for this has been completed'. On these texts, see Göller (1933), 87 ff. On the latter two see J. Morin (1702), Book VI, ch. 13, § 7 and 8.

71 F. Probst (1896), 112–13.

contrast between *oratio fidelium* and *oratio catechumenorum* in T 18, and thought it reasonable to interpret the first of these terms as the Prayer of the Faithful rather than the entire Mass of the faithful.[72] Dom Capelle echoed this opinion,[73] and since then the authors have largely spread the idea that T 18 was the last trace of the *oratio fidelium* before Pope Gelasius, successor of Felix III, replaced it with the *Deprecatio Gelasii*.[74] Can we agree with them?

T 19 takes up c. 11 from the Council of Nicea (T 6); χωρὶς προσφορᾶς κοινωνήσουσι τῷ λαῷ τῶν προσευχῶν is translated as 'oblationes modis omnibus non sinantur offere, sed tantummodo saecularibus (popularibus) in oratione socientur'. Participation *at* prayer has become participation *in* prayer; the reality seems identical, given its comparison with the offering of sacrifice. These penitents will no longer be subject to the laying on of hands, but are able to join the ranks of the faithful for prayer; it is not a question of the *oratio fidelium*. However, let us leave the door ajar, because we find that in Italy, 160 years after the Council of Nicea, that liturgical practice has been able to evolve, along with the vocabulary.

The translation of c. 13 (T 7) in T 20 is the same: ἔστω μετὰ τῶν κοινωνούντων τῆς εὐχῆς μόνης has become *habeatur inter eos qui in oratione sola communicant*. The interpretation of the two texts seems to us to be identical; they signify participation in the prayer that is the Eucharist, as opposed to prayer of a more general kind.

Let us now read T 18 in the light of these passages, which provide its immediate context. The punishment for the clergy is very harsh: they are to be ranked among the penitents and cannot have any part in the 'prayer of the faithful', nor even that of the catechumens. Only at the moment of death can they be received back into the communion of the laity. It is certainly tempting to see here a trace of the Universal Prayer(!) — and we have let ourselves be caught up in it for a long time, since the expression almost automatically brings it to mind. And yet we must cast it aside for several reasons.

Let us begin with the least compelling of these. First, the formula *oratio fidelium* which leaps out at the modern reader and encourages him to see here, without further examination, evidence of our prayer, is not ancient. So far we have found it in only two of Augustine's texts, one of which refers to the Our Father, and the other — although in the plural — to the Universal Prayer. In Basil's canons, εὐχὴ τῶν πιστῶν (T 12) indicates the Eucharistic Prayer. It was, therefore, in no way the technical term that it has become to our modern ears.

Moreover, in order to read in the prescriptions of the Synod of Rome a description of precise liturgical elements, Connolly distinguished between an *oratio fidelium* and an *oratio catechumenorum* and argued as if the Roman liturgy at that time was familiar with a 'prayer of the catechumens' before their dismissal,

72 Connolly (1920), 229.

73 Capelle, Tr. lit. vol. 2, (1962), 143–44.

74 Cf. as an example Martimort (1965), 343.

similar to that found in the *Apostolic Constitutions*.[75] But did this prayer exist? Let us note that a few lines further on,[76] with regard to catechumens who had renounced the faith, the Council of Rome decreed that they should spend three years 'inter audientes, et postea cum catechumenis'. It is no longer a question of prayer. The authors who speak of it presume that the East used the same ordinance as the West, and they were happy to quote the precise text of Felix III when he was speaking of the *oratio catechumenorum*. We are going round in circles! For Connolly's assumption to be supported it would be necessary for him to provide us with texts from the period that evidenced the use of the 'prayer of the catechumens' in the East. In the meantime, we cannot believe that this expression refers to a concrete liturgical rite. The backlash is that *oratio fidelium* must be interpreted in the same manner.

The decisive argument lies in the penitential context into which the decrees of the synod are inserted. Pope Siricius[77] and Pope Leo the Great[78] have already informed us that clergy cannot be subjected to public penitence. If, despite this, Felix III charges the bishop, priests and deacons to rank themselves among the penitents, then it cannot be a question of public penitence, but rather of the *secessio privata* of which St Leo speaks. Since they could not celebrate the sacred mysteries and act as if they had not renounced the faith, and since church discipline prevented them from engaging in public penitence, there was only one thing they could do — retreat from the world in order to carry out their penance away from the community into which they could re-enter only at the time of death. As Göller says, 'the fact that even they had to count themselves among the relapsed and could not take part in worship in any way, seems to us, nowadays, as bizarre, but that was what was prescribed and there was no changing it'.[79]

These three arguments are supported by the expression *communio laica* used in T 18 ('quibus communio laica tantum in morte reddenda est'.) This sentence does not mean that only on the death bed are they permitted to commune as lay persons! *Communio laica* is a technical term that refers to membership of the lay community. The reduction of clerics to the lay state, that the Code of Canon Law today calls *reductio in statem laicalem*, was at that time called *reductio in communionem laicalem*.[80] If reintegration into the lay community can only take

---

75 Brightman (1896), 3–4.

76 PL 58, 926.

77 Siricius, *Letter 1 to Himerius*, 14, 18 (PL 13, 1145): 'paenitentiam agere cuiquam non conceditur clericorum'.

78 Leo the Great, *Letter 167 to Rusticus of Narbonne*, (PL 54, 1204): 'Alienum est a consuetudine ecclesiastica ut qui in presbyterali honore aut in diaconii gradu fuerint consecrati, ii pro crimine aliquo suo per manus impositionem remedium accipiant paenitendi; ... Unde huiusmodi lapsis, ad promerendam misericordiam Dei, privata est expetenda secessio, ubi illis satisfactio, si fuerit digna, sit etiam fructuosa'. On this question see Vogel (1952), 55–62, 138–148, 170–74.

79 Göller (1933), 97.

80 Cf. Stiegler, 'Laienkommunion', in LTK 6, 746.

place at the point of death, it is clear that up until then clerics were more or less 'excommunicated'.

The sentence 'nec orationi non modo fidelium sed ne catechumenorum omnimodis interesse' must then be understood in the following manner. Unlike the superior class of public penitents who attend Mass, but without communion, these clerics will not be able to take part in the prayer of the faithful (that is to say, the second part of the Mass). But they cannot even take part in the prayer of the catechumens, otherwise they would be included, together with the *audientes*, with the catechumens and dismissed after the Liturgy of the Word. In short, they were permitted to prayer neither with the faithful nor with the catechumens; they were to be totally excluded from the Eucharist. In a very real sense, they would be ex-communicated.

Having reached this conclusion, we had the pleasure of reading the equivalent in an article by Mgr. Griffe who, to our knowledge, is the only author who has looked into this precise question. Here is what he writes: 'The synodal letter of Pope Felix III in the year 487 or 488, where it is a question of penitents who will be able to attend *nec orationi non modo fidelium sed ne catechumenorum quidem* would lead us to believe that the prayer of the faithful is in opposition to the prayer of the catechumens. Undoubtedly the synodal letter wishes to state that these penitents will not be admitted to take their place neither among the faithful nor among the catechumens'.[81]

Conclusions

Let us bring to an end this long chapter on penitential discipline. For us, *orationi ... interesse* (T 18), *in oratione socientur* (T 19), and *in oratione ... communicant* (T 20) are synonymous expressions that all translate κοινωνεῖν τῶν (προσ)ευχῶν in the Eastern canons, notably those of Nicea. The same applies to the terms used by Siricius: *oratione iungantur* (T4).[82] All of these formulas have a common *Sitz im Leben*: the problem of the participation of penitents at the Eucharist. They indicate more the group of Christians in which the penitent is to be ranked than specify in which prayer he can take part.

It is our opinion, then, that we ought not consider these texts — neither those from the East nor those from the West — as evidence of the *oratio fidelium*. The

---

81 Griffe (1951), 29, n. 33.

82 Note that the translation by Rufin of Aquileia (*c.* 345–410), has, for c. 12 of the Council of Nicea, 'fidelibus tantum in oratione iungantur' (PL 21, 474); and the Antiochan text reproduced in COD: 'fidelibus in oratione communicent'. Let us say that in general the discrepancies between the Latin translations and the Eastern canons prove that the discipline was not identical in East and West. There was nothing that corresponded exactly to the terms used for the penitential stations in the East; the Western legislators had adapted as best they could for their own purposes canons reflecting another disciplinary practice. We should therefore not be concerned about the discrepancies between the formulas we are citing here.

only way we could do that would be to admit a semantic evolution between Nicea and Siricius (or especially Felix III), an evolution that would have meant that by using the terms of the ecumenical Council the pope wanted to indicate with precision the Universal Prayer, where Nicea had indicated only prayer in general. In the absence of clear indications we cannot speculate, especially since in T 18, the second of the pair of clauses does not seem to allude to a precise prayer made with the catechumens.

And so these texts, having been included for more than fifty years in studies on the *oratio fidelium*, must now be excluded from them.

Boniface (418–422)

The oft-cited letter that Boniface I wrote to Honorius clearly witnesses to the fact that the Church prayed for the emperor:

T 21 *Letter 7 to Honorius*: 'Vobis, inquit, religiose imperantibus, modo tutus est populus, tam fidus Deo, quam tibi, principi christiano. Ecce enim inter ipsa mysteria, inter preces suas, quas pro vestri felicitate dependit Imperii, teste apud quem et de cuius sede agitur sancto Petro, sollicitis pro religionis observantia vocibus clamat; cum sollicita petitione miscetur oratio, ne hos in varias res semel evulsa distrahat a cultu solito, tentatore sollicantante, discordia'.[83]

But where is this prayer situated within the celebration? *Inter ipsa mysteria* rather makes us think of the intercessions within the Anaphora, especially if we remember that Innocent I, a close predecessor of Boniface, ordered Decentius, bishop of Gubbio, to name those making the offerings after the *commendatio oblationem*, 'ut inter sacra mysteria nominentur'.[84] Following the study of Dom Capelle,[85] we recognise that this *commendatio* corresponds to the beginning of the *Te Igitur* of the Roman Canon. Despite the evocative commentary of Fr. Connolly on Boniface's text, where the wise Englishman manages to detect the acclamations (*sollicitis … vocibus clamat, cum sollicita petitione*) between the invitatory and the

83 Boniface, *Epistola 7*, (PL 20, 767): 'As long as you reign piously, she [the Church] says, the people are safe, trusting both in God and in you, O Christian prince. For in the midst of the mysteries themselves, in the midst of her prayers made for the well-being of your reign — witness St Peter on whom she is founded and whose seat is in question — she cries insistently for respect for religion; the prayer mingles with the immediate request that the discord once uprooted may not disperse them (the Christian people) in diverse things and, under the promptings of the Tempter, keep them away from traditional worship'. (This final proposition contains a certain contradiction; one might say that the author has tried to say too many things at the one time. The whole letter is written in a somewhat pompous style).

84 Innocent I, *Epistola 20* (to Decentius of Gubbio), (PL 20), 554; ed. Cabié (1973), 22.

85 Capelle (1952), 5–16; Tr. Lit., vol. 2, 236–247.

prayer of the *Orationes sollemnes*,[86] we think that this passage is directed at a prayer for the emperor contained within the Canon.

Moreover, even if this were not the case, this text is too vague to teach us anything about the *oratio fidelium*.

Celestine (422–432)

The same applies to a passage from Letter 23 of Boniface's successor, Celestine I, addressed to Theodosius II after a victory:

T 22 *Epistola* 23: 'Ecce nunc domus Domini orationibus vacant, et vestrum per omnes Ecclesias, Deo nostro oblatis sacrificiis, commendatur imperium'.[87]

This is a letter for a particular occasion, not a specific report. But the expression *oblatis sacrificiis*, and the use of the verb *commendare*, which can be compared with the *commendatio oblationum* of which Innocent I spoke in the letter that we have just cited, makes us think more of the diptychs in this instance than the Universal Prayer.

Putting aside the text of Ambrosiaster (T 3), this Roman example is rather feeble, it must be admitted. One final author, however, will provide us with information of primary importance.

Prosper of Aquitaine († after 455)

Prosper, as his surname indicates, is not a Roman. He lived in the region of Marseilles around 435, where he showed himself to be a staunch supporter of Augustine's teachings against the semi-Pelagian school of Lérins. From there he went to Rome and became secretary to Leo the Great, and somewhat moderated his devotion to Augustine.

A. The Gallic Period (before 435)

Between 431 and 434 Prosper wrote several pamphlets. One of them, *Contra collatorem*, was addressed to John Cassian (*c.* 360–430/35) who by the time of writing his thirteenth *Collatio* 'had become the father of semi-Pelagianism'.[88]

86 Connolly (1920), 227–28.

87 Celestine 1, *Epistola* 23 (to Theodosius II), (PL 50), 544: 'Now the houses of the Lord are devoted to prayers, and in all the Churches your reign is recommended when sacrifices are offered to our God'.

88 Altaner (1961), 629.

T 23 Prosper here affirms that 'the Church prays each day for her enemies, that is to say for those who have not yet come to believe in God'.[89]

And in the section of his *Pro Augustino responsiones* where he refutes the objections of Vincent of Lérins, he comments on the sentence from St Paul: 'God wants to save all people'. He writes,

T 24 [If then,] the Apostle, from whom this sentence comes (1 Tim 2:4) has consistently ordered — and what has been assiduously observed in all the Churches — to beseech God on behalf of all humankind, it follows ...'[90]

Further on, in his responses to the priests of Gênes, he uses the way in which the Church prays as recognition of the fact that grace is indeed a gift of God:

T 25 'Si ergo fides donum Dei non est, frustra Ecclesia pro non credentibus orat, ut credant'.[91]

In short, Prosper teaches us that the Church, or better, that all the Churches, pray each day for all people, following the order given in 1 Tim 2:1–2. The aim of this prayer is primarily faith. He will soon tell us what form this takes.

B. The Roman Period (435–455)

Since the research undertaken by Dom Cappuyns, it has been generally accepted that *De vocatione omnium gentium* (*c.* 450) was an authentic work of Prosper of Aquitaine, along with *Auctoritates (Indiculus) de gratia* also known as *Capitula* (*c.* 435–442), which is sometimes attributed to Pope Celestine.[92] In 1938 he published a study comparing two passages of these writings with the *Orationes sollemnes* (*OS*) of Good Friday.[93]

The first of these texts is the one where Prosper launches the famous adage 'Legem credendi lex statuat supplicandi'. St Augustine had already used the 'liturgical argument' to prove to his adversaries that their doctrine was in opposition

---

89 Prosper of Aquitaine, *Contra collatorem*, 12, 3, (PL 51), 235: 'Ecclesia quotidie pro inimicis suis orat, id est, pro his qui necdum Deo crediderunt'.

90 Prosper of Aquitaine, *Pro Augustino responsiones*, 2, (PL 52), 179B: 'Siquidem Apostolus, cuius ista sententia est, sollicitissime praecipit, quod in omnibus Ecclesiis piissime custoditur, ut Deo proomnibus hominibus supplicetur ...'.

91 Prosper of Aquitaine, *Pro Augustino responsiones*, 2, (PL: 51), 193B: 'If, therefore, faith is not a gift of God, then it is in vain that the Church prays for those who do not believe, in order that they may believe'.

92 Cappuyns (1927), 198–226, and (1929), 156–170. On these two works cf. Clavis at nos. 528 and 527 respectively.

93 Cappuyns (1938), 18–31. Cf. also Alfonso (1930), 199–203.

to the prayers of the Church.[94] As a good disciple, Prosper perfects the master's teaching and shapes it into a cut and dried formula. Originally, K. Federer had cleverly detected that *lex supplicandi* did not refer to liturgy in general, nor even to a liturgical prayer, but to the order given in 1 Tim 2:1–2, or more broadly, the command to pray. In other words, the need of prayer to obtain grace is a proof of the necessity of grace.[95] But let us now turn to the text; as an argument against the Pelagian doctrine in addition to the inviolable decrees of the Apostolic See.

T 26 *Capitulum 8*: 'obsecrationum quoque sacerdotalium sacramenta respiciamus, quae ab apostolis tradita in toto mundo atque in omni Ecclesia catholica uniformiter celebrantur, ut legem credendi lex statuat supplicandi. Cum enim sanctarum plebium praesules mandata sibimet legatione fungantur, apud divinam clementiam humani generis agunt causam et, tota secum ecclesia congemiscente, postulant et precantur
ut infidelibus donetur fides,
ut idololatrae ab impietatis suae liberentur erroribus
ut Judaeis, ablato cordis velamine, lux veritatis appareat,
ut haeretici catholicae fidei perceptione resipiscant,
ut schismatici spiritum redivivae charitatis accipiant,
ut lapsis paenitentiae remedia conferantur;
ut denique catechumenis, ad regenerationis sacramenta perductis, caelestis misericordiae aula reseretur.

Haec autem non perfunctorie neque inaniter a Domino peti, rerum ipsarum monstrat effectus. Quandoquidem ex omni errorum genere plurimos Deus dignatur attrahere quos erutos de potestate tenebrarum transferat in regnum filii charitatis suae ...'[96]

94 Cf. above, Section Two, and the bibliography cited therein, to which can be added B. Capelle, 'Autorité de la liturgie chez les Pères', RTAM 21 (1954), 5–22.

95 Federer (1950), 14–18.

96 Prosper of Aquitaine, *Auctoritates de gratia*, cap. 8, (PL 51), 209–10: '... let us look also at the sacred witness of priestly supplications which, transmitted by the apostles, are celebrated in the same way throughout the world and through the Catholic Church, such that the obligation to prayer determines the rule of faith. In fact, when the intercessors of the holy people carry out the mission entrusted to them, they beseech divine clemency on behalf of the human race, and sustained by the sighs of the entire Church, the implore and pray
that infidels may be given the faith,
that idolaters may be freed from their errors and their wickedness,
that to the Jews, once the veil is removed from their hearts, the light of truth may appear,
that heretics may be converted by accepting the Catholic faith,
that schismatics may receive the spirit of renewed charity,
that the lapsed may be given the comfort of penitence,
and finally that to catechumens, led to the sacraments of a new birth, the temple of heavenly mercy may be opened.

Before making any comment, let us read the second extract. Prosper has just cited 1 Tim 2:1–6, and continues:

T 27 *De vocatione omnium gentium* 1, 12: 'De hac ergo doctrinae apostolicae regula, qua Ecclesia universalis imbuitur, ne in diversum intellectum nostro evagemus arbitrio, quid ipsa universalis Ecclesia sentiat, requiramus: quia nihil dubium esse poterit in praecepto, si obedientia concordet in studio. Praecepit itaque Apostolus, immo per Apostolum Dominus, qui loquebatur in Apostolo, fieri obsecrationes, postulationes, gratiarum actiones, proomnibus hominibus, pro regibus ac pro his qui in sublimitate sunt. Quam legem supplicationis ita omnium sacerdotum et omnium fidelium devotio concorditer tenet ut nulla pars mundi sit in qua huiusmodi orationes non celebrentur a populis christianis. Supplicat ergo ubique ecclesia Deo, non solum
pro sanctis et in Christo iam regeneratis, sed etiam
pro omnibus infidelibus et inimicus crucis Christi:
pro omnibus idolorum cultoribus,
pro omnibus qui Christum in membris ipsius persequuntur;
pro Iudaeis quorum caecitati lumen evangelii non refulget,
pro haereticis et schismiticis qui ab unitate fidei et charitatis alieni sunt.

Quid autem pro ipsis petit nisi ut, relictis erroribus suis, convertantur ad Deum, accipiant fidem, accipiant charitatem et, de ignorantiae tenebris liberati, ad agnitionem veniant veritatis. Quod quia ipsi praestare sibi nequeunt, malae consuetudinis pondere oppressi et diaboli vinculis alligati, neque deceptiones suas evincere valent, … misericors et justus Dominus pro omnibus sibi vult hominus supplicari: ut cum videmus de tam profundis malis innumeros erui, non ambigamus Deum praestitisse quod ut praestaret oratus est'.[97]

That this is not asked of the Lord in vain is shown by the effects of these prayers: every time God deigns to draw many out of all kinds of errors. He snatches them from the powers of darkness so that, in his charity, they can pass into the kingdom of his Son …'

This same text is cited in the letter written in 519–550 by Peter the Deacon and the Scythian monks to the African bishops (including Fulgentius of Ruspe) exiled in Sardinia; cf. PL 62, 91; CC 91A, 561. The author of this letter, whoever it may be (cf. Clavis 663), presents our text as an *auctoritatis* under the name of Pope Celestine, although in no way could any practice connected to the *Orationes sollemnes* be drawn from it.

97 Prosper of Aquitaine, *De vocatione omnium gentium* 1, 12: 'With regard to this rule of apostolic doctrine of which the universal Church has been instructed, let us see how this universal Church understands it, lest our judgement be undermined by diverse opinions. There can be no doubt as to the precept, but there must be agreement in how obedience to it is applied. The Apostle commanded, or rather the Lord, who spoke through the Apostle, commanded supplications, requests, favours for all humankind, for kings and for those holding authority. This obligation to pray is so unanimously and faithfully guarded by all priests and all the faithful, that there is no part of the world where prayers of this kind are not celebrated by the Christian people. Everywhere, then, the Church beseeches God not only for the saints and those who are already reborn in Christ, but also for all non-believers and the enemies of the cross of Christ,
for all those who serve idols,

What is this formulary?

According to Cappuyns there is no doubt that there is a relationship between these texts and the *Orationes sollemnes* and that it is indeed on that venerable prayer which Prosper relies to confound the Pelagians. The author notes any lack of a literal quotation is due to the pontifical secretary who, in usages of this type always maintained a remarkable independence of style. Cappuyns then points out the similarities between these two passages, which we don't have to go over here. If the first four prayers of the *Orationes sollemnes* (for the Church, the pope, the clergy, the emperor) are not found in Prosper's text, except by way of summary in T 27 in the expression 'non solum pro sanctis et in Christo iam regeneratis', it is because they deal only with believers and therefore offered nothing of interest to the theological argument, or because it was a matter of showing that even the *initium fidei* was the work of grace. And the monk from Louvain even ventures to justify the fact that the order of the prayers in Prosper is in reverse to that of the *Orationes sollemnes* with a simple explanation: when Prosper seeks from the *oratio fidelium* evidence of the universality of grace, their importance is in inverse order (to that of the prayer of the Church). It begins with the most unlikely of the beneficiaries, while the most likely scarcely warrant attention. That is why … the faithful are neglected by Prosper. It is also why the catechumens are named last of all'.[98] To reinforce this explanation, let us add that Prosper speaks in both these texts of priestly supplications, which corresponds well to the structure of the *Orationes sollemnes.*

But several elements of Prosper's extracts do not have a parallel in the *Orationes sollemnes*; there is in them no mention of the infidels and the *lapsi* (T 26), nor of the *inimici crucis Christi* nor of those who persecute the Church (T 27). Cappuyns attributes their presence in Prosper solely to literary elegance, but the argument does not convince us. 'Moreover', he writes in a footnote, 'it is likely that a collection as well constructed and as archaic as the *Orationes sollemnes* has, in the course of centuries, undergone both additions and reductions'.[99] When we study this formulary in Part Two we will see that this is not true.

The parallels pointed out by this historian of ancient and medieval theology are, however, not negligible. They are even strengthened when we acknowledge that the prayer for the Jews is mentioned only in Rome — in the *Orationes*

---

for all those who persecute Christ in his members,

for the Jews, for whom the light of the Gospel does not shine on account of their blindness,

What does she [the Church] ask for them if not that, rejecting their mistakes, they turn to God, receive faith and charity and, freed from the darkness of ignorance, come to the knowledge of the truth. And since they cannot arrive at this themselves, oppressed as they are by the weight of their bad habits and bound by the devil's ties, and because they cannot overcome their lies…, the merciful and just Lord wants to be beseeched on behalf of all people; so that when we see a large number torn away from such profound evils we have no doubt that it is God who brings about what we have asked him to do'.

98 Cappuyns (1938), 29–30.

99 Cappuyns (1938), 28, n. 2.

sollemnes and the *Deprecatio Gelasii*. It seems that it does not figure at all in the East.

Let us note that Tertullian has already pointed to the prayer for the *lapsi* and for persecutors (Tert. T 7). the *lapsi* are also mentioned by Cyprian (Cyprian T 3 and T 4) and Novatian (Rome T 2).

How are we to synthesise all this information? Originally we were in agreement with Willis who believes that the *Orationes sollemnes* may have once included a prayer for the *lapsi*.[100] Such a prayer would not have disappeared immediately after the cessation of persecutions; we are all familiar with the strongly conservative nature of the liturgy. But a study of the *Orationes sollemnes* themselves does not lead us in this direction.

In earlier days, when the *OS* consisted only of invitatories and the orations had not yet been added, petitions on behalf of the *lapsi* and persecutors could have been composed — and this corresponds well to the historical data of the 3rd century. However, it is very unlikely that once the final form that came about with the addition of the orations at the end of the 4th century it was further varied or subjected to suppressions. It seems more likely, on the other hand, that the literary revision at the end of the 4th century would have adapted the petitions to the circumstances of the period.

Moreover, we think that Prosper may be alluding to several different formularies. Dom Cappuyns sits alongside the bulk of liturgists who have consistently assumed that the *Orationes sollemnes* were the only Universal Prayer text of the Roman Church. In our opinion this assumption is unfounded; the genre of the litany appeared in the West much earlier than is often thought. According to us, the litany *Dicamus omnes* of the Stowe Missal dates from the end of the 4th or beginning of the 5th century.

In short, we consider it probable, although not absolutely certain, that Prosper is alluding to the *Orationes sollemnes*. The variations between his works and the *Orationes sollemnes* can be explained by literary amplification, whether because the theological argument called for it, or because of reference to other Universal Prayer formularies.

Use of These Prayers

Having been convinced of recognising the *Orationes sollemnes* in Prosper's texts, Cappuyns continues; 'In the 5th century, the *orationes sollemnes* of Good Friday became part of the ordinary or daily formulary of the Roman Mass. We know this from indications in the general order [of Mass]. We know it in particular through

100 Willis (1964), 40 adds a reference to St Leo, who in his Sermon 49 (*De Quadragesima 11*) mentions the *lapsi* after the catechumens (PL 54, 303; SC 49, 82). With justified caution the author does not claim to see there any allusion to the *Orationes sollemnes*. The term *lapsi* was therefore in use at the time of St Leo, which is to say the exact same period as Prosper.

Prosper of Aquitaine who refers to it as the *oratio fidelium* that was celebrated everywhere, every day'.[101] There are several elements in these few lines.

1. Transition from *orationes sollemnes* to *oratio fidelium*.
   Dom Cappuyns does not hesitate to claim, as does Mgr. Duchesne, that the Solemn Orations served as the Universal Prayer in the Roman liturgy. Although Prosper does not mention it at all, we can accept this assertion, given the content of the Solemn Orations and their place in the Good Friday liturgy.
2. We must point out, however, that his reasoning is based on false premises. By 'indications in the general order' he is referring to evidence of the existence of an *oratio fidelium* in Africa (Augustine), Gaul and Rome. For Gaul, he cites only the Council of Lyon in 517, which took place a half-century later, and which speaks of an 'oratio plebis quae post evangelia legeretur': the least that can be said is that this reference is rather imprecise (cf. infra). And for Rome Dom Cappuyns resorts to the classic text of Pope Felix III: 'nec orationi non modo fidelium sed ne catechumenorum omnimodis interesse'. Not only does this text date from 488, around 40 years later than those of Prosper, but we have demonstrated above that he was not indicating the Universal Prayer. Thus it is wrong to rely on these passages to claim the existence of the *oratio fidelium*, and consequently to recognise the formulary in the Solemn Orations!
3. Above all, these conclusions are too broad. The *Orationes sollemnes*, he says, become part of the ordinary or daily formulary of the Roman Mass; and in a footnote he writes that Prosper's insistence on the universality and uniformity of the prayer throughout the world makes him suspect that the Roman form was in use elsewhere, especially in Gaul and probably in Africa. Is it really so clear cut?

With regard to this last point, he relies on the article by Connolly that we have already cited several times, where the English liturgist compares the Solemn Orations with an Augustinian text; we have shown above that this relationship was virtually without foundation.[102] In the absence of more conclusive indications, we cannot accept that the Church of Africa used the Solemn Orations in the middle of the 5th century. As for Gaul, it is probable that the Roman formulary was known there, not — as we will see later — because Prosper says that all the Churches use it, but because his reasoning would have carried little weight if his adversaries (Gallic) had *not* used the *Orationes sollemnes* in their liturgy.

The thing that arouses our suspicion when Prosper affirms that the use of the solemn prayers is daily and universal is first of all historic reality: we have no other proof of this than his declarations! And above all, we note the polemical character of his writing. In order that the liturgical argument be deemed valid in the eyes of his semi-Pelagian opponents, he had to respond to the criteria they demanded

---

101 Cappuyns (1938), 29-30.

102 Cf. above, p. 64.

before a usage might be considered truly traditional, criteria summarised by Vincent de Lérins in his *Commonitorium*: 'quod ubique, quod semper, quod ab omnibus creditum est'.[103] To meet the criterion of antiquity, Prosper turned the Universal Prayer into an apostolic institution by attaching in to 1 Tim 2:1–2.[104] Its universal and unanimous use he affirms without scruple, somewhat exaggerating reality (although for a good cause!) The solemn character with which Prosper invests this prayer is not accidental; his purpose is strictly theological. The detail alone of this order should make us wary: cf. for example, in T 26: 'ab apostolis tradita — in toto mundo — atque in omni ecclesia — uniformiter — tota secum Ecclesia' and in T 27: 'doctrinae apostolicae regula — Ecclesia universalis (twice) — obedientia concordat in studio — praecepit Apostolus, immo per Apostolum Dominus — omnium sacerdotum et omnium fidelium — concorditer tenet — nulla pars mundi — ubique'.

In short, the assertions of the papal secretary as to the universality and daily use of the solemn orations must be toned down, together with their repetition, without sufficient appraisal, by Dom Cappuyns.

Before concluding, let us note a passage from Prosper where the meaning he provides is quite close to what we have already found in Augustine. 'One cannot pronounce on the eternal fate of someone before his death', he writes, 'since conversion is always possible':

T 27 *De vocatione omnium gentium* 2, 37: 'Oret itaque sancta Ecclesia et pro iis qui crediderunt gratias agens, proficientem eis perseverentiam petat; pro iis autem qui extra fidem sunt, poscat ut credant'.[105]

Thanksgiving for the faith of believers, prayer that non-believers may believe and that believers may persevere, are to be found in abundance in Augustine's writings.[106] We come across the expression *proficientem perseverentiam* in his Letter 217 (Augustine, T 33). Does this mean that Augustine and Prosper are using the same formulary of the *oratio fidelium*? The link between these two men is too limited for us to be entitled to draw such a conclusion in the absence of any further clue. It should also be noted that Letter 217 is where Augustine developed most fully the liturgical argument; undoubtedly his disciple drew on this and it is no surprise when we read in his works expressions borrowed from his master.

---

103 Vincent de Lérins, *Commonitorium* I, 2; (PL 50), 640.

104 Let us remember that Ambrosiaster had already described this passage as *regula ecclesiastica*, which the priests of his Church obeyed faithfully, placing before God prayers of supplication on behalf of all people.

105 *De vocatione omnium gentium* 2, 37; (PL 51), 722: 'This is why the holy Church prays: giving thanks for those who have the faith, she asks that they might grow in perseverance; and for those who are still outside the faith she asks that they might believe'.

106 Cf. p. 74-75 above.

C. Summary

Let us summarise Prosper of Aquitaine's contribution. Going back to Augustine's liturgical argument, he has framed it within the adage *Legem credendi lex statuat supplicandi*. The *supplicatio* on which he relies is probably the Solemn Orations, thus providing us with the first evidence of them. In order to be able to serve as a touchstone in a question as important to our author as the theology of grace, it would be essential that this prayer be in common use at the time in Rome. It goes without saying that it was not reserved as it is today for Good Friday, with which it has no particular attachment. And in order for it to be presented as an apostolic institution, it had to have been known for some time already; in no way could it be a novelty or innovation. It is therefore reasonable to assume that it served as an *oratio fidelium*; besides, it is not clear what other function it could have fulfilled.

Moreover, for the argument to hold up against his adversaries, it must be assumed that the Solemn Orations had been in frequent use for some time in Gaul as well, at least in Provence.

Were they the daily form of the Prayer of the Faithful in these Churches, as Dom Cappuyns concludes? We do not know, but in any case we need not take Prosper's assertions, at the end of the letter, that all the Churches used it every day. Personally, we are rather inclined to believe that, with regard to the Universal Prayer, this formulary is but one among others.

Conclusion of Section Three

The most original part of this inquiry into the field of the liturgy of the Roman Church is certainly where we have laid out the Eastern canonical background to the prescriptions of Siricius and Felix III concerning the participation of public penitents in the Eucharist. But for our purposes it ended up being of little help, and the text of Felix III (predecessor of Gelasius!) can no longer be considered as the last evidence of the ancient *oratio fidelium* before its replacement by the *Deprecatio Gelasii*.

What have we determined with certainty? 'Hipploytus' is the only author who places our prayer in the unfolding of the liturgy, provided we can assume, on the basis of what Justin wrote a century before, that the baptism described in the *Apostolic Tradition* took the place of the Liturgy of the Word.

Novation's letter has not been of much assistance to us, and then we had to wait more than a century before Ambrosiaster lets us know that the priest made supplication for several categories of person, thereby obeying the *regula ecclesiastica* found in 1 Tim 2:1–2. But here we are faced — and probably for the first time — with a fixed formulary, where the themes at least are common to the texts that we will study in Part Two; certainly, he was familiar with at least the invitatories of the *Orationes sollemnes*. In any case, and most importantly from our point of view, this text of Ambrosiaster proves that the Universal Prayer was in use in Rome at the end of the 4th century and can even assist us in knowing its content.

In the middle of the 5th century, Prosper of Aquitaine placed such importance on the *oratio fidelium* that he based all his arguments against the semi-Pelagians on it. His works most probably allude to the *Orationes sollemnes*. The way in which Prosper speaks of them presumes that they were already well known before that date, and even extended as far as Gaul. We will examine this later.

Despite the enormous gaps in the documentation,[107] the points of reference provided by Justin, 'Hippolytus', Ambrosiaster and Prosper of Aquitaine, incline us to accept that the *oratio fidelium* did indeed exist in Rome during the 3rd, 4th and 5th centuries. What form did it take? The first two witnesses do not give us any clue. Ambrosiaster uses expressions that we will find later in the litanies; does this mean that this liturgical form was already known in Rome at the end of the 4th century? The indications are too tenuous to claim this with any certainty, but it would not be all that surprising. Finally Prosper provides for us what is most likely an echo of the *Orationes sollemnes*; in any case, in their regard the internal criticism is formal; they certainly existed at the end of the 4th century. For now, that information may be enough for us.

As for its content, Novatian (in so far as his testimony refers directly to the Universal Prayer) points to the immediate needs of a community at the time of the persecutions by asking prayer for the *lapsi* and the *stantes*: this is not far from the earliest African texts.

Ambrosiaster indicates, following 1 Tim 2:1–2, prayer for
kings, so that peace might reign;
leaders and rulers, that they might govern with justice and truth;
the needy, that, once freed, they might give praise to God.

Prosper's texts call for a discerning exegesis, for they constitute part of a theological argument that proves the need of grace for those who wish to believe. Moreover, the prayers mentioned focus on conversion and the gift of faith. Here we find the same issue that faced Augustine, the intellectual guide of the pontifical secretary. These passages make no allusion to prayers for the various needs of the community or for the diverse categories of people such as are found in

---

107 Saint Jerome does not seem to provide any information; besides, it is difficult to know to which liturgical tradition this great traveller is referring. Two texts that are sometimes cited actually concern the diptychs (*In Ezechielem* 6, 18; PL 15, 175; CC 75, 238, and *In Jeremiam* 11, 15; PL 24, 755; CC 74r, 116).

We have not found any reference to the works of St Leo, even though a good part of his writings consist of homilies, in which one might expect to find allusions to the *oratio fidelium* that follows [the homily]. Professor Chavasse, having just published the sermons of Leo the Great in *Corpus Christianorum*, has confirmed for us that he did not uncover any indication concerning our prayer; we thank him for this.

the invitatories of the *Orationes sollemnes*, but which are, nevertheless, probably implied in these extracts. Given the theological context, we cannot, in any case, conclude that these petitions did not exist and that petitions for faith were the only ones to be expressed.

Section Four

The Church of Milan (Saint Ambrose)

Introduction

Is it appropriate to analyse the sources from Milan in a separate section? In other words, do we consider that the Milanese liturgy of the end of the 4th century was independent of that of Rome? It is not up to up to us to *a priori* answer this question. We have presented the Roman and Milanese texts in different sections out of respect for their particular origins, but this methodological division makes no pre-judgment on links that existed between the two cities on the liturgical level. This division does, however, seem justified by the fact that we have found no pertinent link between Rome and Milan with regard to the *oratio fidelium*.[1] Two important studies have been dedicated to Saint Ambrose (340–397). In his Master's thesis presented at the Catholic University of Louvain, R. Gryson states unambiguously that he has not 'discovered any clear trace of the *oratio fidelium* in the works of St Ambrose'.[2] And in a work centred on the Eucharist according to the Milanese doctor, R. Johanny, without considering the question head on, is of the same opinion.[3]

Absence of a List of Intentions

Any list of intentions similar to those we have found in the preceding authors is not to be found in the works of the bishop of Milan. He certainly says, with regard to levels of faith, that there are also levels of prayer, depending on whether one is praying for a particular person or from a particular standpoint:

T 1 *Expositio psalmi 118*, 22, 15 (389–390): Sunt etiam orationis dignitates, si pro vidua roges, si roges pro pupillo, si roges pro misericordi, roges pro nimium devoto ac fideli, si roges in tribulatione, roges cum dolore, si maesto et ipse qui rogas compatiaris affectu. Intrat oratio tua dei gratiam, intrat domum eius, si tecum ecclesia deprecetur, si populus universus imploret, ut domini inclinet favorem.[4]

1 As well as the works cited earlier, there is an abundant bibliography on the liturgy of Milan in Borella (1964), 475–92.
2 Gryson (1968), 269. Footnote 47.
3 Johanny (1968), 60 and 64–65.

But this is not, strictly speaking, a list of intentions, it is more an enumeration, in a fairly free manner, of the different possibilities for prayer and the conviction with which such prayer can be addressed to God. What is more, the context here is not at all liturgical.

Prayer for the Emperor

Fairly often, it is true, one comes across testimony of a prayer that the Church makes for the emperor. As an example, we cite this passage from Letter 12, addressed by the Council of Aquileia (381) to Emperors Gratian, Valentinian and Theodosius:[5]

T 2 *Epistola 12, 2*: Sed tamen etsi beneficia vestra verbis explicare non possumus, votis tamen concilii compensare desideramus: qui licet per singulas quasque ecclesias quotidianas apud Deum nostrum pro imperio vestro celebremus excubias, tamen conducti in unum, ..., Deo nostro omnipotenti et pro imperio, et pro pace ac salute vestra gratias agimus, quod per vos nobis pax et concordia ita sit refusa.[6]

But other texts clearly claim that the name of the emperor was read in the diptychs, recognizable from the formula *pro te offerre*. Here are some texts;

T 3 *Epistola 40, 1*, to the Emperor Theodosius: 'Nam si indignus sum qui a te audiar, indignus sum qui pro te offeram'[7]

T 4 *Epistola 41, 28*, to his sister Marcellina (388): 'Deinde, cum aliquandiu starem, dico imperatori: Fac me securum pro te offerre ... Et ita ad altare accessi ... Et vere tanta oblationis fuit gratia, ut sentirem etiam ipse eam Deo nostro commendatiorem fuisse gratiam'[8]

---

4 Ambrose, *Expositione psalmi 118, 22, 15*; (CSEL 62, 496): 'There also exists levels of prayer, if you are praying for a widow, if you are praying for an orphan, if you are praying for a person open to mercy, if you are praying for a person of deep faith and deep piety, if you are praying in time of affliction, if you are praying with sorrow, if you yourself are overcome with sadness. Your prayer enters the grace of God, it enters his house, if the Church prays with you, if the entire people beg with tears, to sway the benevolence of the Lord'.

5 If this letter cannot be attributed to Ambrose with complete certainty, it nevertheless reflects his thought, since he was the 'leading light' of the Council of Aquileia; cf. Gryson (1968), 38–39. Moreover, from our point of view, this passage is all the more important because it is not echoing merely the Church of Milan.

6 Ambrose, *Epistola 12, 2*, (PL 16, 987): 'And nevertheless, while words are not enough to express your good deeds, we desire to compensate for this by the prayers of the Council; while in every church we daily address prayer to God on behalf of your governing, we gather in unity ... and we give thanks to our almighty God and for your empire, and for your peace and well-being, since thanks to you, peace and harmony are also granted to us'. //p//Cf. also *Epistola 1, 2*; 18, 8; *De Sacramentis*, 4, 14, ed. Faller (CSEL 73); *pro regibus* (cf. infra, T 8).

T 5 *De obitu Valentiniani*, 78 (392): '... omnibus vos oblationibus frequentabo. Quis prohibebit innoxios nominare ...?'[9]

The prayer for the emperor took place, in all probability, during the diptychs. None of it proves, however, that there was an *oratio fidelium*.

Prayer for the Penitents

Alongside the prayer for the emperor, Ambrose often noted that the entire Church prayed for penitents. For example:

T 6 *Expositio evangelii secundum Lucam*, 7, 225: 'Sed etsi Deus novit omnia, vocem tamen tuae confessionis exspectat ... Confitere magis, ut interveniat pro te Christus, quem advocatum habemus apud patrem, roget pro te ecclesia, inlacrimet populus'.[10]

Unfortunately, none of these passages situate this prayer in an exact place in the liturgy. Nor does the following, which affirms that the Christian prays for all members of the Church:

T 7 *De Cain et Abel*, 1, 39 (*c.* 378): 'Orandum autem praecipue et pro populo doceris, hoc est pro toto corpore, pro membris omnibus matris tuae, in quo mutuae caritatis insigne est. Si enim pro te roges, tantummodo pro te rogabis, et si pro se tantum singuli orent, minor precatoris quam intercedentis est gratia; nunc autem qui singuli orant pro omnibus, etiam omnes orant pro singulis ... Ita magna remuneratio est, ut orationibus singulorum adquirantur singulis totius plebis suffragia'.[11]

---

7 Ambrose, *Epistola 40*, 1, 1148; 'For if I am not worthy of being listened to by you, I am not worthy of offering [prayers] on your behalf'.

8 Ambrose, *Epistola 41*, 28, (PL 16, 1168–9): 'Then, as I stood before him one day, I said to the emperor, "Make sure that I may sacrifice on your behalf in safety" And so I went up to the altar ... And such was the grace of this offering that I myself felt that the favour I had received had made me more acceptable to our God'.

9 Ambrose, *De obitu Valentiniani*, 78; (CSEL 73, 365): 'I name you in all the oblations. Who will prevent me from mentioning the innocent?'

10 Ambrose, *Expositio evangelium secundum. Lucam*, 7, 225, (CSEL 32, 383): 'But although God knows everything, he is waiting for you to make your confession to him ... Confess rather that Christ, whom we have as our advocate with the Father, may intervene for you, so that the Church may pray for you, so that the people may weep [for you]'. Cf. *Exp. ev. Luc.*, 5, 11, 92, and 7, 208; *De Paenitentia* 1, 80–81; 90; 92; *De Paenitentia* 2, 54–57; *Expositio psalmi* 37, 10 (cited by Gryson (1968), 281, footnote 114).

11 Ambrose, *De Cain et Abel* 1, 39, (CSEL 32, 372): 'You are taught above all to pray for the people, that is, for all humankind, for all members of your family; this is a sign of your mutual love. For if you petition for yourself, then you pray merely for your own self, and if each one were to petition only on

Even if we want to highlight *nunc autem*, by understanding it as a description of what is in fact practised in the Milanese Church, we cannot draw anything from it for our purpose, since this 'prayer' remains vague and indeterminate.

De Sacramentis 4, 14

It is only from a description of the Eucharist that we can learn more. Do we find one in Ambrose's writings? A text from *De Sacramentis* is often cited in this regard: here the bishop is explaining to catechumens the heart of the Eucharistic mystery:

T 8 De Sacramentis 4, 14 (*c.* 390–391): 'Quomodo potest qui panis est corpus esse Christi? Consecratio igitur quibus verbis est et cuius sermonibus? Domini Iesu. Nam reliqua omnia quae dicuntur in superioribus a sacerdote dicuntur: laus deo, defertur oratio, petitur pro populo, pro regibus, pro ceteris; ubi venitur ut conficiatur venerabile sacramentum, iam non suis sermonibus utitur sacerdos, sed utitur sermonibus Christi'.[12]

How should we understand the sentence: 'laus deo defertur oratio petitur pro populo pro regibus pro ceteris?' Scholars divide themselves into two camps on the matter.

The first group considers this sentence to be referring to the *oratio fidelium*. According to J. H. Srawley, it is possible that Ambrose is not following strictly the order of the celebration and that the prayer in question describes the Prayer of the Faithful, since no prayer for the king exists in the Canon of the Gelasian sacramentary, while it *is* found in the *orationes sollemnes.*[13] Connolly has taken up this suggestion in his study which we have cited several times already, and reinforces it: 'After my article', he writes, 'it is difficult to believe that these prayer for the people, for kings and for others, can be anything other than the *orationes sollemnes* prayed after the gospel. I therefore conclude that the author, beginning from the words of Institution, names the oldest elements of the Mass in reverse order'.[14] This 'reverse order' was taken up by Jungmann. Dividing the sentence into two and placing the caesura after *defertur,* he sees in the *oratio petitur* an invitation to

his own behalf, the grace bestowed on the one who prays is less than on the one who intercedes; but now that each one prays for all, all also pray for each one ... Thus great is the recompense whereby all are accorded the benefits acquired by the prayers of each individual'.

12 Ambrose, *De Sacramentis* 4, 14 (SC 25/2, 108–111; CSEL 73, 52): 'How is it possible that what is bread can be the body of Christ? By what words is this consecration carried out, and whose words are these? They are the Lord Jesus' words. For all the rest that are said beforehand are spoken by the priest: we praise God, we offer prayer to him, we petition on behalf of the people, for kings, for everyone else. But when it comes to enacting the venerable sacrament, then the priest uses not his own words, but the words of Christ'.

13 Thompson and Srawley (1950), 87.

14 Connolly (1920), 231.

the people that would be rather strange within the Canon. His conclusion is that it must therefore be the Universal Prayer.[15] For his part, A. Paredi considers that the *laus* must be a hymn of the *Gloria in excelsis* type and that the prayer for the people and other benefactors is none other than the ancient *oratio fidelium*.[16] This is also the position held by P. Borella.[17]

In the opposite camp we find F. Probst, who sees in this prayer the intercessions of the Anaphora.[18] Similarly, V. L. Kennedy considers untenable the 'inverse order' hypothesis put forward by Connolly. In his opinion Ambrose signifies by *laus* the preface and by *oratio* the end of the *Te Igitur*.[19] Agreeing with Callewaert,[20] L. Lavorel thinks that reference is here being made to the beginning of the Eucharistic Prayer; before reaching the *Fac nobis* of the Canon, such as we found in *De Sacramentis*, 'the priest would have then sung praise to God (*laus Deo*), then presented an *oratio*, and finally recited a prayer *pro populo, pro regibus, pro ceteris*. Perhaps the expression *oratio* here describes a formula of offering, for the demonstrative *Fac* ***hanc*** *oblationem* clearly implies that a previous formula referred to an offering of gifts placed on the altar. This prayer of offering corresponds to our current *Te Igitur*'.[21] This is also the opinion held by R. Johanny.[22] Finally, R. Gryson thinks that these petitions form part of the Eucharistic prayer.[23]

Which is it then? A preliminary problem concerns the punctuation. Is the sentence to be broken into two, with a comma after *defertur*, or into three, as we did in T 8? The expression *oratio defertur* is common,[24] occurring in *De Sacramentis* itself (I, 18) while the passive form *petere* is often used with a personal subject. Let us remember that the two most recent editors of the work, P. Faller and Dom Botte, have both opted for the tripartite division; so let us rely on the philologists!

Having dealt with the question of punctuation, it would seem that the context steers us towards the second solution. Without exhaustive discussion, it deals with consecration, but the expression 'reliqua omnia qui dicuntur in superioribus a sacerdote dicuntur' cannot possibly encompass the entire celebration, otherwise you would have to suppose that the readings too were read by the celebrant! These words can just as easily mean 'all that has just been said' in the Eucharistic prayer, beginning from the Preface (*laus*) as was well explained by Lavorel. It must be admitted that 'the inverse order' envisaged by Connolly is scarcely convincing, lacking argument (apart from agreeing with his own article). And to say, as

15 Jungmann (1962), vol. 2, 68–69.
16 Paredi (1940), 78–79.
17 Borella (1949), 41.
18 Probst (1893), 249.
19 Kennedy (1963), 23, footnote 41.
20 Callewaert (1949), 102.
21 L. Lavorel (1956), vol. 1, 14.
22 Johanny (1968), 65.
23 Gryson (1968), 269, footnote 47.
24 Cf. Blaise and Chirat (1954), 246, third meaning.

Srawley did, that the passage can be regarded as an *oratio fidelium* because the prayer for the king is found in the Solemn Orations, seems to us to be a rather hasty conclusion.

We rely, therefore, on the context of this fourth Eucharistic catechesis and on the structure of the Roman Canon (to which that of *De Sacramentis* is related) to affirm that this passage should not be seen as pointing to the Universal Prayer. We must remember that the words 'a sacerdote dicuntur' are not of themselves proof that they are actually anaphoric intercessions, since thus far we have found few mentions of the deacon in the West, and Ambrose does not ascribe any important role to them. If the Universal Prayer did exist, it was probably pronounced by the celebrant himself.

Commentary on 1 Tim 2:1

In another passage of *De Sacramentis* (6, 22–25) dedicated to prayer, Ambrose comments on the famous passage from the Epistle to Timothy. It insists on the order to be followed when addressing God: begin with praise and then move on to supplication, request and thanksgiving (§ 22). And the Milanese doctor shows us that this is also the pattern of the Our Father (§ 24) and Psalm 8 (§ 25). No allusion is made to the Universal Prayer.

Oratio pro salute omnium

One further text remains to be analysed:

T 9 *De virginibus* 3, 3, 11 (377): ... et tu, cum legitur aliquid quo Christus aut venturus annuntiatur aut venisse ostenditur, noli fabulando opstrepere, sed mentem admove. An quidquam est indignius quam oracula divina circumstrepi, ne audiantur, ne credantur, ne revelentur, circumsonare sacramenta confusis vocibus, ut impediatur oratio pro salute deprompta omnium?[25]

Do not these final words describe our prayer? It would seem not, since the text distinguishes between the *oracula divina* and the *sacramenta*, which in all probability corresponds to the two parts of the Mass. Moreover, a few lines further on we read:

---

25 Ambrose, *De virginibus* 3, 3, 11; ed. Faller (1933), 68; (PL 16), 223B: 'and you, when any passage is read announcing that Christ will come or showing that he has come, do not make a noise by chattering, but keep your mind attentive. Is there anything more unworthy than to drown out the divine words with such noise that they cannot be heard, be believed or made known, or surrounding the sacraments with such confused murmuring of voices that it hinders prayer that is offered for the salvation of all?'

T 10 *De virginibus* 3, 3, 14: Frequens sermo est cum plurima ranarum murmura religiosae auribus plebis opstreperent, sacerdotem dei praecepisse ut conticescerent ac reverentiam sacrae deferent orationi.[26]

But *sacra oratio* is clearly describing the Eucharistic prayer in the following passage:

T 11 *De Fide* 4, 10, 125 (380): Nos autem quotienscumque sacramenta sumimus, quae per sacrae orationis mysterium in panem transfigurantur et sanguinem, mortem domini adnuntiamus.[27]

In short, T 9 cannot serve as evidence for the existence of the Prayer of the Faithful.

Conclusions

What can we conclude? In the absence of any feasible list of intentions and especially any description of the Mass, we are reduced to silence. Nevertheless F. Probst, who has reconstructed the Milanese liturgy from the writings of St Ambrose, claims not only the existence of a Prayer of the Faithful, but even a prayer for the catechumens prior to their dismissal.[28] But this is more fiction than history! Lavorel is somewhat wiser; he considers the presence of an *oratio fidelium* as a possibility, but adds 'there is no explicit text by our author in this regard'.[29]

On our part, we consider that we ought to suspend judgement. Unless we bring new texts to the table for consideration, we cannot know if the Church of Milan was familiar with the *oratio fidelium*.

---

26 Ambrose, *De virginibus* 3, 3, 14; 'It is often told how, when the excessive croaking of frogs was filling the ears of the faithful people, the priest of God ordered them to be silent and show their respect to the sacred prayer'.

27 Ambrose, *De Fide* 4, 10, 125: CSEL 78, 201: 'Each time that we partake of the sacramental elements, which by the mystery of holy prayer are transformed into the body and blood, we announce the death of the Lord'.

28 Probst (1893), 241–250.

29 Lavorel (1956), vol. 1, 10.

Section Five

The Church of Gaul

The evidence that comes to us from Gaul[1] is much more recent that what we have analysed so far. The first text *ad rem* is none other than that of Prosper, which we read in the section on the Church of Rome. The available texts are also less numerous since, beyond this text from Prosper, we have only the terse order of a Council. We shall see what can be gleaned from that.

Hilary of Poitiers (315–367)

Hilary provides us with proof of prayer for the emperor. In the first book to Constance II († 361), the bishop of Poitiers writes that at the heart of the Eucharistic celebration Christians offer prayers for the well-being and happiness of the emperor;[2] but he does not provide any supplementary detail.

In his commentary on Psalm 140, he cites the text of 1 Tim 2:1–2, after which he distinguishes four types of prayer, but he makes no reference to the liturgy.[3]

As for his commentary on Ps 58,[4] which is sometimes cited, it is not *ad rem*. This sentence lists the requirements of the Gospel, but makes no appeal to any liturgical situation and so carries little weight with regard to our question.

---

1 On the Gallican liturgy, consult the following:

E. Griffe, *La Gaule chrétienne à l'époque romaine*, 3. vols, Paris, 1964; see particularly vol. 3, ch. 5: 'La liturgie de l'église cathédrale', 164–213.

E. Griffe, 'Aux origins de la liturgie gallicane' in *Bulletin de litterature ecclésiastique*, vol. 52 (1951), 17–43; see 28–31 for some very pertinent remarks on the Prayer of the Faithful.

Th. A. Vismans, 'Oud-gallicaanse liturgie' in LW 2, 2048–94.

A. G. Martimort, 'La liturgie de la messe en Gaule' in *Bulletin du comité des études de Saint-Sulpice*, vol. 22 (1958), 204–222.

On literary evidence from 6th century authors, see H. Beck, *The Pastoral Care of Souls in South-East France during the sixth Century*, Rome, 1950.

2 Hilary of Poitiers, *Ad Constantium Augustum*. 1, 2: (PL 10, 559; CSEL 65, 183): 'pro incolumitate et beatitudine tua offerant preces'.

3 Hilary of Poitiers, *Tractatus super psalmos*, 140, 2; (PL 9, 825; CSEL 22, 790).

4 Hilary of Poitiers, *Tractatus super psalmos*, 58, 2; (PL 9, 374C; CSEL 22, 182): 'Et idcirco iras et simultates et inimicitias evangelium conpressit, cum … et inimicos non solum diligendos (Mt 5: 22–23), sed pro his orandum esse decernat' (Mt 5:44).

John Cassian (*c.* 360–430/35)

In his ninth *Collatio*, the monk of Lérins also speaks of the different degrees of prayer, following the Epistle to Timothy. He writes extensively, but without any reference to public worship, limiting himself instead to the 'interior life'.[5]

Prosper of Aquitaine († 455)

In the section on the Church in Rome we analysed the liturgical argument used by Prosper against the semi-Pelagians of Lérins before the middle of the 5th century, an argument which probably leant heavily on the Solemn Prayers of Good Friday. We noted that to be fully justified, this reasoning supposes that these prayers were known in the south of Gaul, and even used in the liturgy for a sufficiently long time for them not to appear any longer as a novelty.[6] There is no positive indication available to support this deduction, but logic obliges us to present it as at least a strong probability.

According to Dom Alfonso, 'it is logical to imagine that by writing to the Gallican bishops, the author means at least that in Rome and Gaul the Prayer of the Faithful was quite similar, and derived from the same source'.[7] According to him, however, Gaul did not know the *Orationes sollemnes*, but the *orationes paschales*, the text of which we will provide later in Part Two of this work. We consider these *orationes* to be much later, and that they owe their liturgical form to the *Orationes sollemnes* which by then would have crossed the Alps.

Gennadius of Marseilles († 492/505)

In chapter 30 of his *De ecclesiasticis dogmatibus*, Gennadius takes up the text of the passage we have cited from *Capitulum* 8 of Prosper of Aquitaine.[8] This text proves that Prosper's argument was widespread in Gaul and had born fruit, since it figures in a kind of catechism that was written in Provence. Can we, then, conclude from this with any certainty that the Solemn Prayers were still in use in this region at this period? No, since this passage is merely a literal copy of *Capitulum* that Gennadius cites because of its doctrinal value and not for the liturgical allusion it contains.

---

5 John Cassian, *Collationes* 9, 7; (PL 49, 780ff; SC 54, 71ff).
6 Cf. Section Three above, Prosper of Aquitaine.
7 Alfonso (1928), 75.
8 Gennadius, *De ecclesiasticis dogmatibus* 30, (PL 58, 987–88). Cf. above, p. 107, T 26.

The Council of Orleans (511)

In his treaty *De synodalibus causis et disciplinis ecclesiasticis*, Regino of Prum (+ 915) places two canons related to the *oratio fidelium* one after the other. The first is the translation of c. 19 of the Council of Laodicea,[9] the second is a text of unknown origin.[10] Both probably refer to an ancient practice: this is obviously so for the first text which is describing a practice unknown in the West.

What interests us here is that a century later, the canonist Burchard of Wurms (965–1025) repeats these two canons in his *Decretorum libri XX* and names the second as c. 3 from the Council of Orleans (held in 511).[11] At the end of the 11th century, Ivo of Chartres (+ 1092) discarded the Laodicean canon, undoubtedly judged as too archaic, to cite only the second, which he too attributed to the Council of Orleans.[12]

Mansi cites this canon in relation to the Universal Prayer in an appendix to the Council of Orleans, with the notation: *Ex Burchardo*.[13] But the manuscripts from this Council contain no trace of this text.[14] There is no doubt that it is a fanciful attribution on the part of Burchard, which, notes his modern editor, is not uncommon.[15]

In short, the Council of Orleans does not speak about the *oratio fidelium*.

Council of Lyon (518–523)

This Council condemned a certain Stephen, accused of incest with Palladia, and subjected him to penitence. Thanks to the intervention of Emperor Sigismond, the sentence was reduced, and in an appendix on the Council decisions we find the following:

> 'Domni quoque gloriosissimi regis sententia secuti id temperamenti praestitemus, ut Stephano praedicto vel Palladiae usque ad orationem plebis, quae post evangelia legitur, orandi in locis sanctis spatium praestarimus'.[16]

---

9 Council of Laodicea (end 4th century), Mansi 2, 568 (in the year 320); Brightman (1896), vol. 1, 520, 25 ff.

10 Regino of Prum, *De synodalibus causis et disciplinis ecclesiasticus*. 1, c. 191 and 192; (PL 132, 224); ed. Wasserschleben (1840), 98–99. Also cited by Molin (1967), 333–34.

11 Burchard of Wurms, *Decretorum 1, XX*, 2, 69 and 70; (PL 140), 638.

12 Ivo of Chartres, *Decretum* 2, 120; (PL 161), 193.

13 Mansi 8, 361.

14 Cf. *Concilia Galliae*, ed. de Clercq;(CC 148A), 3–19.

15 Wasserschleben (1840), 99, in a footnote: 'hanc inscriptionem Burch., deficiente apud Reginonem fontis allegatione, ex more sibi finxit'. Cf. also Molin (1967), 334. For further details refer to Fransen (1969), 111–18.

16 Council of Lyon, (CC 148A), 41: 'Following the order of the very glorious king, we decide on this relaxation of the sentence: we give the said Stephen and Palladia the opportunity to pray in the holy places until the prayer of the people, which is read after the Gospel'.

Along with most other scholars, we recognize here a proof of the existence of an *oratio fidelium*, but the text says nothing about its liturgical form.

Conclusions

These rare snippets of evidence are not enough to satisfy our curiosity. We know nothing of the *oratio fidelium* in Gaul prior to the *Capitula* of Prosper of Aquitaine and the letter from Pope Celestine to the bishops of Gaul, both of which probably leant on the *orationes sollemnes* to demonstrate the need for grace. Therefore we think that this form must have been known there, at least in Provence, in the middle of the 5th century. A single text from the Council of Lyon of 517 informs us of an *oratio plebis* after the gospel. Apart from that we have only a testimony of prayer for the emperor from Hilary of Poitiers. Perhaps the Solemn Prayers endured for a certain time. Abruptly, the Council of Vaison (529) introduced the *Kyrie eleison*; but that is another story.[17]

---

17 There are no ancient patristic sources that inform us of the possible existence of a Universal Prayer in Spain. But our study of the texts will detect some archaic elements among them. Without being able to devote a section to Spain, we refer the reader to pp. 288–290.

Conclusions from Part One

At this point we shall stop the gathering of texts and analyses of allusions to the *oratio fidelium* that we have found in the Fathers and the ecclesiastical writers of the first five centuries. We will not present general conclusions at the moment, but limit ourselves to summarizing the data already presented and respond to the questions that were asked at the beginning of this first part of the study.

A. Existence of the Universal Prayer

No simple and universally valid answer can be formulated in this regard. The gaps in the documentation as well as the historical reality itself impel us to qualify our judgements.

It is striking to note, from the earliest days of the Church, prayers of petition for different categories of people. It is undeniable that the text of 1 Tim 2:1–2 has been influential in this regard. Following its recommendation, Christian have made 'petitions, prayers, supplication, thanksgiving for all humankind, for kings and all those in authority, in order to lead a calm and peaceful life in all holiness and dignity'.

And certainly from St Justin we see that this custom has taken the form of a liturgical rite: between the readings and the Eucharist, Christians prayed 'common prayers'. Even if all the texts that speak to us about the prayer of petition are not necessarily an allusion to the Universal Prayer, they affirm, nevertheless, the soil that nourished it.

In the Church of North Africa everything leads us to believe that Tertullian indicates the existence of such an *oratio fidelium*. While the texts of Cyprian may be less clear in this regard, nevertheless the convergence of various clues leads us to acknowledge that the Bishop of Carthage was also familiar with it. As for Augustine, there is no hesitation in saying that he knew it; it is on the content of this prayer that he bases his proof to the Pelagians that grace is necessary to arrive at faith.

It is in the Church of Rome that the existence of the Universal Prayer is most assured. Justin, 'Hippolytus', Ambrosiaster and Prosper of Aquitaine are reliable witnesses. The first two show us the place where it occurred during the liturgy; the second two probably let us hear the echo of particular formularies.

Ambrose of Milan, on the other hand, leaves us scarcely any trace of the *oratio fidelium*. It is certain that the Milanese Christians prayed for specific people, including the emperor and the penitents, but there is no indication that this took the form of any particular rite other than the diptychs.

Finally, in Gaul — or at least in Provence — the *orationes sollemnes* were probably borrowed from the Christians of Rome before the middle of the 5th century, but it was not until the beginning of the 6th century that we learn with any certitude of a 'prayer of the people' being prayed after the gospel.

We have to recognize that we cannot be as categorical as some have been. The evidence is not as conclusive as some encyclopedias and dictionaries like to claim. Yes, the early Church was familiar with the Universal Prayer, but perhaps not everywhere, neither in its origins nor throughout the first five centuries. And it probably owes its origin more to the order given in 1 Tim 2:1–2 than to Jewish liturgical influences.[1]

B. Its Content

1. For the Emperor

One of the most frequent petitions, especially among the earliest examples, concerned the emperor and those in public authority. There is nothing surprising about that, since this is the first petition cited in 1 Tim 2:1, and is also attested by the letter of Clement of Rome.[2] From this we draw two principal meanings.[3]

The first is an apologetic meaning: Christians prayed for the emperor as a proof of their good will towards him. We are good citizens, they affirmed, for it is the true God whom we invoke on behalf of the emperor and not just some vain idol.

The second is a more general meaning, and broader than we would believe today. For the emperor represents more than just himself as an individual; he is the embodiment of power. In praying for him, they were praying for the peace of the world and the safety and security of the citizens. Let us look a little more closely at this.

The expressions *pro salute imperatorum* (Tertullian T 5), *pro incolumitate imperatorum* (Cyprian T 6) are taken from the Roman religion and its worship of the emperor.[4] A. Stuiber[5] has studied the formula *pro salute et incolumitate* which is also to be found in the Roman Canon. He cites numerous inscriptions where this phrase — or one or other of its elements — can be found; among these, eleven

---

1 At least this is the impression gained from reading the patristic texts. But it must be said that the Fathers do not cite Jewish liturgical sources and prefer wherever possible to make reference to scriptural texts.

2 Cf. Mikat (1973), 455–471.

3 On all this see Biehl (1937).

4 Wissowa (1912). *Salus* was a goddess of ancient Italy, cf. p. 131.

5 Stuiber (1954), 127–146.

are pagan, five are Christian. L. Eizenhöfer has followed up this research[6] and has provided us with an extensive list of texts, among which the extracts from the *Acta Fratrum Arvalium* (nos 534–40) are of particular note. These passages furnish us with the exact equivalent of the intentions found in the earliest examples of the *oratio fidelium*. As Stuiber states, *salus et incolumitas* are the two words which recur repeatedly to indicate prosperity, particularly in the political domain, upon which the prosperity of the individual citizens depends entirely. For — and this is important for an accurate interpretation of our texts — according to the imperial ideology of the Late-Empire, the *incolumitas* of the emperor is the basis of the safety of his subordinates: 'ex cuis incolumitate omnium salus constat'.[7] This is exactly what we have seen in Athenagorus, and in Ambrose (T 2): 'per vos (imperatores) nobis pax et concordia sit refusa'. The Christians took these very terms from the ancient Roman cult. Christine Mohrmann notes that among the rare words in the Canon that are considered to be influenced by pagan prayer is the expression *pro salute et incolumitate*.[8]

We have come across similar formulas in Tertullian (T 5 and *Ad Scapulam*), Cyprian (T 6), Boniface and Celestine (Rome T 21 and 22), and Ambrose (T 2).[9] The presence of the couplet *salus et incolumitas*, Christianised by the addition of *spes*, in the diptychs of the Roman Canon, strengthens the conclusion that the greater part of these texts refer back to the diptychs and not to the Universal Prayer.

In short, in praying for the emperor, Christians were praying largely for the peace and security of everyone. We must compare this with opinion that existed in the mentality of the period, which viewed the end of the world as dependent upon the end of the Roman Empire (cf. Tertullian T 6).

2. For the Current Situation of the Church and of Christians

In time of persecution Christians prayed for the perseverance of believers and the return of those who had given up their faith. Tertullian, Cyprian, and Novatian cite the *stantes* and the *lapsi*; these last are also mentioned by Prosper of Aquitaine (T 26). Justin too (T 7) reported on 'bad Christians'.

3. For the Conversion of Unbelievers and the Faith of Believers.

This theme, which is so dominant in Augustine and Prosper that it overshadows all the others, is controversial, as we have pointed out, but that does not mean

6 Eizenhöfer (1966), nos. 352–381, 473–484, 490, 493, 513–558.
7 Stuiber (1954), 132. This last text comes from an inscription; see Eizenhöfer (1966). n. 535.
8 Mohrmann (1950), vol. 4, 1–19.
9 And also in Hilary, cf. p. 125, footnote 2.

that it did not correspond to reality. Justin (T 10) also mentions the prayer for the Jews; this is a rare petition, known only in the *Orationes sollemnes* (cf. also, however, *Deprecatio Gelasii* X)

4. For All People, Especially the Needy.

Universalist petitions are often encountered, following 1 Tim 2:1. However, they are often concretised in a list of those with particular needs: children, travellers, all those in danger … so that, once freed, says Ambrosiaster (T 3), they can give praise to God. These petitions will be developed in the litanies.

5. For Enemies

We must point out the influence of Christ's commandment (Mt 5:44): 'Love your enemies, pray for your persecutors'. This was remembered in times of persecution and put into practice.

We would point out that there are few petitions concerning material needs; only Cyprian speaks of rain and seeks protection from enemies (T 2–3). It was people more than things that were prayed for (even if this is a false opposition, since it is always for people that we seek benefits).

The dead are never mentioned.

C. Formularies Used

Probably only two of our authors made reference to fixed formularies. It is highly likely that Prosper of Aquitaine is copying the *Orationes sollemnes* in his controversy with the semi-Pelagians. And at the end of the 4th century Ambrosiaster gives us the themes which will find numerous expressions in the litanies, but we cannot know for sure that he himself was aware of this liturgical form.

The existence of a formulary as broad as that of the *Orationes sollemnes* before the middle of the 5th century show us just how important the *oratio fidelium* was in the eyes of the early Christians. If it is true the most important liturgical texts were finalized first, then we can say that at Rome the Universal Prayer occupied a prime place. This is confirmed by Augustine and Prosper, who make it the touchstone in a theological debate they both considered of primary importance.

The other pieces of evidence do not permit us to determine any constituted formularies. The priest expresses in the prayer the petitions that we have cited in the previous paragraph, and no doubt many others as well, according to the needs of the moment and his own faith insights.

D. The Liturgical Form

We will study the form of the *Orationes sollemnes* and the litanies in Part Two.

For the rest, the nature of the documentation does not allow us to draw any conclusions. To notice that these petitions were introduced by *pro* does not constitute a discovery! We can scarcely detect in Augustine's texts the structure *orare pro … ut …*: it is an invitatory developing into a final proposal, like those of the *Orationes sollemnes*.

We also observe that, apart perhaps from Augustine, nowhere have we found any mention of the deacon.

Part Two

Study of the Texts

Introduction

Having studied the pre-history of the *oratio fidelium*, that is to say the period which provides only allusions to the prayer, we now come to its actual history, analyzing and comparing the oldest forms that are preserved for us.

The State of the Question

Just what is it? For a long time scholars have published their random discoveries of this or that text; they have even pointed out parallels in use in another Church. Thus, for example, we find in the complete works of Thomasius († 1713), the edition of the *Deprecatio Gelasii* according to the two traditions that we know, followed by that of the two so-called Milanese litanies.[1] But these authors have been content to collate and publish the texts without further analysis.

In his *Histoire du bréviaire*, Dom Bäumer has dedicated a dozen well-documented pages to the *oratio fidelium*.[2] A number of texts are presented, ranging from the end of the Epistle of Clement of Rome to the *preces* of the Office, comprised of biblical verses. Apart from the *Deprecatio Gelasii*, the main versions are covered.

A more systematic study was undertaken at the beginning of the 20th century by the German philologist Wilhelm Meyer. In an important article published in 1912,[3] he edits the *Deprecatio Gelasii* and compares it with other texts. He is the first, we believe, to provide a methodical inventory, and distinguishes three categories of text:

1 The *pro*-series ('Pro-Reihen') that includes
  - the litany from the Stowe Missal,
  - the Milanese litanies,
  - the *Deprecatio Gelasii,*
  - the Franco-Gallican *Dicamus omnes.*

2 The Solemn Prayers of Good Friday, that he attributes to Gregory the Great, thereby radically distorting all his comparative conclusions;

---

1 Thomasius-Vezzosi (1747) vol. 2, 570–72.
2 Bäumer-Biron (1905), vol. 2, 1905, Appendix 2, 429–41.
3 Meyer (1912), Appendix II, 87–108.

3 The Gallican and Hispanic *Orationes paschales*, most often based on the same outline as their precedents.

Four years later, Wilhelm Bousset completed this study by including the Eastern parallels of these formularies.[4]

In 1928, Dom Pio Alfonso published a small book[5] in which he tries to cover the entire question of the *oratio fidelium*, from both East and West, and to uncover the most primitive schemas. The real value of this work lies in the fact that it provides the most important texts in a single, convenient collection.

Finally, Dom Capelle systematically works through this collection in a famous article,[6] in which his main interest are the Western litanies, which he names as the source of the current *Kyrie* of the Roman Mass. Since then, this has been regarded by liturgists as the classic work on the subject.

It is along this same line that our own research has been directed. In our Licentiate thesis,[7] prior to tracing the history of studies dedicated to the *oratio fidelium*, we drew up an inventory of the ancient texts that have come down to us. These are the formularies belonging to all the ancient Latin liturgies that we have assembled here, to edit, analyse and compare. Here is the list, with the acronyms that will identify them in the future. We have simply classified them according to the liturgical families from whose sources they have come down to us, without making any pre-judgement about their origin or their age:[8]

1 Celtic liturgy:
Irl¹ = *Dicamus omnes* from the Stowe Missal.
Irl² = anaphoric intercessions from the Stowe Missal ('Canon dominicus papae gilasi').

2 Milanese liturgy:
M¹ = *Divinae pacis*
M² = *Dicamus omnes*

3 Roman liturgy:
OS = Solemn prayers of Good Friday
DG = *Deprecatio Gelasii*

4 Gallican liturgy:
FG¹ = Franco-Gallican *Dicamus omnes*
FG² = Franco-Gallican *Kyrie eleison, Domine Deus omnipotens patrum nostrorum*
Orationes paschales of the

4 Bousset (1916), 135–163.
5 Alfonso (1928).
6 Capelle (1934), 126–144; Tr. Lit, vol. 2, 116–134.
7 De Clerck (1967), typewritten thesis.
8 Precise references to manuscript or published sources will be given below, before the edition of the text.

Missale Gallicanum Vetus (= MGV)
Missale Gothicum (= Go)
Bobbio Missal (= Bo)

5 Hispanic liturgy:
Ha = Orationes in vigilia Paschae, tradition A.
Hb = Orationes in vigilia Paschae, tradition B.

It must be noted that not all these texts appear in these manuscripts as formularies of the Universal Prayer: *Irl*[1] is situated in the Canon of the Mass, as an insertion into the *Memento* for the living, The final five, each bearing the title of *orationes paschales*, are used during the Easter Vigil, sometimes even (as in Spain) between the readings. Finally, only one of the manuscripts of the *Deprecatio Gelasii*, the most altered of them all, places it in the Mass (in the Milanese tradition). In what capacity, then, do we present these texts in the context of a study of the *oratio fidelium*?

Given their antiquity, supported by patristic evidence, the content of the existing texts and the absence of any other *Sitz im Leben* with which to connect them, we think that, more or less, they all have their origin in the *oratio fidelium*. Without wanting to enter at this point into the delicate problem of the link between these and the anaphoric intercessions, we note that in the East both share the same literary genre and develop the same set of themes, repeated in our Western forms. Even if the manuscripts present the Hispanic texts to us as *orationes paschales*, a quick glance is enough to detect in them the same intentions as in the other litanies. We find ourselves in the presence of the same vein of inspiration. To neglect these texts would be to deprive ourselves of a large part of the documentation which, despite appearances, is very ancient. Even if their function has changed in the course of history, their source remains, in our eyes, the ancient *oratio fidelium*.

In short, without claiming that *Irl*[2], in its current form, has ever served as the Universal Prayer in the Celtic Church, we nevertheless think that it is in some way derived from it. Therefore, we have retained all the texts which, in their content and literary form,[9] enjoy the guarantee of antiquity.

Research Undertaken to Expand the Documentation

It will be noted that this list includes several titles beyond those of the authors previously cited. So how then did we proceed?

In the first instance we have been able to more aptly classify these documents in the light of recent research. For example, we have, for the Hispanic texts,

9 We have not retained those formularies where the responses take the form of psalm versicles; this is a later literary form, perhaps originating with the Irish monks: cf. Section Five.

adopted the two-tradition distinction proposed by Père Bernal.[10] Then we made the connection between classical texts and others in a similar vein, such as *Irl*[2] and *FG*[2].

We have also undertaken a research project with the goal of finding new texts or new examples of known formularies. On the advice of Père Gy we conducted an investigation into the processional manuscripts; and without being exhaustive this has proved to be full of interest and rich in learnings. From the list of documents that Père Gy had examined, with a view to the publication of a Directory of Ritual Manuscripts conserved in the Public Libraries of France, we have identified all the Processionals and other liturgical books likely to contain *preces*. From this, four main sources have emerged: Paris, Cambrai, Verdun and Autun. We have examined all the Processionals from these, together with several Graduals and some *libri precum*. This second category of documents has shown to be as fruitful in litanic texts as the first. We have also viewed all the Processional manuscripts in the Bibliothèque Royale of Brussels and we took advantage of a trip to Switzerland to carry out the same procedure at Saint-Gall. With regard to printed Processionals, we have been content to examine those from the Bibliothèque Royale in Brussels, the Abbey of Mont César in Louvain and the Centre National de Pastorale Liturgique in Paris.[11]

It is always at the Rogation Days that the texts that concern us have been preserved. When a Church uses them they are still sometimes found in books

10 Bernal (1964), 283–347.

11 To avoid unnecessary work for those who would like to continue the research, we will also indicate the negative results of our survey. Of the 150 manuscripts examined, we did not find any of the texts cited in the list (apart from the *Orationes sollemnes*) in:

AUTUN, Bibl. Mun. S 181.

BESANÇON, Bibl. Mun. 79, 131, 140.

BRUXELLES: none of the Processionals of Bibl. Roy. contained any *preces*, apart from 4836 (641) in *FG*[1], while IV 60 (f. 57) referred to this same piece without providing any text.

CAMBRAI, Bibl. Mun. 55, 67, 70, 72 to 76, 79, 82, 83.

HAUTECOMBE, Abbey of Saint Madeleine, Gradual of Valence.

MADRID, Acad. Hist. 18;

B.N. 1361;

Pal. Nac. II. D. 3.

PARIS, B.N. — lat. 931, 1086, 1122 to 1124, 1132, 1136, 1154, 1210, 1240, 1331, 1336, 9467, 9478, 10517, 10518, 10581, 12584, 13159, 13256 to 13258, 18050.

– nv. acq. lat. 387, 422.

ROME, Bibl. Vat. Palat. At. 489

ROUEN, Bibl. Mun. 222 to 224, 242, 253, 255, 3030.

SAINT-GALL, Stiftsbibl.: no processional, nor any of the manuscripts that we examined (15, 97, 339, 349, 360, 395, 443, 473) contained our litanies.

VERDUN, Bibl. Mun.: neither the processionals nor the manuscripts 12, 127, 130, 131, 149 to 151, 153, contained our litanies.

As for the printed processionals none of those from the Bibliothèque Royale of Brussels, nor the abbey of Mont César in Louvain, contain any. According to Père Gy, we have, at least for France, dealt with around 90% of the existing sources.

printed not so long ago; thus, for example, the *Processionale turonense*, edited in Tours in 1827 contains *FG*[2].

What were the results of this survey? Given the locations at which we carried it out, we have found new examples only for the Franco-Gallican *preces* (*FG*[1] and *FG*[2], which we will point out as we deal with them). By chance, we also discovered a new text from *Irl*[2]. On no occasion did we come across the so-called Milanese litanies, nor the *DG*, which matches perfectly with the conclusions of Père Molin[12] who, in studying the manuscript tradition of the *DG*, notes that apart from its presence (altered) in an Ambrosian liturgical book, this item is found only in books of private prayers (*libelli precum*). We think, as he does, that if we wish to uncover new examples of the *DG* we must search in manuscripts of the same genre.

The result of this research was rather meagre with regard to the list of texts given below. On the other hand, we have come across several *preces* of more recent origin, more hymnic than litanic, which allow us to further clarify our chronological framework.

Chronological Limits

Since ancient liturgical texts can be incorporated into more recent liturgical books it is essential that the age of the sources be distinguished from the age of the texts themselves. With regard to the sources, we have not imposed any limit, and we will refer as happily to manuscripts from the 8th century as to a Processional edited in Tours in 1827. With regard to the texts, we will range from roughly the second half of the 3rd century up to the time of Charlemagne.

Technical Vocabulary Used for Classification

It remains to clarify the terms that we will use in the study of these texts. It is most helpful to develop an exact technical vocabulary which can serve as an analytical tool. This might seem a little pedantic, but our intention is only to forge a scientific instrument for classification, not to extend these terms to liturgical practice.

The necessity for this has become apparent to us for several reasons. First, we have already noted that in the liturgical tradition our ancestors have not always clearly distinguished the liturgical forms they employed. For example, so many times we find the ending, *Per Dominum* at the end of an invitatory addressed to the people, as if it were actually a prayer. At other times we find invitatories that have been transformed into prayers. The study of liturgy itself, while generally concerned with distinguishing between different euchological

12 Molin (1976), 113–48.

forms, is nevertheless far from consistent in using identical and unequivocal vocabulary to label these forms, leading to a great deal of confusion. Moreover, in the realm of pastoral liturgy, many pastors are unaware of the structure of the texts that they are using, and we think that liturgists would be doing a good service in better classifying the euchological formularies by providing precise definitions. We hope, too, that this attempt, while limited to the question that now occupies us, can be improved and expanded so as to initiate a more general attempt to systematically classify liturgical forms. Our main concern in the development of this vocabulary has been precision. In the first place it was a question of seeing how the formularies differed, being careful not to confuse the basic composition with the presence of a non-essential element, isolating the simple elements and dismantling their combinations. Next, it was a case of allocating a unique and distinguishing term for each reality, whether foundational or composed. We have also sought a certain linguistic symmetry between parallel elements belonging to the two different euchological types; thus were we led to forge the term 'invocatory' to correspond to 'invitatory'.

On principle we have avoided taking up the terminology used in the manuscripts — for example, *preces* or *orationes*; our forefathers were not concerned with systematization and often designated different realities with the same rubric. This will also prevent us from projecting our own classificatory schemas onto documents simply by reading their titles, which are often misleading.

This attempt at clarification will have shown to be successful if, at the end of this study the reader has the impression of mastering the material presented. In that case, far from being a straitjacket, this vocabulary will have been proven to be an effective tool.

At the outset, it is essential to distinguish clearly the semantic core from the grammatical forms that it assumes.

- *At the semantic level*, whatever the language or turn of phrase used, there are five fundamental elements:
  1. The subject of the action, which, in the liturgy, is the assembly or a minister;
  2. The function, explained essentially by the verb, which, in this case, is supplication;
  3. The beneficiary of the request, either an individual or a group;
  4. The aim of the petition;
  5. The one to whom the words are addressed, which, in this case, is God or the assembly.
- *At the grammatical level*, very different expressions can carry the same semantic value. To explain the subject of a request and its beneficiary, we can say
  - 'pro conservatione Ecclesiae oramus te'.
  - 'pro Ecclesia, ut conservetur, oramus te'.
  - 'ut Ecclesiam tuam conservare digneris oramus te'.

Grammatically these expressions are very different, but semantically they have the same value: none of the three teaches us more than the other two.

This distinction is fundamental. We are of the opinion that it is superfluous to designate an unambiguous word for each grammatical form, especially for the most elementary, as long as their semantic value is clearly articulated. Thus, for example, each sentence of a litany that begins with the preposition *pro* is sometimes called an 'intention', but if we look closely at this intention we find that sometimes it designates the beneficiary of the request ('pro rege nostro'; 'pro sancta Ecclesia') and sometime the aim of the request ('pro remissione peccatorum'). Moreover, the same reality can reside in quite different grammatical forms, for example, 'ab omni malo (libera nos Domine)'; 'ut nobis parcas (te rogamus audi nos)'; 'mortificatam vtiis carnem (praesta Domine)'.

This allows us to avoid false oppositions that lack any real foundation, such as that of prayer for persons ('pro navigantibus') and prayer for things ('pro aeris temperie'). The latter explicitly names only the aim of the petitions, but its beneficiaries are, of course, implied — good weather is prayed for so that the harvesters can reap a fine harvest and so that the members of the assembly (or most of them) will benefit. Conversely, the prayer for persons names only the beneficiaries but the aim is more or less obvious: we pray for sailors so that there are no storms and that they might reach port in a timely manner. To put such petitions in opposition to each other is unproductive.[13]

From a practical point of view it is important to take account of two aspects: the semantic and the literary. We propose the following classification:

I *At the semantic level*

1) *Liturgical types*, determined by the function of the generalized liturgical expression. All our formularies are of the '*common prayer*' type, which is to say, prayer organized in such a way as to favour the maximum interaction between the group leader and the participants. The 'common prayer' is distinguished from the 'priestly prayer' where the presider of the assembly has the role of transmitter, or of being the spokesperson for the participants. Similarly, it differs from other forms, such as 'reading' or 'acclamation'. An exhaustive classification of liturgical types still remains to be developed.[14]

2) *The subjects of the action*

All liturgical action is the work of an *assembly*, which can be divided into two groups:

- the *leading group*, composed either of a single person (priest, deacon) or of several people (e.g. choir);

13 The work of Berger (1965), has not been a great help to us despite its title ('Die Wendung "*offerre pro*" in der römischen Liturgie'); it seeks to place things on a more theological level.

14 Some useful elements can be found in L. Duchesne (1925), 110–111, and in Martimort (1965), 135–147.

– the *participating group*, which is to say the members of the assembly who do not lead (including the priest when a proclamation is being made by the deacon, for example).

3) *The person addressed*

All liturgical pronouncements are addressed either to God (or the saints); or to the assembly. We also distinguish two basic euchological types:
– *invocative*, which is addressed to God,
– *invitative*, which is addressed to the assembly.

II *At the literary level*

1) The *liturgical forms*, or general structures for pronouncements. In the 'common prayer' type we find two:

a) the *litie*,[15] or ensemble comprising several 'litiques'. A litique is a two-part pronouncement made up of an invitatory followed by a prayer. These two elements can eventually be separated by an admonition.
Example: the *Orationes sollemnes* forms a litie comprised of 9 litiques.

b) the *litanie* or ensemble calling for the constant interaction of two groups:
– the leader formulates the announcements (either 'invocative' or 'invitative' in style);
– the participants respond after each of these with their response.
Generally (but not always), the litany includes an introduction of the 'invitative' type (e.g. *dicamus omnes: Domine miserere*) and a final prayer.
For example: *M*[1].

2) *The elements* that make up these forms:

2.1. The *response* or refrain repeated by the participants at the end of each pronouncement by the leader.
e.g. 'Kyrie eleison'.
The term 'response' does not mean that the participants 'reply' to the leader himself; but as in the case of the psalms, it follows immediately after the intervention of the leader. In a Universal Prayer form, the 'response' is necessarily of the 'invocative' type.

---

15 Not finding any term to accurately describe this liturgical form, we have taken the word 'litie' (from the Greek λιτή) from which comes 'litany'; and so from the same root, which indicates belonging to the same genre, we get two sufficiently differentiated terms that we can clearly indicate the particular meaning of each of them.

In the Byzantine liturgy the litie describes a procession which, during the singing of the tropes, proceeds from the sanctuary to the narthex; the term, then, can be considered a synonym of the Latin *litania*.

Concerning the sense of these words in Greek and Latin, see G. Knopp (1970), 187–188. See also OR 50, chapters 35 and 36 (Andrieu (1961)).

2.2. Elements of the 'invocative' type:

2.2.1. The *admonition* or communication to the participants of a directive concerning posture (physical or spiritual) to be assumed, or an action to be carried out.

e.g. 'Flectamus genua'
'Levate' (the admonition or directive)

2.2.2. The *invitation* or announcement inviting the participants to pray, but indicating neither the subject nor the beneficiary of the prayer.

e.g. 'Oremus'
'Salvatorem Dominum supplicamus' (attributive invitation)

2.2.3. The *invitatory* or announcement inviting the participants to pray, indicating either the aim or the beneficiaries of the prayer, or both.[16]

e.g. (aim): 'pro remissione peccatorum' (nominal invitatory)
e.g. (beneficiary): 'Oremus pro sancta Ecclesia' (verbal invitatory)
e.g. (both): 'Oremus pro catechumenis nostris ut deus adaperiat aures praecordiarum ipsorum'

2.3. Elements of the invocative type:

2.3.1. the *invocation* or announcement addressed to God but indicating neither the subject nor the beneficiary of the prayer.

e.g. 'Oramus te'
'Exaudi nos in omni oratione nostra' (imperative invocation)

2.3.2. the *invocation* or announcement addressed to God by the leader and indicating either the aim, or the beneficiary, or both.

e.g. (aim): 'pro altissima pace invocamus te'[17]
e.g. (beneficiary): 'pro rege nostro oramus te'
e.g. (both): 'ut Ecclesiam tuam conservare digneris te rogamus'
'pro infidels ut credant oramus te'
'ab omni malo libera nos Domine'

2.3.3. the *prayer* or announcement addressed to God in the name of the participants by the single presider (not just any leader) who is exercising his role as mediator.

The prayer could be more or less developed but comprises at the least:

- an address,
- the aim of the petition and the favour being sought and its beneficiary,
- a formulary of mediation ('per Dominum'),
- an involvement by the participants ('Amen').

3) The various *modalities* that may be included in these elements.
An announcement is described as:
3.1. *Verbal* if it includes a verb;

---

16 This definition does not therefore include, despite the accepted usage, the psalm 'invitatory' of Matins.

17 While it is not specifically indicated, the beneficiary is often, as in this case, the subject of the verb.

e.g.: 'pro pastore nostro imploramus te' (verbal invocation)

Nominal if it does not include a verb; in fact the verb is 'understood' or included in the response.

e.g.: 'pro pastore nostro et omni clero eius'

3.2. *Attributive* if it qualifies God:

e.g. 'Domine Deus omnipotens patrum nostorum' (attributive invocation)

Descriptive if it qualifies those praying:

e.g. 'peccatores, te rogamus audi nos' (descriptive invocation)

3.3. *Imperative* if the verb is in this mode, thereby expressing a wish or an order;

e.g. 'Exsurge, Domine, adiuva nos' (imperative invocation)

Indicative if the verb is in this mode, thereby expressing a statement;

e.g. 'Lord, we seek you' (indicative invocation).

Now we are equipped to undertake the study of the texts. For each of them we will establish the list of source references and provide both the critical edition and the Eastern parallels.[18] We will analyse their liturgical form and in a commentary will review the studies that have been dedicated to them, then finally, we will present our conclusions.

18 In giving the references we will use the method employed by Capelle: the numbers refer to the pages in Brightman (except for the *Apostolic Constitutions*) and the letters that precede them indicate the liturgical family from which they have been borrowed: CAp = *Apostolic Constitutions*, that we cite according to the division of the text into books and paragraphs; J = the Greek liturgy of St James; B = Byzantine liturgy; M = liturgy of St Mark; E = Egyptian liturgy (Coptic).

For the Eastern formularies see Hanssens (1932), vol. 3, 230–260 (n. 1047–82). See also Baumstark (1922), 53–72; according to him the background of these items dates back to the time of the persecutions.

Section One

The Solemn Orations (OS)

The first text to read and analyse is probably the most beautiful of them all, as much for its content as for its stylistic quality. It is one of the earliest of all the Latin liturgical texts that have been preserved. At first sight the 'Solemn Orations' are quite different, especially in their liturgical form, from other formularies of the Universal Prayer, but we will see that this is really an optical illusion. An in-depth study of this 'litie' would be very long. Here we confine ourselves to our current objective, which is to refer the reader to the works that have been devoted to this prayer.

A. The Sources

Since this formulary is still in use today, we will cite only the most ancient examples. Three liturgical traditions will provide them for us:

Gelasian:

V ROME, Bibl. Vat. Reg. lat. 316 (*c.* 750), f. 63^{v}–66^{r},
= Old Gelasian Sacramentary, ed. Mohlberg, 64–67.
(Claves 1899 Bourque 8 Gamber 610).

R ZURICH, Bibl. Centre. Rh 30 (*c.* 800),
= *Sacramentary of Rheinau* (8th century Gelasian), ed. Hänggi-Schönherr, 126–29.
(Clavis 1905t Bourque 29 Gamber 802).

S SAINT-GALL, Stiftsbibl. 348 (*c.* 790–817), 149–53,
= *The Sacramentary of St Gall* (8th century Gelasian), ed. Mohlberg, 78–80.
(Clavis 1905g Bourque 24 Gamber 830).

A PARIS, B. N. lat. 816 (*c.* 800),
= *The Sacramentary of Angoulême* (8th century Gelasian), ed. Cagin, 43–44.
(Clavis 1905d Bourque 23 Gamber 860).

Gallican:

ROME, Bibl. Vat. Palat. lat. 493 (*c.* 700), f. 47^{r}–50^{v},
= *The Old Gallican Missal*, ed. Mohlberg, 27–29.
(Clavis 1922 Bourque 519 Gamber 212–14).

Gregorian:

C CAMRAI, Bibl. Mun. 164 (olim 159) (of 812), f. 57–61,
= *The Sacramentary of Hildoard*, ed. Lietzmann, 47–49 Deshusses 176–80.
(Clavis 1904 Bourque 53 Gamber 720)

O ROME, Bibl. Vat. Ottob. lat. 313 (9th century)
= Alcuinianum, Variations in Wilson, Lietzmann and Deshusses.
(Bourque 72 Gamber 740)

B. Edited Version

Here, with minor modifications, the critical edition given is Willis;[1] we will not indicate the solely orthographical variations that he cites in his apparatus.

ITEM POST LECTIONEM EUANGELII

ORATIONES SOLEMNES[2]

I

Oremus, dilectissimi nobis, in primis[3] pro ecclesia sancta dei, ut eam[4] deus et dominus noster pacificare adunare[5] et custodire dignetur toto orbe[6] terrarum, subiciens ei principatus et potestates, detque nobis tranquillam et quietam[7] vitam degentibus glorificare deum patrem omnipotentem.

OREMUS.[8] Omnipotens sempiterne deus, qui gloriam tuam omnibus[9] in Christo gentibus reuelasti, custodi opera misericordiae tuae, ut ecclesia tua[10] toto orbe diffusa stabili fide in confessione tui nominis perseueret. per dominum nostrum.

---

1 Willis (1964), 14–17.

2 ITEM POST LECTIONEM EUANGELII ORATIONES SOLEMNES *Gall.*
ITEM SECUNTUR ORATIONES SOLEMNES *Gel* (*S*).
ORATIONES QUAE DICENDAE SUNT VI FERIA MAIORE IN HIERUSALEM *Greg.* Item sequitur lectio et responsorium. Inde vero legitur passio domini. Ipsa expleta incipit sacerdos orationes solemnes quae sequuntur *Gel* (*VRA*).

3 in primis *om Greg.*

4 eam] etiam *Gel* (*V*).

5 adunare] multiplicare *Gall. om Greg* (*C*).

6 toto orbe *Gall Gel* (*RS*) *Greg* (*C*), per universum orbem *Gel* (*VA*) *Greg* (*O*).

7 tranquillam et quietam] quietam et tranquillam *Greg.*

8 OREMUS + *Et dicit diaconus.* Flectamus genua. *Postquam orauerint dicit* Leuate *Gel* (*S*).
+ *Adnuntiat diaconus.* Flectamus genua. *Iterum dicit.* Levate *Gel* (*VRA*) *Greg* (*O*).
deinde + postea dicit sacerdos orationem *Greg* (*O*).

9 omnibus] in omnibus *Gel* (*V*).

10 tua *om Gall Greg* (*C*).

II

Oremus et pro beatissimo[11] papa nostro,[12] ut deus omnipotens[13] qui elegit eum[14] in ordine episcopatus saluum et incolumem[15] custodiat ecclesiae suae sanctae ad regendum populum sanctum dei.

OREMUS. Omnipotens sempiterne deus, cuius aeterno[16] iudicio[17] uniuersa fundantur, respice propitius ad preces nostras et electrum nobis antistitem[18] tua pietate conserua, ut christiana plebs quae tali gubernator auctore[19] sub tanto pontifice[20] credulitatis suae meritis augeatur. per.

III

Oremus et pro omnibus episcopis, presbyteris, diaconibus, subdiaconibus,[21] acolytis, exorcistis, lectoribus, ostiariis, confessoribus, uirginibus, uiduis, et pro omni populo sancto dei.

OREMUS. Omnipotens sempiterne deus, cuius spiritu totum corpus ecclesiae sanctificatur et regitur, exaudi nos pro uniuersis ordinibus supplicantes, ut gratiae tuae munere ab omnibus tibi gradibus[22] fideliter seruiatur. per.

IV

Oremus et pro christianissimis imperatoribus nostris[23] ut deus et dominus noster[24] subditas illis faciat omnes barbaras nationes ad nostrum perpetuam pacem.[25]

---

11 beatissimo] famulo dei *Gel* (*VA*).
12 nostro] illo *add Gel* (*S*) *Greg.* sedis apostolicae illo et pro antistite nostro illo *add Gel* (*VRA*).
13 omnipotens] et dominus noster *Greg.*
14 eum] eos *Gel* (*VRA*).
15 saluum et incolumem] saluos et incolumes *Gel* (*VRA*), saluum atque incolumem *Greg.*
16 aeterno *om Greg.*
17 iudicio] inditio *Gall.*
18 electum ... antistitum] electos ... antistites *Gel* (*VRA*), a te *add Gel.*
19 tali ... auctore] talibus ... autoribus *Gel* (*VRA*).
20 tanto pontefice] tantibus pontificibus *Gel* (*RA*), tantos pontifices *Gel* (*V*).
21 subdiaconibus *om Gall.*
22 tibi gradibus *om Gel* (*V*).
23 christianissimis imperatoribus nostris *Gel* (*S*), christianissimo imperatore nostro *Greg.* christianissimis imperatoribus nostris uel rege nostro *Ill. Gell* (*R*). christianissimo imperatore nostro uel rege nostro *Illo Gel* (*V*). christianissimo imperatore uel rege nostro *illo Gel* (*A*). christianissimis regibus *Gall.*
24 et dominus noster] omnipotens *Gel* (*VA*).
25 per *add Gall.*

OREMUS. Omnipotens sempiterne deus, in cuius manu sunt omnium temporum[26] potestates et omnia iura regnorum,[27] respice propitius[28] ad Romanum[29] benignus imperium, ut gentes que in sua feritate confidunt potentiae tuae dextera[30] conprimantur. per.

V

Oremus et pro catechumenis nostris, ut deus et dominus noster adaperiat aures praecordiarum ipsorum[31] ianuamque[32] misericordiae, ut per lauacrum regenerationis accepta remissione omnium peccatorum digni[33] inueniantur in Christo Iesu domino nostro.

OREMUS. Omnipotens sempiterne deus, qui ecclesiam tuam noua semper prole fecundas, auge fidem et intellectum catechumenis nostris, ut renati fonte baptimatis adoptionis tuae filiis adgregentur. per.

VI

Oremus, dilectissimi nobis, deum patrem omnipotentem ut cunctis mundum purget erroribus, morbos auferat, famem depellat, aperiat carceres, uincula dissoluat, peregrinantibus reditum, infirmantibus sanitatem, nauigantibus portum salutis indulgeat.

OREMUS. Omnipotens sempiterne[34] deus, maestorum consolatio, laborantium fortitudo, perueniant ad te preces de quacumque tribulatione clamantium, ut omnes sibi in necessitatibus suis misericordiam tuam gaudeant adfuisse. per.

VII

Oremus et[35] pro hereticis et schismaticis, ut deus et[36] dominus noster eruat eos ab erroribus uniuersis et ad[37] sanctam matrem ecclesiam catholicam atque apostolicam reuocare dignetur.[38]

---

26 temporum *om Greg.*
27 in cuius … regnorum *Gall Greg.* qui regnis omnibus aeterna potestate dominaris *Gel.*
28 propitius *om Greg.*
29 Romanorum *Gall Gel* (*VA*) *Greg* (*C*). romanorum *Gel* (*RS*). christianum *Greg* (*O*). siue Francorum *add Gel* (*VA*). atque Francorum *add Gel* (*R*).
30 potentiae tuae dextera *Gall Greg Gel* (*RS*). dexterae tuae potentia *Gel* (*V*). dexterae potentia *Gel* (*A**). dexterae maiestatis tuae potentia *Gel* (*A*[c]).
31 ipsorum] eorum *Gel* (*RS*[c]).
32 ianuamque] genuamque *Gel* (*V*).
33 digni] et ipsi *Gall Greg.*
34 sempiterne] et misericors *Gel* (*S*) *Gall.*
35 et *om Gall Gel* (*SA**. et *post* pro *A*[c]).
36 et *Gel* (*VA*), ac *Gel* (*RS*) *Gall Greg.*
37 ad *om Gall* (*lapsu*).
38 per *add Gel* (*V*) *Gall.*

OREMUS. Omnipotens sempiterne deus, qui omnes saluas[39] et neminem uis perire, respice ad animas diabolica fraude deceptas, ut omni heretica prauitate[40] deposita[41] errantium[42] corda[43] resipiscant et ad ueritatis tuae redeant firmitatem.[44] per.

VIII

Oremus et pro perfidis iudaeis, ut deus et dominus[45] noster auferat uelamen de[46] cordibus eorum, ut et ipsi cognoscant[47] Christum Iesum[48] dominum nostrum.[49]

OREMUS. Omnipotens sempiterne deus, qui etiam iudaicam perfidiam a[50] tua misericordia non repellis, exaudi preces nostras, quas tibi[51] pro illius populi obcaecatione deferimus, ut agnita[52] ueritatis tuae luce, quae Christus est, a suis tenebris eruantur. per.

IX

Oremus et pro paganis, ut deus omnipotens auferat iniquitatem[53] a[54] cordibus eorum, et relictis idolis suis conuertantur ad deum[55] uerum et unicum filium eius Iesum Christum[56] dominum nostrum,[57] cum[58] quo[59] uiuit et regnat cum Spiritu sancto.[60]

OREMUS. Omnipotens sempiterne deus, qui non[61] mortem peccatorum sed uitam semper inquiris, suscipe propitius orationem nostrum et libera eos ab

39 omnes saluas *Gel VA*). saluas omnes *Gel* (RS) *Gall Greg.*
40 prauitate] peruersitate *Gel* (*VA*).
41 deposita] depulsa *Gel* (*VRA*).
42 errantium] et errantium *Gel* (*S*).
43 errantium corda *om Gall.*
44 firmitatem] unitatem *Greg.*
45 deus et dominus] dominus et deus *Gel* (*S*).
46 de] a *Greg* (*O*).
47 cognoscant] agnoscant *Greg.*
48 Christum Iesum] Iesum Christum *Gel* (*A*) *Greg* (*O*). Iesum *om Gel* (*S*).
49 qui uiuit et regnat *add Gall.*
50 a *om Gall.*
51 tibi *om Gall Greg.*
52 agnita] cognita *Gel* (*R*).
53 iniquitatem] iniquitates *Gel* (*S*). iniqua *Gall.*
54 a] de *Gel* (*S*) *Gall.*
55 deum] uiuum et *add Gel* (*S*). *Greg.*
56 Christum] deum ac *add Gel* (*S*). deum et *add Greg* (*C*).
57 dominum nostrum *om Gall.*
58 cum … sancto *om Gel* (*A*).
59 cum quo] qui cum eo *Greg* (*O*).
60 cum Spirito sancto *Gall Greg* (*C*). cum sancto Spiritu *Greg* (*O*). Deus in unitate spiritus sancti *Gel.* In saecula saeculorum *add Gall.* Deus per omnia saecula saeculorum amen *add Greg* (*O*) *Gel* (*RS*[c]).
61 non] uis *add Greg* (*O*).

idolorum cultura, et adgreda ecclesiae tuae sanctae ad laudem et gloriam nominis tui. per.

C. Eastern Parallels

To our knowledge, only Baumstark[62] has so far compared the *OS* with the Eastern litanies; their similarity is apparently less obvious due to the difference between their liturgical forms. The subject matter is, however, strongly comparable, as the following texts testify (we present only the truly relevant texts):[63]

I for the Church: a petition present in all the litanies, but without any strict parallel; 'tranquillam et quietam vitam' is a quotation from 1 Tim 2:2 that is found in CAp VIII 13, 5 (cf. 12, 42) and *J* 55.

Flectamus genua — *Levate* = *E* 159 Κλίνωμεν τὰ γόνατα — Ἀναστῶμεν.

II for the *pope* (in the sense of bishop); no strict parallel. Cf. *M* 121.

III for the ecclesiastical orders; CAp VIII 10 and in particular 12 cite them in the same way, apart from acolytes, exorcists, porters and confessors; *M* 126 and *M* 138 mention the people (πάντων τῶν λαῶν and φιλοχρίστου λαοῦ).

IV for the emperor; *J* 45 ὑπὲρ τῶν εὐσεβεστάτων καὶ θεοστέπτων ὀρθοδόξων ἡμῶν βασιλέων; *B* 363 ὑπὲρ τῶν εὐσεβεστάτων καὶ θεοφυλάκτων βασιλέων ἡμῶν;
'ut deus et dominus noster subditas illis faciat omnes barbaras nationes ad nostrum perpetuam pacem': cf. *J* 55 ὑπόταξον αὐτοῖς (βασιλεῦσι) πάντα τὰ πολεμικὰ καὶ βάρβαρα ἔνθη ... ἵνα ἤρεμον καὶ ἡσύχιον βίον διάγωμεν ... (1 Tim 2:2).

V for the catechumens; found in CAp and *M*, but not in *J* or *B*; 'adaperiat aures praecordiarum ipsorum' = CAp VIII 6, 5 διανοίξῃ τὰ ὦτα τῶν καρδιῶν αὐτῶν; the same is in the Antioch liturgy, according to the writings of John Chrysostom, Br 471, 8;
'lavacrum regenerationis' = Tit 3:5 = CAp VIII 6, 7 and others;
'accepta remissione omnium peccatorum' = CAp VIII 6, 7: ἀφέσεως τυχόντες τῶν πλημμελημάτων.

VI for the needy; this is one of the most universal petitions; all the categories are found in the Easter litanies, apart from deliverance from hunger.

VII for the heretics and schismatics; a much more original request; those approaching closest to it are CAp VIII 10. 17 and 12, 46: τῶν ἔξω ὄντων καὶ πεπλανημένων and *J* 56: παῦσον τὰ σχίσματα τῶν ἐκκλησιῶν καὶ τὰς τῶν αἱρέσεων ἐπαναστάσεις.

VIII for the Jews; this appears nowhere else (even in the West).

XI for the pagans; also original. cf. VII.

---

62 Baumstark (1969), 65–71.

63 Here and for all the following texts, the acronymns used in the commentary refer to the corresponding passage of the edition.

So it is that we find two passages literally parallel: IV and *J* 55; V and CAp VIII, 6, 5. We can conclude that, despite their literary form of a litie, the *OS* engage in the same subject matter as the Eastern litanies. We are accustomed to comparing the Western litanies with their Eastern sisters, but the parallels that we have just provided show that there is no reason to exclude the *OS*. No doubt, all these texts draw from the same arsenal of petitions, constituted in the East. Apart from their literary form, the most apparent difference is that the *OS* concentrate into two invitatories (III and VI) what the litanies cover in several, and they devote four invitatories to categories of people absent from the litanies or included in other petitions.

Study

1. The Oldest Text of the OS

The most ancient of the *OS* text is not, as one might expect, that of the ancient Gelasian manuscript, but rather the text given in the *Missale Gallicanum Vetus* that dates from around 700. Antoine Chavasse has shown[64] that it would have come from an even older Roman source, which had reached Gaul before the arrival of either the Gelasian or the Gregorian and which represented an independent tradition.

2. The Current Liturgical Form

The *OS* constitute the example par excellence of the litie, and are composed of nine 'litiques'. Between the invitatories and the prayers, the current usage — already attested by the Gelasian tradition and the manuscript *O* (Gregorian) — prescribes two admonitions by the deacon: *Flectamus genua* — *Levate.*

An analogous literary form is found in the three solemn prayers of the Coptic and Ethiopian rites, recited three times in the course of the Eucharistic celebration. The first of these is for the peace of the Church, the second for the patriarch, the third for the assembly. Each one begins with an invitatory by the priest, taken up briefly by the deacon in the form of a command. In the Coptic rite the people respond with *Kyrie eleison*, after which the priest follows with his invocation.[65] In Lent, the Coptic rite is also familiar with the admonitions κλίνωμεν τὰ γόνατα — Ἀναστῶμεν.[66]

64 Chavasse (1958), 634–35.

65 For the Coptic rite, see Brightman (1896), 150–51 and 160–61; for the Ethiopian rite see Brightman (1896), 210–11, 216 and 223–25.

66 Brightman (1896), 158–59; cf. Hanssens (1932), vol. 3, (233–34), no. 1051.

Furthermore, the Nestorian liturgy has retained a form of the *oratio fidelium* that is undoubtedly very ancient, where the deacon announces a series of invitatories that the people interrupt with an *Amen* placed between the naming of the beneficiary of the petition and the aim of the petition (Br 263–66). We may have here a distant ancestor of the *OS*.

3. Ancient Liturgical Form

a) Invitatories and Prayers

Willis is the first, we think, to have suggested that the invitatories and prayers could not have been of the same age and that the invitatories would have been older than the prayers, with the two being bracketed together later. Here are the reasons proffered by this author:[67]

1. The invitatories are as developed as the prayers, sometimes even more so, and in almost all cases are more detailed. Both fulfil basically the same function: they list the beneficiaries (except III, where the *ut* of the invitatory is missing), specifying the aim of the petition.
   The prayers, by contrast, tend to be more general in their requests and are clad in the sobriety characteristic of Latin Collects of the golden era.
2. Their style is different.
   The prayers are carefully composed, respecting the rules of cursus that prevailed between the fourth and seventh centuries, which indicates to us that the prayers do not predate the fourth century.
   The invitatories on the other hand rarely conform to cursus and so can be dated prior to the fourth century.

Willis here provides a series of examples that gain our support. He concludes that the very striking difference in the rhythmic structure of the invitatories and the prayers establishes beyond all doubt that they were composed separately and subsequently combined into this form of intercession.

On our part, we would be happy to add some details we have observed that confirm this thesis:

- The presence of closing formulas at the end of the invitatories: *per (Dominum …)* in IV (*Gall*) and VII (*V* and *Gall*); *qui vivit et regnat* (*Gall*) in VIII; *in saecula saeculorum* in IX (*Gall*; *Amen* add. *ORS*). It might be objected that this is not a particularly strong argument since these manuscripts date from a time when there was no longer a vivid awareness of the difference between an invitatory and an oration. If, however, this mistake (or distraction) is committed, it is because quite spontaneously

67 Willis (1964), 45–47.

we no longer expect anything after the invitatories which are complete in themselves. Basically, the prayer is superfluous.

The clearest example appears in invitatory IX, which concludes with the ancient doxology. This is obviously a conclusion; our formulary probably terminated at this point in its primitive version.

- certain invitatories strongly resemble the prayers, notably V and VIII, which each include two final clauses; only III and VI are without these.

If, therefore, the invitatories are composed by different hands and in different eras, what would the original literary form of our piece have been?

If the invitatories had existed from their beginning in the form that we know them today, it is hard to imagine that they would have been followed by a response, especially since there is no stereotypical ending to remind the people that the invitation is over and it is up to them to join in. The only participation by the people would seem to us to be silent prayer.[68] If the *Oremus* at the end of the invitatories (which is to be found in all the manuscripts) is original, then this would reinforce the hypothesis. Perhaps a prayer concluded the formulary. This structure exists in fact in the *orationes paschales* in the Bobbio Missal, where a single prayer completes a set of twelve invitatories.[69]

With or without a final prayer, the original formulary, then, is constructed quite differently from the current litie, with a somewhat lighter quality. The addition of the prayers has given it a grave and solemn character which does not lend itself to daily use.

It should be noted, however, that the manuscripts have not preserved any trace of this separation of invitatories and prayers, and that they were joined together prior to the diverging of the Gelasian, Gallican and Gregorian traditions. On the other hand we find in the patristic writings a small clue that could corroborate this theory of an earlier period of invitatory and prayer. Indeed the commentary of Ambrosiaster (second part of the 4th century) on 1 Tim 2:1–2[70] undoubtedly alludes to the fourth invitatory of the *OS*. But let us tread carefully. The lack of any reference to the prayers does not prove that he had no knowledge of them. The two texts of Prosper of Aquitaine[71] contain allusions to prayers as well as to invitatories; if it is indeed to the *OS* that they refer, then they must have existed already in their present form around 450.

We can see that the fusion was carried out in an intelligent manner; although the prayers never literally repeat the invitatory, they have generally been inspired by them. It will suffice for us to note the parallels between the two elements of the first litique:

68 As was Baumstark's intuition. See Baumstark (1953), 84.
69 *The Bobbio Missal*, ed. Lowe (1919), vol. 2. 67–69; cf. infra, pp. 264–66.
70 Cf. Part One, p. 81, T 3.
71 Part One, Section Three, The Church of Rome, T 26 and T 27.

Omnipotens, first word of the prayer, takes up the last word of the invitatory;
gloriam is linked to *glorificare* at the end of the invitatory;
opera misericordiae tuae serves to provide a concrete description of the Church, the subject of the prayer, as suggested by the final clause;
toto orbe diffusa corresponds to *toto orbe terrarum.*

b) The Diaconal Admonitions: Flectamus Genua — Levate

Did the usual form of the *OS*, when it was not reserved for Good Friday, include these admonitions? We find them in the Gelasian manuscripts (*VRAS*) and *O*, while *C* (the most ancient of the Gregorian manuscripts) and *MGV* omit the rubric entirely. Willis considers it likely that this last tradition is the oldest; the rubric would only have been inserted in the 6th century, when the people no longer knew enough about the rite and were therefore in need of the admonition.

If this argument seems lame to us, we think, nevertheless, that the author is right. Baumstark considers these admonitions ancient,[72] based on the parallel offered by a Coptic Lenten litany. But there has not, in our opinion, been enough insistence on the fact that it is a Lenten formulary; the *OS* would have been able to take it back to penitential times. When one is familiar with the ancient canonical prescriptions about kneeling,[73] it is unimaginable that the *OS* would have included this admonition of the deacon outside the times of penitence.

The manuscripts *S* and *O* include, after the *Flectamus genua*, the rubric *postquam oraverint, dicit Levate.* Meyer considers this *overint* as referring to the priestly prayer that follows,[74] but Willis[75] along with most authors believes that it is a silent prayer, reinforcing the theory that we proposed above about the ancient literary form of this prayer.

4. Commentary

This marvelous text, masterfully laying out the great theology of the Church in impeccable style, deserves an in-depth commentary which, to our knowledge, has not yet been provided.

Willis has initiated it,[76] but his enterprise needs to be completed. Let us note just a few points pertinent to our study.

---

72 Baumstark (1953), 87.

73 Council of Nicea, c. 20: 'Seeing that certain people kneel for prayer on Sundays and during the days of Pentecost, it falls to this council, so that in all places things may be observed uniformly, (to decree that) prayers to the Lord are to be made while standing'. Cf. COD, 15.

74 Meyer (1912), 97.

75 Willis (1964), 45.

76 Willis (1964), 39–45.

I. — The superlative *dilectissimi* corresponds to the ancient usage in the Roman Church; it predates the expression *fratres carissimi* that is found, for example, in the *Exsultet*. This archaism occurs frequently in the sermons of St Leo; it also figures twice in the 'Leonine' sacramentary, during the Ordinations,[77] but it is very rare that it is followed, as in the *OS*, with *nobis*.

The *OS* contain several superlatives (*pro beatissimo papa, pro christianissimis imperatoribus*). It is important to note that they do not carry the pompous sense that a (bad) literal translation into French would provide. In his study on Roman epistemography, A Bastiaensen[78] wrote that for Roman ears, 'the superlative indicated intimacy at least as much as the objective eminence of a determined quality'. He researched this extensively in funeral epigraphy, for example. In another example this philologist notes the curious comment of Delehaye giving *sanctus* as an epithet for gods, but *sanctissimus* by contrast for mortals[79] — which just goes to show the often unsuspected importance of the affective nuance of these expressions.

- *Pro ecclesia sancta Dei*. '*Ecclesia Dei*' is used frequently by St Paul at the beginning of the Letter to the Galatians. 'Sancta Ecclesia' is not found in the New Testament apart from Eph 5:27, where the Apostle says that Christ was given up for the Church in order to render her 'holy and immaculate'. A cursory study of the ancient Creeds shows that they all speak of 'holy Church'. Some add 'catholic', but the expression is not found in the *OS*. However, the qualification 'holy' *is* often found in the *OS*, especially in the invitatories:
- 'pro ecclesia sancta dei', I, invitatory
- 'ecclesiae sanctae', II, invitatory

  'ad regendum populum sanctum dei', II, invitatory
- 'pro omni populo sancto dei', III, invitatory

  'totum corpus ecclesiae sanctificatur', III, prayer
- 'sanctam matrem ecclesiam catholicam atque apostolicam', VII, invitatory
- 'adgrega ecclesiae taue sanctae', IX, prayer.

Here we are in the presence of a less important development than what will be found in the later texts; we note particularly the absence of 'catholica' which is found however in the *Te igitur* of the Roman Canon[80] and in *OS* VII. The expression of our invitatory has an undeniably archaic flavor.

---

77 *Sacramentarium Veronense*, ed. Mohlberg, nn. 949 and 952.

78 Bastiaensen (1964), 24–28 and 40–43. The remark is made a propos to Cyprian, but the author notes (p. 25) that it holds for all Roman epistolography.

79 Delehaye (1927), 20 ff.

80 This first invitatory, coming close to the end of the *Te igitur*, has numerous parallels in the anthology of texts collected by Eizenhöfer (1966), 51 ff.

– *deus et dominus noster* is an expression dear to the editor of the invitatories; he uses it at least five times (I, II *Greg.*, IV, V, VII, VIII), compared with at least a single use of *deus omnipotens* (II *Gel.*, IV *Gel.*, IX). The author of the prayers, meanwhile, makes use each time of the majestic formula 'Omnipotens sempiterne deus' (except perhaps in VI).

– *detque nobis tranquillam et quietam vitam degentibus* goes back, according to Baumstark, to the persecutions rather than to any desire for world domination. The fact that this may be a quotation from 1 Tim 2:2 just increases the difficulty of interpretation in our eyes!

– *toto orbe diffusa* is encountered in Cyprian's works.[81]

II. Willis rightly notes that the term *papa* was at one time not at all reserved for the bishop of Rome. At the beginning of the 6th century the tendency to appropriate it developed, but it did not become a strict rule until the end of the 7th century. Also, three manuscripts from the Gelasian family, *VRA*, have specified: 'pro famulo dei papa nostro sedis apostolicae ·illo· et pro antistite nostro ·illo·'. We come across the same evolution in the *Te igitur* of the Roman Canon, where the Bobbio Missal and the Stowe Missal have both added after 'papa nostro', 'episcopo sedis apostolicae'.

This information will be useful when we comment on other formularies.

III. We have already noted that apart from acolytes, exorcists and porters, all these orders are to be found in the East. To situate our piece, we provide below, in five columns, first the numbering found in CAp VIII 12, 43, then our invitatory, the sequence of chapters from the *Apostolic Tradition*, the terms used in 251 by Pope Cornelius in his letter to Fabius of Antioch to inform him of the composition of the Christian community in Rome,[82] and finally, the list of the *officiales* of the *Statuta Ecclesiae antiqua* (*c.* 476–485):[83]

CAp VIII 12, 43	***OS*, III**
1. patriarchs	
2. prophets	
3. judges	
4. apostles	
5. martyrs	
7. bishops	*bishops*
8. priests	*priests*
9. deacons	*deacons*

81 Cf. Eizenhöfer (1966), 55 ff.

82 In Eusebius, *Histoire ecclésiastique* VI, 43, 11, ed. Bardy, vol. 2 (SC 41), 156.

83 Munier (1960), 95–100 and commentary, 170–76.

	CAp VIII 12, 43	OS, III
10.	sub-deacons	*sub-deacons*
		acolytes
		exorcists
11.	lectors	*lectors*
		porters
6.	confessors	*confessors*
12.	cantors	
13.	virgins	*virgins*
14.	widows	*widows*
15.	laypersons	*all the holy people of God*

	Apostolic Tradition, 1–8	Cornelius	*Statuta Ecclesiae antiqua*
1.	bishops	bishop	bishop
2.	priests	priests	priest
3.	deacons	deacons	deacon
8.	sub-deacon	sub-deacons	sub-deacon
		acolytes	acolyte
		exorcists	exorcist
6.	lector	lectors	lector
		porters	porter
			psalmista, id est cantor
4.	confessors		
7.	virgin		virgin
5.	widows	widows	widows
		people, great beyond number	

The *Statuta* have only been included here so that it is possible to understand the errors made in the past with regard to the meaning of the term *confessor*; they date from the second half of the 5th century and are not Roman.

The parallelism of the *OS* with the *Apostolic Tradition* and the text of Cornelius, both from the middle of the 3rd century is striking. The 'minor orders' that are not mentioned (apart from lector and sub-deacon) in the *Apostolic Tradition* (undoubtedly already outdated) receive a mention from the pope several years later. The absence of confessors and virgins in the papal letter can be explained by the fact that the pope explicitly mentions clerics, distinguishing them from the people 'great beyond number'. Mention of the widows at this point is not clear.[84] In any case, the editor of our invitatory would have been able to complete it thanks to the *Apostolic Tradition*. We think that these Roman texts sufficiently shed light on the *OS* without the need to have recourse to the CAp, which cannot be dated before the end of the 4th century.

The main thing is to know if these parallels oblige us to date the *OS* from the 3rd century. Any comparison with the *Statuta* must be approached with caution; let us not forget, however, that its editor had a clear concern for archaism. But nothing is excluded that the *OS* did not share with it!

We do not believe this, however, for the function of these texts is quite different. The *OS* were neither a polemical writing, nor a dogmatic treaty that must not omit anything. This invitatory is not the work of a later historian wisely recapitulating all the orders that the Church has known in the past; it is the prayer of a pastor interceding with his people for the concrete needs of their Church. We cannot imagine that at the time of its creation these different orders were not living realities.

This clarifies for us the meaning that must here be given to the term *confessor*. We know the Dom Morin, based on the equivalence suggested by the *Statuta* between the *confessor* and the *psalmist*, felt obliged to give it the meaning of 'cantor'.[85] This seems untenable for several reasons. First, it is improbable that three different terms (*confessor, psalmist* and *cantor*) would have described the same function. But even more, there is no trace of the existence of an order of cantors in the Roman Church; this was a function, but not a clerical order. The ordination of the *psalmist* is probably an invention of the editor of the *Statuta*, whose presbyteral tendencies are well known.[86] Finally, even if in Spain *confessor* could be used to describe a monk, no Roman text gives it this meaning.[87]

In short, *confessor* here has the ancient sense of 'one who confesses the faith'.[88] This conclusion receives external confirmation from the *Apostolic Tradition* which also associates confessors with widows and virgins. (Let us point out here that the widows in question are indeed ministers of the Church and not simply all women who have lost their husbands).

If this is the case, then this invitatory could well date from the 3rd century, as Baumstark, followed by Jungmann[89] and Willis, asserts. It is not without benefit

---

84 The Greek text reads χήρας σὺν θλιβομένοις ὑπὲρ τὰς χιλίας πεντακοσίας.

85 G. Morin ((1912), (1912), 82–84. The equivalence between *confessor* and *psalmist* perhaps comes from the East. It is striking to note that CAp VIII 10 and 12 both quote ψάλται at the place where the *OS* and the *Statuta* place the *confessor* and the *psalmist* respectively. But this is an error, for the CAp earlier mentions (before the bishops!) the ὁμολογηταί, who immediately follow the μάρτυρες: thus the sense of 'confessors of the faith' is imposed.

86 Cf. Botte (1939), 223–241.

87 Botte (1941), 137–48. Here we also rely on the (oral) course of Christian Latin received from this professor at the Institut Supérieur de Liturgie in Paris.

88 We also reject as lacking foundation the sense of *monk* that Righetti (1956), vol. 3, 263 gives to *confessor*; it is one of arguments for dating the *OS* in the 5th century.

89 Jungmann (1962), vol. 1, 616.

to refer here to a passage of the letter written to Cyprian in 250 by 'Moses and Maximus, priests, and Nicostratus and Rufinus and others who with them are confessors'. In the body of the letter these Roman recommend that the case in question be considered with caution, 'consultis omnibus episcopis presbyteris diaconibus confessoribus et ipsis stantibus laicis'.[90] However, in the 4th century there were still confessors enjoying particular considerations as well as Christians (not the least, Athanasius, for example) who were being persecuted.

IV. The variations between the manuscripts of this invitatory are explained in a satisfactory manner by historical circumstances. The term *rex* is not a Roman word, but Frankish; it does not, therefore, appear before the second half of the 5th century.

Wilson, and his group of equally competent masters such as Andrieu and Bourque,[91] thought that the plural *pro christianissimis imperatoribus nostris* must indicate two emperors of the West, and therefore indicate a precise date: either the period of time between September 813, when Louis the Debonair joined forces with Charlemagne, and 28 January 814 when the latter died, or the year 817 when Louis the Debonair in turn joined forces with his son Lothar in the empire. But J. Deshusses has shown that this plural is found in several manuscripts, notably the *Missale Gallicum Vetus*, antedating the Carolingian era by a century! Moreover, he thinks that since the plural in question is the 'pre-Gelasian, primitive form of the prayer; would it not be explained by the double empire of East and West?'[92] In our eyes, this plural can designate either, at the earliest, the 'tetrarchy' established by Diocletian in the years 286–293, or the two emperors who shared the empire following the death of Theodosius in 395.

For its part, the superlative *christianissimus* was not conceived of before the peace of the Church, nor probably even before 379, the date of the accession of holy Theodosius, who declared Christianity to be the religion of the State. Here we are again at the end of the 4th century! It is possible that this adjective, together with the plural, dates from this era, which is when the orations were composed. It may be that the orations were accompanied by a revision of the invitatories.

The final clause of this invitatory seems to be the expression of a people harassed by its enemies and worn out from battle; at what period is this to be located?

It is at the heart of the 3rd century that the frontiers of the Roman Empire began to fracture and that the Germanic attacks became more and more frequent and vigorous. In the East, Sapor I (242–273), the second Sassanid emperor, showed himself to be particularly aggressive and dealt a heavy blow to Roman prestige when the Emperor Valerian was taken alive into his hands (260). It is also known that the middle of the 3rd century was marked by a serious internal crisis, which ends only with the ascension of Diocletian (284). Perhaps it is in this particularly sombre era that our invitatory takes root. But how then can we explain the strict parallel of its vocabulary with *J* 55?

---

90 Cyprian of Carthage, *Letter* 31, 6, 2; ed. Bayard, vol. 1, 77 and 81; tr. Donna, (FC 51), 83.

91 Wilson (1894), xliii–xliv. Andrieu (1922), 205. Bourque (1952), Part 2, vol. 1, 128–29.

92 Deshusses (1961), 201–02.

While the first litique opened up clearly universalist perspectives, the fourth one purely and simply equates the enemies of the Empire with the enemies of God.

V. The prayer for the catechumens does not provide any clue as to date. But the oration indicates a pastoral experience: it asks that the catechumens, once baptized, might remain joined to the community.

VI. All these categories of the needy are found in both Eastern and Western litanies. There is one exception, however: nowhere else have we found a petition about hunger. Perhaps this might be a clue to dating?[93]
On the other hand, our invitatory does not speak of the forced work in the mines (*in metallis*) mentioned in the East (CAp VIII, 10, 55; *J* 55; *M* 126) and in the West (*M[1]* and *Go*) and generally considered as a sign of antiquity, since Tertullian has already made reference to this.[94]
It should be noted that these are more likely to concern Christians imprisoned for their faith than just any prisoner. Two clues point in this direction: the first petition of this invitatory asks God to deliver the world from error (as opposed no doubt to Christian truth); on the other hand the three final litiques of the *OS* concern people who are outside the Church. Baumstark argues that the *OS* date from the times of persecution. Willis follows him on this path.

VII. Heresies and schisms allude to the great Trinitarian and Christological controversies of the 4th and 5th centuries. In contrast to invitatory I where the Church is qualified only by the adjective *sancta*, here it is gifted with three other descriptors: *ad sanctam matrem ecclesiam catholicam atque apostolicam. Catholica* depicts the Great Church as opposed to sects, and is an ancient appellation, while *Apostolica* is less so.[95] Even if the term had already been applied to the Church by Tertullian,[96] it would be necessary to wait until the 4th century before the adjective, as used here, became part of an ecclesiological formulary. It does not seem to have been forged at the Council of Nicea (at least the textual tradition is unsure); this will be done at the Council of Constantinople in 381.[97] Dewailly notes that most of the Eastern formularies also inserted it, while the Latin Church does not seem to have adopted it as a common expression until later. However, the expression does not impose itself as a stereotypical formula into the language; it is still only used when wanting to emphasise the relationship that connects the Church and the apostles'.[98]

But in the Eastern parallels we twice find the adjective 'apostolic' in the expressions ὑπὲρ τῆς ἁγίας καθολικῆς καὶ ἀποστολικῆς ἐκκλησίας (CAp VIII, 10, 4 and *J* 45). Could this be borrowed? No Eastern formulary describes the Church as 'mother', the ancient and biblical image (Gal 4:26), which is, moreover,

93 Tertullian, however, had already written that prayer 'nourishes the poor' in a list of intentions (*De Oratione*, 29, 2) that we have cited in Part 1, Section 2: The Church in Africa, T 7.
94 Tertullian, *Apologeticum*, 39, 6, ed. Dekkers, (CC 1), 151.
95 On the history of the term 'apostolic' see Dewailly (1948[1]), 'Mission de l'eglise', 2–37; and (1948[2]), 'Note sur l'histoire de l'adjectif apostolique', 141–52.
96 Tertullian, *De praescriptione*, XX, 7–8, ed. Refoule (CC 1), 202.
97 Denzinger-Schönmetzer, n. 150.
98 Dewailly (1948[2]), 9.

developed in the prayer for the catechumens (V: 'qui ecclesiam tuam nova semper prole fecundas').

It could also be a later retouching, with 'atque apostolicam' being added perhaps under the influence of the Nicene-Constantinople Creed.

VIII. The prayer for the Jews, that we have already read in Justin, but that we will no longer find anywhere else (cf. however *DG* X), can only be a sign of extreme antiquity or date from a time when the Jews were in great number in Rome.

IX. Whatever the etymology of the term *paganus*, this litique is concerned with non-Christians. The doxology of the invitatory (*cum quo vivit et regnat cum Spiritu sancto*) predates the classic formulation *in unitate Spiritus sancti* attested to by the Gelasian tradition of the *OS*. This last phrase, according to the investigations of Dom Botte, is exclusively Latin; its first appearance, somewhat uncertain, dates back to 420, in a sermon by Gaudentius of Brescia.[99] Our invitatory is, therefore, dated before the middle of the 5th century.

5. *Attempt at Dating*

1. Since the work of Dom Cappuyns,[100] it is generally accepted on the basis of the testimony of Prosper of Aquitaine, that the OS as we know them today constituted the usual form of the *oratio fidelium* in Rome around 450.
2. The similarity between invitatory III on the one hand, the *Apostolic Tradition* and the letter of Pope Cornelius to Fabius of Antioch on the other, leads us to place the *terminus post quem* of the invitatories around 250.
3. The *terminus ante quem* of the invitatories ought to be fixed at the beginning of the 4th century, the date at which the persecutions ended and where the cursus begins to be established.

These invitatories, then, can be dated to the period from about 250 to 320.

However, several elements cannot be explained by such a remote date. We mention, for example, the designation of the emperors as *christianissimi* and the literal parallel with a passage of the CAp, which dates at the latest from the end of the 4th century. How can we explain these facts?

We are inclined to believe that at the end of the 4th century or the beginning of the 5th there was a revision of the formulary (which at that time, let us remember, was only an invitatory). This consisted in modifying its literary form by the addition of the orations, thus passing from a series of invitatories to a series of nine litiques, undoubtedly following the example of the Coptic liturgy.[101] It

99 Gaudentius of Brescia, *Tractatus*. 16, 12 (CSEL 68, 140). On this matter see Botte and Mohrmann (1953), 133–39.

100 Cappuyns (1938), 18–31. Cf. Part One, Section 3.

101 Brightman (1896), 150–51; cf. supra, *Current liturgical form*.

would have also provided the opportunity of adapting to the circumstances of the period,

1. in dedicating a particular litique (VII) to the heretics and schismatics. By describing the Church as 'apostolic' the invitatory would have taken account of the dogmatic formulae proclaimed at the recent Council of Constantinople (381);
2. in calling the emperors *christianissimi*, since, from the time of Theodosius (370), they had become champions of the Christian religion;
3. in letting themselves be inspired by the Eastern models, notably
   - in the invitatory for catechumens (V), which translated a phrase of CAp VIII 6, 5, compiled at the earliest around 385;
   - in the invitatory for the emperors (IV) that takes up a phrase of *J* 55;
4. in omitting from the list of the needy (VI) the workers *in metallis*, since the Christians were no longer condemned to this work;
5. in lightly restructuring the division of the petitions, notably by grouping all the needy into VI.

This is confirmed by examining the style of the invitatory; it is only here[102] that there is any trace of the traditional metrical cursus:

– VII errróribus univérsis (velox)
revocáre dignétur (planus)

in this invitatory that we consider to be later for reasons of internal criticism; and

– VI púrget erróribus (tardus)
famem depéllat (planus)
infirmántibus sanitátem (velox)
salútis indúlgeat (tardus)

in this invitatory that would probably have been modified so as to reorder those classified as needy.[103]

This hypothesis allows an explanation of the facts. It also takes account of the allusions to the *OS* that we have found in the authors studied in Part I; Ambrosiaster (second half of the 4th century)[104] may have known only the invitatories of

102 With one exception (which proves the rule!) in I: 'toto órbe terrárum' (planus).

103 It is perhaps not fanciful to put this restructuring in relation to the presbyteralist wave that came at the end of the 4th century, of which Jerome (347–420) became the champion (*Comm. In Tit.*, PL 26, 596–98). The ancient invitatories were perhaps proclaimed by deacons, but in their concern to reduce the role of these latter, the priests undertaking the revision of the *OS* would have reserved to themselves both the invitatory and the prayer; in this the formulary was made more cumbersome.

104 Cf. Part One, Section 3: The Church of Rome.

the *OS*, while Prosper of Aquitaine, in the middle of the 5th century, is dealing with the complete form of the litie.

While maintaining the essence of this hypothesis, another one could also be presented. To resolve the problem of the astonishing similarity between all the Eastern and Western texts, we could consider the existence of a common source. Even if the compositor of the CAp shows a certain originality, it is obvious that he is also using traditional documents, among which may have been a litany known also to the first compiler of the *OS*.[105] To verify this hypothesis it would be necessary to undertake a methodical comparison of the Eastern formularies.

6. Use of the OS

Given the reservation of the *OS* to Good Friday and the way that Prosper of Aquitaine speaks about them, we have no hesitation in considering them to be a customary formulary[106] of the Roman *oratio fidelium* used (at least as far as its invitatories are concerned) since the second half of the 3rd or the beginning of the 4th century.

Following the reference made to them by the papal secretary around 450, we lose any trace of them until we find them again on Good Friday in the sacramentaries. (We cannot take any assurances from the single mention of *flectamus genua* by Caesarius of Arles that he had the *OS* in mind).[107]

The *Ordines Romani* attest them to be a fixture between the 8th and 10th centuries; the most ancient record is in *Ordo XXIII* (first half of the 8th century).[108] *Ordo XXIV*, from the second half of the 8th century, is the first witness that also includes Holy Wednesday, at Terce, with a prayer for the king of the Franks followed by one for the emperor, but without any genuflection and prayer for the Jews.[109]

105 If he had lived in the second half of the 3rd century it is not surprising that he knew Greek; he may have even composed the invitatories in that language.

106 See the reservations noted above on the opinion of Cappuyns who sees the *OS* as a *daily* formulary of the Roman Universal Prayer.

107 Cf. Part One, Section 2: The Church of Africa.

108 Andrieu (1951), vol. 3, 271–72.

109 Andrieu (1951), vol. 3, 287–88. On this and the whole tradition of the OS, see Willis (1964), 17–19.

Section Two

A First Wave of Litanic Texts: Translations

It is usually said that in asking the (Roman) Church to sing the *Deprecatio* for the needs of the universal Church that pope Gelasius (492–496) introduced the form of the litany into the Roman, that is to say Western, liturgy. After a meticulous examination of the texts we have cause to question this assertion. In our opinion there are other formularies of the litanic type that predate the *Deprecatio Gelasii* (*DG*).

Two successive waves appear distinguishable in the introduction of litanies to the West. The first are the translations, where the Eastern models were translated into Latin without too much concern for stylistic considerations. In this first stream, which extends from the end of the 4th to the end of the 5th century, are included the litany *Dicamus omnes* that is to be found in the Stowe Missal (*Irl*^{1}) and the first of the litanies offered to us by the Milanese books (*Divinae pacis, M*^{1}), as well as two sources whose existence we are led to assume.

Towards the end of the 5th century the texts then in use will be revised, first of all to improve their quality and then to adapt them to new circumstances. This second wave, beyond *DG* which is the flagship, gave birth to a second litany from Milanese sources (*Dicamus omnes, M*^{2}), to the two Franco-Gallican formularies (*Dicamus omnes, FG*^{1}, and *Kyrie eleison, Domine Deus omnipotens partum nostrorum, FG*^{2}), and to an item located nowadays in the canon of the Stowe Missal (*Irl*^{2}).

1. The So-Called 'Irish' *Dicamus Omnes* (*Irl*^{1})

A. The Sources

S = DUBLIN, Royal Irish Academy, D. II. 3 8th century; f. 16v–17
= *Stowe Missal*, ed. Warner, 6–7.
(Clavis 1926 — Bourque 527 — Gamber 101)

F = The Irish Missal of FULDA, today lost, but partially copied by G. Witzel, *Exercitamenta sincerae pietatis*, Mayence 1555 (the example held in the National Library of Paris does not include page numbers).
(Bourque 528A — Gamber 102)

B. Edited Version

Since we have not found any new sources, we could have made use of the edition prepared by Dom Capelle.[1] However, because of several errors that it contains, particularly in the ordering of the responses, we have decided to begin afresh.

Our edition is based on *F*, which seems better to us for several reasons; it includes the complete responses twice; the distribution of the text of the invitatories seems to be more exact, and the beginning is more logical since it links 'ex toto corde' to *dicamus*, rather than to *oremus* ahead of the invocation *qui respicis*.

We will place between ⟨ ⟩ what we think should be added to the text, even if the manuscripts do not mention it.

a/[2] Dicamus omnes[3] ex toto corde et ex tota[4] mente:
Domine exaudi et miserere[5]
⟨Domine exaudi et miserere⟩

b/ Qui respicis super terram et[6] facis eam tremere
oramus te
Domini exaudi[7] ⟨et miserere⟩

I Pro altissima pace et tranquillitate temporum nostrorum
oramus te
Domine[8] ⟨exaudi et miserere⟩

II Pro sancta ecclesia catholica quae est[9] a finibus usque ad terminus orbis terrae
oramus te
Domine[10] ⟨exaudi et miserere⟩

III Pro patre nostro[11] episcopo et[12] omnibus episcopis et presbyteris et diaconis et omni[13] clero
oramus te
Domine[10] ⟨exaude et miserere⟩

1 Capelle (1934), 120–22.
2 Deprecatio sancti martini pro populo incipit amen deo gratias *add S* (*alt. manus*).
3 *Hic add S* Domine exaudi et miserere. Domine miserere.
4 et ex tota *S*. totaque *F*.
5 Domine exaudi et miserere *om S*. ô *praem F*.
6 et *S*. ac *F*.
7 te Domine exaude *om S*.
8 oramus te Domine *om S*.
9 est *om S*.
10 te Domine *om* S.
11 patre nostro *F*. pastore *N. S*.
12 et *S*. pro *F*.
13 et omni *S*. omnique *F*.

IV Pro hoc loco et habitantibus[14] in eo
oramus te
Domine[8] ⟨exaudi et miserere⟩

V Pro piissimis imperatoribus et toto[15] Romanorum[16] exercitu
oramus te
Domine[10] ⟨exaudi et miserere⟩

VI Pro omnibus qui in sublimitate constituti sunt
⟨oramus te
Domine exaudi et miserere⟩

VII Pro virginibus, viduis[17] et orphanis
oramus te
Domine[10] ⟨exaudi et miserere⟩

VIII Pro peregrinantibus,[18] iter agentibus ac[19] navigantibus
oremus te
Domine[8] ⟨exaudi et miserere⟩

IX Pro paenitentibus et catechumenis
oramus te
Domine[10] ⟨exaudi et miserere⟩

X Pro his qui in sancta ecclesia fructus misericordiae largiuntur domine Deus virtutum exaudi preces nostras
oramus te
Domine[10] ⟨exaudi et miserere⟩

XI Sanctorum apostolorum et[20] martyrum memores simus[21] ut orantibus eis pro nobis veniam mereamur
oramus te
Domine[10] ⟨exaudi et miserere⟩

XII Christianum ac[22] pacificum nobis finem concedi
a domino comprecemur[23]
praesta, Domine, praesta

XIII Et divinum in nobis permanere vinculum caritatis
sanctum[24] dominum comprecemur[23]
praesta, Domine, ⟨praesta⟩[25]

---

14 habitantibus *F.* inhabitantibus *S.*
15 toto *F.* omni *S.*
16 Romanorum *F.* romano *S.*
17 viduis *S.* viduisque *F.*
18 et *add S.*
19 ac *S.* atque *F.*
20 et *F.* ac *S.*
21 simus *S.* sumus *F.*
22 ac *F.* et *S.*
23 comprecemur *F.* deprecemur *S.*
24 sanctum *om F.*
25 Domine praesta *om S.* praesta *om F.*

XIV Conservare sanctitatem et catholicae fidei puritatem[26]
sanctum Deum[27] comprecemur[23]
praesta, Domine, ⟨praesta⟩[25]

c/ Dicamus omnes: Domine exaudi et miserere.[28]

C. Eastern Parallels

These are particularly numerous.[29]

a/ – Εἴπωμεν πάντες ἐξ ὅλης τῆς ψυχῆς καὶ ἐξ ὅλης τῆς διανοίας εἴπωμεν: κύριε ἐλέησον B 373 (cf. Mk:12:30). The uncertainty of the Latin texts, which make of this sentence one or two invitations, is already found in the East. While the Εὐχολόγιον τὸ μέγα (Venice 1869) reproduced by Brightman has a single invitation, the older versions in Armenian[30] and Arabic,[31] have two, separated by a Κύριε ἐλέησον after εἴπωμεν πάντες.

– δεόμεθά σου ἐπάκουσον καὶ ἐλέησον B373.

b/ ὁ ἐπιβλέπων ἐπὶ τὴν γῆν καὶ ποιῶν αὐτὴν τρέμειν CAp VIII, 7, 7 (in the priestly prayer that follows the litany for the possessed) = Ps 103:32 (LXX).

I ὑπὲρ τῆς ἄνωθεν εἰρήνης *J* 34, 36, 39; B 362. ὑπὲρ ... καὶ καιρῶν εἰρηνικῶν B 363 (including good weather).

II ὑπὲρ τῆς ἁγίας καθολικῆς καὶ ἀποστολικῆς ἐκκλησίας τῆς ἀπὸ γῆς [περάτων] μέχρι τῶν περάτων αὐτῆς *J* 45.

III ... καὶ παντὸς τοῦ κλήρου CAp VIII 12, 41; *J* 34, 36; B 363; *M* 138.

IV ὑπὲρ τῆς πόλεως ταύτης καὶ τῶν ἐνοικούντων CAp VIII 12, 45.

V ὑπὲρ τῶν εὐσεβεστάτων καὶ ... βασιλέων, παντὸς τοῦ παλατίου καὶ τοῦ στρατοπέδου αὐτῶν *J* 45; B 363.

VI ὑπὲρ τοῦ βασιλέως καὶ τῶν ἐν ὑπεροχῇ καὶ παντὸς τοῦ στρατοπέδου CAp VIII 12, 42 and 13, 5; = 1 Tim 2:2.

VII ὑπὲρ ... παρθένων χηρῶν τε καὶ ὀρφανῶν CAp VIII, 10, 10. μεμνημένων τῶν πενήτων χηρῶν καὶ ὀρφανῶν *J* 45.

---

26 et ... puritatem *S.* ac puritatem catholicae fidei *F.*

27 sanctum Deum *F.* dominum *S.*

28 omnes ... miserere *om S.*

29 The first person to supply these is, to our knowledge, Duchesne (1925), 212, note 2. He was followed by Bousset (1916) who, from p. 154–59 gives, in six parallel columns, the Latin texts compared with five Greek litanies. All of this was then revised by Dom Capelle (1962 reprint), 120–23. We are updating and correcting this.

30 ed. Aucher (1908), 380.

31 ed. Bacha (1908), 453.

VIII	ὑπὲρ πλεόντων ὁδοιπορούντων ξενιτευόντων χριστιανῶν καὶ … *J* 46; ὑπὲρ πλεόντων καὶ ὁδοιπορούντων CAp VIII, 10, 15 and 12, 45; B 363.
IX	ὑπὲρ τῶν κατηχουμένων τῆς ἐκκλησίας καὶ ὑπὲρ … καὶ ὑπὲρ τῶν ἐν μετανοίᾳ ἀδελφῶν ἡμῶν CAp VIII, 12, 47.
X	ὑπὲρ τῶν καρποφορούντων ἐν τῇ ἁγίᾳ ἐκκλησίᾳ καὶ … CAp VIII, 10, 12.
XI	τῶν θείων καὶ πανευφήμων ἀποστόλων, ἐνδόξων προφητῶν καὶ ἀθλοφόρων μαρτύρων καὶ πάντων τῶν ἁγίων καὶ δικαίων μνημονεύσωμεν ὅπως εὐχαῖς αὐτῶν καὶ πρεσβείαις οἱ πάντες ἐλεηθῶμεν *J* 35, 48.
XII	Χριστιανὰ ὑμῶν τὰ τέλη CAp VIII, 6, 8; 36, 2; 38, 2. χριστιανὰ τὰ τέλη τῆς ζωῆς ἡμῶν ἀνώδυνα ἀνεπαίσχυντα εἰρηνικὰ … παράσχου κύριε *J* 39, B 382; cf. *M* 129.
XIII	'We ask of you the unceasing love that is the bond of perfection'. Nestorian liturgy, Br. 266, 1.17; = Col. 3:14. Cf. *DG* XVI.
XIV	'For the sake of our faith, we beg the Lord may grant us to please him and to keep the faith in its purity'. Ethiopian liturgy, Br 206, 1.23–24.

This is an impressive table. Altogether we have eight parallels with CAp, seven with the liturgy of St James, six with the Byzantine liturgy, one with that of St Mark, one with the Nestorian liturgy and one with the Ethiopian liturgy. Moreover, the division into two parts (I–X and XI–VIX) is affirmed by the *oratio fidelium* of Vespers and Lauds in CAp VIII, 36 and 38, and repeated (with practically identical expressions) in *J* 39 and B 381. In the West, only *Irl*[1] and *DG* possess this bipartite structure. Indeed, *Irl*[1] cannot be other than a translation from a Greek text.

D. Liturgical Form

Here we are in the presence of a litany that comprises:

1. *Introduction*
   a/ descriptive invitation, indicating and introducing the response;
   b/ attributive invocation.
2. *First part*: I–X verbal invocations; strangely X inserts an imperative invocation before the verb.
3. *Transition*: XI is an invitatory that is ended, curiously, with a verb of invocation.
4. *Second part*: XII–XIV verbal invitatories.
5. *Conclusion*: invitation that reprises a/ and includes it.

E. Commentary

a. The Responses

1) The Response in the First Part

The manuscripts do not clearly apprise us of the text of the response.

- *S* has the leader say, 'Dicamus omnes: domine exaudi et miserere', but following immediately after is 'Domine miserere',[32] which seems to be the response. In what follows, the response is never indicated.
- F puts into the mouth of the leader, 'Dicamus omnes ... ô Domine exaudi et miserere; after b/ he has "Domine exaudi"; in I–XI he stops after "Domine", but in c/ he again takes up "Domine exaudi et miserere."'

First of all, it seems clear to us that the leader indicates in a/ what the response is. We would not have thought this, except that we read in *S* that the leader invites [the people] to say, Domine exaudi et miserere' whereas in reality the participants respond, 'Domine miserere'.

In all the other litanies with a Latin response, we read *Domine miserere*, a translation of Κύριε ἐλέησον; *DG* also displays the same confusion as *Irl*[1].

It is also found in the Greek model; B 373 has two invocations that end with 'ἐπάκουσον καὶ ἐλέησον' even though the response may be simply, 'Κύριε ἐλέησον'. Also, we think that initially the response might have been 'Κύριε ἐπάκουσον καὶ ἐλέησον' — *Domine exaudi et miserere*, of which traces still remain in the manuscripts (*Irl*[1] and *DG*); but it would have been shortened, for convenience or by competition, into Κύριε ἐλέησον — *Domine miserere*. In our edition, therefore, we have supplied *exaudi* (between ⟨ ⟩) each time that the manuscripts omitted it.

Egeria, the great lady from the north of Spain who made a pilgrimage to the Holy Places, records in her Diary of Travels (*c.* 381–384) that at Jerusalem the children responded to the deacon with *Kyrie eleison*; she elaborates: 'kyrie eleison, which we say as: miserere Domine'.[33] It seems to us that the expression reflects more than a simple translation (note the inversion of the words), but indicates a response to which the pilgrim would have been accustomed to in the Western Church; this response is not used in our major formularies.[34]

---

32 The same anomaly is found in manuscript *D* of the *DG*!

33 *Itinerarium egeriae*, 24, 5; ed. Franceschini-Weber, (CC 174), 68. We have not found a commentary on this passage in any study on this travel diary.

34 However, one finds *Miserere Domine*, in Spain in the *Breviarium Gothicum* to be exact, but only in remnants of very secondary litanies. It is found once in that form (PL 86, 355) and twice with the ending *et exaudi nos* (PL 86, 345 and 563). However, the predilection of these Spanish compositions for the verb *miserere* should be noted; thus it would seem that the response indicated by Egeria and included in the *Breviarium Gothicum* could be more because of coincidence than of any particular link [with these litanies].

We note that Dom Capelle has poorly separated the invocations from the responses. He begins with *oramus te,* then the invocations remain as a noun phrase. Given invitation a/, our revision is necessary.

2) The Response in the Second Part

From XII to XIV, the response is *praesta, Domine, praesta*; in the East, in parallel texts we find παράσχου κύριε. We think that this is truly a response and not the end of the invitatory pronounced by the leader, to which the participants would have responded, as in the first part, with 'Domine exaudi et miserere'; this would have made the prayer too complicated. The change of response was called for by the move from invocation to invitation and by the absence of *pro* at the beginning of the sentence, so that the participants would not have had any difficulty in going from one reponse to the other.

b. The Structure of XI

In the Eastern parallels, the commemoration of the saints brings the litanies to a conclusion. This, together with the inadequacy of the final *oremus te* after an invitation, makes us think that here we are in the presence of a somewhat awkward transition between the two parts. If the aim was for XI to conclude Part One and be followed by Part Two, then it plays the role of hinge rather badly.

c. Attempt at Dating

The Eastern models are so similar that we must accept either a dependence or a common source. But let us see first of all what the text itself can teach us:

1) Internal Criticism

b/ the use of this psalm verse seems more recent in comparison to the rest of the litany; in the East we find these developed introductions only in B 373.

II we note the absence of the adjective *apostolica,* that is present, however, in the East (*J* 45); but this absence is not significant, particularly in the West, where the text may be prior to the Council of Constantinople (381).[35]

III *S* has *pastore, F* has *patre*; this latter reading seems to us the more ancient, and perhaps translates πάπα: in *Irl*^{2} X, we read in *S*, 'pro domino papa episcopo et omnibus episcopis'. There is no mention of the pope of Rome, which indicates its antiquity and without doubt also its non-Roman origin. Only the 'major orders' are cited. *Clerus* is used by Tertullian and Cyprian.

35 On the term *apostolicus*, cf. supra, commentary on *OS*, VII.

IV *Pro hoc loco* that is also found in *FG*[2] VII (and secondarily in *FG*[1] VI) is perhaps later in comparison with *pro civitate hac* of M[1] V and M[2] V, which translates ὑπὲρ τῆς πόλεως ταύτης. The wording of *Irl*[1] is more general and is adapted, in particular, to monasteries.

V *Pro piisimis imperatoribus* translates ὑπὲρ εὐσεβεστάτων ἡμῶν βασιλέων; Athanasius († 373) has already described Constantine as εὐσεβεστατος.[36] Invitatory IV of the *OS* speaks of *christianissimis imperatoribus*; the general sense is identical. The adjective *romanus* is found only in the two Irish texts and in the *OS*, and never in the East; 'toto Romanorum exercitu' must date from a period where the imperial army was indeed a reality. The phrase, however, does not compel us to concede that the formulary was composed in Rome.

VI This invocation is a citation from 1 Tim 2:2; this petition is not found in any other of the Latin litanies apart from an example in *M*[1] IV.

VII–X Virgins and widows, along with orphans, are placed here among the needy and no longer seem to constitute an 'order'. The same applies to penitents and catechumens, although the invocation reserved for them (IX) may refer to the discipline of canonical penitence which, to some extent, assimilated these two categories of people.

An undeniable evolution can therefore be seen in relation to the *OS*. Confessors are no longer mentioned, nor are prisoners: we are no longer in an era of persecution; 'works of mercy' have replaced martyrdom.

XI Note here the parallel with the *Communicantes* of the Roman Canon: 'sed et beatorum apostolorum ac martyrum tuorum … quorum meritis precibusque concedas ut'.

XIV The purity of the Catholic faith is likely contrasted with the great heresies of the 4th and 5th centuries.

2) *The Evidence Provided by Egeria*

We indicated above that Egeria gives the formula *miserere Domine* as the Latin equivalent of Κύριε ἐλέησον. The argument is somewhat intricate. But nothing more can be derived from it than the following: at the end of the 4th century (389–390), her Church in northern Spain was not familiar with any litany whose response was *Domine miserere*. Neither *Irl*[1] nor any other of the Latin texts could have been in use in these regions at that time.

36 Athanasius, *Apology to Constance*, 33 (SC 56, 128; PG 25, 640B); cf. Lampe (1961), 576.

3) The Title of Irl[1]

In the Stowe Missal *Irl*[1] carries the following title, added by Moelcaich during the 9th century: 'Deprecatio sancti martini pro populo'. Is there any chance that this is authentic? Let's put St Martin into context.[37]

Martin, bishop of Tours, who died in 397, was born in Pannonie around 316–317. Son of a Roman tribune, he was educated at Pavia, joined the Roman army and then left it to become a disciple of Hilary of Poitiers. As missionary and thaumaturg he travelled across Europe; as a spiritual leader, he founded the first French monasteries at Liguge and Marmoutier.

Warren takes this title seriously. In his eyes it proves that, despite its Eastern origin, the litany reached Ireland via Gaul.[38] Following on from this great man of learning, we might be tempted to at least take this title into consideration, even though it is a 9th century addition. Both the era in which Martin lived and his links with the whole of Christian Europe, especially with Hilary who spent several years in exile in the East, merit our attention.

We must note, however, that in OR XIX (775–80), St Martin is regarded as a founder, or at least as a defender of the Gallican liturgy, with Hilary and Germain, just as Ambrose is for the Milanese liturgy.[39] This gives us cause for circumspection.

4) The Eastern Origin

Considering the numerous literary parallels, the Eastern origin of this text cannot be denied. Unless we are going to assume a common source, it is not possible to date the formulary before the end of the 4th century.

Conclusions Regarding the Dating

Consideration of the material leads us to situate the Latin original of *Irl*[1] at the end of the 4th or beginning of the 5th century. In this era we can easily understand the absence of the adjective *apostolica* as applied to the Church, the quality of *piisimi* attributed to the emperors, the movement of the widows and virgins from the category of ministers to that of the needy, and the absence of any reference to persecutions. The Eastern influence has had time to make its presence felt through people like Hilary of Poitiers (died *c.* 367) who in the course of his exile in Asia Minor was initiated into Greek Christian hymnody and subsequently composed Latin hymns; Auxentius of Milan (355–374), the Arian predecessor of Ambrose, who was of Cappadocian origin; or yet John Cassian (*c.* 360–434), who spent a

---

37 Cf. Fontaine, (LTK 7), 118–19.

38 Warren (1881), 251. Note that the author rejects the thesis of an Eastern origin for the Celtic liturgy. Without speaking of the East, Gamber (1967), 214–21, considers *Irl*[1] to be a Gallic item.

39 OR XIX, 39. ed. Andrieu (1951), vol. 3, 225.

number of years in Palestine, Egypt and Constantinople (where he was ordained deacon by John Chrysostom) before returning to the West. Finally, the title that was added in the 9th century indicates at the least that during this period they were still aware of being in the presence of a very ancient text. We do not think that we can ignore this information. If all this is correct, then *Irl¹* is the first litanic formulary in the Latin language. We can no longer say that it was Pope Gelasius who introduced the litanic form to the West.

As for the geographic origin of *Irl¹*, the reference to Martin no more links it to Gaul than to another part of Europe. Nothing in the text particularly suggests the Celtic Church. We must admit that we do not know anything about its geographical origin.

d. The Place of the Litany in the Stowe Missal

How was our formulary used? Strangely, *S* places it after the epistle, where it is followed by psalm verses (Gradual) and two short prayers; this follows *Irl¹* which ends with a prayer, as the primitive text has disappeared under Moelcaich's additions.

An odd placement, we might say. And yet it is affirmed in the East by the Liturgy of St James[40] and in the West by the Hispanic liturgy.[41] The question of the placement of the litany in the Gallican liturgy is very complex. At this point we allow ourselves to refer the reader to the hypothesis recently proposed by Abbe Mouret.[42] On the basis of c. 17 of the Council of Orange (441) forecasting that the gospel would be read to the catechumens,[43] the author supposes that before 441 there existed in Gaul a diaconal prayer situated between the Epistle and the Gospel, preceding the dismissal of the catechumens. By being repositioned after the Gospel, the dismissal of the catechumens has doubtless brought with it this diaconal prayer which will be transformed from a prayer for the catechumens into the prayer *pro populo*, mentioned by Pseudo-Germain. The Stowe Missal will become a witness to this ancient ordinance.

We point out, however, that we have found no trace in the West of any *oratio catechumenorum*. The text of Felix III that uses this expression does not indicate a particular prayer but rather the category of persons with which one is permitted to pray (cf. Part One, Section Three).

40 Brightman (1896), 36–38.

41 For the first five Sundays of Lent the Hispanic liturgy includes a litany placed between the two first readings (Old Testament) and the last two (Epistle and Gospel), cf. PL 85, 298–373.

42 Mouret, 'La prière universelle en Gaule. La disparition et le remplacement de l'oratio fidelium', (article to be published). The author kindly allowed us to read a copy of his study, for which we are very grateful.

43 Council of Orange, c. 17, ed. Munier, (CC148), 83; Mansi, vol. 6, 439 (shown as c. 18!), plus the notes at col. 447.

II. The So-Called Milanese 'Divinae Pacis' (M^1)

The sources of the Milanese liturgy include two litanies for the first Sundays of Lent,[44] both situated at the *Ingressa*, between the *Dominus vobiscum* and the *Oratio super populum*. The first of these, which is also the older, begins with *Divinae pacis*. Examples of this are reasonably numerous, and the manuscript tradition in remarkable agreement.

A. Sources (List Not Exhaustive)

A MILAN, Bibl. Ambr. A24 bis inf. (late 9th c. –early 10th c.), f. 65r-v;
= *Sacramentary of Biasca*, ed. Heiming, 41–42.
(Clavis 1909 — Bourque 556 — Gamber 515).

B MILAN, Bibl. Ambr. Trotti 351 (late 10th c. –early 11th c.);
= Sacramentary of Milan, given here following the Tables of Sacramentaries of Bergamo.
(Bourque 561 — Gamber 520).

Berg BERGAMO, Bibl. S. Alessandro in Colonna, 242, (Second half 9th c.), f. 91v–92r;
= Sacramentary of Bergamo, ed. Paredi, 108.
(Clavis 1908 — Bourque 558 — Gamber 505).

C MILAN, Bibl. Ambr. A 24 inf. (10th c.–11th c.);
= Sacramentary of Lodrino, originally of St Stephen of Milan, following the Tables of the Sacramentary of Bergamo.
(Bourque 562 — Gamber 519).

D MILAN, Bibl. Ambr. D 87 sup. (12th c.)
= Sacramentary of Bedero following the same Tables.

E MILAN, Bibl. Capitulaire D 3, 2 (mid 11th c.), f. 51r;
= Pontifical Sacramentary of Aribert, ed. Paredi, 366–67.
(Clavis 1909a — Bourque 559 — Gamber 530).

F BERGAMO, Bibl. Civica Γ III. 18
(Antiphonary late 11th c.), f. 41v–42v.[45]

J MILAN, Bibl. Capit. D 3.3 (*c.* 900), f. 25v–26v;
= Sacramentary of S. Simpliciano, ed. Frei, 179
(Bourque 563 — Gamber 510).

L LONDON, Brit. Mus. Add. 34.209 (early 12th c.), f. 131–32;
= *Ambrosian Antiphonary*, ed. Cagin, *Paléographie musicale*, vol. 5 (Plates) and vol. 6 (transcription), Solesmes, 1896–1900.
(Clavis 1942 — Gamber 555).

---

44 In the manuscripts and editions prior to 1560, these are found on the 2nd and 3rd Sundays of Lent, after the *Dominica in caput Quadragesimae*. After 1560 they are situated on the 1st and 2nd Sundays; cf. *Missale ambrosianum*, Milan, 1913, 121, note 17.

45 We were informed of this manuscript by M. Huglo, Leader of Research at CNRS; a photocopy of it was supplied by Mgr L. Chiodi, Director of the library. We extend thanks to both of them.

O MILAN, Bibl. Ambr. I 127 sup.;
= Sacramentary of Milan, cited by Heiming in the edition of the Sacramentary of Biasca, p. xli.

Tr ZURICH, Bibl. Centr. C 43 (early 11th c.), f. 53v–54r;
= *Sacramentarium Triplex*, ed. Heiming, 64–65.
(Clavis 1907 — Bourque 565 — Gamber 535).

Vr VERCELLI, Arch. Capit. 136 (11th c.);

Sacramentary of Milan, following the Tables of the Sacramentary of Bergamo.

[*R* = ROME, Bibl. Vat. Palat. lat. 506 (14th c.), f. 52v ff. Ambrosian Missal. Described by Gerbert (1774), 528; cf. Ehrensberger (1897), 440. This manuscript, whose text we have not seen, is not included in our edition.]

The two editions provided by Thomasius-Vezzosi could also be added:

- *T2* = vol. 2, 572–73.
- *T7* — vol. 7, 304 = 5, following a Vatican manuscript. Unfortunately it does not indicate the source manuscripts

Finally we note the two editions taken up in the *Missale ambrosianum*:

- *1751* = editio puteobonelliana
- *1902* = editio typica.

B. Edited Version[46]

a/ Divinae pacis et indulgentiae munere supplicantes,
ex toto corde et ex tota mente
precamur[47] te
Domine miserere

I Pro ecclesia tua sancta catholica
quae hic et per universum orbem diffusa es
precamur te
Domine miserere[48]

II Pro papa[49] nostro · illo ·[50] et omni clero eius[51]
omnibusque sacerdotibus ac minbistris
precamur te
Domine miserere

46 Improved from that given in Capelle (1934), 121–23.
47 precamur] deprecamur *T7*.
48 te … miserere *om ABerg semper; om D infra semper; om F qui saepius habet* precamur domine.
49 papa] antistite *F*.
50 et pontifice nostro ·illo· *add T2, 1751, 1902*.
51 eius] eorum *T2, T7, 1751, 1902*.

III Pro famulo tuo · illo · imperatore [et famula tua · illa · imperatrice[52]]
et omni exercitu eius[53]
precamur te
Domine miserere

IV[54] Pro pace ecclesiarum, vocatione gentium[55]
et quiete populorum
precamur te
Domine miserere

V Pro civitate[56] hac et conversatione eius
omnibusque habitantibus in ea
precamur te
Domine miserere

VI Pro aerum[57] temperie ac[58] fructu[59]
et[60] fecunditate terrarum
precamus te
Domine miserere

VII Pro virginibus, viduis, orphanis,
captivis et paentitentibus
precamur te
Domine miserere

VIII Pro navigantibus, iter agentibus, in carceribus,
in vinculis, in metallis, in exiliis[61] constitutis
precamur te
Domine miserere

IX Pro his qui diversis infirmitatibus detinentur
quique spiritibus vexantur inmundis
precamur te
Domine miserere

X Pro his qui in sancta tua ecclesia[62]
fructus misericordiae largiuntur
precamur te

---

52 pro … imperatrice *codd. nisi T7 qui add* nostro *et F qui habet*: pro imperatore nostro . illo . ; pro famulis tuis . N . imperatore et . N . Rege, Duce nostro *1751–1902*; pro famulis tuis . illis . regibus et famulabus tuis ·illis· reginis *J*.

53 eius *Berg D¹ Tr*. eorum *ABCD²EJLVr, T2, T7, 1751, 1902* et ipse *F*.

54 *Ante* IV *add T2*: Pro famulo tuo ·illo· Rege et Duce nostro et omni exercitu ejus …; *add T7*: Pro famulo tuo . N . Rege nostro et omni exercitu ejus, et omnibus qui in sublimitate sunt.

55 gentium] Haereticorum, Judaeorum et Gentium *T7*.

56 civitate] plebe *AC²*. civitate-plebe *L*.

57 aerum] aeris *T2, T7, 1751*.

58 ac] hac *AF*.

59 fructu *T2, T7, 1751, F*; fructuum *ABBergCDELTrVr 1902*.

60 et *om 1902*.

61 exiliis] eliis *F*.

62 catholica *add F*.

Domine miserere

b/ Exaudi nos Deus in omni oratione
atque deprecatione nostra
precamur te
Domine miserere

c/[63] Dicamus omnes: Domine miserere

d/ Kyrie eleison — Kyrie eleison — Kyrie eleison.[64]

C. Eastern Parallels

a/ The incipit is original; we have not come across any parallel, either Eastern or Western. A similar phrase is found, however, at the end of the Exsultet: 'ineffabili pietatis et misericordiae munere, dirige'

ex toto corde ... = B 373.

I ὑπὲρ τῆς κατὰ πᾶσαν τὴν οἰκουμένην ἁγίας σου καθολικῆς καὶ ἀποστολικῆς ἐκκλησίας *J* 54.

II ... καὶ παντὸς τοῦ κλήρου CAp VIII 12, 41; *J* 34; B 363; *M* 138.

III τῶν εὐσεβεστάτων καὶ φιλοχρίστων ἡμῶν βασιλέων, τῆς εὐσεβοῦς καὶ φιλοχρίστου βασιλίσσης, παντὸς τοῦ παλατίου καὶ τοῦ στρατοπέδου αὐτῶν ... *J* 55.

IV ὑπὲρ τῆς εἰρήνης τοῦ σύμπαντος κόσμου καὶ ἑνώσεως πασῶν τῶν ἁγίων τοῦ θεοῦ ἐκκλησιῶν *J* 34, 36, 39.

V ὑπὲρ τῆς πόλεως ταύτης καὶ τῶν ἐνοικούντων CAp VIII 12, 45; cf. *J* 55, B 363.

VI ὑπὲρ εὐκρασίας ἀέρων, εὐφορίας τῶν καρπῶν τῆς γῆς ... B 363. *Temperies* traduit εὐκρασία.

VII ὑπὲρ (ἀναγνωστῶν, ψαλτῶν), παρθένων, χηρῶν τε καὶ ὀρφανῶν CAp VIII 10, 10; cf. *J* 45.

VIII ὑπὲρ πλεόντων καὶ ὁδοιπορούντων δεηθῶμεν, ὑπὲρ τῶν ἐν μετάλλοις καὶ ἐξορίαις καὶ φυλακαῖς καὶ δεσμοῖς ὄντων CAp VIII 10, 15; cf. *J* 55, *M* 126.

IX ὑπὲρ τῶν ... νοσούντων καμνόντων καὶ τῶν ὑπὸ πνευμάτων ἀκαθάρτων ἐνοχλουμένων *J* 45; cf. B 565, *M* 126; cf. Mt 4:23; Mk 1:34; Lk 6:18.

X ὑπὲρ τῶν καρποφορούντων ἐν τῇ ἁγίᾳ ἐκκλησίᾳ καὶ ποιούντων τοῖς πένησι τὰς ἐλεημοσύνας CAp VIII 10. 12; ὑπὲρ τῶν καρποφορούντων καὶ καλλιεργούντων ἐν ταῖς ἁγίαις τοῦ θεοῦ ἐκκλησίαις *J* 36; cf. B 373.

b/ ὑπὲρ τοῦ εἰσακουσθῆναι καὶ εὐπρόσδεκτον γενέσθαι τὴν δέησιν ἡμῶν ἐνώπιον τοῦ θεοῦ *J* 47.

---

63 c/ *om T7*; c/-d/ *om F*.

64 Kyrie eleison *ter AEJLT2, T2, 1751, 1902; semel BergTr.*

D. Liturgical Form

M[1] constitutes a good example of the invocative type of litany. Here is its structure:

a/	descriptive invocation, introducing the response;
I–X	verbal invocations, all beginning with *pro* and concluding with *precamur te*;
b/	imperative invocation;
c/	invitation picking up the response; originally it would probably repeat the earlier incipit of the litany and form an inclusion with it.
d/	The three-fold *Kyrie eleison* (unique in *Berg Tr*) poses a problem of identification; is it an invocation pronounced solely by the leader, or an ancient response, or a chant by the whole assembly? We shall return to this.

E. Analysis

a) The Response

The edited version clearly indicates that the response is *Domine miserere*, introduced each time by the ending of the invocation: *precamur te*. Dom Capelle made this last phrase the beginning of the response, which then became: *precamur te, Domine miserere*. Our trimming of the response is confirmed by the music for the piece, such as is found in *L* and in the new edition of the Ambrosian Antiphonary.[65] Regardless of the period during which it was composed, it is unlikely that the music did not follow the text which, we must remember, is still in use in the Milanese Church; a melody that distorted the traditional responses would not have been accepted. Moreover, from a pastoral point of view, it is very convenient to conclude each petition with the same formula, so that the participants know when they are being asked to respond. The final *precamur te* is easily understood.

b) The Incipit

In earlier times the litany would have begun with *Dicamus omnes: Domine miserere*. We have two proofs of this:

1 The more convincing proof is invitation c/; it only makes sense as a repetition of the incipit with which it forms an inclusion.

---

65 *Antiphonale missarum mediolanensis* (1935), 105–09. This edition has in any case used manuscript *L*.

2 The formula *Divinae pacis …* has no parallel, either in the East or the West. But the descriptive element that follows it, *ex toto corde …*, comes from the East (B 373) where it is introduced by εἴπωμεν πάντες!

Thus the banal invitation *Dicamus omnes* would have been replaced with a more novel invocation *Divinae pacis et indulgentiae munere supplicantes.*

c) Commentary

I. Here we have an exact parallel with the first intention of the Eucharistic celebration given by the *Te igitur* of the Roman Canon. What a pity that we do not have the beginning of the Canon conserved in *De Sacramentis*! We note the absence of the adjective *apostolica*, just as in Irl^1 II.

II. What sense it given here to *papa*? We know that the term, borrowed from the Greek (πάπα) originally referred to the bishop alone. From the middle of the 5th century on, beginning at Rome, the word tends to be reserved for the successor of Peter, a meaning that is definitely accepted by the middle of the 7th century.[66] Moreover, Dom Botte does not think that he knows any liturgical use of *papa* other than for the bishop of Rome. In what sense should it be understood here? Let us examine two possibilities:

– either *papa* refers to any bishop; in this case the addition *et pontifice nostro* in the printed examples dates from the time that *papa* is reserved to the Bishop of Rome and is witness to the semantic evolution of the term. Originally, there would not have been any special prayer for the successor of Peter.

– or *papa* does refer to the bishop of Rome; in this hypothesis, the origin of the text would have to have been this city, for we could scarcely imagine that M^1 would fail to include an invocation for the bishop of the place while it contains one for the city and its inhabitants (V) The addition of *et pontifice nostro* gives witness to the use of this formulary outside of Rome.

Would M^1, which is found only in Milanese sources, be of Roman origin? The history of relations between the various Western liturgies is not sufficiently developed to be able to enlighten us on this point. Scholars have not yet had the last word on the links between Rome and Milan for example.[67]
What arguments do we have in favour of a Roman origin?

– the addition *pro pontifice nostro,* made with the bishop of Milan in mind, reveals that previously *papa* described the Bishop of Rome and that the

66 Cf. Leclercq, article 'papa', DACL 13/1, 1097–1111 and the bibliography cited there.
67 See the state of the question in Borella (1964), chapters 1–5.

formulary therefore came from that city. This would be so if *papa* had not undergone a semantic evolution.

- the invocation for the civil authorities speaks of the emperor and not of the king as is the case with FG^1 and FG^2; but this is more an indication of date than of place, and can moreover have been easily altered subsequently.

- the phrase *sacerdotibus ac ministris*: in the Latin litanies, we do not come across this apart from here and in *DG*, which is certainly Roman, before it occurs in all the Gallican and Hispanic litanies. It may be that Gelasius took it from M^1 which therefore if it did not originate in Rome had at least to be known there. In Cyprian, however, the two words were already paired together.[68]

In short, a Roman origin for M^1 is possible but not certain. The two stiques (lines) of this invocation are parallel with regard to sense; the first prays for the bishop of the place and his clergy, the second for all bishops and other ministers.[69] The idea corresponds with that expressed in I: the Church is scattered 'here and throughout the universe'.

III. Mention of the empress, unique to M^2 in the West, apart from the parallel with *J* 55, can be explained by the Roman origin of the formulary. However it would not be surprising in Milan, which was often the imperial residence once Maximian installed his capital there at the end of the 3rd century.

The word *eius* retained in the manuscripts (*Berg*, D^1, *Tr*) that name both emperor and empress indicates, as noted by Dom Heiming,[70] that originally they would have prayed only for the emperor. It could certainly be assumed that in the spirit of the redactor the army belonged to the emperor alone, but the phrase is then grammatically incorrect.
We point out the variant found in *T7*: *et omnibus qui in sublimitate sunt* (1 Tim 2:2), appears in Irl^1 VI.

IV. The mention of Churches in the plural is certainly a sign of antiquity. Since the same invocation seeks tranquility for the peoples, the peace of the Churches should undoubtedly be understood on the basis of doctrinal disputes.

The prayer for calling pagans to Christianity is rare; it does not exist in the East. Alone among the Latin texts, the *OS* contains a litique (IX) for the

68 Cyprian, *Epistola* 1, 2, 1–2, ed. Bayard, vol. 1, 3; tr. Donna, (FC 51), 4; cf. Part One, Section Two, T 13.

69 From the second half of the 4th century until the 6th century, *sacerdos* normally meant the bishop; cf. Gy (1957), 125–45. As for *minister*, it sometimes referred specifically to deacons; here it has a broader meaning, equivalent to *clerus* in the first part of the invocation.

70 Heiming (1969), xli.

pagans and *DG* (X) prays for the *gentili superstione perfusi*. This missionary intention is therefore well established in Rome.

V. The term *conversatio* is attested universally by all the sources. We cannot understand why Dom Capelle has preferred *conservatio,* which is certainly a *lectio facilior,* at least for those who speak French!

M^2 V has the same invocation, without *et conversatione eius*; this typically Latin phrase does not figure in the Eastern sources; might it have been added in M^1 V by its editor in order to get the ternary structure of invocations III–VI?

The very detailed study that P. Hoppenbrouwers has devoted to *conversatio*[71] can assist us in determining its sense in this invocation. Amongst the different meanings that *conversatio* offers, two would seem germane to our context:

a) understood in a 'plurilateral sociative' sense the term can mean *societas conversantium* and designate a community, a group of people who live together, the collectivity of a city. In this case our invocation contains three terms that are almost synonymous: the city, its collectivity (global aspect), its inhabitants (individual aspect).
b) understood as '*naming the act of interaction*' it can designate a 'way of living' and more precisely life in a particular state. Later, especially from the 6th century onwards this referred to living in a Christian state of life, or even more precisely in the state of *conversus,* that is to say the life of a monk or virgin (from the 5th century onwards).
   Following this hypothesis, the invocation refers to three distinct groups: the city, the *conversi* that it shelters, and more broadly, all the inhabitants.
   M^1 does not seem to recognize the monks; nothing leads us to understand *conversatio* in such a restrictive sense. We consider that here the term is used in the sense of community, collectivity.

VI. This invocation surely translates B 363; moreover, the majority of the examples use *fructuum,* as in *Irl*^{2} III. Only *F* and three printed versions use *fructu,* which is more logical since, in all cases, the conjunction *et* separates *fructuum* (*fructu*) from *fecunditate.* Thus the evolution would be as follows:

1. '...ac fructuum fecunditate terrarum': as contained in Irl^2 III, but nowhere in M^1, apart from the *edition typica* of 1902.

2. '...ac fruc*tuum et* fecunditate terrarum', the reading given in all the M^1 manuscripts apart from *F*. Undoubtedly this preposition would have been added to obtain an invocation with the same tripartite structure as those preceding it (II–V).

---

71 Hoppenbrouwers (1964), 45–95.

3. '...ac fructu et fecunditate terrarum', an adaptation made by *F* and three other versions in order to obtain a more satisfactory meaning; *fructu* has become a generic term, in the ablative, in parallel with *temperie* and *fecunditate*.

FG[2] VII and *M*[2] VI have resolved the problem in a different way, by dropping the term *fructus*.

VII–VIII. Virgins and widows are no longer regarded as members of the ecclesiastical 'orders' but are included among the needy, along with orphans. The same applies to penitents. This leads us to think that captives, prisoners and exiles in question are no longer so because of their faith, as was the case before the Peace of the Church. Do workers *in metallis*, for example, correspond to a real situation when this invocation was translated from Eastern formularies? If so, we do not think they were exclusively Christians.

IX. The first part of this invocation will 'come into its own' in the Latin texts, especially in the Gallican and Hispanic lities.

d/ The triple *Kyrie eleison* (unique to *Berg Tr*, which has to be considered as an abbreviation) poses two problems: its appearance in *M1*, and the use that has been made of it. These difficulties have a significance for the history of liturgy that might not be evident at first glance. We know that Dom Capelle linked the introduction of the *Kyrie* in the West to the use of litanies, and more particularly with the *DG*. According to him, *Kyrie eleison* was the response to the latter, but this conclusion will be challenged by the analysis of the *DG* presented below. It is therefore advisable to record with caution the first traces of the Kyrie and to proceed in a very methodical manner.

1. Inclusion of the Triple 'Kyrie eleison' in M[1]

Has this litany always included the ending that we currently find there? To tell the truth, we just don't know! There are two likely possibilities:

- the *Kyrie* did not originally belong to the litany but it was linked to it at a later date — perhaps quite quickly, or perhaps when *M*[1] was introduced in the *Ingressa* of the Milanese liturgy, the date of which we are not aware.
- the triple *Kyrie* forms the earliest conclusion in *M*[1], in which case it would be the first trace of the *Kyrie* in the West. Indeed, we know that the first verifiable mentions of the *Kyrie* are in canon 3 of the Council of Vaison (529) and Chapters 3 and 17 of the Rule of St Benedict, which date from exactly the same period. The Council of Vaison states explicitly that it was introduced in Provence, following the example of the *consuetudo* that was as much Roman as it was Eastern and Italian.[72] Thus the *Kyrie* would

72 Council of Vaison, c. 3, ed. De Clercq, (CC 148A), 79; Mansi, vol. 8, 729. Cf. infra, p. 310.

have existed in the Western Churches from at least the beginning of the 6th century.

What are we to make of this? With all our examples coming from the Milanese liturgy, it is impossible to decide the question. The only certain thing is that all the examples (apart from *F*) have the *Kyrie* at the end of the formulary; everything else remains in the realm of hypothesis. With this clearly in mind, we think that the most obvious explanation is that the triple *Kyrie eleison* was part of *M¹* from the beginning. We will draw our conclusions from this to propose a dating.

2. *Function of this Triple 'Kyrie eleison'*

Was it chanted by the leader alone, or by the whole assembly? Or is it an ancient response of which only a trace has been conserved? This last proposition can be discarded, since we have just said that the *Kyrie* was already known in the West in an earlier time; in no way is it a vestige of the time when the liturgy was celebrated in Greek.

As for the first option, we think that this *Kyrie* would have been chanted by the whole assembly, thereby repeating with particular insistence the litany's invocation. Perhaps an examination of the music that accompanied this text in the manuscripts will confirm or weaken this theory.[73]

d) Attempt at Localisation and Dating

The Roman origin of *M¹* seems to us possible (cf. commentary, II), but not at all certain. With regard to the age of the text we have few specific references. Even if it includes a barrage of terms that fit well with the era of persecutions, it does not give the impression of being so old, given the order in which it places these ancient elements, and especially taking into account the invocation for the imperial couple and the numerous Eastern parallels.

In comparing *M¹* and *Irl¹*, it would seem to us that the first of these is the more recent. Indeed, its response is clearly and directly *Domine miserere*, without any further dithering with *Domine exaudi et miserere*. The incipit *Divinae pacis* has replaced the earlier *Dicamus omnes* as we have already noted. *M¹* also omits the catechumens who are frequently mentioned in the Eastern sources.

Only the triple *Kyrie* ending remains to be considered. We said above that with all the examples (apart from *F*) affirming this, we lean towards its belonging to the litany from the beginning. But let us remember that this is only a hypothesis. If this turns out to be correct, we would hold both ends of the chain: the *terminus*

---

73 If it were to be verified, there might be an argument against the Roman origin of *M¹*. Indeed, in the famous passage of a letter to John of Syracuse, Gregory the Great affirms that in Rome they do not say and have never said the *Kyrie* as do the Greeks, who say it all together; 'apud nos autem a clericis dicitur et a populo respondetur'. (PL 77, 956; cf. Section Six.) But St Gregory lived a good century later.

post quem would be established by Irl^1, certainly the older of the two, that we have situated at the end of the 4th or the beginning of the 5th century; the *terminas ante quem* would be the year 529, the date at which Provence adopted the *Kyrie* following the example of the Roman and Italian Churches. Considering the overall content of M^1, we find that it contains many elements that will be abandoned by the second wave of Latin litanic texts, that came to birth at the end of the 5th century, and so we must reject the 6th century as a possible date. In the absence of a *Kyrie*, we would date M^1 from the first half of the 5th century; but is it possible that this innovation, retained in the Greek language, would have left no trace before 529 if it was already in use a century before? Taking this into account we think we must date it from the second half of the 5th century. This latter date, closer to the start of the new wave of litanies and adaptations, also provides an explanation for the change of incipit of M^1 as well as the modifications that were imposed for stylistic reasons (tripartite structure of the invocations III–VI). Strictly speaking, M^1 does not belong to translations of Easter texts; it serves as a transition between them and their various adaptations.

e) Use of $\mathbf{M^1}$

M^1 has been retained in the *Ingressa* for the first Sunday of Lent (cf. p. 155, n. 44) in the Milanese liturgy. Whatever may be the use of *preces* on Lenten Sundays, and its analogous use in the Hispanic liturgy, we think that M^1 is an ancient form of the *oratio fidelium*. To us, this seems to be indicated as much by the function of the Eastern sources as by the literary form of all the Latin litanies. Besides, what other role would they have to fill? As it is possible that M^1 is of Roman origin, it follows that the liturgy of this city (or one of the liturgies of this city) may have used litanic forms for the Universal Prayer before the *DG*.

Section Three

A Second Wave of Litanic Texts: Adaptations

1. The 'Deprecatio Gelasii' (*DG*)

Here we are in the presence of the most elaborate litany from the literary point of view. With the *OS* it is undoubtedly one of our most beautiful texts, although it is less dense than the *OS* and theologically less rich. Following the work of Dom Capelle it constitutes a centrepiece in the history of the *Kyrie eleison* of the Roman Mass. From this standpoint, the examination of the *DG* in a way forms the crux of this book and so we must pay careful attention to it.

1. *The State of the Question*

To our knowledge, Edmund Bishop is the first to undertake a study of the *DG*[1] He considers it to be a Roman formulary (cf. his arguments below, Commentary, XIV) which he unhesitatingly attributes to Pope Gelasius (492–496).[2] He compares it with Irl^1 and estimates that both draw their material and inspiration from the litanies of Constantinople. To him *DG* seems slightly older than Irl^1, which depends on it. Finally, he holds that a century before St Gregory the Roman Mass was familiar not only with the response *Kyrie eleison*, but also with petitions of the type found in the Greek litanies; it is to this that St Benedict was alluding when he spoke of the *supplicatio litaniae, id est Kyrie eleison*. We do not have any grounds, however, for asserting that the intentions of the *DG* were those accompanying the *Kyrie* of the Mass at the time of St Gregory and the period before him. 'In a word, we know nothing about the matter', concludes Bishop, with a caution that will not, unfortunately, be exercised in what follows.

A year later, Wilhelm Meyer, the eminent philologist from Göttingen, looks in turn (independently?) at the *DG*.[3] He supports the judgement of the English liturgist and concludes that it accords well with the times and circumstances in which its name and title place it. He undertakes a comparison of the ancient Latin litanies, distinguishing three groups:

1 E. Bishop (1911), 406–13.
2 On Gelasius, see Pomares (1959), 15–19.
3 Meyer (1912), 87–108.

- the 'pro series' ('die Pro-Reihen'): *Irl*^{1}, *M*^{1}, *M*^{2}, *DG*, *FG*^{1};
- the Gallican and Hispanic *Orationes paschales*, which most often take the form of lities;
- the *OS*, which he attributes to Gregory the Great (since they are found in the Gregorian Sacramentary…), which radically distorts the study.

Meyer edits our piece following Paris B.N. lat. 1153, and gives the variants of Rome, Bibl. Angelica 123. The first of these is the manuscript that was used for Duchesne's edition (Quercetanus) in 1617. This was reprised by Froben in 1777 and reproduced by Migne, PL 101, 510 ff. As the beginning of the manuscript is missing, Duchesne titled it *Officia per ferias* and attributed it to Alcuin; it was with good reason that Meyer rejected this attribution.[4]

These two initial contributions will be completed shortly after by Wilhelm Bousset[5] who repeats Meyer's conclusions. His main contribution consists in broadening the field by indicating the Eastern parallels, which his predecessor did not even mention.

After this the *DG* fell into virtual oblivion for about twenty years. In the fifth edition of *Origins of Christian Worship*, Mgr Duchesne devoted a footnote to it,[6] where he rejected its attribution to Gelasius (cf. below, Commentary XIV). Fr Connolly, in an article on the literary traditions of the *OS*,[7] seems not to be aware of it; in any case he makes no mention of it.

Nor does it feature in the synopsis of the litanic prayers published by Dom Alfonso.[8] Dom Cabrol cites it, without providing the text, and once more, despite Duchesne's objections, attributes it[9] to Gelasius.

The article by Dom Capelle on *Le Kyrie de la messe et la pape Gélase*[10] marks a turning point. The author props up the conclusions of Bishop and Meyer, pointing out similarities from various phrases within the litany, with the works of Gelasius. He edits the *DG*, correcting Paris 1153 on the basis of Angelica 123, and situates the piece in its context, publishing the litanies *Irl*^{1}, *FG*^{1}, *M*^{1} and *M*^{2} in four parallel columns and supplying Eastern sources for all of them. This excellent work receives the acclaim it deserves. Taken up again and revised by the author,[11] it would become a classic. But in addition to this remarkable documentation the abbot of Mont César defends, unduly in our opinion, the thesis of a relationship between the *DG* and the *Kyrie eleison* of which the sources speak, a connection against which Bishop had cautioned some twenty years earlier. This is not the

4 Cf. Wilmart (1936), 259–299, particularly 263–64.
5 Bousset (1916), 135–162.
6 Duchesne (1925), 211, n. 2.
7 Connolly (1920), 219–32.
8 Alfonso (1928).
9 Cabrol, DACL9.2, 1540–71.
10 Capelle (1934), 126–44; Tr. lit., vol. 2, 116–34.
11 Capelle(1939), 24–34; Tr. lit., vol. 2, 135–45; Capelle (1951), 129–144; Tr. lit., vol. 2, 146–160; Capelle (1952), 5–16, Tr. lit., vol. 2, 236–47; Capelle (1955), 181–91; Tr. lit., vol. 2, 236–47.

place, in this examination of texts, to develop further the thesis of the Leuven liturgist on the transfer of the *DG* to the current place of the *Kyrie* and on the birth of the *oratio super sindonem*; we will come back to this in Section Six.

Since then, two more manuscripts have been discovered. One is pointed out by Capelle himself in his second article.[12] The other was detected by the tireless researcher, Père Molin, who not only kindly informed us about it, but has also given permission for us to report on it in his place.[13] Since our research of the processional manuscripts has not thrown up any new examples, we agree with Père Molin in thinking that it would be better to look for them in the booklets of private prayers (*libelli precum*), the literary genre to which the three Paris manuscripts belong.[14]

2. The Sources

They are divided indisputably into two families.

a) The Gallican Tradition

B = PARIS, B.N. lat. 1153, f. 48^{v}–49^{v}, originally from the Abbey of St-Denis (Paris), *c.* 850, a book of psalms for private use, given the title *Officia per ferias* by Quercetanus (1617). It is reproduced in PL 101, 509–612 according to the Froben edition; the *DG* is found at columns 560–61, with several inaccuracies in relation to the manuscript. It has also been edited by Thomasius-Vezzosi, vol. 2, 571, with corrections, with the final verbs in the subjunctive and the double response *Domine exaudi et miserere.* It is also published by Meyer (1912), 110–11

C = PARIS, B.N. lat. 1248, f. 100^{v}–102^{r}, Saint-Martial de Limoges, 9th century,[15] among some fragments taken from Alcuin; it has been described by Andrieu (1931), OR, vol. 1, 265–69

---

12 Capelle (1939), 138. It deals with Paris, B.N. lat. 1248.

13 This is Paris, Bibl. Mazarine, 512.

14 Cf. Molin (1976), 113–48. We warmly thank Père Molin for having communicated to us the essential elements of his conclusions. We must point out that the *DG* is not found in the four manuscripts edited by Wilmart (1940), *Precum libelli quattuor aevi carolini.* On this genre, great profit can be gained by consulting the article by the same author (1936), 259–99, on *Le manuel de prières de saint Jean Gualbert*, as well as Chazelas (1959), *Les livrets de prières privées du IXe s.*

15 This manuscript consists of several parts. The passage that interests us we owe to the hand that copied ff. 89–116^{v} of the current manuscript. The Lauer Catalogue dates the collection in the manuscript from the 10th–12th centuries; Père Molin, who is familiar with these texts, has indicated to us that he would be happy to date the folios containing the *DG* from the 9th century. M. Jean Vezin, of the Bibliothèque Nationale of Paris, when consulted on this matter, gave the following response: 'Perhaps the texts date from the 10th century, but, as with Père Molin, I would rather place them in the 9th. It is often very difficult to say if a manuscript is from the 9th or 10th century'. (Comment received in a letter dated 6 October, 1975, for which I am very grateful).

D = PARIS, Bibl. Mazarine 512, f. 23r–24r, Saint-Eloi de Noyon, *c.* 850 (and not 9th century as indicated by the Catalogue de Molinier); private euchology contents analogous to the *Officia per ferias*. This example was discovered by Père Molin.

b) The Milanese Tradition

A = ROME, Bibl. Angelica lat. 123 (olim B. 3. 18), f. 213r-v, Gradual and Tropary of Bologne, 11th century.[16] This manuscript has been published in facsimile, with an introduction by Dom J. Froger, *Le codex 123 de la Bibliothèque Angelica de Rome,* (*Paléolographie musicale,* 18), Berne, 1969; the bibliography is also found there.

3. Edited Versions

Dom Capelle edited the *DG* on the basis of *B*, with corrections from *A*. It has been our preference to edit the Gallican and Milanese traditions separately, the better to show the superiority of the former (cf. infra). Where *A* has retained the better reading, we have put the Gallican text between square brackets []; in order to reach what we think to be the original text, it suffices to replace the words between brackets with their equivalent in *A*.

This process has the advantage of not mixing the two different families too hastily, and therefore avoiding any regrettable confusion.

a) Gallican Tradition

a/[17] Dicamus omnes: Domine exaudi et miserere[18]

b/ Patrem unigeniti et Dei filium genitoris ingeniti[19]
et sanctum domini[20] spiritum fidelibus animis invocamus
⟨Domine exaudi et miserere⟩[21]

I Pro inmaculata Dei vivi ecclesia, [sacerdotibus ac ministris]
divinae bonitatis[22] opulentiam deprecamur
⟨Domine exaudi et miserere⟩[23]

---

16 The *DG* is here set down for the Second Sunday of Lent; for the First Sunday the manuscript offers *M*2. We are, then, dealing with a book in the Milanese tradition, but one which curiously upsets the pattern of the Lenten prayers; usually *M*1 is found on the First Sunday of Lent and *M*2 on the Second. *M*1 does not feature at all in this manuscript.

17 Deprecatio quam papa Gelasius pro universali Ecclesia constituit canendam esse *BC*. Deprecatio quam papa Gelasius pro universali deprecando Ecclesia constituit quamque sancti et beati patres pro omni christiano populo deprecantes in publicis et privatis orationibus cantare solebant *D*.

18 miserere: Domine miserere *add D*.

19 ingeniti] ingenitum *C*.

20 domini *codd.* deum *edd.*

21 *Hoc responsum conjicio sicut Thomasius, vol. 2, 571.* Domine miserere et miserere *D*.

22 bonitatis] pietatis *D*.

23 *Hoc responsum conjicio,* Domine miserere *D*.

II Pro sanctis Dei magni[s][24] sacerdotibus et ministris
cunctisque Deum verum colentibus populis
Christum dominum supplicamus
⟨Domine exaudi et miserere⟩[19]

III Pro universis recte tractantibusverbum veritatis
multiformem verbi[25] Dei sapientiam peculiariter obsecramus
⟨Domine exaudi et miserere⟩[19]

IV Pro his qui se mente et[26] corpore propter caelorum regna castificant
et spirituali[27] labore desudant
largitorem spiritalium munerum obsecramus[28]
⟨Domine exaudi et miserere⟩[19]

V Pro religiosis principibus omnique militia eorum
qui iudicium et iustitiam diligunt
domini[29] potentiam obsecramus
⟨Domine exaudi et miserere⟩[19]

VI Pro [iocunditate et serenitate] pluviae
atque aurarum vitalium blandimentis ac prospero diversorum
[operum] cursu
rectorum mundi dominum[30] deprecamur
⟨Domine exaudi et miserere⟩[19]

VII Pro his quos[31] prima[32] christiani nominis initiavit agnitio
quos iam desiderium[33] gratiae caelestis accendit[34]
omnipotentis Dei misericordiam obsecramus
⟨Domine exaudi et miserere⟩[19]

VIII Pro his quos humanae fragilitatis infirmitas[35] et quos
nequitiae spiritalis invidia vel varius saeculi[36] ⟨error⟩[37] involuit
redemptoris nostri misericordiam imploramus
⟨Domine exaudi et miserere⟩[19]

IX Pro his quos peregrinationis necessitas
aut iniquae potestatis impietas[38] vel hostilis vexat aerumna

---

24 magnis *C, et B ubi em. alt. m. in* magni; sacerdotibus magnis *D.*
25 verbi] *om D.*
26 et] vel *D.*
27 spirituali *D,* spiritalium *BC.*
28 obsecramus] imploramus *D.*
29 domini] Dei *D.*
30 dominum *om C.*
31 quos] quibus *C.*
32 prima *B.* proxima *D om C.*
33 desiderium *B.* desiderio *CD.*
34 accendit] poscit *C.*
35 fragilitatis infirmitas *D.* infirmitatis fragilitas *BC.*
36 saeculi *om C.*
37 error *Thomasius et Capelle.* horror *codd.*
38 impietas] impressio *D.*

salvatorem dominum supplicamus
⟨Domine exaudi et miserere⟩[19]

X Pro iudaica falsitate ⟨...⟩[39] aut heretica pravitate deceptis
vel gentili[40] superstitione perfusis
veritatis dominum deprecamur
⟨Domine exaudi et miserere⟩[19]

XI Pro operariis pietatis et his qui necessitatibus laborant⟨i⟩um
fraterna caritate subveniunt
misericordiarum dominum deprecamur
⟨Domine exaudi et miserere⟩[19]

XII Pro omnibus intrantibus[41] in haec[42] sanctae domus domini[43] atria
qui[44] religioso corde et supplici devotione convenerunt
dominum gloriae deprecamur
⟨Domine exaudi et miserere⟩[19]

XIII Pro emundatione animarum corporumque nostrorum [omnium ac
venia peccatorum
clementissimum dominum supplicamus[45]
⟨Domine exaudi et miserere⟩[19]

XIV Pro refrigerio fidelium animarum praecipue sanctorum[46] domini
sacerdotum qui huic ecclesiae praefuerunt catholicae
dominum spirituum et universae carnis iudicem[47] deprecamur
⟨Domine exaudi et miserere⟩[19]

XV Mortificatam vitiis carnem et viventem fide animam
praesta, Domine, praesta

XVI Castum timorem et veram dilectionem
praesta, Domine, praesta[48]

XVII Gratum vitae ordinem et[49] probabilem exitum
praesta, Domine, praesta

XVIII Angelum[50] pacis et solacia sanctorum
praesta, Domine, praesta

---

39 *post* falsitate *lacunam unius verbi suspicitur Capelle.*
40 gentili *D*. gentilium *BC*.
41 intrantibus *om D qui add* qui.
42 in haec] huius *C*.
43 domini *om D*.
44 qui *om BD*.
45 supplicamus] deprecamur *D*.
46 sanctorum *om D*.
47 iudicem *om C*. dominum *add. D*.
48 praesta *om D*.
49 et *om D*.
50 angelum] angelus *C*.

c/ Nosmetipsos et omnia nostra quae orta quae acta[51] per dominum
ipso auctore[52] suscipimus[53] ipso custode retinemus
ipsiusque[54] misericordiae et arbitrio providentiae[55] commendamus
Domine ⟨exaudi⟩ et miserere

d/[56] Dicamus omnes: Domine exaudi et miserere[57]
Domine ⟨exaudi⟩ et miserere.

b) Milanese Tradition

a/ Kyrie eleison

b/ Deum patrem filiumque eius dominum Iesum Christum
et spiritum sanctum devotis animis invocemus
Kyrie eleison

I Pro catholica dei vivi ecclesia per totum orbem constituta
misericordem dominum deprecemur
Kyrie eleison

1. Pro domno ·illo· apostolico et universali papa,
misericordem dominum deprecemur
Kyrie eleison

2. Pro domno ·illo· imperatore nostro, iudicibus et exercitibus eius
qui iustitiam et rectum iudicium diligunt,
misericordem dominum deprecemur
Kyrie eleison

3. Pro domno ·illo· archiepiscopo nostro et sacerdotio eius,
omnipotentem dominum deprecemur
Kyrie eleison

4. Pro domno ·illo· episcopo nostro et sacerdotio eius
omnipotentem dominum deprecemur
Kyrie eleison

II Pro sacerdotibus et ministri⟨s⟩ sacri[s] altari⟨s⟩
et cunctis verum Deum colentibus populis,
domini potentiae⟨m⟩ deprecemur
Kyrie eleison

IX Pro his quos peregrinationis necessitas
aut iniquae potestatis oppressio
vel hostilitatis vexat aerumna,|

---

51 acta *codd.* aucta *Thomasius — Meyer — Capelle.*

52 ipso auctore] ipsum auctorem *C.*

53 suscipimus *B.* suscepimus *D.* suscipiamus *C.*

54 ipsiusque] ipsius *D et Meyer.*

55 arbitrio providentiae[arbitrii providentia *D.*

56 miserere] et miserere *add. D.*

57 d/ *om C, Thomasius, Meyer et Capelle; apud Frobenium (et PL) incipit d/ orationem sequentem.*

conditoris nostri misericordiam deprecemur
Kyrie eleison

VI Pro iocunditate serenitatis et opportunitate pluviae
atque aurarum vitalium blandimentis
[h]ac diversorum temporum prospero cursu,
omniptentem dominum supplicemus
Kyrie eleison

XIV Pro requie[m] fidelium animarum
praecipue sanctorum domini sacerdotum qui huic ecclesiae praefuerunt,
dominum spirituum et universae carnis iudicem imploremus
Kyrie eleison

XIII Pro emundatione animarum corporumque nostrorum
et omnium venia[m] peccatorum,
conditorem mundi dominum supplicemus
Kyrie eleison

5. Pro civitate hac et omnibus habitantibus in ea,
misericordem dominum deprecemur
Kyrie eleison

Merit of the Two Traditions

Without any beating round the bush Cappelle claims that manuscript *A* 'shows itself to be clearly superior'.[58] This judgement is based on invitatory VI, where the matter is clear. We can add to it the reading *per totum orbem constituta* included by *A* in I, as well as *omnium venia peccatorum* in XIII, a phrase which better respects the cursus. But apart from these three cases, which are exceptions, *A* is, on the contrary, clearly inferior! Here are the reasons why:

- b/ is composed in a more banal manner than in the Gallican tradition, which certainly offers a 'lectio difficilior';
- the final verbs of each invitatory are in the subjunctive, more 'normal' than the indicate of *BCD*. They are less varied in *A* which most often used *deprecemur*. The discriminating redactor of *DG* would not have been content with such monotony;
- between I and II, *A* interpolates four invitatories that this same manuscript also places in M^2.
- *sancti altaris* in II seems secondary;
- the omission of *catholicae* in XIV reveals an adaptation made beyond Rome (cf. below, Commentary XIV);
- *A* omits III–V, VII–VIII, X–XII and the entire second part;
- *A* adds at the end a petition for the city taken from M^2.

58 Capelle (1934), 125.

We do not understand why the abbot of Mont César could have written: 'perhaps this one (*A*) represents a more direct tradition than that of Alcuin'.[59] This judgement is again taken up by Père Molin. In our eyes, *A* represents, on the contrary, a secondary text, altered by Milanese influences. But *A* is the only manuscript where the response is *Kyrie eleison.*

Relations Between the Three Gallican Manuscripts

These three manuscripts belong without doubt to the same family. We will content ourselves with indicating as proof the presence of the title and the interpolation *sacerdotibus ac ministris* in I. Among them, *D* is the least good; the variation of its title seems to be a scholarly explanation by the compiler to justify the resumption of a dead text and the words *impressio* in IX and *arbitrii providentia* in c/ have little chance of being original, the same being said for the formulation of XII which omits *intrantibus.*

B and *C* are nearer to each other. *C* is certainly later and contains several errors that distance it from the original, such as *ingenitum* in b/ and *poscit* in VII. In our opinion *B* is the best example and it is on this that we have based our edition.

D is probably not dependent on *B*, but both must arise from a lost intermediary (*X*). By contrast, there is every chance that *C* does depend on *B*. Thus we propose the following line of descent:

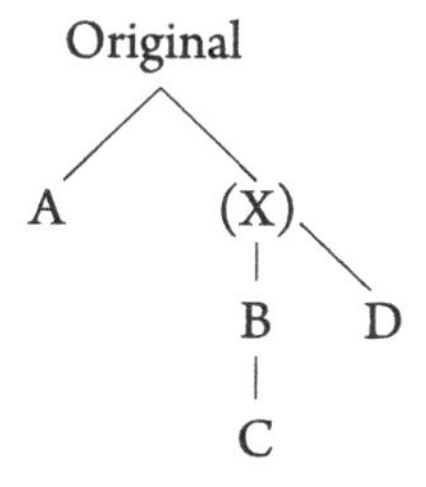

4. Literary and Liturgical Forms

The *DG* is written in very careful language, which fits well with the description that the *Liber pontificalis* gives us of Gelasius and his style: 'Fecit etiam et sacramentorum praefationes et orationes cauto sermone et epistulas fidei delimato sermone multas'.[60]

59 Capelle (1939, 138, n. 22.
60 LP, vol. 1, 255.

In both the first part (46 times) and in the second (4 times) the cursus — a literary device that was used, as we have already said, between the 4th and 7th centuries — has been respected. The three customary rhythms are found there:

´ _/_ ´ _ (planus)
´ _/_ ´ _ _ (tardus)
´ _ _/_ _ ´ _ (velox)

The pauses are thus indicated by the accents, and final words of more than four feet are avoided.
But an interesting observation is made by Meyer (p, 108), that sometimes the ending is trispondaic: ´ _ / _ _ ´ _; however, in his work on the rhythm of medieval Latin,[61] this philologist, who was very interested in these matters, noted that this rare rhythm was favoured by Ennodius and Gelasius! Meyer provides three examples:

- III vérbum veritátis
- XII devotióne convenérunt
- c/ custóde retinémus

We would add:

- I órbem constitúta,

the wording in manuscript *A*; this would be further proof, if any was needed, of the superiority of this expression when compared to the 'sacerdotibus ac ministris' of *BCD*. In short, the literary analysis of the piece indicates that the *DG* is the work of a single author, a person of taste, with a subtle and fine pen.

The liturgical form of the *DG* is a litany, composed in the following manner:

–	title, without doubt added later;
a/	invitation, indicating the response
b/	attributive invitation that develops a Trinitarian formula at some length, and not without theological subtleties;
I–XIV;	fourteen invitatories, each containing not only the announcement of the purpose and beneficiary of the prayer, but also an attributive invitation, always different and sometimes adapted to the petition.[62] We note that the Gallican tradition has retained the verb in the indicative, probably for a good reason;
XV–XVIII;	four invocations (relatively insignificant, but compensated by the response)
c/	commendation of the assembly and its goods to God, Creator and Provider;
d/	invitation making an inclusion with a/.

61 Meyer (1905), 260.

While in *Irl*[1] the first part consists of invocations and the second of invitatories, *DG* offers us exactly the opposite.

5. *Study*

1) The Title

The title is probably not from the hand of the redactor himself; so we did not include this in the apparatus. Only *Irl*[1] and *DG* include one; we note that both begin with the word *deprecatio,* a term that is found at the end of the celebrated passage on the *Kyrie* in Gregory the Great's letter (598) to John of Syracuse:[63] 'ut in his *deprecationis* vocibus paulo diutius occupemur'. With Capelle[64] one might wonder if *deprecatio* is considered as a technical term.

2) The Response in the First Part

This seemingly banal point is in fact crucial for the rest of our study and for the history of the *Kyrie.* Without even questioning the response of the Gallican tradition, Dom Capelle has taken up the *Kyrie eleison* of manuscript *A,* which he wrongly considered to be superior. In his edition, he places it between brackets, and points out in a footnote that this response exists only in the Angelica manuscript. Without explanation, he links the *Kyrie* to the *DG,* to the point of identifying the one with the other and assuming the *DG* wherever the sources say only *Kyrie eleison.* In this passage he may have done it unconsciously. In any case, he does not make any specific reference to it, which may explain all the criticism it has received. What can we say about it?

- Manuscript *A* gives the response *Kyrie eleison;*
- the other three manuscripts include invitation a/, omitted by *A,* which usually introduces the response[65] which would be *Domine exaudi et miserere;*
- *B* and *C* do not have a response after the invitatories; which could explain why Capelle, basing himself on *B,* has taken the response from *A;*
- *D* follows each [invitatory] with *Domine miserere et miserere;*
- we find *Domine miserere* in *B* after c/ and d/
in *C* after c/ (it omits d/)

62 Callewaert (1942), 20–45, emphasises (p. 27) that the end of the 5th century was the period of the full flowering of antiphonal chant and that the influence of the chant *schola* was apparent in the organisation of the liturgy. He also suggests that this attributive invitation was reserved to the *clerici* of the *schola,* after the deacon had chanted the first phrase of the invitatory, while the response was taken up by the people. Willis (1964), 21–24, repeated this hypothesis; in his edition, the section for the *schola* is printed in italics. The only certain thing is that this 'attribution' is found only in *DG.*

63 PL 77, 956; or MGH, *Epist.,* vol. 2, 1899. Cf. infra, p. 314.

64 Capelle (1934), 133.

65 Cf. pp. 168–70, concerning *Irl*[1].

in *D* after d/ and also after a/,

while the leader has just proposed the double response. Is it a curious fact or simply coincidence that the same succession is found in the Stowe Missal (*Irl*[1] *S*)?

The conclusion is clear; as we have already stated with regard to *Irl*[1] a/, the response would originally have been *Domine exaude et miserere*, traces of which are still to be found in Irl[1]; this will be shortened to the *Domine miserere* that we find in *M*[1] and *FG*[1]. We believe that the redactor of *DG* has, undoubtedly out of respect for the ancient text, taken up the old and long response. Here are two proofs of this: the invitation a/, taken up in d/; and the defective expression *Domine miserere et miserere* in manuscript *D*, relic of the double phrase.[66] Subsequent users of the *DG* will be content to use the short response, as testified by *BCD* in the places we have already indicated above. In our own edition we have re-established, with the appropriate indications, the response that we consider to be original.

Whatever the situation, it is patently clear from our current documentation that the *Kyrie eleison* is not linked intrinsically to the *DG*. This constitutes a major step forward. To read canon 3 of the Council of Vaison as replacing — as Capelle does — *Kyrie eleison* by the *DG* thus constitutes a poor methodology. We will shortly draw out the consequences.[67]

3) Commentary, Eastern and Western Parallels

a/ is Eastern (cf. p. 138); the wording of *D* is found literally in *Irl*[1] *S*. This invitation is omitted by *A* which commences *ex abrupto* with *Kyrie eleison*, as does *FG*[2].

b/ is written in a style that we have not found in the preceding texts; this literary quality characterizes the entire *DG*, the work of a refined redactor. There is no Greek parallel. The reading of *A* is a later watering down; it has not taken up the theological subtleties of the original which testify to a sophisticated religious culture.

The reading *domini* is in all three manuscripts; even apart from this decisive argument, it would be preferable to the *Deum* of the editors, a term that already features in Christological attributes. Such an expression reflects the trinitarian controversies of the 4th century and would have dated from the end of the century, after the Council of Constantinople (381).

The 'description' *fidelibus (devotis A) animis* is the equivalent of the traditional *ex toto corde...*, omitted by the *DG*.

---

66 The original of *D* would have had the correct reading, *Domine exaudi et miserere*. Perhaps the copyist of *D* (or of a related manuscript), swept along by the simple response he was accustomed to chanting, wrote *Domine miserere* and then, continuing to follow the manuscript he was copying, added *et miserere*.

67 On the response in the second part, compare with what we have said about *Irl*[1].

I As in the principal tradition (*Irl*^{1} II, *M*^{1} I) the invitatory for the Church comes at the beginning. According to Dom Capelle, the replacement of *sancta* by *immaculata* arose from the concerns of Gelasius who always put the 'immaculate' Church in opposition to the 'defilement' with which heresy attempted to dishonour her.[68] The Milanese tradition is more banale; it includes *catholica*. 'Ecclesia Dei vivi' = 1 Tim 3:15.

Sacerdotibus ac ministris is a poor reading; it has its place in II — perhaps the copyist has skipped a line. As Meyer wrote (p. 103), the phrase *per totum orbem constituta* from *A* would be preferable, since it is more traditional and offers a trispondaic ending, favoured by Gelasius (cf. supra, literary form). The term *constituta* has no doubt been chosen for purposes of rhythm. This word does not necessarily carry the strong sense of 'constituted' or 'established'; in later periods we frequently find it with the weak meaning of 'being' or 'finding' in a number of places.[69]

II This invitatory brings together all the orders to which all Christian peoples are joined in a rather universalist way (*Irl*^{1} VII and IX; *M*^{1} VII)

Magnus Deus = Tit 2:13. This is the first time that we find *sancta* describing the clergy; although this had to be one of Gelasius' concerns, since his instruction in the *Liber pontificalis* uses it twice.[70]

The doublet *sacerdotibus et ministris* has already appeared in *M*^{1} II; the Milanese tradition of *DG* has taken it up and given *sacri altaris* as its ending, which probably reveals a secondary liturgical concern. As with *M1* II, *sacerdos* here refers to the bishop, a fact confirmed by the use of this word in invitatory XIV; *minister* probably describes all the other ministers of the Church.

Manuscript *A* interpolates four invitatories between I and II, as also occurs in *M*^{2}; the ending of the second of these, for the emperor, is inspired by V. It is clear that manuscript *A* has adapted the ancient formulary of the *DG* to the Milanese liturgy.

III = ὑπὲρ πάσης ἐπισκοπῆς τῆς ὀρθοτομούσης τὸν λόγον τῆς ἀληθείας CAp VIII 12, 40, a quotation of 2 Tim 2:15 that is often found in the Eastern litanies, cf. CAp VIII 10, 6: *J* 55; *M* 130; the Ethiopian liturgy, Br 207, 1, 1–2; *Testamentum Domini*, (Rahmani edition, p. 85). In the West, the Gallican *DG* is the only one to include this prayer.

The attributive invitation at the end of the invitatory is an adaptation of it. Meyer (p. 104) does not consider this as an 'attribution' but as the object of the prayer. Because the petition seeks 'the multifaceted wisdom of the Word of God' for bearers of the Word, he writes, then we must be talking about theological scholars. But the parallelism with the ending of the other invitatories clearly

68 Capelle (1934), 131; As proof of this, he includes three quotations from Pope Gelasius.

69 Cf. Thesaurus, vol. 4, 523–24.

70 LP, vol. 1, 255; 'Hic … et clerum ampliavit… Sub huius episcopatu clerus crevit'.

indicates that the wisdom referred to here is a divine attribute and not the object of the petition. Meyer's argument is rendered null and void.

But who are the beneficiaries of this petition? In the East it is the episcopy, charged with ministry of the Word, and is named explicitly. Here it is less clear. Should we see in it a kind of doublet of II, or is it about theologians (as Meyer thinks), or missionaries?

IV This is probably an allusion to Mt 19:12: 'et sunt eunuchi qui se ipsos castraverunt propter regnum caelorum' ('and there are eunuchs who have made themselves so for the sake of the kingdom of heaven'), softened and adapted for those who in the same way master their spirit.

Cf. ὑπὲρ εὐνούχων ὁσίως πορευομένων δεηθῶμεν, ὑπὲρ τῶν ἐν ἐγκρατείᾳ καὶ εὐλαβείᾳ CAp VIII 10, 11; ὑπὲρ τῶν ἐν παρθενίᾳ καὶ ἁγνείᾳ καὶ ἀσκήσει *J* 46.
We think particularly of the monks. IV does not feature in *A*. The wording *spirituali* of *D* is to be preferred, given the repetition of *spiritalium* in the following line. Cf. also X.

V Prayer for the authorities. This is the first time that the adjective *religiosus* occurs, and above all, the term *princeps*. It is not a matter of the leading ecclesiastics, as might be thought at first reading; the rest of the invitatory makes this quite clear. The word *princeps* is perhaps in reference to the time of Gelasius, where they could no longer pray for the *imperator*, who had been gone from the scene for twenty or so years. We could imagine that the pope of Rome would have had qualms about failing to name the new *reges*. It is perhaps useful to recall that it was Pope Gelasius who, in his letter to the emperor Anastasius, set out the doctrine known as the 'two powers'.

All the Latin litanies use the word *exercitus*; *DG* uses *militia*; Meyer (p 89) considers that here this term describes the senior functionaries; the rest of the text seems to validate this. This meaning, he says, is well suited to the time of Pope Gelasius.
Dom Capelle has preferred the reading of *A* 2: 'qui iustitiam et rectum iudicium diligunt'.

VI Here manuscript *A* is clearly better; *pro iocunditate et serenitate pluviae* fails to offer any satisfactory meaning, while *pro iocunditate serenitatis et opportunitate pluviae* is easily translated: 'for the pleasantness of clear skies and timely rain'. The wording of the Gallican manuscripts probably results from a 'jump from the same to the same' owing to three nouns in a row ending in *-itate*(*-is*).

We can perhaps recognise in this invitatory a free translation from the Greek parallels (CAp VIII, 12, 48; *J* 47; B 363).
Aura means light breath or gentle breeze; its translation by *vitalis* is classic; 'vivit et aetherias vitales suscipit auras' writes Lucretius (*De rerum natura* 3, 406), and Virgil favoured 'auras vitales carpere'.
The reading *temporum* of *A*, in the sense of 'seasons', is better than the *operum* of the Gallican tradition; so, do we put this latter in square brackets, just as at the beginning of the invitatory? The attribution *rector mundi* is well suited.

VII — The prayer for catechumens in found in the West only in *OS* V and *Irl*^{1} IX; manuscript *A* makes no mention of them. Here it is written in an idiosyncratic way, with an archaic flavour; note, for example, the consciousness of the Christian 'name'. The wording *desiderio* must be a corruption; the normal use of the verb *accendere* does not allow for the translation 'inflamed by the desire of grace'.

VIII — This petition for those who have spiritual difficulties is missing from *A*. The wording *humanae fragilitatis infirmatias* of *D* seems better than the *humanae infirmatiatis fragilitas* of *BC*. Indeed

- the *Veronense* uses *humana fragilitas* six times, while *humana infirmitas* features but a single time;[71]

- *humanae fragilitatis infirmitas* is found explicitly in an Hispanic *Inlatio* and in the *Missale mixtum*,[72] while a Gallican *Expositio symboli* speaks of *fragilitatis infirmitas*.[73]

The second *quos* serves no purpose since the verb is the same; perhaps it owes its presence (in all the manuscripts) to reasons of rhythm. Thanks to this *quos* the invitatory contains, after *pro his*, three clauses of four words each, just as the following two contain three clauses of three words; the editing has been done with great care!

Horror, which is found in all the manuscripts, offers little satisfactory meaning; Thomasius has proposed the correction *error*, an amendment appreciated by Meyer and taken up by Capelle. We will fall in line behind these masters.

This invitatory seems to us better placed on the spiritual rather than the corporal level; we therefore doubt the parallels of *M*^{1} IX and *FG*^{1} VIII suggested by the German philosopher and by the liturgist of Leuven.

IX — As Meyer observes (pp. 105–06), *DG* combines in IX what had been the subject of different petitions in the preceding litanies (*Irl*^{1} VIII; *M*^{1} VIII–IX). Do the *impietas* (or the *oppression A*) of an unjust power and the misery caused by enemies reflect the Roman situation after the fall of the Empire?

X — *DG* pick ups in this invitatory, omitted by *A*, the litiques VII–VIII and IX of *OS*, which must have been known by its redactor. The Jews are only mentioned here and in *OS* VIII, and never in the East. The heretics are named in *OS* VII (where the formulation is very similar: 'respice ad animas diabolica fraude *deceptas*, ut omni *heretica pravitate* deposita … ad *veritatis* tuae redeant firmitatem') and in the *Missale Gothicum* VIII (*hereticus et infidelis*, cf. p. 220). The superstitious pagans are named in *OS* IX, while *M1* IV prays more positively for the call to the nations. It is clear that the redactor must have been familiar with the *OS*.

---

71 Bruylants (1948), 227–28 and 280.

72 *Liber mozarabicus sacramentorum*, ed. Ferotin, no. 59 (c 31); *Missale mixtum*, PL 85, 855A. Cf. Manz (1941), no. 478.

73 *Bobbio Missal*, ed. Lowe, no. 185 (p. 57).

Must we see here allusions to the events that marked the pontificate of Gelasius, and read into the prayer for the heretics all the controversy with Acacius on the interpretation of Chalcedon, and in the petition for the pagans, the energetic interventions of the pope against the Lupercales?[74]
Given the ternary structure of the invitatory, Capelle supposes that a participle has been omitted after *falsitate,* which would provide symmetry with *deceptis* and *perfusis*. It is not therefore a question about a prayer for the Jews, but only for the victims of Jewish unbelief.[75] The adjectives *iudaica* and *heretica* make us prefer *gentili* to the genitive *gentilium* of *D*; cf. *spirituali* in IV.

XI The same petition for those who give alms is found, although differently formulated, in *Irl*^{1} X and *M*^{1} X. It comes from the East and is missing in *A*.

XII = ὑπὲρ τοῦ ἁγίου οἴκου τούτου καὶ τῶν μετὰ πίστεως εὐλαβείας καὶ φόβου θεοῦ εἰσιόντων ἐν αὐτῷ of B 363, freely translated, as is the custom with our redactor. *A* omits this item and includes instead that of *M*^{2} V. Together with *Irl*^{2} VI, it is the only prayer for the assembly that we have come across. *B* omits the *qui,* introducing the relative clause, but *C* (generally very similar to *B*) includes it. *D* replaces *intrantibus* with *qui,* thus making the whole invocation a relative clause, an error without doubt. Froben (PL) rectifies this by replacing *convenerunt* with *convenienter.*

XIII = ὑπὲρ ἀφέσεως τῶν ἁμαρτιῶν καὶ συγχωρήσεως πλημμελημάτων ἡμῶν ... *J* 34; συγγνώμην καὶ ἄφεσιν τῶν ἁμαρτιῶν καὶ τῶν πλημμελημάτων ἡμῶν ... αἰτησώμεθα *J* 39; cf. CAp VIII 12, 47; B 373 and 381; *M* 130 and 138. Pardon for sinners is here sought for the first time; it appears in a form close to *FG*^{1} X, *FG*^{2} VIII and *Irl*^{2} VIII. All three have the noun *emendatio,* while *DG* uses *emundatio*. This cannot be a coincidence!

A's reading of *et* omnium *venia peccatorum* is better with regard to both meaning and rhythm. Meyer has already made this observation (p. 101). Capelle follows him and we do likewise.

XIV = ὑπὲρ ... ἀναπαύσεως τῶν προκεκοιμημένων πατέρων τε καὶ ἀδελφῶν *J* 47; cf. B 373; *M* 120 and 128. This is the first time that we encounter this petition for the dead, missing from *OS, Irl*^{1} and *M*^{1}. *Refrigerium* is undoubtedly archaic, or purposely made so. *A* has replaced it with *requies,* which is used also in *Irl*^{2} VIII and *FG*^{1} X. The second part of the invitatory is original. In a 'Liturgy Bulletin', E. Bishop has demonstrated, in a long footnote, that the expression 'sacerdotes qui huic ecclesiae praefuerunt catholicae' corresponds with the manner in which the papal chancellery described the Church of Rome between 466 and 540.[76] For Meyer too (p. 107) the expression can only be describing the popes. L. Duchesne has contested this.[77] According to him, this description is not reserved to Rome, and the adjective *catholicus* is used in a particularly polemical

74 Cf. the notes of the editor in Pomares (1959), 20–51.
75 Willis (1964), 24, n. 1.
76 E. Bishop (1911), 408–09.
77 Duchesne (1925), 211, n. 2.

sense, in opposition to those who oppose heterodoxy. According to Bishop, however, the overall style of the *DG* clearly confirms its Roman origin.[78]

The abbot of Mont César took up the assertions of the English liturgist and has extended them.[79] Recently, Dom H. Marot has taken even further the study of the episcopal vocabulary of the 5th to the 7th centuries and confirms Bishop's views in a very scholarly note.[80] We agree with this, adding as proof that manuscript *A* most likely omitted *catholicae* in order to be able to adapt the invitatory to the Church of Milan.

XV The second part begins here. It is omitted entirely by *A*. Among the Latin texts, only *Irl*^{1} includes this second part, although it occurs frequently in the Eastern models (CAp VIII 36 and 38; *J* 39; B 381).

Mortificatam vitiis carnem is a doublet with IV. The subject is equivalent to *Irl*^{1} XIV. As for the response, *praesta, Domine, praesta,* we can refer to what I have said about *Irl*^{1}.

XVI *Castium timorem* is perhaps taken from CAp VIII 6, 5: ἐγκαταφυτεύσῃ ἐν αὐτοῖς τὸν ἁγνὸν αὐτοῦ καὶ σωτήριον φόβον. *Veram dilectionem* may be compared with *Irl*^{1} XIII (*vinculum caritatis*).

XVII *Gratum vitae ordinem* is perhaps inspired by CAp VIII 12, 42; ὅπως ἐν ἡσυχίᾳ καὶ ὁμονοίᾳ διάγοντες τὸν πάντα χρόνον τῆς ζωῆς ἡμῶν... Or from *J* 39: Τὸν ὑπόλοιπον χρόνον τῆς ζωῆς ἡμῶν ἐν εἰρήνῃ καὶ ὑγιείᾳ ἐκτελέσαι. The second part of this invocation takes up the petition Χριστιανὰ τὰ τέλη τῆς ζωῆς ἡμῶν ἀνώδυνα ἀνεπαίσχυντα ... αἰτησώμεθα *J* 39, B 382; cf. CAp VIII 6, 8; 36, 2; 38, 2.

XVIII The angel of peace is mentioned in the West only in the *DG*, but it is a traditional theme in the East; we find it in CAp VIII 36, 3 (see note 3 of Funk, p. 545), in *J* 39, B 381. John Chrysostom was certainly familiar with it (Br 471, 1. 27; 478, 1. 38–39).

Solacia sanctorum might be an abridgment of Irl^1 XI, traditional in the East.

c/ Commendation of those praying is classic in the East: Τῆς παναγίας ... ἑαυτοὺς καὶ ἀλλήλους καὶ πᾶσαν τὴν ζωὴν ἡμῶν Χριστῷ τῷ θεῷ παραθώμεθα *J* 40, B 363. Here, however, it is developed in a typically Latin sentence; we entrust ourselves to God the creator and his providence.

Finally, it should be noted that *DG* does not include the traditional petitions for the *altissima pace*, for the city (or the locality) and its inhabitants (cf. however *A* 5, the Milanese petition that is found in *M*^{1} V and *M*^{2} V), nor for *omnibus qui in sublimitate sunt* (*Irl*^{1} VI, and *M*^{1} V according to *T7*), nor for the ancient orders. It gathers together in (VIII and) IX the ancient list of the needy.

---

78 E. Bishop, *Kyrie*, (1918), 124, n. 2.
79 Capelle (1939), 139–40.
80 See *Note sur l'expression: 'Episcopus Ecclesiae Catholicae'* following Marot (1965), 59–98.

Conclusion

This exploration convinces us that *DG* belongs to the second wave of texts. It is not one of the earliest translations of the Greek formularies, but a recasting in the highest quality Latin of materials which, for the most part at least, were already in circulation in Latin.

Indeed, the numerous redactional retouches indicate a later period: *inmaculata* in place of *sancta*, and the addition of *vivi* in I; the adjective *sanctus* to describe priests in II; the whole of invitatory V, with *religiosis principibus* and especially *militia* to describe not the army but the senior Church functionaries; XIII being absent in the ancient formularies (*Irl*[1], *M*[1]) but present in the more recent (*FG*[1], *FG*[2], *Irl*[2]); XIV making use of a papal chancellery formula that was used between 466 and 540.

To this are added later elements such as the attributive invitation at the ending of each invitatory, the subject of IV, and invitation b/, which, despite being a formulation that could date from the end of the 4th century, cannot be an early element of the *oratio fidelium*.

On the other hand, *DG* contains more than a few seemingly ancient elements: a/ with its double response; III for those who preach the Word; VII for catechumens; the intercession for victims of the Jews in X; the term *refrigerium* in XIV. To these we add the fact that *DG* is comprised of two parts as in the East (as evidenced by CAp), and in *Irl*[1].

As it is easier to explain the survival of ancient elements in a more recent time than the presence of later elements in earlier times, we think that the former are to be considered as archaisms close to the heart of the redactor, one of those Romans who is probably rather nostalgic for the grandeur of yesteryear.

4) Attribution

Does this mean that we attribute the piece to Pope Gelasius (492–496)? We see no reason to doubt it.

The arguments are as follows:

- the title (absent from *A*) explicitly mentions Gelasius and suggests, by using the verb *constituit*, that the use of this text was ordered by a *Constitutio*; this reinforces the idea that it indeed is the work of a pope;
- Invitatory XIV uses a formula of the papal chancellery between 466 and 540;
- the very careful way in which the piece has been assembled agrees with what the *Liber pontificalis* reveals to us with regard to the language of this pontiff (cf. supra, literary form); and most of all, the use (four times) of the trispondaic endings which are rare but known to be favoured by Gelasius (cf. literary form, above);

– to which we can add a series of expressions in the *DG* that are also found in the works of Gelasius; Dom Capelle cites an entire page of examples.[81]

This attribution, made independently by Bishop and Meyer, has never been called into question.[82] Dom Botte also subscribes to it. We have not discovered any new indication in favour of Gelasius himself, but in studying all the litanies and comparing them, we have seen that from the second half of the 5th century onwards the ancient texts were revised so that the Latin flowed more naturally and did not appear so much as a translation. *DG* fits perfectly into this movement, whereby Gelasius' masterpiece finds its *Sitz im Leben*.

5) Sources

What sources did Gelasius use? Among the Western texts, he would have been familiar with the *OS*; its mention of the Jews in X and the concentration into a single invitatory of litiques VII–VIII (inverted) and IX of the *OS* persuades us of this. Did he have *Irl*[1] at hand? The division of *DG* into two parts and the invitation a/ with its double response could make us believe this to be the case, but no such convincing is needed, since these elements are taken directly from the East. He might have been familiar with *M*[1], with which *DG* has several elements in common — as well as the petition for good weather (VI) which is absent in *Irl*[1], that for benefactors (XI) and the formula *sacerdotibus et ministris* (I and II).

Did Gelasius make use of the Greek sources or did he only reshape the Latin models? The question leaves us perplexed. Dom Capelle has not attempted to answer it. The single invitatory translated from the Greek and not attested by the Latin litanies is III, for those who preach the Word.

But the analysis of *FG*[1] and *M*[2] leads us to assume the existence of Latin sources *Q* and *Y* that are no longer extant; and so we are unable to answer the question we have asked, since it is possible that one and/or the other source included this prayer. We might add that given the animosity that Gelasius shows towards the East in the case of the schism of Acacius, it is unlikely that he made any great attempts to locate the Greek originals. It is much more likely that he would be happy to present in refined language a set of traditional petitions, already present in the Latin liturgy for around a century. In any case, it seems certain to us that it was not Gelasius who introduced the litany genre into the

81 Capelle (1934), 131–32.

82 Only Gamber (1966), 1966, 123, states that the *DG* clearly has nothing to do with Gelasius. We await his arguments. He considers it (not without basis it must be said) as a later form ('Spätform') of *Irl*[1]. He repeats these two assertions in a subsequent article, (1967), 214–21; he considers that both *DG* and *Irl*[1] represent 'late forms of the Gallican "Deprecatio" after the Gospel' which is confirmed, in his eyes, by the typically Gallican response *Domine exaudi et miserere* used in place of *Kyrie eleison* (p. 218).

West. *Irl*[1] and *M*[1] are certainly older; and if one or the other (or both) of these litanies is Roman, which is quite possible, then the *DG* would not be the first Roman litany.

6) Use of the DG

For what purpose did Gelasius compose this prayer? The three Gallican manuscripts present it to us as a private work, in the 'books of prayers' for pious persons. This was not its original destination.

Both the title and the content of *DG* confirm to us that it was indeed, initially at least, a formulation of the *oratio fidelium*. The relationship of ideas between the Greek and Latin litanies leaves no doubt about the matter. And the title explicitly affirms that 'Pope Gelasius ordered (by Constitution) the singing of this "deprecation" for the universal Church'. E. Bishop is mistaken when he holds as fiction that Gelasius prescribed the use of this litany *by* the universal Church;[83] *pro* never introduces a possessive clause! Dom Capelle has since rectified this blunder.[84]

But, we might ask ourselves, was the Church of Rome familiar with an *oratio fidelium* during the period of this pope (492–496)? Indeed all the manuals indicate that the last trace of it is provided by Gelasius' predecessor, Felix III (483–492). In this the authors commit two errors.

The first mistake is almost implicit. Reading the expression *oratio fidelium* in a letter by this pontiff, they more or less unconsciously projected onto it the *OS* of which Prosper of Aquitaine has spoken some thirty years earlier. This error is understandable since the *OS* was the only Roman formulation with which the liturgists were familiar. On the basis of our study, we can say this could well have referred to *M*[1], or one of the sources whose existence must assume, or even *Irl*[1]. The *OS* did not exercise a monopoly; they were competing amidst diverse litanies.

The second error is more serious, and results from too rapid a reading of the passage by Felix III dealing with the discipline to be followed toward rebaptised clerics:

> 'Sed quia idem Dominus atque salvator clementissimus est, et neminem vult perire, usque ad exitus sui diem, in paenitentia (si resipiscunt) iacere conveniet; nec orationi non modo fidelium sed ne catechumenorum omnimodis interesse'.[85]

83 E. Bishop (1911), 410.

84 Capelle (1934), 132.

85 Felix III, Epistola 7, (PL 58), 925: 'But since the same Lord and Saviour is most merciful and wills that no one should perish, it is fitting that, until the day of his death, they should remain as penitents (if they repent); nor may they take part in the prayer not only of the faithful but also of catechumens in any way'. Eng. tr by J.O'Brien.

We showed in Part One that all this discipline was based on the decisions of Councils in the East. It is with this in mind that we have to situate the passage in order to make a correct interpretation. In light of this it would appear that *oratio fidelium* does not here refer to the rite of the Universal Prayer, as opposed to an *oratio catechumenorum*; rather, these two expressions refer to the two parts of the Mass: the Liturgy of the Word (or 'Mass of the catechumens') and Liturgy of the Eucharist (or 'Mass of the faithful'), and more precisely yet, to the category of persons who are entitled to pray each part. The clerics in question may not pray with the faithful, nor even with the catechumens, says Felix III. This means that they are excluded from the Eucharist, a fact confirmed by the following passage:

> 'quibus communio laica tantum in morte reddenda est'.[86]

So nothing prevents us from supposing that Gelasius composed his *Deprecatio* to serve as a Universal Prayer, along with the *OS* and any other Latin litanies already in use.

II. The Gallican 'Dicamus Omnes' (*FG¹*)

Dom Capelle has edited this text[87] on the basis of two sources (Rome, Bibl. Vallicellana D 5, one of the manuscripts from OR 50, already published in Thomasius-Vezzosi, vol. 5, p. 113; and Vienna, Nationalbibl. lat. 1888). Our own research has led us to uncover numerous other examples of *FG¹*; indeed this formulary has been repeated in the Rogations of OR 50 and is also found in a similar place in many Processionals and sometimes even in the Graduals of the Middle Ages. The list that we provide here, despite its length, is far from being exhaustive.[88]

A. The Sources

The sources are divided into three families, a division we will justify below. We will use the same letter for identical or quasi-identical sources, but will distinguish them by means of a superscript number. An asterisk indicates that the letter refers to a group of manuscripts.

86 Felix III, Letter 7, (PL 58), 925: Communion of the laity may be given to these [clerics] only at the moment of death'. Eng. tr by J.O'Brien. On this matter, cf. Part One, Section III above.

87 Capelle (1934), 120–22, with the acronym GA.

88 The expression *Dicamus omnes*, that opens this litany, was very popular and served as the incipit for various formularies (*Irl¹*, *DG*, *FG¹*, *M²*). The Spanish liturgical books also offer many fragments of litanies introduced by *Dicamus omnes*; we can find a list of them in Ferotin, *Liber ordinum*, Tables, p. 634. But just reading the incipit does not allow us to know which piece is which, leading to a good deal of confusion about the litanies. For this reason, in his notes on the Ordinal de St.-Vedast (vol. 1, 68), Dom Brou confuses *FG¹* with *DG*.

a) The Pure Family (α)

A = all the manuscripts from OR 50 (apart from *Z*: Vienna 1817), which we have taken from the critical edition provided by Andrieu, vol. 5, p. 310; we have disregarded the variants which are minor in nature. Manuscript *D5* of the Vallicellana cited by Capelle is one of this family. OR 50 was compiled at Mayence around the year 950.

B = VIENNA, Nationalbibl. lat. 1888 (late 10th c.), f. 110r. Rituel de Saint-Alban de Mayence; ed. Gerbert (1779), 89, reproduced in PL 138, 1085–6; description of the manuscript can be found in Andrieu, OR, vol. 1, 404–19.
(Bourque 475 — Gamber 1580)

C = AUTUN, Bibl. Mun. S 12 (12th c.), f. 89r-v.
Gradual from the north of France.

D = BRUSSELS, Bibl. Royale, 4836 (Cat 641) (14th c.), f. 6v–8v.
Processional of unknown provenance but used probably by the Augustinians.[89]

D' = ARRAS, Bibl. Mun. 230 (years 1307–8), f. 42r–43.
= Ordinal of St.-Vedast of Arras, ed. Brou (1957), 194.

W = a manuscript from the abbey of Werden (on the Ruhr), transcribed by Martène (1788), vol. 3, 185.

We must add the manuscript of ASCHAFFENBOURG, Hofbibl. MS 43, a 14th c. Processional from the collegiate church of Sts Peter and Alexander of Aschaffenbourg (diocese of Mayence).[90] As all we know about this formulary is the order of the petitions, we will not include it in our edition; it is very similar to *A* and *W*.

b) The 'quia' Family (β)

E = three manuscripts from Saint-Martial of Limoges:[91] PARIS, B.N. lat. 909 (11th c.), f. 8r-v among the various pieces before the Tropary;
ibid. 1120 and 1121 (first third 11th c), f. 171r-v and 163r-v respectively (identical text), Processionals.

F = PARIS, B.N. lat. 903 (beginning 11th c.), f. 136r. Gradual of Saint-Yrieix (diocese of Limoges).

G = AUTUN, Bibl. Mun. S 183 (13th c.), f. 56r-v. Processional of Saint-Martin of Autun.

---

89 As with *FG¹* and *FG²*, this manuscript is almost identical to *D'*, from Arras. It is therefore probable that it came from this region.

90 This information was sent to us by M. Huglo, whom we thank warmly; He points out that a similar text appears in the more recent Processionals of the Stiftsbibl. Perg. 32, 33, 34 and 36, of the same origin.

91 On the Saint-Martial manuscripts you can read a good article by Stäblein (1963), 1262–72.

**G'* = AUTUN, Bibl. Mun. S 98 and S 188 (identical text) (16th and 15th c.), f. 63–67 and 96–98^{v} respectively. Processionals of Autun.

H = CAMBRAI. Bibl. Mun. 78 (late 11th c.), f. 42. Processional of the cathedral of Cambrai.

**H'* = CAMBRAI, Bibl. Mun.: 6 identical texts, all from Cambrai:
60, f. 102^{v}, 12th c., Gradual;
68, f. 44–46^{v}, Processional (then Antiphonary) of the cathedral, 15th–16th c.;
71, f. 145, 15th c. Processional of the cathedral, 15th c.;
77, f. 79, 13th–14th c. Processional of the cathedral, 13th–14th c.;
80, f. 43, Processional of 1755;
131, f. 53^{v}, Processional of the cathedral from the beginning of the 14th c.

N = MADRID, B.N. 136 (14th c.), f. 51^{v}–52^{v}. Processional of Saint-Saturnin of Toulouse.

S = *Variae preces*, Solesmes, 1896, 257–58, without indication of source.

c) The Mixed Family (γ)

I = BESANÇON, Bibl. Mun. 119, f. 142–45. Processional of Besançon, dating from 1704.

I' = PARIS, Bibl. Mazarine 541, f. 57. Processional of Châlons-sur-Marne, dating from 1544.

**J* = LANGRES, Grand Séminaire 312, f. 139. Missal of South-West of France, early 13th c.
LONDRES, Brit. Mus. Harleian 4951, f. 233^{v}–234. Gradual of Toulouse, 11th c.
PARIS, B.N. lat. 776, f. 83^{v}–84. Gradual of Saint-Michel-de-Gaillac (sur le Tarn), 11th c.

J' = PARIS, B.N. nv. acq. lat. 3001, f. 26^{r}–27. Monastic Processional from South-West of France (13th c.)[92]

M MADRID, Acad. de la Hist. 45, f. 54^{v}–55^{r}. Spanish Gradual, perhaps from San-Millan de la Cogolla, early 12th c.

M' MADRID, Acad. de la Hist. 51, f. 147^{v}–148^{r}. Gradual of San-Millan de la Cogolla, 11th–12th c.[93]

---

92 The origin of this manuscript is not indicated in the catalogues. But these *preces* are identical to those of B.N. lat. 776, of Saint-Michel-de-Gaillac; moreover, these two manuscripts have all their *preces* in the same order, which is rare indeed. Perhaps MS 3001 originates in the same abbey, a hypothesis that could be confirmed by comparing other parts of these two manuscripts.

93 We have found only two items in *FG*^{2} that *FG*^{1} does not include; they concern the manuscript PARIS, B.N. lat 780, Gradual of Narbonne, 11th–12th c., and the *Processionale turonense*, of Tours, 1827. In his book, *Les Tonaires*, Paris, 1971, M. Huglo carries out a classification of Aquitaine tonaries. On the basis of the schematic formulas and the antiphon-types of each tone, he distinguishes a Toulouse group and a Limousin group. Our classification of litanies found in the Aquitaine manuscripts corroborates that of Huglo, since the manuscripts of family β (Paris, B.N. lat. 909 and 1121) belong to the Limousin group, while those of the family γ (Paris, B.N. lat. 776 and London, Brit. Mus. Harl. 4951) are originally from the region of Toulouse. The same goes for *FG*^{2}, 214–15.

B. Edited Versions

We have put this heading in the plural as it seems to us beneficial to furnish several editions of the text. The first will be based on all the sources cited and will endeavour to come as close as possible to the original text.

The other three will present each of the three identified families. The characteristics of each group, as well as the varying order of the invocations, will appear more clearly in this way, and will also make it easier in the future to classify new items in one of the three families (or in still others) eventually. And a final advantage is that the local peculiarities of the liturgy are better respected, thus laying the foundation for a history of the liturgy by region.[94]

General Edition

This is based on the thirty examples studied. We will place between square brackets [] the invocations that seem to us not to be original. We prefer not to exclude them from the apparatus so that the reader (and the manuscript researcher) can see at a glance the petitions that *FG*[1] sometimes contains and to know our opinion of them.

a/ Dicamus omnes: Domine miserere[95]

b/ Ex toto corde et ex tota mente oramus[96] te
Domine miserere[97]

I[98] Pro altissima pace[99] et benigna constitutione invocamus[100] te
Domine miserere

II Pro sancta[101] ecclesia catholica quae est in toto orbe diffusa[102] supplicamus[103] te
Domine miserere[104]

94 Among the sources of *FG*[1] many are notated; we will find melodies printed in the *Variae preces* of Solesmes (*S*) and also in Gastoue (1937), 170, or in Gastoue (1904), 70.

95 Chorus repeats: Domine miserere *add S*. Domine *add M'*.

96 oramus *ABDD'W*. deprecamus β. invocamus *CII'*. imploramus *JJ'MM'*.

97 Domine miserere *om W*.

98 I *om* α. pro perpetua pace et benigna constitutione rogamus te *CDD' post* II.

99 pace *om N*.

100 invocamus β *JJ'MM'*. deprecamur *II'*.

101 sancta *om C*.

102 diffusa α *HH'*. constituta β (*praeter HH'*) γ.

103 supplicamus *ABW*. obsecramus *CDD'*. invocamus *E*. deprecamur *FNM*. adoramus *HH'*. oramus *GG'S* γ (*praeter M*).

104 Domine miserere] Dicamus omnes *DD' alternatim cum* Domine miserere.

III[105] Pro pastore nostro et omni clero[106] eius[107] imploramus[108] te[109]
Domine miserere

[IV[110] Pro abbate[111] nostro et omni congregatione eius[112] flagitamus[113] te
Domine miserere]

V[114] Pro rege[115] nostro et omni[116] exercitu eius[117] obsecramus[118] te[119]
Domine miserere

[VI[120] Pro loco nostro et omnibus habitantibus in eo[121] deprecamur[122] te
Domine miserere]

VII[123] Pro aeris temperie et fecunditate terrae precamur te[124]
Domine miserere

VIII[125] Pro his qui infirmantur ac[126] diversis languoribus detinentur exoramus te[127]
Domine miserere

---

105 III *om SJJ'*. III *post* V *CDD'G'HH'* γ (*praeter JJ'*).
106 clero] congregatione *CFMM'*.
107 eius] suo *G'*.
108 imploramus *ABWII'*. rogamus *C*. precamur *DD'*. deposcimus *MM'*.
109 imploramus te] quia potens es β (*praeter HH'*). quia magnus es *HH'*.
110 IV *add* α (*praeter AW*)*NJJ'*. *AW habent* pro pontifice (antistite *W*) nostro et grege sibi commisso flagitamus (obsecramus *W*) te. *Hoc ponit W post* V.
111 abbate] doctore *N*.
112 omni congregatione eius *NJJ'*. grege sibi commisso *B*. omni clero eius *C*. omni congregatione nostra *DD'*.
113 flagitamus *A*. obsecramus *BW*. precamur *D*. exoramus *DD'*. deposcimus *NJ*. deprecamur *J'*.
114 V *om* B. *et S qui add* pro pace regum et quiete populorum quia magnus es. V *post* II *CDD'G'HH'*γ.
115 rege] imperatore *AI*.
116 et omni] et pro omni *D'*.
117 exercitu eius] populo christiano *FN*. exercitu christiano *M*. exercitu christianorum *M'*.
118 obsecramus *A*. supplicamus *DD'*. flagitamus *W*. deprecamur *JM'*. deposcimus *J'*. rogamus II'. oramus *M*.
119 obsecramus te] quia magnus es β (*praeter HH'*). quia potens es *HH'*. rex regum *C*.
120 VI *add CEFNM*. VI post VIII *E*. VI *post* X *M*.
121 omnibus habitantibus in eo] et conversatione eius *C*.
122 deprecamur] adoramus *C*.
123 VII α (*praeter W*). *om* β γ. VII *post* VIII *DD'*.
124 precamur te *AB*. flagitamus te *DD'*. largiter bone *C*.
125 VIII *om WSJJ'*. VIII *ante* VII *DD'*. VIII *ante* VI *E*. *ante* VIII Pro omnibus sanctae (sancta *M'*) dei ecclesiae (ecclesiae dei *M*) ordinibus et utriusque (variiusque *M'*) sexus fidelibus clamamus te *add MM'*.
126 ac] et α *G'HH'*.
127 exoramus te *AB*. imploramus te *DD'*. sana eos *C* β (*praeter HH'*)*II'M'*. quia clemens es *HH'*. flagitamus te *M*.

IX[128] Pro remissione peccatorum vel[129] emendatione morum[130] rogamus te[131]
Domine miserere

X[132] Pro requie defuntorum et[133] indulgentia paenitentium imploramus te[134]
Domine miserere

c/ Exaudi nos Deus in omni oratione[135] nostra[136] quia[137] pius[138] es
Domine miserere

d/[139] Dicamus omnes: Domine miserere.[140]

2. Particular Editions[141]

a. The Pure Family'
Germanic group: *ABW*
Gallican group: *CDD'*

a/ Dicamus omnes: Domine miserere

b/ Ex toto corde et ex tota mente oramus[142] te
Domine miserere[143]

II Pro sancta[144] ecclesia catholica quae est in toto orbe diffusa suplicamus[145] te
Domine miserere[146]

128 IX *om HH'* γ.
129 vel *ABW*, et *CDD'* β (*praeter HH'*).
130 morum *BDD'W*. eorum *AC* β (*praeter HH'*).
131 rogamus te *ABW*. adoramus te *CDD'*. deprecamur te *EGG'*. invocamus te *FN*. quia clemens es *S*.
132 X *om* α *H*, *ante* X Pro captivis et afflictis peregrinis orphanis ac viduis adsis eos *add M'*.
133 et *EFG'N* γ. vel *GH'S*.
134 imploramus te *M*. quia pius es β *JJ'M'*. quia clemens es *II'*.
135 oratione] tribulatione *C*.
136 nostra α *HH'*. ista β (*praeter HH'*) γ.
137 quia] qui *W*.
138 pius α (*praeter C*). clemens *CG'* γ (*praeter II'*). potens β (*praeter G'*) *II'*.
139 d/*CDD'GHH'I'*. *om ABWEFG'NS* γ (*praeter I'*).
140 Domine miserere *DD'H'*. *om CGHI'*.
141 The Roman numerals always correspond to the same invocations, both in the general edition, whose order they reproduce, and in the particular editions; for example, I always indicates 'pro perpetua pace'. The order of the invocations in the manuscripts is retained but the corresponding Roman numeral matches that of the general edition. Thus in family α, II precedes I, signifying that these manuscripts all begin with invocation II and that I follows, contrary to the order in the general edition.
142 oremus] invocamus *C*.
143 Domine miserere *om W*.
144 sancta *om C*.
145 supplicamus *ABW*, obsecramus *CDD'*.
146 Domine miserere] Dicamus omnes *DD' alternatim cum* Domine miserere.

I[147] Pro perpetua pace et benigna constitutione rogamus te
Domine miserere

III[148] Pro pastore nostro et omni clero[149] eius imploramus[150] te
Domine miserere

IV[151] Pro abbate nostro et omni congregatione eius[152] flagitamus[153] te
Domine miserere

V[154] Pro rege[155] nostro et omni[156] exercitu eius obsecramus te[157]
Domine miserere

VII[158] Pro aeris temperie et fecunditate terrae precamur te[159]
Domine miserere

VIII[160] Pro his qui infirmantur et diversis languoribus detinentur exoramus te[161]
Domine miserere

IX Pro remissione peccatorum vel[162] emendatione morum[163] rogamus[164] te
Domine miserere

c/ Exaudi nos Deus in omni oratione[165] nostra, quia[166] pius[167] es

d/[168] Dicamus omnes: Domine miserere.[169]

---

147 I *om ABW*.
148 III *post* V *CDD'*.
149 clero] congregatione *C* (*confusio cum* IV).
150 imploramus *ABW*. Rogamus *C*. precamur *DD'*.
151 IV *om AW qui habent*: Pro pontifice (antistite *W*) nostro et grege sibi commisso flagitamus (obsecramus *W*) te. *Hoc ponit W post* V.
152 omni congregatione eius *conjicio*. grege sibi commisso *B*. omni clero eius *C*. (*confusio cum* III). omni congregatione nostra *DD'*.
153 flagitamus *A*. obsecramus *BW*. Precamus *C*. exoramus *DD'*.
154 V *om B*; *ante* III *CDD'*.
155 rege] imperatore *A*.
156 et omni] et pro omni *D'*.
157 obsecramus te *A*. flagitamus te *W*. supplicamus te *DD'*. rex regum *C*.
158 *Ante* VII *add C*: pro loco nostro et conversatione eius adoramus te. VII *om W*. VII *post* VIII *DD'*.
159 precamur te *AB*. flagitamus te *DD'*. largitor bone *C*.
160 VIII *om W*. VIII *ante* VII *DD'*.
161 exoramus te *AB*. imploramus te *DD'*. sana eos *C*.
162 vel *ABW*. et *CDD'*.
163 morum *BWDD'*. eorum *AC*.
164 rogamus *ABW*. adoramus *CDD'*.
165 oratione] tribulatione *C*.
166 quia] qui *W*.
167 pius] clemens *C*.
168 d/ *om ABW*.
169 Domine miserere *om C*.

β The 'quia' Family

a/	Dicamus omnes: Domine miserere[170]
b/	Ex toto corde et ex tota mente deprecamur te
	Domine miserere
I	Pro altissima pace[171] et benigna constitutione invocamus te
	Domine miserere
II	Pro sancta ecclesia catholica quae est in toto orbe constituta[172] oramus[173] te
	Domine miserere
III[174]	Pro pastore nostro et omni clero[175] eius[176] quia potens[177] es
	Domine miserere
V[178]	Pro rege nostro et omni exercitu eius[179] quia magnus[180] es
	Domine miserere
[VI[181]	Pro loco nostro et omnibus habitantibus in eo deprecamur te
	Domine miserere
VIII[182]	Pro his qui infirmantur ac[183] diversis languoribus detinentur quia clemens es[184]
	Domine miserere
IX[185]	Pro remissione peccatorum et emendatione eorum deprecamur te[186]
	Domine miserere
X[187]	Pro requie defunctorum et[188] indulgentia paenitentium quia pius es
	Domine miserere

170 Chorus repetit: Domine miserere *add S.*
171 pace *om N.*
172 constituta] diffusa *HH'.*
173 oramus *GG'S.* adoramus *HH'.* deprecamur *FN.* Invocamus *E.*
174 III *post* V *G'HH'. om S.*
175 clero] congregatione *F.*
176 eius] suo *G'.*
177 potens] magnus *HH'.*
178 V *ante* III *G'HH'. om S qui add*: Pro pace regum et quiete populorum quia magnus es.
179 exercitu eius] populo christiano *FN.*
180 magnus] potens *HH'.*
181 VI *add EFN.* VI *post* VIII *E. ante* VI Pro doctore nostro et omni congregatione eius deposcimus te *add N.*
182 VIII *ante* VI *E. om S.*
183 ac] et *G'HH'.*
184 quia clemens es *HH'.* sana eos *EFGG'N.*
185 IX *om HH'.*
186 deprecamur te] invocamus te *FN.* quia clemens es *S.*
187 X *om H.*
188 et *EFG'N.* vel *GH'S.*

c/ Exaudi nos Deus in omni oratione ista[189] quia potens[190] es
Domine miserere

d/[191] Dicamus omnes: Domine miserere.[192]

γ. The Mixed Family

a/ Dicamus omnes: Domine miserere[193]

b/ Ex toto corde et ex tota mente imploramus[194] te
Domine miserere

I Pro altissima pace et benigna constitutione invocamus[195] te
Domine miserere

II Pro sancta ecclesia catholica quae est in toto orbe constituta oramus[196] te
Domine miserere

V Pro rege[197] nostro et omni exercitu eius[198] rogamus[199] te
Domine miserere

III[200] Pro pastore nostro et omni clero[201] eius imploramus[202] te
Domine miserere

IV[203] Pro abbate nostro et omni congregatione eius deposcimus[204] te
Domine miserere

VIII[205] Pro his qui infirmantur ac diversis languoribus detinentur sana eos[206]
Domine miserere

---

189 ista] nostra *HH'*.
190 potens] clemens *G'*.
191 d/ *om EFG'NS*.
192 Domine miserere *om GH*.
193 miserere] Domine *add M'*.
194 imploramus] invocamus *II'*.
195 invocamus] deprecamur *II'*.
196 oremus] deprecamur *M*.
197 rege] imperatore *I*.
198 eius] christiano *M*. christianorum *M'*.
199 rogamus *II'*. deprecamur *JM'*. deposcimus *J'*. oramus *M*.
200 III *om JJ'*.
201 clero] II. congregatione *MM'*.
202 imploramus *II'*. deposcimus *MM'*.
203 IV *om II'MM'*.
204 deposcimus *J*. deprecamur *J'*.
205 VIII *om JJ'*. *ante* VIII Pro omnibus sanctae (sancta *M'*) dei ecclesiae (ecclesiae dei *M*) ordinibus et utriusque (variisque *M'*) sexus fidelibus clamamus te *add MM'*.
206 sana eos] flagitamus te *M*.

X[207] Pro requie defunctorum et indulgentia paenitentium quia pius es[208]

Domine miserere

c/[209] Exaudi nos Deus in omni oratione ista quia clemens[210] es

Domine miserere[211]

Why, in our general edition, have we placed IV and VI between square brackets? In the first place, IV is specifically monastic, even if it is not attested by all the extant sources from abbeys (it is lacking in *AWEFMM'*). Secondly, we must remember that OR 50 (source *A*) 'constitutes part of the original categories of materials in the Roman-Germanic Pontifical (around 950)',[212] and it uses in a significant way *pro pontifice nostro*, which *N* corrects to *pro doctore nostro*. For all these reasons we do not think that IV would have been part of the original formulary, but would have been added later, according to monastic usage.

As for VI, it is only weakly affirmed (in *C*, the most complete formulary, only X is missing; *E* = Saint-Martial; *F* = Saint-Yrieix; *N* = Saint-Saturnin de Toulouse; *M* = San-Millan de la Cogolla) even though it is an integral part of FG^2. We consider that here it is a corruption of FG^1 by FG^2.

C. Eastern Parallels

a/ – b/ cf. supra Irl^1, a/

I *Pro altissima pace*: cf. Irl^1 I.

et benigna constitutione: this expression is the exact reproduction of the term εὐστάθεια, that we find in CAp VIII, 10, 3; ὑπὲρ τῆς εἰρήνης καὶ τῆς εὐσταθείας τοῦ κόσμου καὶ τῶν ἁγίων ἐκκλησιῶν, or in B 362: ὑπὲρ τῆς εἰρήνης τοῦ σύμπαντος κόσμου, εὐσταθείας τῶν ἁγίων τοῦ θεοῦ ἐκκλησιῶν…

II cf. Irl^1 II. M^1 I, *DG* I.

III cf. Irl^1 III.

IV The monastic inspiration itself could have been copied from the East; indeed it features in B 363: ὑπὲρ τῆς ἁγίας μονῆς (ἢ πόλεως ταύτης) and in B 373: ὑπὲρ τῶν ἀδελφῶν ἡμῶν τῶν ἱερέων ἱερομονάχων ἱεροδιακόνων καὶ μοναχῶν…

V cf. Irl^1 V and M^1 III; *DG* V.

VI cf. Irl^1 IV.

VII cf. M^1 VI; *DG* VI.

207 *Ante* X Pro captivis et afflictis peregrinis orphanis ac viduis adsis eos *add M'*.
208 quia pius es *JJ'M'*. quia clemens es *II'*. imploramus te *M*.
209 *Ante* c/ Pro loco nostro et omnibus habitantibus in eo deprecamur te *add M*.
210 clemens] potens *II'*.
211 Dicamus omnes *add I'*.
212 Cf. Vogel (1986), 187.

VIII	cf. *M*[1] IX.
IX	cf. *DG* XIII.
X	cf. *DG* XIV.
c/	cf. *M*[1] b/.

While the parallels are as numerous as for the litanies already examined, the style is more flowing. We are indisputably in the presence of a secondary composition, no longer adapted from the Eastern originals, but already from Latin texts.

D. Characteristics of Each Family

Three criteria allow us to distinguish each family: the presence or absence of a particular petition; redactional details, and above all, the endings of the invocations.

α. The Pure Family

We have given this family its name because all the invocations regularly end with a verb of petition in the first person, governing the pronoun in the second person, while the β group has been distorted at the commencement of its ending by the 'quia potens es' that completes the imperative invocation c/; it seems as if this ending has turned back the flow of the litany and returned to its beginning (or almost the beginning).

The manuscripts of the α family fall into two groups which, for the sake of brevity, we will name as the Germanic group (*ABW*) and the Gallican group (*CDD'*).

The characteristics of this family are as follows:

II	always makes up the first petition and always uses the word *diffusa*;
I	lacks the phrase *altissima pace,* a beginning common to both β and γ groups; the Gallican group compensates by adding *pro pace et benigna constitutione,* unknown in the other families;
III—IV—V	are all present (or slightly modified);
VI	is omitted, apart from *C*;
VII	is peculiar to α (apart from *W*); it is not present in either β or γ;
VIII	is present, with the verb of petition in the first person plural, while β and γ have a different ending; the ending in γ (*sana eos*) also features in *C*!
IX	\is found here, but four out of the six manuscripts have *morum* in place of *eorum,* as in β and γ;
X	is missing, in contrast to β — γ;
c/	always includes *nostra,* in contrast to β — γ, which has *ista* (except Cambrai).

Manuscript *C* is the most irregular of the family; twice (V and VII) it replaces the verb with an attributive invocation linking it with the petition (*rex regum, largitor bone*); it adds VI; in VIII it ends in the same way as γ with *sana eos*; finally, in IX we read the bland *eorum*.

β. The 'quia' Family

This title arises, as we have just explained, from the distortion at the end of each invocation, and this constitutes the major characteristic of this family.

It brings together three groups of sources:

- The manuscripts of Cambrai, all originally from the cathedral or the city parishes;
- The manuscripts of Autun, similarly originally from the cathedral or the parishes of this ancient city, to which the text printed in the *Variae preces* are linked;
- Finally five monastic manuscripts: three from Saint-Martial, one from Saint-Yrieix and one from Saint-Saturnin de Toulouse.

The Cambrai group often stands alone when compared with the other two: in II it uses *diffusa* and not *consituta*; in VIII it remains faithful to *quia* instead of ending with *sana eos*; finally, in c/ we find *oratione nostra*, whereas the other manuscripts have *ista*.

We move now to the characteristics common to β, which offers the longest text of the three families:

I	is the obligatory beginning;
II	uses *constituta* (as with γ), apart from Cambrai (*diffusa*, as with α);
III	inaugurates the series of invocations that have *quia* at the end;
IV	is always missing, despite the monastic origins of *EFN*;
V	is included here as in every group; *S* has a different wording, taken from *FG*², but nevertheless well integrated here, and ending with *quia*;
VI	features in the monastic group, but not in the others (apart from *CM*); it occurs without *quia*. This shows that it not been well integrated; undoubtedly it was taken from *FG*²;
VII	is never included, in common with γ, in contrast to α[213]

213 This prayer for good weather exists in family α, where all the manuscripts are originally from northern countries with less clement climates. It is understandable that this invocation has been omitted in the South (le Midi), the place of origin for *EFN* in family β and *JJ'MM'* in family γ; its absence is less understandable in Autun (*GG'*) and especially Cambrai (*HH'*). We think, however, that we can use this indicator to affirm that these last two cities received their *preces* from the South.

We will meet another example of meteorological influence later on; in *FG*², a manuscript from Narbonne inserts a particular petition for rain!

VIII is included, with *sana eos* (as with γ), apart from Cambrai (*quia* is integral) which has no doubt reta ined the preferredwording;

IX has the 'lectio facilior' of *eorum*; IX is missing from Cambrai, and lacks any *quia*. Is it perhaps an interpolation?

X is included, in common with γ, in contrast to α;

c/ has *ista* (as does γ) apart from Cambrai (*nostra*, as with α)

γ. The Mixed Family

This family has the shortest text (*JJ'* has a mere five invocations) and is called 'mixed' because it has as many similarities with the 'pure' family as with the 'quia' family.

Compared to α, the differences are marked especially by

- the sequence I–II in γ, as opposed to II–I in α (Gallican group);
- in the use of the word *constituta* in II;
- the omission of VII;
- the imperative *sana eos* in VIII;
- the absence of IX;
- the presence of X;
- and finally, the use of *ista* in c/

With regard to similarities, α and γ are united by

- the verb of petition at the end of each invocation (apart from VIII and X in γ);
- the presence (partial) of III–IV-V;
- the omission of VI.

When compared with β the differences are:

- the absence in γ of *quia*, apart from X (omitted by α);
- the omission of IX, and the presence of IV in the monastic manuscripts *JJ'*.

In common with γ, β has:

- the same incipit in I;
- the word *constituta* in II;
- *sana eos* in VIII;
- the presence of Xl
- *ista* in c/.

However, this division of families should not be set in concrete, since some manuscripts belonging to different families present some points in common; thus γ and the manuscripts of Cambrai have *pro rege* (V) before *pro pastore* (III), and both omit IX.

E. Liturgical Form

FG[1] is a litany without any introduction or conclusion by a priest.
It consists of:

a/	an invitation indicating the response;
b/	a descriptive invocation;
I–X:	from five to ten verbal invocations, whose order sometimes varies slightly;
c/	an imperative invocation;
d/	reprise of the initial invitation.

F. Analysis

1. Commentary

I. Family α omits *pro altissima pace,* attested unanimously by β and γ. Three examples from α however are in two minds and replace it with *pro perpetua pace.* There is no reason to doubt the word *altissima,* of Eastern origin and present in *Irl*[1], nor the original character of this invocation in *FG*[1]. It is α that is responsible for the omission, and sometimes introduces *perpetua* in place of *altissima,* whose meaning (clearer in Greek it must be said) was perhaps no longer understood.

Benigna constitutione is equivalent to the Greek εὐστάθεια; any translation has to take this into account. The expression offers a scarcely satisfactory meaning, and we think that originally it would have been determined by a genitive (cf. infra, Origin of *FG*[1])

The verbs of petition that end each invocation are varied; the formularies try not to repeat them. This is typical of the care with which the second wave of texts was produced. *DG* does the same.

II. The β families (except Cambrai) and γ families have the variant *constituta.* As with *diffusa,* it could originate from the Greek ὑπὲρ τῆς κατὰ πᾶσαν τὴν οἰκουμένην ἁγίας σου καθολικῆς καὶ ἀποστολικῆς ἐκκλησίας (*J* 54). Two reasons can explain the presence of *constituta*: first, the influence of the noun *constitutio* in I; next, its use in *DG* I, where this adjective seems to have been chosen to obtain a particular rhythmic effect (cf. supra, *DG* I).

III. This seems to concern solely the local bishop and his clergy; none of the texts mention the bishop of Rome nor any other bishops. We note that the prayer for the king frequently precedes that for the pastor (*CDD'G'HH'* γ).

From this point on, family β ends each invocation with an argument presented in the form of a causal clause: *quia pius (clemens, potens...) es.* This ending cannot be original; it will be petition X (which in γ also ends with *quia pius es*) that through retroactive influence will little by little impose this ending onto each invocation. The first two, however, resisted contamination and their archaisms were preserved. Moreover, the second of these has not even submitted to the binary structure that characterises the invitations of this litany: the later redaction was not able to extend its grip to this venerable formulary.

IV. The invocation for the Abbot and his family of monks is a monastic addition and is not present in all the manuscripts originating in monasteries (it is missing in *AWEFMM'*). We consider that it is not original and have placed it in brackets.

V. Present in all the examples, this prayer for the king twice uses the variant *imperatore* (*AI*); in *A* (= OR 50), it can be explained by the constitution of the German nation by the Holy Roman Empire in 962. There is no question about it referring to any emperor from ancient times, since they had disappeared (476) or did not exercise sufficient authority at the place that *FG¹* was redacted to merit mention as the civil authority.

VI. is only attested to by seven of the sources, including the extravagant *C* which has the variant *et conversatione eius* (cf. *M¹* V). It became an integral part of *FG²* which never omitted it. As *FG¹* and *FG²* were both used for the Rogation Days in the Middle Ages, it could well be that VI is a contamination of the second by the first, so we have put this in brackets as well.

VII. does not feature in family α (apart from *W*); perhaps the meteorological conditions excluded it from the warmer countries (cf. n. 213, p. 183). We note the simplifications made in relation to *Irl¹* III and *M¹* VI, thanks to the omission of *fructu(um)* (whose textual variations in *M¹* VI attest to the difficulties it caused). Our invocation could well depend on *M¹* VI, with its complicated construction, rather than on *Irl²* III. The absence of *fructus* in *FG¹* also indicates a lack of direct dependence on the East. It is not possible to arrive at our invocation by beginning from any of the Eastern petitions (at least those that remain extant today); indeed, all of them speak of 'fruits', and only one (B 363) mentions the earth, but then simply as a descriptor of 'fruits'.

VIII. The hypothesis of a dependency of *FG¹* on *M¹* or an equivalent litany is reinforced by examination of this petition. While there exists no exact Eastern parallel, *FG¹* VIII and *M¹* IX offer such similarities in vocabulary as to exclude coincidence. The evolution would have been as follows: *FG¹* would have wanted to remove the prayer for those possessed; however, a reconstruction of the invocation would have been necessary if they wished to remain faithful to the binary rhythm adopted throughout the entire litany. The noun *infirmitatibus* of *M¹* gave birth to the verb *infirmantur* from the first part of *FG¹* VIII; the adjective and the verb that accompanied it (*diversis — detinentur*) moved into the second part, enriched by the term *languoribus*. You only have to look in the gospels for a summary of the activity of Jesus, for example Mt 4:23, and you will find that *languor* and *infirmitas* appear there together.

IX. is encountered also in *Irl²* VII. They are direct translations of their Eastern parallels. They were more aware of using *eorum* rather than *morum*, which is less often chosen, but retained, nevertheless in the edition as a *lectio difficilior*.

X. *Irl*^{2} VIII contains the first part of this; the second (*indulgentia paenitentium*) does not feature in the East. Undoubtedly it was called for by the binary structure of the invocations; the penitents were mentioned in both *Irl*^{1} IX and in *M*^{1} VII.

c/ = *M*^{1} b/ shortened by the removal of *deprecatione* but enlarged by a conclusion: *quia pius es.*

2. Use of the Litany

As we have said, OR 50 situates *FG*^{1} on the Monday of the Rogation Days; it was sung going out of the church, after two antiphons.[214] The liturgical books of the Middle Ages give us abundant testimony of this usage, but often they designate different days.[215]

The sources do not indicate any other use of the litany. But its liturgical form and its content prove to us that it is very old. There is a clear difference between *FG*^{1} and the later *preces* that accompany it in OR 50 (*Humili prece* pp. 326–30, *Clamemus omnes* p. 333, *Omnes o sancti* p. 337) which are, by nature, hymnic. Could we be seeing in this medieval use the original function of *FG*^{1}? In other words, is it feasible that this piece never served as an *oratio fidelium*, but that it was redacted directly for the Rogation Days, which emerged in Gaul around 470 thanks to the pastoral zeal of Mamert, the bishop of Vienna?[216] In that case, the redactor would have drawn on the common pool of petitions, that we are beginning to know very well, to compose a prayer destined for this new pastoral need, the penitential processions. Our sources from the 10th century would then not be introducing anything new by chanting *FG*^{1} during the Rogation Days; we would have to consider them as the first witnesses of a usage from the end of the 5th or the beginning of the 6th century.

Frankly, we do not think that such a hypothesis has any foundation. Mamert indeed organised the ‘minor litanies’ during earthquakes. But nothing in *FG*^{1} evokes similar catastrophes; it prays the traditional intentions (more or less universal) for the Church and the world. No specifically penitential intent is detected.

It is most unlikely that OR 50, which is our oldest witness (around 950) was responsible for introducing *FG*^{1} to the Rogation Days. If this were the case it would be hard to understand how only half a century later the manuscripts of a completely different country, from Saint-Yrieix (*F*) and Saint-Martial de Limoges (*E*), include this very *FG*^{1} in a significantly different version.

---

214 OR 50, ch. 36, 8; ed. Andrieu, vol. 5, 317–18.

215 There is ample confusion here, as much in the studies as in the sources themselves, for certain manuscripts use *Feria II* to indicate the second day of the *week* (Monday) and others the second day of the *Rogation days* (Tuesday)! Sometimes only the indication of the final day as *Feria V* allows us to know whether they are counting according to the days of the week or according to the three days of the Rogation Days.

216 On the minor litanies (= Rogation Days) see Moeller (1938), 75–91.

It is more like that OR 50 simply continued on an older custom (of that period?) using, on the days of minor litanies, the formularies that had fallen into disuse with the disappearance of the *oratio fidelium*. Moreover, in reading the manuscripts we get the impression that the Rogation Days constituted a kind of 'hold-all', in which had been accumulated a series of antiphons and diverse pieces of sufficient number to cover the distance between one 'station' and the next. We could easily come to this conclusion by reading chapter 36 of OR 50.

In short, we do not hesitate to recognise in *FG¹* one of the formularies of the ancient Universal Prayer.

3. Origin of FG¹: the Source Q

The formulary is not necessarily of monastic origin. As we have said, the prayer for the Abbot must be an interpolation, and nothing else leads us to see here the work of the monks; only the penitential spirit of IX–X could set us along this path.

What does seem certain to us, on the other hand, is that *FG¹* is an adaptation of another Latin text. A first wave of texts (*Irl¹*, *M¹*) would have been content to translate the Greek formularies. A second wave, to which *FG¹* belongs, reworked these rather crude attempts and tried to improve and beautify them; sometimes however the original meaning was not understood and degenerated into banalities.

Of what did the work of this redactor consist? First of all he reorganised the material of each invocation into a binary structure, drawing the line only at II which was too traditional to undergo reform. This work is particularly apparent in petitions III–V where each time we have *pro … nostro et omni … eius*. It would have been an improvement to vary the final verb of each invocation. He might have taken the idea of such a stylised systematisation from a text like *M¹* where a ternary structure is often displayed (III–VI).

In I we immediately recognise the intervention of the redactor. We admit that *pro … benigna constituione* does not make much sense; however, we can understand that, joined to 'peace', the *constitutio* here in question must mean stability or some similar quality. But if we look at the Eastern parallels, we note that εὐσταθεία (translated as *benigna constitutione*) is determined by τοῦ κόσμου καὶ τῶν ἁγίων ἐκκλησιῶν (CAp VIII 10, 3); or, as we read in B 363: ὑπὲρ τῆς εἰρήνης τοῦ σύμπαντος κόσμου, εὐσταθείας τῶν ἁγίων τοῦ θεοῦ ἐκκλησιῶν… It is unthinkable that the translator would have left the term *constitutio* without any descriptor; it is at least necessary to supply *mundi* or *ecclesiarum*. It is most likely that our redactor omitted this genitive so that this invocation would have the same rhythm of the invocations that followed it.

This work on style was accompanied by pruning and adapting translations from the Greek to new circumstances. If the model on which our redactor was working was a text similar to *Irl¹* or *M¹* it would have dropped the following:

- the prayer for all the bishops, an important sign of the communion of all the local Churches; *FG¹* prays only *pro pastore nostro*;

- eventually a prayer for the authorities (Irl^1 VI);
- perhaps a petition for the call to the pagans and the peace of the peoples (M^1 IV);
- especially the detailed list of the [ministerial] orders or of the needy (widows, virgins, orphans, captives…) who are mentioned in only two variants of San-Millan (*Pro omnibus sanctae Dei ecclesiae ordinibus* in *MM'*; *Pro captivis et afflictis peregrinis orphani ac viduis* in *M'*). Catechumens are deleted; penitents are probably understood in a different, more individual sense;
- the invocation for benefactors.

In short, we see here narrower perspectives. At the ecclesial level the vision is less universal, less catholic; at the secular level, their concerns are more limited. This must correspond to new circumstances. We seem to have left Antiquity, or at least an environment of advanced civilisation; another world has been born.

But which model has our redactor transformed? Several clues suggest a direct line of descent in relation to M^1. M^1 VI became FG^1 VII; M^1 IX in particular was adapted into FG^1 VIII; M^1 b/ is transformed into FG^1 c/; and the variant of *M'* that we were citing just now, (*pro captivis…*) immediately reminds us of *M'* VII–VIII. However, it is not possible to explain all the invocations of FG^1 as coming from M^1, which, notably, is missing *pro altissima pace* (FG^1 I). Nor can Irl^1 have served as a likely source for the Franco-Gallican text, for while the *pro altissima pace* is certainly included, the prayer for the sick is not, and neither do we find there the prayer for good weather.

Are we therefore justified in assuming the existence of a text (*Q*) that the sources have not conserved for us (or that we have not yet found)? *Q* would be a translation directly from the Greek, as with Irl^1 or M^1, whose content would not be substantially different from a synthesis of those two litanies and which would include at least the eight petitions that the redactor of FG^1 has transformed into its own eight original invocations.

We have situated Irl^1 at the end of the 4th or beginning of the 5th centuries, and M^1 in the 5th, probably the second half of the century. Since FG^1 does not mention the widows, virgins or the needy, we cannot be sure that model *Q* contains them; it is possible that *Q* could even be slightly more recent. We would therefore place it roughly in the second half of the 5th century.

4. Attempt at Dating

Let us gather together the elements at our disposal. Both a/ and b/ are ancient, as are I and II; the traditional formulation of II has even resisted the rhythmic structure imposed by the redactor.

V, which once petitioned for the emperor but now speaks only of the king, can be dated before the middle of the 5th century. Even if the Empire did not officially fall until 476, the imperial powers would have already been greatly weakened for several dozen years, while lordships existed in several places. We would claim 450 as an approximate *terminus post quem.*

IX attests to a penitential concern (and a moral one too if we accept the reading *morum*) but this may be secondary in the overall scheme of liturgical piety. In any case it does not feature in either *Irl*[1] or *M*[1]. The second part of X probably uses the mention of penitents in the same way; from Christians who subjected themselves to the earlier forms of penance we have passed to those who (individually) repent of their sins.

If Q were to be a source in this instance, it would again lead us to around the second half of the 5th century.

The conclusion, then, is not difficult to draw. We consider it reasonable not to date *FG*[1] before the middle of the 5th century; its older formularies can be explained by the model Q. As for a *terminus ante quem*, the absence of monastic elements invites us to situate it not too far into the 6th century. Therefore we propose that the date of redaction of *FG*[1] based on Q, in the period between the middle of the 5th and the middle of the 6th centuries.

5. Attempt at Location

Internal criticism does not teach us anything about *FG*[1]'s region of origin. Only mention of the king could indicate that the text is not Roman, since the notion of the king is typically Germanic. Moreover, in the capital of the ancient empire, we cannot suppose that they would have prayed only for the king, since the imperial fiction remained alive.

The manuscript tradition, on the contrary, is unanimous; *FG*[1] appears only in manuscripts originating in the Germanic or Gallic regions (Gaul included Aquitaine, whose musical influence extended beyond the Pyrenees up to the Middle Ages). We think that *FG*[1] would have served as an *oratio fidelium* formulary in one or other Church from these regions (hence its acronym *FG* = Franco-Gallican). After the disappearance of the Universal Prayer, it would have fallen into oblivion, until by good fortune it was guaranteed a new 'career' by being placed in the Rogation Day prayers.

III. The So-Called Milanese 'Dicamus Omnes' (*M*[2])

A. Sources

On the second Sunday of Lent (cf. n. 44, p. 177), the Milanese liturgy has retained in the *Ingressa* a litanic piece whose incipit, once again, is *Dicamus omnes*. The response, on the other hand, is one we have not yet encountered; it is none other than *Kyrie eleison*. As was the case with *M*[1], and for the same reasons, we consider that *M*[2] originally served as an *oratio fidelium*.

The list of sources is almost the same as that for *M*[1], to which we can refer. Here, we provide an abridged version.

A	= *Sacramentary of Biasca*, f. 75^r^, ed. Heiming, 46–47.
B	= Sacramentary of Milan, following the Tables of the Sacramentary of Bergamo.
Berg	= *Sacramentary of Bergamo*, f. 102^v^–103^r^, ed. Paredi, 118–19.
C	= Sacramentary of Lodrino, following the same Tables.
D	= Sacramentary of Bedero, also following the same Tables.
E	= *Sacramentary d'Aribert*, f. 55^r^, ed. Paredi, 371.
+ *G*	= ROME, Bibl. Angelica lat. 123 (olim B. 3.18), f. 212^r-v^, Gradual and Tropary of Bologna, 11th c.;[217] M^2 is indicated for the first Sunday of Lent; for the second Sunday, the manuscript gives the *DG*; it was not familiar with M^1. The piece is edited in Thomasius-Vezzosi, vol. 5, 241
J	= *Sacramentary of S. Simpliciano*, f. 40^v^–41^r^, ed. Frei. 184–85.
L	= *Ambrosian Antiphonary*, f. 132, ed. Cagin, 312–14.
O	= Sacramentary of Milan, following Heiming, ed. Biasca, p. xli.
Tr	= *Sacramentarium Triplex*, f. 59^v^–60^r^, ed. Heiming, 71–72.
Vr	= Sacramentary of Milan, following the same Tables.
[*R*	= Ambrosian Missal, f. 59 ff.]
T 570	= Thomasius-Vezzosi, vol. 2, 570.
T 572	= Thomasius-Vezzosi, vol. 2, 572.

The editor does not indicate the source manuscripts.

1751	= edition puteobonelliana
1902	= editio typica.

Curiously, manuscript *F* (Bergamo, Bibl. Civica Γ III. 18) that contains the text of M^1 does not include that of M^2.[218]

The textual tradition is in agreement; only *G* and *T570* offer any variations.

B. Edited Version[219]

a/[220] Dicamus omnes;[221] Kyrie eleison[222]

b/ Domine Deus omnipotens patrum nostrorum

Kyrie eleison

c/ Respice de caelo[223] et de sede sancta tua

Kyrie eleison

---

217 For more details, see p. 192.

218 At least this is what Mgr Chiodi, Director of the Library, has informed us, following 'an accurate check of the codices'. We thank him for this information.

219 Improved in comparison to that given by Capelle (1934), 121–23.

220 a/ *om T 570*.

221 Dicamus omnes *om G*.

222 Kyrie eleison *om Tr*.

223 Deus *add T 572*.

I[224] Pro ecclesia tua sancta[225] catholica quam conservare digneris

Kyrie eleison

II[226] Pro papa nostro ·illo·[227] et sacerdotio eius[228]

Kyrie eleison

III[229] Pro universis episcopis, cuncto clero et populo

Kyrie eleison

IV[230] Pro famulo tuo ·illo· imperatore [et famula tua ·illa· imperatrice][231] et omni exercitu eius[232]

Kyrie eleison

V Pro civitate[233] hac omnibusque[234] habitantibus in ea

Kyrie eleison

VI[235] Pro aerum[236] temperie[237] et fecunditate terrarum

Kyrie eleison

d/[238] Libera nos qui liberasti filios Israël

Kyrie eleison[239]

e/ In manu forti et brachio excelso[240]

Kyrie eleison

---

224 I *lac L.*
225 ecclesia tua sancta] sancta ecclesia *G, T 570.*
226 II] pro domno ·illo· apostolico et universali papa *G, T 570.*
227 et pontifice nostro ·illo· *add T 572, 1751, 1902.*
228 eius] eorum *T 572, 1751, 1902.*
229 III *post* pro domni ·illo· episcopo *G.*
230 IV] pro domno ·illo· imperatore nostro, iudicibus et exercitibus eius — Kyrie eleison *G, T 570 post* II.
Pro domno ·illo· archiepiscopo nostro et sacerdotio eius — Kyrie eleison *add G, T 570.*
Pro domno ·illo· episcopo nostro et sacerdotio eius — Kyrie eleison *add G.*
IV] pro famulo tuo ·illo· rege et famula tua ·illa· regina … *J.* pro famulis tuis ·N· Imperatore et ·N· Rege, Duce nostro … *1751–1902.*
231 et … imperatrice *om A.*
232 eius *ABBergCEOTr.* eorum *DJLVr, T 572, 1751, 1902.*
233 civitate] plebe *A.* civitate-plebe *L.*
234 omnibusque] et omnibus *G, T 570.*
235 VI *om G, T 570.*
236 aerum] aeris *T 572, 1751.*
237 ac fructu *add T 572.*
238 *ante* d/ Ut concordiam veram et pacem bonam nobis omnibus donare digneris — Kyrie eleison *add G, T 570.*
239 Kyrie eleison *om Tr.*
240 excelso] extento *G, T 570.*

f/ Exurge Domine adiuva nos et libera nos propter nomen tuum
Kyrie eleison, Kyrie eleison, Kyrie eleison.[241]

C. Eastern Parallels

Eastern sources are becoming more familiar to us. Thus we can refer to the texts cited in connection with the preceding litanies without having to repeat them each time. It seemed useful to us to provide Western parallels at the same time, so as to suggest at the outset the possible links between the formulary and its Latin counterpart.

a/ cf. *J* 36, *Irl*[1] a/. *DG* a/.

b/ Κύριε παντοκράτορ ὁ θεὸς τῶν πατέρων ἡμῶν; *J* 36, B 373 (cf. 2 Chron 20:6).

c/ cf. *Irl*[1] b/ = Ps 103:32 (LXX); cf. Ps 79:15: 'Respice de caelo et vide et visita vineam' or again, Dt 26:15: 'Respice de sanctuario tuo et de excelso'; cf. also Is 63:15; Bar 2:16; Ps 32:13–14.

I cf. *M*[1]; *quam conservare digneris*: ὑπὲρ ... ἐκκλησίας ... ὅπως ὁ Κύριος ἄσειστον αὐτὴν καὶ ἀκλυδώνιστον διαφυλάξῃ καὶ διατηρήσῃ ... CAp VIII 10, 4; cf. CAp VIII 12, 40; 13, 4.

II cf. *Irl*[2] X; *M*[1] II; *sacerdotium* = πρεσβυτέριον CAp VIII 12, 41; 13, 4; B 363.

III *OS* III; *Irl*[1] III; *M*[1] II; ὑπὲρ πάσης ἐπισκοπῆς παντὸς πρεσβυτερίου ... CAp VIII, 13, 4; ὑπὲρ ... παντὸς τοῦ κλήρου καὶ τοῦ λαοῦ B 363.

IV *M*[1] III; *J* 55.

V *M*[1] V; CAp VIII 12, 45; cf. *J* 55; B 363.

VI *M*[1] VI; *FG*[1] VII; *Irl*[2] III.

d/ cf. Jos 22:31: 'Et liberasti filios Israël...'

e/ Dt 5:15; Ps 135:12, etc.

f/ Ps 43:26; 78:9.

D. Liturgical Form

M[2] is a litany of the invocative type, without introduction or conclusion by the priest, and is characterised by multiple biblical verses at the beginning and end. It comprises:

241 Kyrie eleison *ter BergEGJL, T 570, T 572, 1751, 1902. bis A. semel Tr.*

a/	an invitation indicating a response;
b/	an attributive invocation;
d/	an imperative invocation; b/ and c/ are biblically inspired, even if they are not direct scriptural quotations.
I–VI	six nominal invocations; it is clear that they are indeed invocations, given b /c/ d/f/I (*tua-digneris*) and IV (*tuo-tua*).
d/– f/	imperative invocations, in the form of biblical verses.

The whole thing is concluded, as in M^1, with a triple *Kyrie eleison*. The ending does not echo the incipit; for this reason we do not find the customary process of inclusion.

E. Analysis

1. The Response

This is the first time that we have encountered *Kyrie eleison* as a response; moreover, it is repeated three times at the end of the litany, just as in M^1. In the formularies analysised up till now, the Greek response has always been translated by *Domine (exaudi et) miserere*. Is this *Kyrie* long-standing? Was it always maintained in Greek in the West, concurrently with its translation into Latin, or is it, on the other hand, a recent addition, under a pretense of archaism? Let us continue our examination before coming to any decision.

2. The Biblical Verses

Apart from a/, which is taken from the Eastern liturgies, the beginning (b–c) and the end (d–f) of M^2 are made up of verses which, if they are not direct quotations from the Bible, are clearly inspired by it. Comparing this with other Latin liturgies, we note the absence of the descriptive 'ex toto corde et ex tota mente' of Eastern origin. *Irl*^{1} b/ does include a psalm verse, the first part of which develops the same theme as M^2 c/; but M^2 has systematised this usage, framing the invocations with a symmetric number of verses.

Judging from the subsequent development of our literary genre, we can say that here we are faced with a secondary phenomenon. Indeed in the 6th century the custom arose in Gaul of concluding the Hours with verses, the *capitella de psalmis*. In the 7th century we find some litanies with responses composed from such verses; perhaps this genre was spread by the Irish monks (cf. Section Five).

We note, however, that that *Gloria in excelsis* (the oldest manuscript of which dates to the 5th century) and the *Te Deum* (manuscript from the 7th century) which are part of Morning Prayer, both have such psalm verses at the end.[242]

Even if the genre was in existence, it seems to us that its more ample introduction in a formulary of the *oratio fidelium* is secondary; indeed this misrepresents the primary function of the introduction since these verses make no explicit mention of either the purpose or the beneficiary of the prayer.

3. Commentary

I The first part is identical to M^1 I and to the *Te igitur* of the Roman Canon. Striking is the fact that the relative clause that follows is also found in this first intention of the *Te igitur*, with a different, but certainly very comparable verb (*conservare*). This verb will, moreover, be repeated in the Litanies of the Saints of the Church, in the petition, 'Ut Ecclesiam tuam sanctam regere et conservare digneris, to rogamus audi nos', where it is linked with *regere* which also features in the *Te igitur*.

Was *conservare* the only verb that replaced what was unnecessary in this prayer? In any case, the phrase of this invocation could be ancient. The objection could be made that this relative clause is unique in the formulary, and that it does not match the rhythm of the other invocations. But all the litanies examined so far also have a relative clause in the prayer for the Church, and the difference in rhythm could be put down to an ancient formulary which has resisted the revisions of the redactors.

We observe that M^2 is the only litany (apart from Irl^2 which omits this petition) where the invocation for the Church does not include one of the venerable ancient phrases describing its universality.

II The *papa* cited here must surely be the local bishop; the adjective *nostro* indicates this. But is the place itself Rome? The problem arises in exactly the same way as it did for M^1. We shall solve it in the same way, supporting the possibility of a Roman origin for the formulary. That *papa* had been understood as signifying the bishop of Rome is confirmed by the variant of *G* and *T 570*: 'pro domno ˙illo˙ apostolico et universali papa'. Here there is no possible doubt, for these sources add (after IV) an invocation for the archbishop and his clergy, and *G* adds one for the bishop and his priests. *G* is the only Latin text so explicit and so complete. We note that it could not have been redacted in Rome, unless it was proposing several invocations from which one or other would be chosen according to the circumstances. It could only have come from a diocese that was governed by an archbishop, otherwise it would be supplying two invocations for the same person.

---

242 The edition of the oldest examples of these hymns may be found in Warren (1895), vol. 2, 78–79 and 93–94 respectively.

We point out that the terms *apostolicus* and *universalis papa* indicate the theological issue of the 9th century encountered by Nicholas I, Adrian II and John VIII.[243] Undoubtedly this variant dates from this period.

III ... *et populo* is perhaps a translation from the Greek, or even an echo of *OS* III. M^2 and *OS* are the only Latin texts (along with some manuscripts from the β and FG² families) that mention the people.

IV The word *eius* is employed more often in the manuscripts where the emperor's spouse is mentioned alongside the emperor than in M^1 II. This would have been a later addition (see the commentary on M^1 III). The wording of manuscript *G*, 'pro domno ˙illo˙ imperatore nostro, iudicibus et exercitibus eius' is paralleled in *DG* V which combines together princes, justice and the *militia*. *J* at this point speaks of the king and queen, which may be a later addition. Both editions that mention the *Duce* are more recent.

V This invocation is identical to M^1 V, apart from the fact that the latter adds *et conversatione eius* between the two phrases. This may be an interpolation, in which case M^2 would be the older of the two.

VI As in FG^1 VII, this invocation omits the terme *fructu(um)* which caused difficulty in M^1 VI. We have already said with regard to the Franco-Gallican formulary that this omission reveals that we are not in the presence of a well-adapted translation of an Eastern text, but of an adaptation, probably made previously from a Latin formulary that was considered confusing. Must we conclude that M^2 also depended on *Q*, whose existence we must assume in order to understand FG^1? We will examine this question below. We note that two small differences separate M^2 VI and FG^1 VII: *aerum* in place of *aeris* (attested by two other sources), and *terrarum* (also in Irl^2 II and M^1 V) in place of *terrae*.

At this point *G* and *T 570* add, 'Ut concordiam veram et pacem bonam nobis omnibus donare digneris — Kyrie eleison', which is similar to the current Litany of the Saints where we read 'Ut regibus et principibus christianis pacem et veram concordiam donare digneris, te rogamus audi nos'. We must see this as an interpolation. We note that the expression *domnus apostolicus* used in II by those two manuscripts is also encountered a little earlier in the same part of the Litany of the Saints, while three petitions further on is the prayer for the fruits of the earth (cf. VI)! Nothing changes!

d/– f/ perhaps allude to an imminent danger from which they are asking God to save them. The literary form of these verses does not match up with the rest of the litany; if they are original, M^2 would have to be fairly recent.

We note that M^2 includes no invocation for peace, which does not even merit a mention. It omits completely the list of the needy (travellers, prisoners, the sick) and the ancient ecclesiastical orders (virgins, widows, penitents). In the previous Latin litanies the latter were already misrepresented and reduced to the

243 Cf. Congar (1968), 71, 210, 232 ff.

rank of the former; M^2 omits them straight out. It is probably a case of adapting to circumstances, but is, nevertheless, a substantial loss for the Universal Prayer whose horizon is narrowing. Finally, we note that there is no monastic influence.

4. Origin of M^2: Source Y

The commentary has made us aware of alternately old and more recent aspects to M^2. Considering it as a whole, however, we feel that we are here in the presence of a piece belonging, like FG^1, to what we have called the 'second wave', that is, it is no longer a case of translations from the Greek but of a reworking of Latin texts.

The arguments in favour of a redactional adaptation are as follows:

1. The omission of *fructu(um)* in invocation VI, which reveals — as we have shown with regard to FG^1 VII — a Latin intermediary;
2. The absence of petitions for the (ecclesiastical) orders and the needy that characterise the ancient texts;
3. Finally, the presence of biblical verses, which seem to be a more recent fashion that does not match the original function of the *oratio fidelium*.

On the other hand, certain elements are older, notably the themes of invocations I–VI. How can we explain this? In our eyes, M^1 is not the source of M^2, even though this relationship may be asserted here and there in some studies. The formulation of I–II (plus III in M^2) differs on points whose modification would have made little difference (*clero-sacerdotio* for example); and even if the historical circumstances of the 6th century called for M^2 to omit the invocations for the orders and the needy (M^2 VII–VIII), that does not explain why they would have neglected M^1 IX which prays for the sick, or even M^1 X. Moreover, all the biblical verses are different. And finally, the responses are not the same. We no longer think that source *Q* is the common origin of FG^1 and M^2 since too many differences separate these two litanies.

Thus we are led to presume the existence of a source *Y*, lost today, which would have been reworked by the redactor of M^2. This would have had a liturgical form analogous to M^1 and belonged without doubt to the first wave of formularies dating from the 5th century. It would have included the ancient elements retained by M^2 and perhaps already contained c/, whose theme is found in Irl^1 b/.

By rejecting the relationship of M^2 with M^1, we agree with the judgment of Dom Alfonso,[244] for whom the biblical verses and the *Kyrie eleison* are the decisive arguments. In his view the verses indicate a Western style, of Irish origin, while the *Kyrie eleison,* despite the apparent contradiction, leads us to Rome. We know from the Council of Vaison that at the beginning of the 6th century Rome and Italy (which Alfonso details in his writing as 'Milan') had introduced the frequent repetition of the *Kyrie eleison* into both the Mass and the Office.

244 Alfonso (1925), 89–91.

'It seems evident to me', writes the Italian liturgist, 'that from the beginning the *Kyrie eleison* consisted of simple repetitions of these words, both according to the terms of the Council (of Vaison) and its function in the tradition preserved in the Office and the Ambrosian Mass and in the ancient Gallican liturgy'. In Rome, this repetition of the *Kyrie eleison* will be transformed and give birth to the stational litany (conceived as a type of Litany of the Saints); in Milan, it will develop into M^2. More precisely, according to Alfonso, the biblical verses of M^2 are 'direct invocations' similar to those of the Litany of the Saints ('libera nos Domine'; cf. M^2 d/), while the invocations must surely owe their existence to a desire to imitate M^1. In his opinion, the redactor of M^2 would have wanted to imitate this litany and would have interpolated the other invocations between the *Kyrie eleisons*; thus this response would have developed, just as others had done in Rome, but in a different way.

What are we to think of all this? We are in complete agreement with Alfonso on the origin of the *Kyrie* in the West. However, the fanciful thoughts that he builds around it are quite without foundation. The earliest trace of the Litany of the Saints dates back to the end of the 7th century,[245] and on the other hand, all the texts parallel to M^2 clearly prove that it is the litanies that attracted them to the *Kyrie eleison* and not the *Kyrie eleison* that has developed into a form of litany.

5. Attempt at Dating

In M^2 we have detected ancient elements whose presence we attribute to the influence of source *Y*, and later elements for which the redactor is responsible. But certain other characteristics of M^2 leave us perplexed; should we see in it a sign of antiquity or, on the contrary, something new? This is the first appearance of the phrase *quam conservare digneris* (I). While it is found, with regard to the Church itself, in the *Te igitur*, it will become very popular later, in the Litany of the Saints. But above all we have here the problem of the *Kyrie eleison*! As we recalled with regard to the ending of M^1, liturgical scholarship has, since E. Bishop, considered it as a latecomer in the West; the first solid traces both date from 520 (the Council of Vaison and the Rule of St Benedict).

Here it appears under two forms: as a final triple invocation and as a response. We voted in favour of the original character of the triple *Kyrie* in M^1; as M^2 is a later work, this opinion can only be confirmed by our litany; here it acquires an even higher degree of probability.

M^2 introduces a new element into the debate, since here the response itself is *Kyrie eleison*. Is this an ancient refrain that the redactor would have found in source *Y*, which itself would have been copied from the East? Or is it a new response, adopted in order to give the piece an archaic flavour, at a time when this Greek invocation was becoming fashionable in the West, notably thanks to

245 Cf. E. Bishop (1918), 'The Litany of the Saints of the Stowe Missal', 137–164. Cf. infra, Section Five.

the ending of M^1? As a response, *Kyrie eleison* appears a mere three times in the litanies: here, in the most amended of the *DG* manuscripts, and in the later FG^2. This inclines us to believe that it is the second hypothesis, that of the novelty of the *Kyrie*, that is the better, since it aligns better with the body of facts. In the first proposition it would be incomprehensible that this characteristic response had failed to leave its trace in any source before the 6th century.

Let us summarise the elements of dating that we have so far noted:

- Source *Y* must date from the 5th century, without being possible to be more specific;
- M^2 cannot predate M^1, which we have situated during the second half of the 5th century;
- the *Kyrie eleison*, of which there are no traces before 529, cannot be much earlier than the 6th century.

We therefore conclude that M^2 must date from the beginning of the 6th century. Its redactor, who might be a Roman, like that of M^1, belongs to this second wave of texts that has already produced *DG* and FG^1 and will provide us with yet two more litanies.

IV. The Second Franco-Gallican Litany (FG^2)

Dom Capelle has not edited this secondary and sometimes severely degraded text. It was used in OR 50 for Rogation Days, as was FG^1. Our research into the processional manuscripts and other medieval liturgical books has led us to discover several sources. The list, which is not exhaustive, is for the most part identical to that for FG^1, so we can quote it in a shortened version.

A. Sources

We will divide them into four families, each distinguished by the biblical verses with which they conclude. This classification does not arise from evidence, it merely seeks to bring a little order and clarity; perhaps the discovery of new sources will break the impasse.

α. The 'Libera — Exaudi preces' Family

**A* = all the manuscripts for OR 50 (apart from *Z*: Vienna 1817), which we have taken from the critical edition by Andrieu, vol. 5, 338; there are minor variants (Mayence, around 950)

D = BRUSSELS, B.R. 4836 (Cat. 641), f. 15v–16v, (14th c.)

D' = ARRAS, B.M. 230, f. 52v (dating from 1307–8).

Just three sources, then, instead of the six in the corresponding family of FG^1; indeed, FG^2 is not found in *B* (Vienna 1888), and the extravagant *C* (Autun S 12) here moves into family δ.

β. The 'Libera — Exaudi Preces — Exaudi Nos' Family

E = PARIS, B.N. lat.909, f. 7^v (11th c.)
**E* = PARIS, B.N. lat 1120 and 1121, respectively f. 168^v–169 and 161^v–162 (early 11th c.)
F = PARIS, B.N. lat 903, f. 137^r (early 11th c.)
**G* = AUTUN, B. M. S 183, f. 63 (13th c.) and S 188, f. 99^v–100^v (15th c.)
**H* = CAMBRAI, B.M. 60, f. 101^v–102 (12th c.).
68, f. 36–38 (15th–16th c.)
71, f. 137 (15th c.)
77, f. 76^v (13th–14th c.)
78, f. 41 (late 11th c.)
80, f. 33 (18th c.)
131, f. 51 (early 14th c.)
M' = MADRID, Acad. de la Hist. 51, f. 146^v–147^r (11th–12th c.)

A curious fact: the manuscript AUTUN S 98 which contains FG^1 does not include our litany; the same thing goes for MADRID, B.N. 136.

γ. The Abbreviated Family

**J* = LONDON, Brit. Mus. Harl. 4951, f. 237^v–238^r (11th c.)
PARIS, B.N. lat. 776, f. 85^v (11th c.)
J' = PARIS, B.N. lat. 776, nv. acq. lat. 3001, f. 32 (13th c.)
M = MADRID, Acad. de la Hist. 45, f. 57^v (early 12th c.)[246]
P = J. Pothier, *Prières litaniales ou processionnelles*, in *Revue du chant grégorien*, vol. 9 (1901), 113–14, following a 13th century Pontifical, whose origin is not given by the author. The text is identical to *J'*.

FG^2 is found in neither *I* nor *I'*, nor in manuscript 312 of the Great Seminary of Langres.

δ. The 'Exaudi Preces — Exurge' Family

C = AUTUN, B. M. S 12, f. 95 (12th c.)
K = PARIS, B.N. lat. 780, f. 77^v, Gradual of Narbonne, 11th–12th c.

246 The litany stops at the bottom of f. 57^r with the words, 'Pro rege nostro'; it does not continue on f. 58. According to this fragment, it must belong to the abbreviated family.

L = *Processionale turonense*, Tours, 1827, 117–19.[247]

B. Edited Versions

Below, we establish the critical edition of the four families mentioned. Since they are sufficiently clear and there are few variants, it is not useful to give a global edition as we did for *FG¹*: formulary β is complete and takes its place. Thus all the Roman numerals refer to the order found in β. The square brackets [] enclose those invocations that to us do not seem original; while they crop up in several families, we have only indicated the brackets in β.

a. The 'Libera — Exaudi Preces' Family

a/ Kyrie eleison
b/ Domine Deus omnipotens patrum nostrorum
Kyrie eleison[248]
c/ Respice de caelo et de sede sancta tua
Kyrie eleison
V Pro pace regum et quiete populorum
Kyrie eleison
VII Pro loco nostro et habitantibus in eo
Kyrie eleison
d/ Libera nos qui liberasti filios Israël
Kyrie eleison
e/ Exaudi preces supplicantium te, Christe
Kyrie eleison.

---

247 According to Gastoue (1937), 173, *FG²* also features in PARIS, B.N. lat. 1118, f. 12, the Tropiary from the region of Auch, subsequently handed on to Saint-Martial, dating from the 10th–11th c; having checked, we have found that this is not so.

Many of the manuscripts are notated; we can find the melodies for *FG²* in the article by Gastoue cited above or in his *Cours théorique et pratique de plain-chant romain grégorien*, (1904), 70.

As with *FG¹*, our classification matches that of M. Huglo (1971), which is based on musical criteria; the Aquitaine manuscripts of group β (Paris, B.N. lat. 909 and 1121) represent Limousin, those of family γ (LONDON, Brit. Mus. Harl. 4951 and Paris, B.N. lat. 776) are originally from the Toulouse region; while PARIS, B.N. lat. 780, from group δ, form part of the manuscripts 'linked to the Toulouse group', according to Huglo's terminology.

248 Kyrie eleison *om A semper nisi post* e/.

β. The 'Libera — Exaudi Preces — Exaudi Nos' Family

a/ Kyrie eleison

b/ Domine Deus omnipotens patrum nostrorum
Kyrie eleison

c/ Respice de caelo et de sede sancta tua
Kyrie eleison

I Pro sancta ecclesia catholica quae est in toto orbe constituta[249]
Kyrie eleison

II[250] Pro papa nostro et omni plebe[251] eius
Kyrie eleison

III[252] Pro pastore nostro et omni clero eius
Kyrie eleison

[IV[253] Pro rege nostro et omni exercitu eius
Kyrie eleison]

V[254] Pro pace regum et quiete populorum
Kyrie eleison

[VI[255] Pro abbate nostro et omni congregatione eius
Kyrie eleison]

VII[256] Pro loco nostro et[257] habitantibus in eo
Kyrie eleison

VIII[258] Pro remissione peccatorum et emendatione eorum
Kyrie eleison

d/[259] Libera[260] nos qui liberasti filios Israël
Kyrie eleison

---

249 constituta] diffusa *H*.
250 II *om GH*.
251 plebe] clero *M'*.
252 III *om F*.
253 IV *add H*.
254 V *post* VII *G*.
255 VI *add FM'*.
256 VII *post* VIII *FM'*, *ante* V *G*.
257 et] et omnibus *FM'*.
258 VIII *om H*. *post* d/ *EE'G*. *ante* VII *FM'*.
259 d/ *ante* VIII *EE'G*.
260 Libera *GH*. pro ut liberes *EE'FM'*.

e/ Exaudi voces[261] deprecantium te, Christe
Kyrie eleison

f/[262] Exaudi nos Deus in omni oratione ista
Kyrie eleison.

γ. The Abbreviated Family

a/ Kyrie eleison

b/ Domine Deus omnipotens patrum nostrorum
Kyrie eleison

c/ Respice de caelo et de sede sancta tua
Kyrie eleison

I Pro ecclesia catholica quae est in toto orbe constituta
Kyrie eleison

IV Pro rege nostro et omni exercitu eius
Kyrie eleison

II Pro papa nostro et omni clero eius
Kyrie eleison

VI Pro abbate[263] nostro et omni congregatione eius
Kyrie eleison

VII Pro loco nostro et omnibus habitantibus in eo
Kyrie eleison.

δ. The 'Exaudi Preces — Exurge' Family

a/ Kyrie eleison

b/ Domine Deus omnipotens patrum nostrorum
Kyrie eleison[264]

c/ Respice de caelo et de sede sancta tua
Kyrie eleison

---

261 voces] preces *EH*.
262 f/ *om H*.
263 abbate *del J' em* conventu. conventu *P*.
264 Kyrie eleison *om C semper nisi post* g/.

V[265]	Pro pace regum et quiete populorum
	Kyrie eleison
[II[266]	Pro papa nostro et apostolatu eius
	Kyrie eleison]
IV	Pro rege nostro et omni exercitu eius
	Kyrie eleison
III[267]	Pro pastore nostro et omni clero eius
	Kyrie eleison
VII	Pro loco isto[268] et habitantibus in eo
	Kyrie eleison
e/[269]	Exaudi preces confitentium te, Christe
	Kyrie eleison
g/	Exurge Domine adiuva nos et libera nos propter nomen tuum
	Kyrie eleison.[270]

C. Characteristics of Each Family

More than the purpose of the petitions, it is the closing biblical verses that provide the criteria for distinguishing each family.

α. The 'Libera — Exaudi Preces' Family

This is the shortest, having only two of the invocations (V and VII) that constitute the common core of the four families (one other exception is that family γ omits V).

β. The 'Libera — Exaudi Preces — Exaudi Nos' Family

This is the longest of the families and contains up to eight invocations. Apart from V and VII, we read the petitions repeated from *FG¹*, several of which are common with γ (I–II-IV–VI), others with δ (III–IV). Moreover, it adds at the end a biblical verse f/, also taken from *FG¹*.

265 *ante* V Oramus te supplices ut exaudias nos precantes *add C.*
266 II *add K.*
267 III] Pro abbate nostro et omni congregatione eius *C.*
268 isto] nostro *C.*
269 *ante* e/ Aperi caelos deus et da pluviam terrae *add K.*
270 Kyrie eleison *om L.*

γ. The Abbreviated Family

This family merits this description because it contains neither the final biblical verses, nor V which forms part of the common core of the family members. It has no invocation of its own.

δ. The 'Exaudi Preces — Exurge' Family

Apart from the common core, δ offers invocations that feature in both β and γ. It omits d/ and adds a second final verse g/ taken from *M*². Two manuscripts from this family indulge in their own particular whims; *C* adds an introductory invocation: 'Oramus te supplices ut exaudias nos precantes', and *K* adds a third final biblical verse, 'Aperi caelos deus et da pluviam terrae', an original petition that occurs only at Narbonne, a hot and dry region (cf. n. 213, p. 184).

D. Liturgical Form

*FG*² is a litany characterised by the presence of numerous biblical verses, as occurs in *M*² which, moreover, has the same response, *Kyrie eleison*. Lacking both introduction and conclusion by a priest, it consists of:

a/ the response, which is not introduced in the usual way with any admonition such as *Dicamus omnes*;

b/ an attributive invocation;

c/ an imperative invocation;

I–VIII; from two to eight nominal invocations; b/-c/, also with the response, clearly indicating that these are invocations;

d/-g/ two or three imperative invocations in the form of biblical verses, as at the beginning.

E. Analysis

It is not necessary to draw out Eastern parallels any further, since *FG*² does not include any really original invocation. It will be enough for us to comment on the form, noting any relationships with the Latin litanies.

1. Commentary

a/ the omission of an admonition to introduce the response is certainly a later redaction; the other Latin litanies do not leave any doubt in this regard. We note that manuscript *G* of *M*² omitted *Dicamus omnes* and commenced abruptly with *Kyrie eleison*, as happens here.

b/-c/ are identical to the b/-c/ of M^2.

I features in β and γ; it is found in FG^1 II, with the same confusion between *diffusa* and *constituta.*

II the prayer for the pope exists in certain manuscripts of families β — γ — δ; its ending is original (*plebe* β; *apostolatu K*). One curious thing: this invocation features in all the manuscripts from the South of France or from Spain, and only there (*EE'FJJ'KM'*, and *P* whose provenance is unknown). Is this by chance, or does this finding reveal particular trends in theology or popular piety?

III is mentioned by β (apart from *F*) and δ (apart from *C*); it is identical with FG^1 III.

IV–V the first petition for the king occurs in β in the group from Cambrai. γ and δ have it; it is identical with FG^1 V. V also speaks about kings, but the subject of this invocation is actually peace. Is it the proximity of the two mentions of the king that caused V to be suppressed in γ? We note that M^1 IV prayed *pro pace ecclesiarum … et quiete populorum*; the times have changed…

VI features in two manuscripts (the monastic *F* and *M'*) of β, in γ and in *C*. We observe the correction in family γ into *conventu,* probably as a result of the manuscripts being used in a religious community without an abbot. The fact that VI is found only in monastic sources, but not in all, seems to indicate that it did not form part of the original source for FG^2, any more than for FG^1; we therefore place it between square brackets.

VII This invocation, which sometimes features in FG^1 VI, seems really to belongto our litany; it is the one one that we encounter, with minor variants, (*isto* δ except *C*; *omnibus* add γ) in all four families.

VIII is found only in β, where the Cambrai group omits it; it is identical to FG^1 IX.

d/ = M^2 d/' and is omitted by δ (and by γ which has no final verse).

e/ proper to FG^2. We observe the variants *supplicantium* (α), *deprecantium* (β), *confitentium* (δ); cf. Ps 139:7, 57:6.

f/ = FG^1 c/.

g/ = M^2 f/.

2. Sources and Dating for FG²

It is undeniable that our piece belongs to the second wave of Latin texts. But has it been adapted from a source that is today lost to us (*Z*), or can it be explained sufficiently based on the litanies studied previously?

a/-b/-c/-d/-g/could be influenced by M^2, as too the response *Kyrie eleison* and the nominal aspect of the invocations. The purpose of these, however, is far closer to FG^1: I–III-[IV]-[VI]-VIII could derive from it, as also the verse f/. Invocations II (with *plebs*), V (possibly influenced by M^1 IV), VII (which is part of the common core for all families) and verse e/ all remain peculiar to FG^2.

We point out that these four elements cannot have as their sources *Q* or *Y*, whose existence we have been obliged to assume. It is impossible to see how FG^1 and FG^2 could both come from the same source, *Q*, nor how both M^2 and FG^2 could come from source *Y*. Do these four elements call for us to suppose the existence of a source *Z*, which would have contained them, or must we attribute their paternity to the redactor of FG^2?

It is possible that a source *Z* did exist; nothing leads us to deny this … apart from the fact that we have no trace of it. Any sound historical methodology is loath to multiply hypotheses when the facts can themselves provide an explanation. We are willing to believe that the current text of FG^2 is the work of an author who, in composing it, drew on the litanies with which we are familiar, notably M^2 and FG^1. Perhaps he has taken II, V, VII and e/ from a litany that has not come down to us; but it is also possible that in II he replaces *sacerdotio* (M^2 II) with *plebe*, in a period where the notion of the presbyterium had been forgotten; that he transformed the *pro pace ecclesiarum* of M^1 IV into *pro pace regum* when peace was threatened as much by bellicose kings as by doctrinal disputes between Churches; that he modified the *pro civitate hac* of M^2 V into *pro loco nostro*, which is much more general, and which may apply particularly to monasteries, perhaps inspired by Irl^1 VI.

Whatever its origin, FG^2 is certainly a late formulary, which could not have seen the light of day before the 6th century.

3. Usage of FG^2

OR 50 situates FG^2 on Wednesday of the Rogation Days, to be sung leaving the church, in the same way that FG^1 specifies it for the Monday. The medieval Processionals and certain Graduals use it in this way, sometimes for Monday, quite often for Tuesday. Just as with FG^1, and for the same reasons, we do not think that OR 50 initiated this use of FG^2. We have already rejected as implausible the hypothesis that FG^1 was composed directly for use on Rogations Days (instituted at the end of the 5th century) and not as a Universal Prayer; the changes of this being so with regard to FG^2 are about the same.

But can we honestly recognise in this degraded text a formulary of the *oratio fidelium*? Once again, none of our sources indicate this function for it. The similarity between FG^2 and the other litanies show us however that even if it did not serve as a Universal Prayer in its current state, it does certainly retain traces of it; it is for this reason that it is included in this study.

4. Location

We have not come across any indication of a location for FG^2. We have only two elements to guide us: the fact that all the sources are Franco-Gallican, and the probability that the redactor was familiar with both M^2 and FG^1. Nothing beyond this relationship to M^2 leads us on the road to Rome; on the contrary, everything drives us further to the North, towards those Churches that often turned their eyes to the Apostolic See and little by little took up their liturgical traditions. And so we situate *FG*² in one of these Churches that practised what we could call, loosely speaking, the Gallican liturgy.

V. The Second 'Irish' Text (Irl2)

The 'Canon dominicus papae gilasi' of the Stowe Missal includes a long interpolation at the Memento of the living, whose words come close to our formularies, even if the actual form is no longer an *oratio fidelium*.[271] The text is also found in the Fulda manuscript recopied by Witzel. At the beginning of the century, Bannister encountered evidence of it in a fragment from Reichenau. Finally, in manuscript 164 from Cambrai, which contains the Gregorian Sacramentary of Bishop Hildoard, beginning at f. 35ᵛ, we found at f. 34ᵛ a fourth example of this formulary. Here, then, is the list.

A. The Sources

S = DUBLIN, Royal Irish Academy, D. II. 3, f. 24ᵛ–25ᵛ = *Stowe Missal*, ed. Warner, p. 11; (Clavis 1926 — Bourque 527 — Gamber 101). The entire beginning of the Canon is the work of Moelcaich and dates from the 9th century

F = Irish Missal of Fulda, cf. Witzel (1555); (Bourque 528a — Gamber 102)

R = CARLSRUHE, Bad. Landesbibl., App. Aug. CLXVII (fragment MS Reichenau), f. 2ʳ, col. 1–2, 8th–9th c. ed. Bannister, (1904), 64–65; (Bourque 532)

C = CAMBRAI, Bibl. Mun. 164 (olim 159), f. 34ᵛ; Second half of 9th c. ed. Leroquais (1924), vol. 1, 9; (Bourque 53).[272]

271 In the Introduction to Part Two, we have justified the inclusion of this text in our study.

272 In his article, 'On Some Early Manuscripts of the Gregorianum', reprinted in *Liturgica historica*, E. Bishop has already noted (p. 65, note) that Cambrai manuscript 164 carries traces of Irish influence, particularly in its origins. L. Gougaud repeated this judgement in his article *Celtiques (Liturgies)*, DACL 2/2, 2969–3032, and even classifies the manuscript among the Celtic sources (col. 2972). On the other hand, H. Lietzmann (1921, p. xvii) rejects this influence, as does Bourque (no. 53), whereas Gamber no. 720, Vogel (English version of *Introduction*, p. 82, n. 221) and Leroquais (*loc. cit*) make no mention of it.

None of them seem to have noticed our text, still less its relationship with *Irl*², so must we must conclude that Bishop is right. Relying on Traube (1930), 95–119, he highlights the Irish influence on the abbeys of Peronne, Saint-Riquier and Corbie, extending even to Cambrai. Even if *Irl*² was a Gallican text introduced into Irish sources, additional evidence of a link between Gaul and Ireland is nonetheless provided.

B. The Edited Version

Our edition is based on *S*, which has retained in several repeated versions, the noun that *F* has replaced with a verbal adjective. *C* has also been influenced by this last way of doing things; in VI, the reading *venerantium*, which is meaningless, can be explained by the presence in *F* of *celebranda*. The beginning a/ does not form part of the text; we provide it here, following *R*, for purposes of comparison, placing it between square brackets [ ].

[a/[273]		Oremus domini misericordiam
		pro animabus omnium episcoporum nostrorum
		et presbyterorum[274] nostrorum
		et diaconorum nostrorum
		et carorum nostrorum
		et cararum nostrarum
		et puerorum nostrorum
		et puellarum nostrarum
		et paenitentium nostrorum[275]]
A	I[276]	pro[277] statu[278] seniorum[279] et ministrorum omnium puritate[280]
	II	pro integritate virginum et continentia viduarum
	III	pro bona[281] aeris temperie[282] et fructuum fecunditate terrarum[283]
	IV	pro pacis redditu ac fine[284] discriminum
	V	pro incolumitate[285] regum et pace[286] populorum ac redditu[287] captivorum

---

273 a/ *in S* = Secunda pars augmenti hic super oblata (Warner, p. 9)
in *R* = *post* Qui pridie
om CF.

274 presbyterorum *R.* sacerdotum *S.*

275 ⟨ut⟩ cunctis proficiant ad salutem per dominum. Sursum corda *expl S.*

276 I *in S* = Memento vivorum (Warner p. 11)
in F — in Canone (forte etiam Memento vivorum)
in C sine titulo.

277 pro] et in commoni *R.*

278 statu] stratu *alt.m RS.*

279 seniorum *FR.* Seniorum suorum *S.* sacerdotum *C.*

280 ministrorum omnium puritate *CS.* puritate *om R.* puritate ministrorum *F.*

281 bona *om CRS.*

282 temp-/.../pro incolumitate *lac R.*

283 fructuum ... terrarum *CS.* segetum fecunditate *F.*

284 reditu ac fine *F.* redetu et fine *S.* et finis redditu *C.*

285 incolumitate/.../-lorum ac *lac R.*

286 pace] tranquillitate *F.*

287 reditu] liberatione *F.* ac red-/.../-tis adstantium *lac R.*

	VI	pro votis adstantium[288] et[289] memoria martyrum[290]
	VII[291]	pro remissione[292] peccatorum nostrorum[293] et actuum emendatione[294]
	VIII	pro[295] requie[296] defunctorum
	IX[297]	pro[298] prosperitate itineris nostri
B	X	pro[299] domino papa episcopo et[300] omnibus episcopis et presbyteris[301] et omni ecclesiastico ordine[302]
	XI	pro imperio romano[303] et omnibus regibus[304] christianis
	XII[305]	pro fratribus et sororibus[306] nostris
	XIII[307]	pro fratribus in via directis[308]
	XIV[309]	pro[310] fratribus quos de caliginosis huius mundi[311] tenebris dominus arcessire dignatus[312] est ut eos in aeterna summae lucis quiete[313] divina[314] pietas suscipiat

288 exaudiendis *add F*. adstan-/…/-tirum *lac R*.
289 et *C*. pro *FS*.
290 celebranda *add RS*. venerantium *add C*.
291 VII] pro remittendis atque emendandis peccatis nostris F.
292 omnium *add C*. pro re-/…/nostrorum *lac R*.
293 nostrorum *om C*. et/…/et pro requie *lac R*.
294 eorum *add S*. (⟨r⟩eorum *susp Mac Carthy*).
295 pro *F*. ac *CS*. et pro *R*.
296 omnium fidelium *add C*. requie d-/…/itineris *lac R*.
297 IX *usque XV* om *C*.
298 pro *F*. et *S*.
299 pro *FS*. et/…/episcopis *lac R*.
300 domino papa episcopo et *S*. romano pontifice ac *F*.
301 et presbyteris] presbyterisque *F*. episcopis e-/…/-astico ordine *lac R*.
302 ordi-/…/et omnibus *lac R*.
303 romano *om F*.
304 regibus] principibus *F*. regib-/…/directis *lac R*.
305 XII *om R*.
306 et sororibus *S*. sororibusque *F*.
307 XIII *post* XIV *F*.
308 directis] dirigendis *F*.
309 XIV *ente* XIII *F*.
310 et pro/…/-ginosis *lac R*.
311 huius mundi] mundi huius *S*. huius/…/-cessire *lac R*.
312 dig-/…/-ce et quiete *lac R*.
313 in aeterna summae lucis quietae *S*. ⟨in aeterna lu⟩ce et quiete *R*. in aeternam summamque lucem et quietem *F*.
314 divina pietas] pietas divina *S*. di-/…/pro fratribus *lac R*.

XV	pro fratribus qui variis[315] dolorum generibus affligantur[316] ut[317] eos[318] divina pietas[319] curare dignetur[320]
[XVI[321]	pro spe salutis et incolumitatis suae.][322]

C. Eastern and Western Parallels

Strict Eastern parallels with *Irl²* are scarce. While its general subject matter is always held in common with the Eastern litanies, its dependence is nevertheless more marked in relation to Latin texts. We shall note some similarities:

I	*senior* translates πρεσβύτερος.
III	= B 363, *M¹* VI, *FG¹* VII, *M²* VI. *Temperies* as usual translates the Greek εὐκρασία; we note that *F* has 'pro *bona* aeris temperie', which is probably an exact transliteration of εὐ-κρασία.
V	cf. *FG²* V. 'redditu captivorum' is very similar to *J* 46 where the invitatory for the needy ends with the petition εἰρηνικῆς ἐπανόδου αὐτῶν.
VI	τῶν ἁγίων μαρτύρων μνημονεύσωμεν. CAp VIII, 13, 6; *J* 35, 48; cf. *Irl¹* XI.
VII	cf. *DG* XIII, *FG¹* IX, *FG²* VIII.
X	ὑπὲρ τοῦ ἀρχιερέως ἡμῶν πάπα ἀββᾶ *M* 121.
XI	cf. *Irl¹* V.
XV	cf. *M¹* IX, *FG¹* VIII.

D. Liturgical Form

In its current form, *Irl²* is a 'priestly prayer'; it is lacking the response that a litany requires. Neverthless we consider, on the basis of its nearness to other Latin formularies, that it was originally a litany, and it is on these grounds that we present it here.

As we have already said, a/ did not form part of the original text:

---

315 va-/.../gemitibus *lac R.*
316 generibus affligantur *FS.* gemitibus *R.*
317 ut/.../-are dignetur *lac R.*
318 in aeternum *add F.*
319 pietas *S.* bonitas *F.*
320 dignet-/.../*lac R.*
321 XVI *om FR.*
322 suae *om C.*

- it is missing in *C* and *F*;
- in *S* it is situated before the Preface and forms part of a prayer entitled 'secunda parts augmenti hic super oblata';
- in *R* alone it comes immediately before our formulary.

In the same way, XVI belongs to the Commemoration of the living.

The remainder of the text comprises two pieces placed side by side: I–IX and X–XV. We have several indications of this:

1. *C* effectively contains only the first part;[323]
2. X appears like a new beginning; the prayer for the ministers is, in effect, found among the first petitions, and not in the middle of the formulary;
3. Several petitions are expressed twice: X is a repeat of I, XI of V, XIII of IX, XIV of VIII;
4. We also discern variations in the vocabulary; I speaks of *senior*, X of *presbyter*, but both of them have their origin in πρεσβύτερος.

We therefore estimate that the two litanies were put end to end, probably at a time when the Universal Prayer had fallen into disuse and where its function had been taken over by more developed anaphoric intercessions.

Schematically, the liturgical form is as follows:

[a/invitatory for the dead];
A. First part, composed of nine nominal invitatories (I–IX);
B. Second part, composed of six nominal invitatories (X–XV);
[XVI belongs to the Commemoration of the living.]

We are dealing with invitatories since, in addition to a/ which is explicitly so, XIV and XV speak of God in the third person and there is no sense of invocation here.

E. Commentary on the First Part (I–X)

I. The term *senior* (πρεσβύτερος) is peculiar to *Irl*²; but what significance does this give it? In the Christian literature, it reflects mainly two meanings. In the earliest days it was synonymous with *presbyter*; this ministerial meaning is found in

323 Although *C* contains only the petitions I–VIII, we consider that IX forms part of the first litany rather than the second, where XIII is also a prayer for travellers and would therefore constitute a doublet; moreover, there is nothing of an incipit for IX.

Tertullian,[324] Cyprian,[325] and Leo the Great.[326] Later, in the monastic sphere, *senior* had the commonplace meaning of elder, or person of experience.[327] In the Commemoration of the dead from the Stowe Missal (what is near to it in historical time is pertinent), the expression 'offert senior noster ·N· praespiter pro se'[328] seemed rather to describe the father abbot of a monastery, but we are of the opinion that here, in *Irl*^{2}, *senior* refers to priests, seeing that ministries are mentioned in the same petition, and in light of the variant *sacerdotum* that is found in *C*.

The prayer for the *puritas* of the ministers seems to us to be more recent. This petition is never found in the East, and reflects an evolution in the understanding of priesthood.

We note the clearly Latin construction of these petitions (*pro* + ablative, indicating the purpose of the prayer, + genitive that indicates its beneficiary). Indeed Latin prefers abstract terms (*puritas, integritas*...) while the Greek makes better use of concrete words. This affirms that our formulary is not a direct translation from the Greek, but belongs to the second wave of texts.

II. The place occupied by this prayer for virgins and widows takes us back to the early period in the Church when they were included in the ministries. However, we believe that the order of petitions has undergone a metamorphosis: good weather comes ahead of peace and both of these come before kings — scarcely the traditional pattern.

III. The second part of the invitatory faithfully translates B 363 and has preserved the ancient Latin formula; we have seen, on the other hand, that with *M*^{1} VI this petition has been subjected to modifications.

V. *A* is closer to *FG*^{2} V: 'pro pace regum et quiete populorum'; *incolumitas* is peculiar to *Irl*^{2}. There is nothing to indicate that the captives in question here are Christians imprisoned for their faith.

VI. The first part of this invitatory is a prayer for the assembly; the only place where we have encountered a similar petition is in *DG* XII.

The commemoration of the saints is an Eastern theme, as *Irl*^{1} XI has already attested.

IX. The prayer for travellers is quite common, but the wording of this invitatory is original.

---

324 Tertullian, *Apologeticum*, 39, 5; ed. Dekkers, (CC 1), 150: 'Praesident probati quique seniores'.

325 Cyprian, *Epistola* 75, 4, 3; ed. Bayard, vol. 2, 291: 'qua ex causa necessario apud nos fit ut per singulos annos seniores et praepositi in unum conveniamus...' Tr. Donna (FC 51), 297: 'For this reason, it happens necessarily among us that, through the years, we older men and prelates assemble together...'.

326 Leo the Great, *Sermo 60*, 7; (PL 54), 341B: 'Nunc etenim et ordo clarior levitarum, et dignitas amplior seniorum, et sacratior est unctio sacerdotum'.

327 John Cassian, *Institutes III*, 5, 1; ed. Petschenig, (CSEL 17), 40; ed. Guy, (SC 109), 106: 'haec a senioribus nostris sollemnitas instituta est'.

328 *Stowe Missal*, ed. Warner, 14.

Attempt at Dating

This formulary appears to be an example of the second wave of texts. It uses old material (*senior*; III is well preserved; the inclusion of captives in V; the commemoration of the martyrs in VI), but it is evident that this source has been reworked to accommodate a more recent period. It may even be a much more recent period, as evidenced by such elements as *puritas* of the ministers (I), the *integritas* of the virgins and the *continentia* of the widows (II), all terms that reveal a concern for good morals, and the petition to grant the prayers of the assembly (VI), which never appeared in the first formularies.

It is possible that *Irl*^{2} *A* has undergone two revisions. The first would have continued to include a response which provided a balanced rhythm (*pro* + abstract ablative + concrete genitive). The second would have transformed this litany into a priestly prayer (current text); this latter transformation probably dates from the time when the *oratio fidelium* had disappeared, an undefined period, but certainly prior to the Sacramentaries. We will roughly date the first revision to the 6th century and the second to the 7th.

F. Commentary on the Second Part: X–XV

The litany that serves as the second part of *Irl*^{2} has been shortened at the beginning. We do not find there any prayer for peace — frequent in this literary genre — and above all it lacks the petition for the universal Church, always present in litanies of this type.

X What meaning ought we give to *papa*? At first sight, it is describing the local bishop; the placing of the term *episcopo* immediately after seems to indicate this, even if this has been added, as a detail, in a period when *papa* tended to be reserved to the bishop of Rome. This is confirmed by the parallel offered by *M* 121 (ὑπὲρ τοῦ ἀρχιερέως ἡμῶν πάπα ἀββᾶ) as well as by *Irl*^{1} III: 'pro patre nostro episcopo'. The absence of a prayer for the pope of Rome is not an argument against this interpretation; it was missing in many of the ancient texts.

In the second hypothesis, which would be held by Dom Botte, *papa* would indicate the bishop of Rome; certainly the variant *F* states it with all the clarity one could wish for: *pro romano pontifice*. A comma would separate *papa* from *episcopo*; there would be no qualifying term, such as *nostro*, to designate the local bishop, unless of course the text itself comes from Rome, and we have no indication of that. The 'pro imperio romano' of XI cannot be taken as proof of the argument, for the words following immediately after are *et omnibus regibus christianis*.

Once again we are confronted with the difficulty of interpreting these liturgical texts with precision. They have traversed the centuries with terms

whose meaning has evolved; sometimes they have been reshaped and ancient material has been given a different meaning, so that often we are incapable of giving an exact meaning of a text that is present in the manuscripts available to us today. In this case, however, the rest of the piece will clarify things for us.
– *Et omni ecclesiatico ordine*: the word *ordo* is only encountered in our texts here and in the third prayer of the *OS* ('pro universis ordinibus'.)

XI *Pro imperio romano*; this is the only text, along with *Irl*[1] VI, to speak of the Roman empire. Is this a clue to their origin? *Et omnibus regibus christianis* cannot be dated before the end of the 5th century; perhaps it is an adaptation of the first petition, following the collapse of the Empire.

XII–XV These four petitions pray *pro fratribus*; we think that here we are confronted with a monastic formulary, despite the difficulty of knowing who might be the 'sisters' in question. This is confirmed by:

XIII *pro fratribus in via directis*; Chapter 67 of the Rule of St Benedict is entitled *De fratribus in viam directis*; cf. also chapters 50 and 55.

XIV It is from a very dark period that the Lord seems to call the brothers into his light. This invitatory and the one following specify the subject of the prayer, thanks to a final clause.

XVI does not form part of this piece but belongs, rather, to a Commemoration of the living.

Conclusion

The second part of *Irl*[2] is the most degraded of the formularies among those that we have examined so far.

In an earlier version, that we assume was litanic, it would have included at least invitatories X–XI and probably the content of XIII and XIV, and certainly a response. It is comparison with the ancient litanies that leads us to suppose this.

In its current form, *Irl*[2] *B* has been subjected to Benedictine influence, and so certainly cannot be dated prior to 529. It is no longer the formulary of an *oratio fidelium*: invitatories XIV and XV have been reworked and no longer match the characteristic rhythm of the older litanies. A date is very difficult to determine, but the 7th century would not seem to be too late. Thus the *dominus papa* in X of the current version could certainly refer to the bishop of Rome; as for *episcopo*, this would have to be attached to *papa* and translated: 'for our holy father pope, bishop (of Rome)'. The absence of a prayer for the local bishop (if the monastery is not Roman) would not be catastrophic in a monastic text. If *episcopo* were indeed to refer to the local bishop, it would be necessary to underline *nostro*, having first placed a comma after *papa*.

As for the provenance of the formulary, we could take XI as a weak indicator in favour of its Roman origin.

Conclusion of the First Three Sections

We have read and analysed eight of the oldest texts of the Universal Prayer to have been preserved. Before arriving at any general conclusions, we would benefit by first considering the pieces presented in the fourth section. But at this point we can already gather together some impressions.

This study can only provide us with an inadequate idea of the state of the Universal Prayer in ancient Christianity, since it only offers us eight formularies. So many others have been lost to us, or were never written down in the first place. From these comes the majestic *OS*, obviously the richest and most beautiful of these prayers, and also the oldest, since their invitatories date back to the second half of the 3rd century.

New information arising from our study concerns the date when these litanies appeared in the West. While we speak in general terms of the *Deprecatio* of Gelasius (492–496) as the first litanic prayer in Latin, we have established that it formed part of the second generation of litanies. The first, which dates from the end of the 4th century, was content to translate Greek texts, and we find the oldest material in *Irl*^{1} and *M*^{1}. The second wave attempts to improve this situation; *DG* is its flagship. Together with the *OS*, it is the most developed text that we have read.

But soon these rewritings will come to impoverish rather than improve the ancient formularies; *M*^{2}, *FG*^{2}, and especially *Irl*^{2} bear witness to the cultural collapse of the period. Liturgists seek to mine these old treasures and adapt them to new circumstances, but these transformations lead to degradations and soon result in mere refrains. The risk is that the Universal Prayer, the outstanding popular prayer, in the best sense of the term, will degenerate into mere repetition and stereotypical petitions, with very ordinary content. The early writers, on the other hand, did not hesitate to make use of all the resources of literary composition in order to give their prayer a beauty and flow that not only won over the heart but also lifted up the spirit.

Section Four

The Gallican and Hispanic 'Orationes Paschales'

The *orationes paschales* found in the Gallican and Hispanic Sacramentaries take up again, without doubt, the subject matter of the eight texts studied so far. It is for this reason that I feel driven to present them in this work, even though their titles are not related to our topic. In presenting these formularies, our first goal is to provide the reader with a complete set, by gathering scattered, but nevertheless related, texts. Unfortunately we will not have the opportunity to study them as closely as the previous texts. However, by reading them we will be able to get an idea of what the Universal Prayer was like in Gaul and Spain.

In the sources available to us, these items are all used during the Easter Vigil, albeit at slightly different places, which we will indicate each time.[1]

A. The Gallican 'Orationes Paschales'[2]

1. The Missale Gallicanum Vetus (MGV)

This book[3] provides the litie set out below after the *Exsultet*; we have taken it from the text provided by Mohlberg.

Incipiunt orationes in uigilia pascae pro sollemnitate sancta

1 These texts have been known for a long time. They are cited by:
Meyer (1912), 87–108; Alfonso (1928), 67–75; Cabrol, art. 'Litanies', DACL 9/2, 1560 ff.; Willis (1964), 28–31.
Alfonso and Willis only list the invitatories. The best study on this matter is that of Bernal (1964), 283–347 (at 323–47).

2 The bibliography on the Gallican liturgies was given above, Part One, Section Five: The Church of Gaul.

3 ROME, Bibl. Vat. Palat. lat. 493, 8th. Century (Clavis 1922 — Bourque 519 — Gamber 214); ed. Mohlberg (1958). Our piece is found at f. 66r–70r, or pp. 37–39.

a/ Inter prima celebrandae sanctae paschae solempnia uotorum contestatio ex gratiarum actione sumamus[4] exordium, ut passum et immolatum pro nobis Christum credentes, sacris misteriis fidem concinnentibus exultationis plausibus praeferamus; ac per ipsum inque[m] ipsum nostrae sit depraecationis ascensio, manentes in eo et cum eodem diuinitatis gloriae:[5] per.

Collectio sequitur. Respice, domine, ecclesiam tuam quae admirabile[m] nomentuum tota[6] terrarum orbe concelebra[n]t, et super populum tuum uultum tuae pietatis inlumina: per.

I *Pro aeclesiae unitate.* Deum patrem, karissimi fratres, uno spiritu depraecamur,[7] ut omnes fide[8] catholicae uinculis inlegat unum sentiamus in Christo.

Collectio sequitur. Deus, qui unus et uerus es, te suppleces depraecamur, ut in omnibus placita tibi semper fides catholica perseueret: per dominim nostrum.

II *Pro sacerdotibus et omne clero.* Deum nostrum, karissimi fratres, suppleces depraecemur, ut sacerdotes suos quos ceremoniae relegione devinxit, sacri misterii conputes prestet omnemque clerum citra culpam alicuius maculae iubeat permanere: per dominum.

Collectio sequitur. Supplecantibus domus tuae sacerdotibus ac ministris, deum omnium dignitatem,[9] perpetim gratiam benignus infunde. Presta, salvator.

III *Pro regibus et pace.* Apicem omnium potestatum et supereminentem dominationem dominum deprecemur, ut regum nostrorum exercitum ita sua uirtute conroboret, ut per easdem gentibus subdetis uel fugatis deo uiuo iugiter seruiamus: per dominum nostrum.

Collectio sequitur. Respice famulos tuos, domine, quibus orbis regiminum et rerum aduenas[10] dedisti et praesta, ut tua uirtute muniti populum tuum summa felicitate defenda⟨n⟩t, ut pace[m] nobis ubique concessa tibi diebus as noctibus seruiamus.

IV *Pro uirginibus.* Unum uirginis filium depraecemur, ut omnibus castitatis amore[m] flagrantibus perseuerantiae palmas inperciat : per dominum.

Collectio sequitur. Sancte omnipotens deus, eam uirginitatis cultoribus gloriam tribue, quam uirgo mater obtinuit; qui com patre[m].

V *Pro uiduis et orfanis.* Deum, necessitatum omnium consideratorem, dominum postulemus, ut uiduis orfanisque clementiae suae more subueniat: per.

---

4 sumamus] sumat *Bo*.
5 manentes … gloriae] manent … gloria?
6 tota] toto.
7 depraecamur] depraecemur.
8 fide] fidei.
9 dignitate(m *ommitted at end of the line*)] dignitatum.
10 regiminum … aduenas] regimen … habenas.

Collectio sequitur. Religiosa uiduetate poscentes[11] adque orbati paruoli nullo se praesidio distitutus, te, domine, adiuuante nunc sentiant.

VI *Pro egrotantibus*. Medicinae caelestis auctorem dominum, fratres karissimi, ea qua conpetit supplecatione rogemus, ut actus animorum nostrorum corporumque languores uirtutis suae uerbum[12] sanare dignitur: per.

Collectio sequitur. Infirma egretudine[m] laborantibus, omnipotens aeterne deus, paterna miseratione succurre: per.

VII *Pro captiuis uel qui in carceribus detenentur*. Deum, qui mesta⟨s⟩ clades dissoluit, unianimiter deprecemur, ut omnes captiuitatis iugo depressus et in carcerum septa detrusus p[r]ius semper misericordiae largitur absoluat: per.

Collectio. Deus, omnium laborantium insigne presidium, libera carcere clausus adque captiuos, eos presertim qui opem tuae pietatis inplorant.

VIII *Pro peregrinantibus*. Habitatorem caeli inspectoremque omnium regionum dominum pro peregrinantibus unianimiter depraecemur, ut eis pro suae pietatis clementia maturum reditum largiatur: per.

Collectio. Saluatorem omnium, qui es uia et ueritas et uita, it⟨in⟩erantibus angel[or]um ducem, quaesomus, pius pater, adtribue; per.

IX *Pro elimosinis largitore*. Auctorem boni et fidelissimum retributore⟨m⟩ dominum depraecemur, ut omnes qui plenas indigentibus manus aperuit,[13] et hic multiplecato[14] sui operis fructum capiant et in futurum gloriam consequantur aeternam: per.

Collectio. Refice, domine, eorum uiscera benedictione caeleste, qui te pauperem[15] pasto reficiunt. Per.

X *Pro paenitentibus*. Summe pietatis dominum, qui non uult mortem morientium, dummodo renascantur et uiuant, pro paenitentibus dominum depraecemur, ut indulta suorum …[16] remissionis suae plenitudinem largiatur: per.

Collectio sequitur. Tribue, domine, munere fontis exutus,[17] ut fidelis paenitentiae praemiis iterum glorientur: per.

XI *Pro neophitis*. Pro neglegentibus tardisque domini nostri cultoribus, id est neophitis, dominum deprecemur, ut eis desiderium beatae et perpetuae regenerationis infundat.

---

11 poscentes] potientes.
12 uerbum] uerbo.
13 aperuit] aperiunt.
14 multeplecato] multiplicatum.
15 pauperem] pauperum?
16 suorum …] *add* malitia peccatorum.
17 exutus] exutis.

Collectio. Deus, qui semper bona facis inuenire quaerentes, praesta, ut eorum rudimenta tironum mercidem consummati operis consequantur: per dominum.

XII *Pro conpetentibus*. Dominum maiestatis oremus, ut cerui more fonte iam proximo sitientes mox ad[18] caelestis palmae lauream consequantur: per.

Collectio. Siciunt ad te deum uiuum tuorum, domine, corda famulorum: suscipe cupientes saeculo mori, ut tibi, domine, renascantur; da presentem petentibus gratiam, uitam credulis daturus aeternam: per.

Liturgical Form

This is a litie with 13 litiques.

- The first invitatory is a general introduction, which situates the piece in the *paschae sollemnia*. It is the only one not to have a heading and is followed by an oration whose function is not evident.
- Then follow twelve litiques, where each invitatory is preceded by a heading explaining the subject or beneficiaries of the petition.

Remarks

– The first oration seems to fulfil no other need than to match the parallelism of the litiques that follow.

– Several expressions of this formulary feature in the texts we have already studied:

a/ oration: *toto terrarum orbe*: cf. OS I: *toto orbe terrarum*;

II heading: *et omni clero* = *Irl*^{1} III, *FG*^{1} III, *FG*^{2} III.
oration: sacerdotibus ac ministris = M^1 II, DG II.

III invitatory: the *exercitus* of the king is cited in all the texts except *OS*, *Irl*^{2} and *DG* (*militia*);
gentibus subditis matches *OS* IV: 'subditas illis faciat omnes barbaras nationes'.

IV Starting from here, the headings are taken from the lists of the needy in *Irl*^{1} VII–X and *M*^{1} VII–X.

VI The sick feature in *OS* VI, *M*^{1} IX, *FG*^{1} VIII, *Irl*^{1} XV.

X The penitents were mentioned by *Irl*^{1} IX and *M*^{1} VII.

XI–XII The catechumens were cited by *OS* V, *Irl*^{1} IX and *DG* VII.

18 [ad]?

Conclusion

We are inclined to think that this formulary is the result of a restructuring of one or more litanies, influenced by the particular liturgical form of the *OS*. Perhaps the progressive infiltration of the Roman liturgy into Gaul left them impressed by the solemnity of this liturgy; a redactor would have transformed the litanies then in use according to the tastes of the times. His Latin lacks the quality of the model from which he is working.

Has this litie served as a Universal Prayer at Mass (without the first litique), or was it composed expressly to be used as *orationes paschales*? We cannot answer that question at the moment; we will return to it.

2. The Missale Gothicum (Go)

As with *MGV*, it is after the *Exsultet* that the *Go*[19] places this litie, whose text we have again borrowed from Mohlberg:

Oraciones paschalis duodecim cum totidem colleccionibus

a/ *Oracio pro graciarum accione. Praefacio.* Expectatum, frates karissimi, et desideratum nobis paschae diem adepti, gracias agamus omnipotenti deo patri, quod nos in hanc eandem diem per filium suum dominum nostrum Iesum Christum (quem pro nobis hostiam dedit in salutem aeternam) uocauit. Ob hoc fideli graciarum actione laudemus, benedicamus, honorificemus benedictum et beatum nomen dei patris in filio filique in patre et spiritu sancto in saecula saeculorum.

Oracio sequitur. Sancte domine, omnipotens pater, exaudi, tuere ac sanctificare[20] plebem tuam praemonitam[21] signo crucis, baptismate puricatam, crismate delibutam, quos ad celebrandam praesentis sollemnitatis beatitudinem congregasti, uniuersisque noticiam tui particpacionem sancti spiritus propicius infunde: per.

I *Oracio pro exsulibus. Praefacio.* Unianimes et unius corporis in spiritu dei patris omnipotentis domini misericordiam dipraecimur pro fratribus et sororibus nostris captiuitatibus[22] elongatis, carceribus detentis, metallis deputatis, ut eis dominus adiutor, protector et consolator existat neque deesse sibi reputet eos, qui fideli in se[23] innocencia perseuerant.

---

19 ROME, Bibl. Vat. Reg. lat. 317, 8th century (Clavis 1919 — Bourque 516 — Gamber 210); ed. Mohlberg (1961); the text is found at f. 155v–161v, on pages 62–65. For some notes on this formulary by H. M. Bannister, see *Missale Gothicum*, (1919), vol. 2, 55 ff.

20 sanctifica[re].

21 praemonitam] praemunitam.

22 captiuitatibus] captiuitate.

23 fideli in se] fideles (fidelitur?) in.

Oracio sequitur. Tribue, domine, relegatis patriam, uinctis absolucionem, captiuis libertatem, ut plebs tua et in hoc saeculo et in futuro misericordiae tuae munere liberetur.

II *Oracio pro sacerdotibus. Praefacio.* In sanctorum sancta admissi et altaris caelestis sacerdocii aeterni participes effecti, dei patris omnipotentis misericordiam dipraecimor, ut sacerdotes suos ac ministros donis repleat spiritalium graciarum.

Oracio sequitur. Domine deus uirtutum, iustifica et sanctifica pastores et praepositos ouium tuarum, ut aduersarius noster diabulus fide eorum et sanctitate superatus contingere dominicum gregem ac uiolare non audeat: per.

III *Oracio pro uirginibus. Praefacio.* Incorruptae aeternitatis deum et inuiolabilis naturae dominum unianimiter dipraecimor, orantes pro fratribus nostris, qui gloriosam uirginitatem corpore ac mente uouerunt, uti eos usque ad consummacionem propositi sui, misericordiae spiritus prosequatur: per.

Oracio sequitur. Respice, domine, uirgines sacras et spadones uoluntarius id est praeciosas eclesiae margaritas, ut corpora eorum ac spiritum inlaesa castitatis consciencia pari exaestimacione custodiant: per resurgentem.

IV *Oracio pro aelymosinas facientibus. Praefacio.* Sanctum ac benedictum retribucionis deum unianimis,[24] fratres dilectissimi, oracione dipraecimor obsecrantes pro fratribus et sororibus nostris, quorum ministerio atque sumptu inopiam non senciunt, qui in eclesia sunt indigentes, ut isdem dominus spiritalis diuicias communicet, qui fidelium animarum inopiae saecularis substanciae participant facultatem; per resurgentem.

Oracio sequitur. Piis seruorum tuorum praecibus annue, misericors domine, ut quicumque praeceptorum caelestium memores pauperibus tuis quae sunt necessaria subministrant, incorruptibili et caelesti gloria miseracionis tuae et misericordiae[25] coronentur: per.

V *Oracio pro peregrinantibus. Praefacio.* Caelestium et terrestrium et infernorum dominum deum patrem omnipotentem, fratres dilectissimi, dipraecimor, obsecrantes, uti fratres nostros ac sorores, quicumque peregrinacionum necessitatibus subiacent, omnipotens deus auxilio suo comes adiutor reducat ac protegat: per.

Colleccio sequitur. Restitue, domine, peregrinis desideratum patriae solum, ut contemplacione[m] misericordiae tuae, dum ad praesens agunt beneficiis tuis gracias, ciues esse sanctorum ac tui domestici concupiscent. Praesta per resurgentem.

VI *Oracio pro infirmis. Praefacio.* Uniuersae salutis deum et uniuersae uirtutis dominum dipraecimor pro fratribus et sororibus nostris, qui secundum carnem diuersis aegretudinum generibus insultantur, ut his dominus caeleste medicinae suae munus indulgeat: per.

Oracio sequitur. Domine cui uiuificare mortuos facile est, restitue aegrotantibus pristinae sanitati,[26] ne terreni medicaminis remedia desiderent,

---

24 unianimis] unianimes.

25 miseracionis tuae et misericordiae] miseratione tuae misericordiae.

26 pristinae sanitati] pristinam sanitatem *or* aegrotantes pristinam sanitatem.

quicumque medillam caelestis misericordiae tuae dipraecantur: per resurgentem.

VII *Oratio pro paenitentibus.* ⟨*Praefacio.*⟩ Confitentes bonitatis ac misericordiae deum, qui peccatorum mauult paenitenciam quam mortem, communicatis praecibus ac fletibus pro fratribus ac sororibus nostris domini misericordiam dipraecimor, uti eos peccati sui crimina confitentes a bonitatis suae uenia non repellat.

Oracio sequitur. Rex gloriae, qui non uis mortem peccatoris, sed ut conuertatur et uiuat, da nobis peccatorum labe pollutes paenitenciam, simul ut flere cum flentibus et dolentibus et cum gaudentibus gaudire possimus: per resurgentem.

VIII *Oracio pro unitate. Praefacio.* Unum deum patrem, ex quo omnia sunt, et unum dominum nostrum Iesum Christum, per quem omnia, fratres karissimi, dipraecimor, ut unitatem eclesiae suae concordi congregacionis nostrae uoluntate[m] confirmet: per resurgentem filium suum.

Colleccio sequitur. Omnipotens domine, qui es deus bonitatis et totius consolacionis, te supplices dipraecamur, ut hereticus et infidelis a perpetuis gehennae ignibus manifestacione tuae ueritatis eripias, quoniam uis omnis hominis saluos fieri et ad agnicione[m] ueritatis uenire: per.

IX *Oracio pro pace regum. Praefacio.* Dominus dominancium et regem regnancium, fratres karissimi, oracione unianimes dipraecimor, ut nobis populo suo pacem regum tribuere dignetur, ut mitigatis eorum mentibus requies nobis congregacionis istius perseueret: per.

Colleccio sequitur. Carnis spiritum totius sator cunctorumque regnorum mundalium indultor, da regum culmine religi⟨o⟩nis prosperitatem et pacis, ut nobis regno tuo caelesti in terris adhuc positis[27] liberius liceat deseruire: per resurgentem.

X *Oracio pro spiritibus pausancium. Praefacio.* Deum iudicem universitatis, deum caelestium et terrestrium et infernorum, fratres dilectissimi, dipraecimor pro spiritibus carorum nostrorum, qui nos in dominica pace praecesserunt, ut eos dominus in requiem collocare[28] et in parte primae resurreccionis resuscitet: per.

Oracio sequitur. Iesu Christe, uita et resurreccio nostra, dona consacerdotibus et caris nostris, qui in tua pace requiuerunt, exoptatae mansionis refrigerium, et si qui ex his daemonum fraude decepti errorum se multis maculis polluerunt, tu, domine, qui solus potens es, peccata eorum concede, ut quos dampnacionis suae participes diabulus gloriabatur effectus esse, per misericordiam tuam socius tuae beatitudinis ingemiscat, saluator.

XI *Oracio pro caticuminis. Praefacio.* Praecem spei fratrum nostrorum, karissimi, unianimes adiuuemus, uti dominus omnipotens ad fontem eos beatae regeneracionis suae euntes, omnis[29] misericordiae suae auxilio [spiritus] prosequatur.

---

27 positis] posito.
28 collocare] collocet.
29 omnis] omnes *or* omni.

Colleccio sequitur. Creator omnium, domine, et fons aquae uiuae, per lauacrum baptismi peccata eorum dele, quibus iam donasti resurreccionis fidem, ut mortem huius saeculi non timeant, reple eos spiritu sancto, ut formari in illis Christum ac uiuere glorientur: per.

Liturgical Form

The liturgical form is identical to the preceding formulary; here, the invitatory is called *praefacio*, and the collect *oracio* or *colleccio*.

a/ The first invitatory situates the piece in the Easter solemnities.
The heading of this litique *pro graciarum accione* is not to be found in *MGV* a/, but the subject is identical.

I–XI: eleven litiques, whereas *MVG* has twelve; each one is preceded by a heading.

Remarks

1 The first oration, as in *MGV*, is explained, without doubt, by its parallelism with the following litiques.
2 This litie is entirely different from the preceding one, without any relationship or links. We note the large number of biblical citations in *Go*.
3 However, several expressions in *Go* are also taken up in the litanies:
I *pro fratribus et sororibus nostris* is found in *Irl*² XII; the phrase is favoured by *Go* since it recurs again in invitatories III (*pro fratribus nostris*) and IV to VII;
captivitatibus elongatis, carceribus detentis, metallis deputatis is certainly anachronistic by the time of the *Missale Gothicum*; these expressions are obviously borrowed from the litanies:
– captives are named in *M¹* VII and *Irl*² V;
– prisoners in *M¹* VIII; cf. also *OS* VI;
– workers *in metal* are named exclusively in *M¹* VIII.
It would not therefore be surprising to find that *Go* had made use of *M¹*.
II *sacerdotes suos ac ministros*, paired together at least since Cyprian[30] and used by *M1* II, *DG* II, *MGV* II.
III *virginitatem corpore ac mente voverunt* matches *DG* IV: 'qui se mente et corpore propter caelorum regna castificant'. The prayer for virgins appears frequently, as early as *OS* III.

---

30 Cyprian, *Epistola I*, 2; ed. Bayard, vol. 1, 3; tr. Donna, (FC 51), 8; cf. supra, Part One, Section Two, T.13.

V *peregrinacionum necessitatibus subiacent* = *DG* IX, 'peregrinationis necessitas'.
VI *diversis aegretudinum generibus* is very similar to *Irl*[2] XV: 'variis dolorum generibus'.
X *spiritibus carorum nostrorum* = *Irl*[2] a/, 'pro animabus ... carorum nostrorum'. The oration picks up this expression as well.

4 Invitatory I has a parallel in the *A* fragment of REICHENAU discovered by Bannister.[31] There is also a resemblance to a Munich palimpsest decoded by P. Dold;[32] the editor places it at Christmas (?). Unfortunately it has large gaps in it. A striking thing, however, is that a little earlier, this same manuscript uses an expression that is found literally in invitatory IX of *Bo* (cf. infra.)

Bannister observes also that the term *unianimes* appears only three times in the *Missale Gothicum*, and three times in this litie, which seems to prove the same author for both.[33] Taking a closer look, we ourselves found the same term four times, in invitatories I, IV, IX and XI, to which can be added the adverb *unianimiter* in III. This reinforces Bannister's conclusion.

5 The oration *Rex gloriae* (VII) is found in a number of sacramentaries of both Roman and non-Roman origin.[34] It is based on Ezek 18:23, 32 and 33:11.[35]
6 From the end of invitatory VIII to the end of oration X, we have a parallel in the Munich palimpsest already mentioned;[36] the variants are minor.
7 Invitatory X, *Deum iudicem universitatis* is found in the Roman sources since the *Gelasian Vetus* (no. 1616), in the rites for funerals.

Conclusion

This examination reinforces the conclusion that we were led to propose for *MGV*. It seems that, probably as a result of the influence of the *OS* penetrating into Gaul, *Go* transformed litanies such as *M*[1] and *Irl*[2] into a litie. Without having researched the matter too deeply, it seems to us that the language of *Go* is better than that of *MGV*.

31 CARLSRUHE, Bad. Landesbibl., App. Aug. CLXVII, A, f. 2v; ed. Bannister (1904), vol. 5, 61.
32 Dold (1964), 19–20.
33 Bannister, *Missale Gothicum*, vol. 2, 56.
34 Cf. Siffrin (1961), 30 ff.
35 A list of the liturgical passages that echo these verses is provided by E. Bishop, in his commentary on the *Book of Cerne*, ed. Kuypers (1902), 248–49; we must also add nos. 521, 1297 and 1318 of the Sacramentary of Bergamo.
36 Dold (1964), 70–72.

3. *The Bobbio Missal* (Bo)

Always on Holy Saturday, but before the *Exsultet* this time, the Bobbio Missal[37] has the following formulary, which we quote from Lowe:

Incipiunt orationes in uigiliis pascae

a/ Inter prima celebrande pascae sollemnia uotorum consecratio ex graciarum actione sumat exordium ut passum et immolatum pro nobis christum credentis et sacri ministerii princepim confitentis consono ore prosequamur per.

I *Oratio pro his qui custodiarum uigiliis*[38] *et captiuiuate detenti pascha interesse non possunt* Dei patris omnipotentis clemenciam fratres karissimi deprecimur ut eos quos inuidus diabolus captiuitatis seruicio premit dei nostri misericordia in statum pristinum libertatemque constituat.

II *Pro sacerdotibus ac ministris aeclesiae*
Deum ac dominum nostrum iesum christum pro sacerdotibus ac ministris aeclesie suae fratres karissimi supplices deprecimur ut ingressi santa sanctorum tociusque particeps[39] altares spiritalium graciarum donisabundanciaque multimoda repleamur.

III *Pro uirginebus*
Deum patrem omnipotentem fratres karissimi supplices oremus ut in fratribus ac sororibus nostris qui sanctam et maxime acceptabilem deum uirginitatem decarunt bone conceptum mentis propositum tenentes inmacolati iugiter perseuerint.

IV *Pro his qui elymosinas faciunt*
Deum patrem misericordie suppliciter oremus ut in sanctos et huius saeculi pauperis effusa largicio in celestium diuiciarum opes refluat et carnalium participacio societatem possit munerum spiritalium promerere.

V *Oremus pro peregrinantibus*
Celestium et terrestrium deum patrem supplices deprecimur ut omnes fratris nostros qui peregrinacionum necessitatibus subiacent potencia auxilii sui protegat adque defendat.

VI *Pro egrotis*
Uniuerse salutes dominum deprecimur pro fratribus et sororibus nostris qui secundum carnis infirmitatem diuersis aegritudinum uexantur incummodas uti[40] qui solus potest pro sua pietate omnibus adesse dignetur.

VII *Pro penetentibus*
Deum spei nostre fratres karissimi deprecimur ut timerate precepcionis reus reuersus in uiam rectam ab aspecto serentitatis suae non reiciat neque in aduento suo a rigni celestes ianua condemnandus excludat.

---

37 PARIS, B.N. lat. 13246, 8th century. (Clavis 1924 — Bourque 517 — Gamber 220); ed. Lowe (1920); the text is found at f. 107^{r}–109^{v}, on pp. 67–69.

38 vigiliis] vinculis.

39 particeps] participes.

40 uti] ut is Mabillon. ut his *Go*.

VIII *Pro unitatem aeclesiae*
Bonorum omnium fontem auctorem humane salutis dominum deprecimur ut unitate aeclesiae inuiolatam custodire dignetur ut et presenti proteccione et[41] in futuro perennis iute stipendia consequi meriamur.

IX *Pro pace populi et regum*
Deum ac regem uniuerse condicionis dominum suppliciter oremus ut regibus ac potestatibus huius mundi eorumque ministris supplicem inter se amorem et concordiam largiatur.

X *Pro spiritibus pausancium*
Deum patrem omnipotentem fratres karissimi pro cummemoracione defunctorum supplices oremus ut eisdem dominus adtinuatis que merito aspera sunt culpe piaculis clementissime remissionis suae refrigeria largiatur.

XI *Pro competentibus*
Dei patris misericordiam pro competentibus fratres karissimi supplices deprecimur ut eos dominus omnipotens ad fontem regeneracionis suae euntes omni celestes misericordie auxilio prosequatur.
Collectio
Auctur uniuersitatis ac domine te deprecamur et quaesumus ut mortificatus terrenis uiciis in nouum hominem tibi seruire paciaris per resurgentem a mortuis dominum nostrum iesum christum.

1. Commentary

a/ is the same as the beginning of *MGV* a/

I elevates to the spiritual level the litiques of *MGV* VII and especially *Go* I, both of which pray for the needy, using formularies borrowed from the ancient litanies. The evolution is clear: while *MGV* VII prays for them, without anything further, *Go* I entitles this litique *pro exsulibus*; then *Bo*, building on the heading of *Go* I, and no doubt considering that reasons other than imprisonment led to the absence at the Easter celebrations, has spiritualised the subject by praying for those who are 'captives of the devil'.
in statum pristinum libertatemque = hendiadys for *libertatis*.

II The traditional pairing of *sacerdotibus ac ministris* (Cyprian, *M*[1] II, *DG* II) is maintained in the heading. The second part seems to be related to *Go* II, or perhaps they both arise from a common inspiration; our text is certainly secondary, since *totiusque participes altaris* scarcely renders a satisfactory meaning. *Donis abundantiaque*: hendiadys.

III differing from *MGV* and *Go*, this invitatory contains the expression *fratribus ac sororibus* found in *Irl*[2] XII and favoured by *Go* (five times). The construction *ut in fratribus ... perseverint* is flawed.

41 et] in Mabillon.

IV this is without connection to the two preceding texts, but is to be vouched for in *Irl*[1] X, *M*[1] X and *DG* XI.

V This sentence is a poor abridgement of *Go* V; *protegat atque defendat* in *Bo* (cf. the oration after the antiphon *Asperges me*) is inferior to *reducat ac protegat* (*Go*), since it is concerned with travellers. We shall see further on that the Hispanic tradition *A* (*Ha* X) has retained a superior text; cf. p. 286.

VI It seems that we have the same link here between *Bo* and *Go* as in the preceding number; however the reading *secundum carnis infirmitatem*, also to be found in the Hispanic tradition *A* (*Ha* V), would seem to be better than the *secundum carnem* found in *Go* VI. The ending has been corrupted. *Ha* V, which also has *ut qui solus potest* is, unfortunately, incomplete. *FG*[1] VIII prays 'pro his qui infirmantur et diversis languoribus detinentur'.

VI This invitatory, which has nothing in common with either the litanies or the other *orationes paschales*, proves that at that time not much importance was attached to the endings of nouns.

VIII Without relationship to the preceding texts.

IX differing from *MGV* and *Go*, this invitatory — or more precisely, the expression *regibus ac potestatibus huius mundi* — nevertheless has a parallel in the palimpsest of Munich cited above with regard to *Go* I and VIII ff.[42] The text is set down for Christmas (?), but it is incomplete and, in the end, not very enlightening. It is curious to see that several lines further on, this manuscript has 'pro ... exsulibus', the heading of *Go* I!

X Same heading as *Go* X; missing in *MGV*.

XI the ending of this invitatory has the same source as that of *pro caticuminis* of *Go* XI; the text of *Bo* is even better.

The final *collectio* picks up the paschal theme of the first invitatory.

2. Current and Ancient Liturgical Forms

Despite the title '*Orationes* for the Easter Vigil', a term taken up before the caption for I and underlined again with an *Oremus* before V, here we are not face to face with orations, but with a series of a dozen invitatories, enclosed within a single *collectio*. The first places the piece within the Easter Vigil, as with the two preceding texts. The headings there are also the same. In his commentary, Lowe[43] suggests that they are not simply headings, but are the remains of a diaconal admonition such is found in the Hispanic liturgy. This is quite possible; we will speak of it further on, when we study the tripartite structure of the litiques.

Have we preserved the original liturgical form of this formulary? Dom Alfonso thinks not; the redactor, or even someone prior to him, probably confused the

42 Dold (1964), 19.
43 Lowe (1923), 126.

two euchological types, and as a result, not seeing at the time the need for two collects, would have failed to recopy the oration.[44] On the contrary, Mgr Borella tentatively suggests that we have the original form of the text and assumes that a popular invocation was placed after each invitatory.[45] Frankly, we do not see what response can follow these invitatories, except the prayer of silence. The comparison with *Go* and the Hispanic lities would appear to us to show clearly that far from being original, *Bo* has actually shortened a litie formulary; Dom Alfonso was right. Moreover, Meyer was already of this opinion.[46]

3. Relationship Between Bo and Go

A careful reading of *Bo* leads us back to *Go* rather than to the ancient litanies. But does *Bo* depend directly on *Go*, or do they both arise from a common source? Alfonso adopts the second solution, with good cause, in our opinion. On the other hand, he is loath to say whether it is *Go* or *Bo* that deviates furthest from it. In our eyes, it is clearly *Bo* that is secondary, both in its structure (without the oration) and its text. The first invitatory, for example, has not only adapted the list of the needy that must still have included the original list of obstacles that prevented attendance at the Easter solemnities (as is the case with *Go*) but has spiritualised these obstacles to the point that the needy are no longer included! Several expressions found in *Bo* are similarly later additions that show a lack of understanding of the original text.

We notice that the first invitatory of *Bo* forces us to recognize a link between it and its parallel in *MGV*.

Several questions arise with regard to these three texts, especially concerning their origin and their usage. But since the Gallican and Hispanic formularies are very similar, it would be better to present the Hispanic first. In this way we will be better armed to come to a conclusion.

B. The Hispanic 'Orationes Paschales'[47]

In Spain the Easter Vigil contained, after the blessing of the candle, a long prayer of intercession. This was made the subject of a serious study by Fr Bernal, who dedicated a chapter of his thesis to the Hispanic Easter Vigil.[48] The author rightly

44 Alfonso (1928), 69.
45 Borella (1964), 71.
46 Meyer (1912), 91.
47 On the Hispanic liturgy, consult the excellent article by Pinell, 'Liturgia hispánica' in the *Diccionario de histori ecclesiástica de Espãna*, vol. 2, 1303–20, which includes an extensive bibliography.
48 Bernal (1964), vol. 17, 283–347.

distinguishes between two traditions which he calls simply *A* and *B*. We will present the texts of these two traditions, then we will draw our conclusions.

I. Tradition A (Ha)

1. The Sources

GaM = MILAN, Bibl. Ambr. M 12 Sup., 123–40; Sacramentary of the South of France, *c.* 700. Edition, Dold, *Das Sakramentar im Schabcodex M 12 Sup. der Bibliotheca Ambrosiana*, Beuron, 1952, (TA 43), 26*–29*
(Clavis 1917, M 12 — Bourque 522 — Gamber 205)
This sacramentary uses the hispanic formularies, but follows the ordinance of the Gallican liturgy.

V = VERONA, Bibl. Capit. 89, f. 97v–99v, Orational de Tarragone(?), before 731. Edition, Vives *Oracional Visigótico*, Barcelona, 1946, 272–78.
(Clavis 2016 — Gamber 330). This manuscript had previously been edited by J. Blanchini, *Libellus Orationum*, Rome, 1741, 1–136.

L = LONDON, Brit. Mus. Add. 30852, Orational de Silos, 9th century, f. 80b–82d. Edition Vives, (see above.)
(Clavis 2016 — Gamber 331).

O = SILOS, Arch. Monast. 4 (olim C), written in 1052 for Saint-Prudence de Silos,[49] f. 162–65. Edition, Férotin, *Le Liber ordinum*, Paris, 1904, 217–23.
(Diaz 637 — Bourque 552 — Gamber 390).
This manuscript contains only the first eight litiques. Férotin has filled in the gaps with the help of *V* and *L*.

[*A* = Antiphonary of Leon;[50] this includes only the rubrics and the diaconal invitatories; it does not give the text.]

2. Edited Version

Our edited version is based on the four manuscripts cited above.

α[51] [INCIPIUNT[52] ORATIONES, QUAE PER SINGULAS LECTIONES IN VIGILIA PASCHAE DICUNTUR, ID EST,[53] EXPLICITA PRIMA LECTIONE,[54] DICITUR[55] HAEC ORATIO]

---

49 Confusion reigns over the designation of this manuscript. Férotin calls it codex B. Gamber codex 2; here, we use the identification of Millares Carlo, *Manuscritos visigóticos. Notas bibliográficas*, Madrid-Barcelona, 1963.

50 LEON, Arch. Cath. no. 8, 10th century, ed. Brou — Vives (1959), 284.

51 α/*om GaM* (*Dold expl, secundum Bobbio 214*: Incipiunt orationes in vigiliis paschae).

52 incipiunt ... id est *om O*. incipiunt *om L*.

53 id est *om L*.

54 prima lectione *V*. lectione prima *L*.

55 a sacerdote *add O*.

A a	Anniversaria, fratres[56] dilectissimi, festa votis sollemnibus[57] inchoantes, auxilium Domini poscamus e caelis, ut digni habeamur ecclesiasticae functionis officiis,[58] inminet[59] enim[60] cura pro cunctis; illi pro[61] omnibus supplicemus[62] qui mori pro omnium salute dignatus est[63]
b[64]	*Deinde*[65] *clamat diaconus:*[66] Pro sollemnitate paschali precemur Dominum
c	*Collectio eiusdem*[67] Sanctifica, Domine, famulos tuos, ut sanctificatae noctis huius[68] dignis[69] obsequiis serviamus.[70]
I a[71]	Ecclesastica unitate connexi, Deum[72] patrem petamus, ut eandem Ecclesiam concordiae vinculo coherentem, individuae caritatis[73] nunc studiis, post premiis muneretur[74]
b[64]	*Deinde dicit diaconus:*[75] Pro pace ecclesarium et quiete populi precemur Dominum.
c	*Collectio eiusdem:*[76] Deus qui ecclesiae tuae fide et utilitate[77] laetaris, dona ei perfectae religionis affectum, quam sanctae congregationis honore donasti.[78]

56 fratres *om GaM.*
57 festa ... sollemnibus] festivitatis sollemnia *O.*
58 officiis] officio *GaM.*
59 inminet] inminent *GaM* (*Dold in apparatu*: inminente?).
60 illi *add O.*
61 illi pro *om O.*
62 ei *add O.*
63 p.d.n. *add GaM.* cui est honor et gloria *add V.* Amen *add O.*
64 b *om GaM.*
65 deinde *V.* post haec *O.*
66 dicens *add O.* deinde ... diaconus *om L.*
67 collectio eiusdem *V.* alia *L.* collectio *GaM.* post haec dicitur haec oratio *O.*
68 huius *om GaM.*
69 dignis *om O.*
70 per dominum *add GaM.* quia Deus es benedictus. Similiter per ceteras lectiones iste ordo tenebitur *add V.* Post haec salutat episcopus. Et accedens alius, legit hanc lectionem Genesis *add O.*
71 Secunda oratio *add L.* item secunda oratio *add V.* I *LOV* = VIII *GaM.*
72 Deum] Dominum Deum *O.*
73 individuae caritatis *LVGaM.* atque in divina claritate flagrantem *O.*
74 muneretur] munerentur *L.* per dominum nostrum *add GaM.* quia multae miserationis est Dominus *add V.* Amen *add O.* quia multae mi- *add L.*
75 deinde dicit diaconus *VL.* Post haec accredit item diaconus, dicens *O.*
76 Collectio eiusdem] Oratio *O.*
77 utilitate *codd. Dold susp.* unitate.
78 per dominum nostrum *add GaM.* quia deus es gloriosus *add V.* Amen *add O qui semper add lectionem et hic ordinem baptismi.*

IIa[79] Omnipotentem Deum, qui sacerdotes suos ecclesiarum[80] praesules ordinavit supplici oratione poscamus ut[81] fideli[82] nostrae devotionis obsequio suo[83] queamus[84] respondere iudicio[85]

b[64] *Deinde*[86] *dicit diaconus*: Pro sacerdotibus et ministris precemur Dominum

c *Collectio eiusdem*:[87]
Dona, Domine, sacerdotibus tuis ut convenire facias fructum operum cum eminentia dignitatum, ut mercedem potius habeant de labore, quam iudicium de honore.[88]

IIIa[89] Pacem dominicam pacem quoque nostrum, Deum patrem omnipotentem qui pacis auctor est,[90] postulemus ut adsit in ordinatione sua catholicis ducibus et barbaras gentes refrenet; quatenus, rebus omnibus sua lege compositis, eius solummodo[91] imperiis serviamus.[92]

b[64] *Deinde*[93] *dicit diaconus*: Pro prosperitate principum et tranquillitate temporum precemur Dominum[94]

c *Collectio eiusdem*:[95]
Deus qui fidelium pace laetaris, dona servientibus tibi[96] pacem omnesque eorum actus, qui tibi servire cupiunt, placabili[97] miseratione compone.[98]

IVa[99] Deum patrem omnipotetem agentes ipsi gratias postulemus pro his quos saeculi necessitas aut inquietudo detentat[100] ut[101] in hac sollemnitate paschali, quia corporibus absunt, animis et utilitatibus misceantur[102]

---

79 tertia oratio *add L*. item tertia oratio *add V*. oratio *add O*. II *LOV* = I *GaM*.
80 ecclesiarum *GaMO*. in suam ecclesiam *V*. in sanctam ecclesiam *L*.
81 ut] *om GaM*.
82 fideli] fidelis *O*.
83 suo] sui *GaM*.
84 queamus] peramus *GaM*.
85 per dominum *add GaM*. cui est honor *add V*. cui est *add L*. Amen *add O*.
86 deinde] post haec *O*. deinde … diaconus *om L*.
87 Collectio eiusdem *om O*.
88 per dominum *add GaM*. quia deus es benedictus *add V*. Amen *add O*.
89 item quarta oratio *add V*. Oratio de IIII lectione *add L*. III *LOV* = IX *GaM*.
90 auctor est] est auctor *O*.
91 solummodo] solum *GaM*.
92 per dominum nostrum *add GaM*. cuius regnum *add V*. cuius reg- *add L*. Amen *add O*.
93 deinde *V*. et *O*. deinde … diaconus *om L*.
94 Dominum *LV*. *om O*.
95 Collectio eiusdem *om O*.
96 tibi *om L*.
97 placabili] placibili *V*.
98 per dominum nostrum *add GaM*. quia deus es pius in saecula saeculorum *add VL*. Amen *add O*.
99 item quinta oratio *add V*. oratio de V lectione *add L*.
100 vel pro his qui secundum carnis infirmitatem diversis egritudinum generibus afflicantur (affliguntur O) *add OLV qui non habent* V.
101 ut] *om GaM*.
102 misceantur] misceatur *L*. per dominum *add GaML*. condonante Deo nostro, qui regnat in saecula saeculorum *add V*.

b[64] *Deinde*[103] *dicit diaconus*: Pro his qui huic sanctae festivitati[104] interesse non possunt precemur Dominum[105]

c *Collectio eiusdem*:[106]
Deus cui ea quae nobis sunt absentia deesse non possunt, et quae putantur longe sunt proxima, praesta ut famuli tui quorum necessitates[107] ecclesiae sollicitudo commendat pietatis tuae muneribus[108] perfruantur.[109]

V a[110] Universae salutis dominum, fratres depraecamur pro his qui secundum carnis infirmitatem diversis aegritudinum generibus adflictantur ut qui solus potest contra naturam nostrum inbecillem … -ae curationis adcommodet depellat invaliscentes morbos ut qui … -media suis virtutib … verbo … misericordi … ed … -tus salutaris per dominum nostrum

b ⟨*Deinde dicit diaconus*:⟩ Pro pereclitantibus et egrotantibus[111]

c *Collectio eiusdem*:
Precamur te Domine ut nobis in omni passionum genere adiutor protector et consolator adsistas p. d.

VIa[112] Deum fructuum largitorem, aurarum moderatorem, qui in supplementum humani usus terras,[113] fecundavit, creavit fruges, aera[114] temperavit, fratres carissimi, deprecemur, ut omnia haec[115] quae sponte nostris usibus tribuit nostris quoque obsecrationibus largiatur[116]

b[64] *Deinde*[117] *dicit diaconus*: Pro abundantia frugum et tranquillitate aerum precemur Dominum

---

103 deinde … diaconus *VL*. Post haec accredit diaconus, dicens *O*.
104 festivitati *VL*. sollemnitati *O*.
105 -cemur Dominum *om O*.
106 collectio eiusdem *GaMLV*. oratio *O*.
107 vel infirmitates *add LOV*.
108 vel remediis *add LOV*.
109 perfruantur *OV*. perfruatur *GaM*. potiantur *L*. per dominum nostrum *add GaM*. quia tibi soli est omnis honor et gloria in saecula saeculorum *add V*. quia Deus es *add* L. Amen *add O*.
110 V *om LOV*.
111 b *om GaM, sed adest in A* (*post* X) *cum quodam signo deletionis*.
112 item sexta oratio *add V*. oratio de VI lectione *add L*. VI *LOV* = XI *GaM*.
113 terras] terram *L*.
114 aera *GaMV*. aerem *O*. vera *L*.
115 haec *om L*.
116 per dominum nostrum *add GaM*. quia Deus es (est *L*) pius in saecula saeculorum *add LV*.
117 deinde *LV*. post haec *O*.

c *Collectio eiusdem:*[118]
Deus creator omnium bonorum, rogamus immensam misericordiam tuam ut non tam peccatorum quam precum considerator, munera tua quibus et[119] vivimus et vivemus,[120] non quia non meremur[121] neges sed quia precamur amplifices.[122]

VIIa[123] Deum patrem omnipotentem pro sacris[124] virginibus et continentibus[125] deprecemur ut infirmitati corporum adsit robur animorum[126] quo vitam valeant custodire virtutum mortificatione omnium vitiorum[127]

b[64] *Deinde*[117] *dicit diaconus*: Pro virginibus et continentibus precemur Dominum[105]

c *Collectio eiusdem:*[128]
Tribue his, Domine pater sancte,[129] pervenire[130] ad sexagesimi fructus coronam quibus integritatem vovere tu dedisti.
Nulla ex his stultis[131] virginibus misceatur, sed sint in numero[132] sapientium puellarum quarum[133] vasis oleum quo lampades suae inluminentur exuberet.[134]

VIIIa[135] Piae voluntatis retributori Domino[136] supplicemus ut ecclesiam suam bono largitatis accinctam per studium misericordiae ad suam[137] misericordiam iubeat[138] pervenire[139]

b[64] *Deinde*[117] *dicit diaconus*: Pro his qui elemosinas faciunt precemur Dominum

---

118 collectio eiusdem *om LO.*
119 et *om O.*
120 vivemus *susp. Blanchini.* vivamus *codd.* et vivemus *om GaM.*
121 meremur *GaMO.* mereamur *LV.*
122 p. *add GaM.* quia tibi soli est regnum in saecula saeculorum *add V.* quia tu es deus *add L.* Amen. Per gratiam pietatis tuae, Deus noster, qui omnia regis in saecula saeculorum *add O.*
123 item septime oratio *add V.* oratio de VII lec. *add L.* praefatio *add GaM.* VII *LOV* = II *GaM.*
124 sacris] sacratis *GaM.*
125 Et continentibus *om GaM.*
126 animorum] animarum *O.*
127 p. *add GaM.* adiuvante te, Deo nostro, qui gloriatur in saecula saeculorum *add V.* adiubam *add L.* Amen *add O.*
128 collectio eiusdem] oratio *O.*
129 pater sancte] sancte pater *GaM.*
130 pervenire] venire *GaM.*
131 Nulla … stultis *om GaM.*
132 numero] numerum *V.*
133 quarum] quorum *L.*
134 vasis … exuberet *GaMV.* vasa … exuberent *LO.* per dominum *add GaM.* quia Deus es clemens in saecula saeculorum *add V.* quia deus *add L.* Amen *add O.*
135 item octava oratio *add V.* oratio de VIII lectione *add L.* oratio *add L.* VIII *LOV* = III *GaM.*
136 retributori Domino] retributorem Dominum *O.*
137 suam] vivam *GaM.*
138 iubeat] abeat *V.*
139 per dominum *add GaM.* quia Deus est benedictus in saecula saeculorum *add VL.* Amen *add O.*

c *Collectio eiusdem:*[128]
Deus qui elemosynis extingui peccata docuisti, dona famulis tuis sanctam largiendi[140] devotionem; neque enim non habere poterunt possibilitatem, quibus tu dederis voluntatem.[141]

IX a[142] Certi de promissione divina quae[143] ingentia[144] peccata deflentibus indulgendum a se esse promisit, supplices[145] Deum rogemus ut confitentes[146] nomini suo suo[147] iudicio iudicari non in his que ante commissa sunt, sed in his quae fuerint correcta mereantur[148]

b[64] *Deinde dicit diaconus*: Pro penitentibus et confitentibus precemur Dominum

c *Collectio eiusdem:*[149]
Deus qui mutare sententiam per misericordiam tuam nosti, cum se peccator emendatione mutaverit, dona his paenitentiae fructum qui[150] ad tuam misericordiam convolantes[151] recipiendos se[152] in locum revertentis filii crediderunt.[153]

X a[154] Caelestium et terrestrium Deum, fratres dilectissimi, deprecemur, ut[155] fratribus nostris, quicumque peregrinationis necessitatibus subiacent, potenti auxilio suo[156] consolator et redux esse dignetur; neque ab eo peregrinentur qui uni Deo et nati sunt[157] et renati[158]

b[64] *Deinde dicit diaconus*: Pro peregrinantibus et navigantibus precemur Dominum

c *Collectio eiusdem*:
Supplices tibi Domine fundimus preces ut qui per omnia Deus es nos ubique non deseras.[159]

---

140 sanctam largiendi *OV*. sanctam largiendo *L*. istam *GaM*.
141 per dominum nostrum *add GaM*. quia solus cum Deo patre et spiritu sancto vivis et gloriaris Deus in saecula saeculorum *add VL*. Amen. per ineffabilem bonitatem tuam *add O*.
142 item nona oratio *add V*. oratio de VIIII lect. *add L*. oratio *add L*. IX *LOV* = VII *GaM*.
143 quae ... mereantur] pro ingentia peccata deflentibus, piissimum Deum, fratres carissimi, supplices deprecemur, ut indulgentiam mereantur *O qui postea habet lacunam usque in finem.*
144 ingentia] indigentia *L*.
145 supplices] suppliciter *L*.
146 confitentes] confidentes *GaM*.
147 suo *Blanchini*. tuo *LV*. *om GaM*.
148 per dominum nostrum *add GaM*. quia Deus est misericors et regnat in saecula saeculorum *add V*.
149 collectio eiusdem *om L*.
150 qui] quia *L*.
151 convolantes] cumualentes *GaM*.
152 recipiendos se] recipient esse *L*.
153 per dominum *add GaM*. quia multae miserationis est (es *L*) Dominus et regnat in saecula saeculorum *add LV*.
154 item decima oratio *add V*. oratio (de) X lectione *L*. X *LV* = VI *GaM*.
155 in *add V*.
156 auxilio suo] auxilium suum comes *GaM*.
157 sunt *posuit post* renati *GaM*.
158 per dominum *add GaM*. concedente clementia pietatis eius cuius regnum manet in saecula saeculorum *add V*. conceden- *add L*.
159 per dominum *add GaM*. quia Deus *add L*.

XI a[160]	Deum iudicii aeterni, fratres carissimi, pro spiritibus pausantium deprecemur ut eos Dominus aeternae quietis placabilitate susceptos[161] in illa felici beatorum sede[162] constituat, qui, sicut ob hoc renatos[163] esse ut resurgerent, crediderunt, ita se[164] beatificatos, quia resurrexerint,[165] gratulentur[166]
b[64]	*Deinde dicit diaconus:*[167] Pro defunctorum requie et quiete precemur Dominum
c	*Collectio eiusdem:* Precamur te Deus[168] ut defunctorum animae[169] in te credentes ac de tua pietatie sperantes, sic a delictis omnibus absolvantur[170] ut[171] nulla in aeternum confusione obnoxiae teneantur.[172]
XII a[173]	Deum patrem omnipotentem qui per baptismi gratiam delere confugientium ad se peccata consuevit pro his qui sacris fontibus abluendi sunt ⟨deprecemur ut⟩[174] omni faece terrenae, ⟨infect-⟩[175] -ionis abluti, inter matris eccleiae filios eo quo renati fuerint nitore perdurent, per dominum
c	*Collectio eiusdem:* Deus qui sacro lavacro homines pristinae inmortalitati reformas, praesta, ut … tui aquis pere- … -tis tuae munere consecrasti gratias salutis aeternae te sanctificante percipiant per dominum nostrum.

3. Liturgical Form

Ha is a litie, which is made up of:

A	an introductory litique, which places the prayer in the Easter context;
I–XII	Twelve litiques, each of which comprises:
a)	an invitatory;

160 item undecimal oratio *add V.* XI oratio de lectione *add L.* XI *LV* = X *GaM. Hic ponit A* Vb.
161 susceptos] receptos *V.*
162 sede] sed *V.*
163 se renatos] renatus *GaM.*
164 se *posuit post* beatificatos *LV.*
165 resurrexerint] resurrexerunt *L.*
166 per dominum *add GaM.* per dominum nostrum Iesum Christum qui cum Deo patre et sancto spiritu vivit et gloriatur *add V.* per dominum *add L.*
167 deinde … diaconus *om L.*
168 Deus] domine *add GaM.*
169 defunctorum animae *om GaM.*
170 absolvantur] absolvamur *GaM.*
171 ut] et *L.*
172 obnoxiae teneantur] teneamur *GaM.* per dominum *add GaM.* quia multae miserationis es Dominus, et regnas in saecula saeculorum *add V.* quia multe *add L.*
173 XII: *GaM solus.*
174 ⟨…⟩ *susp. Dold.*
175 ⟨infect-⟩ *suspicor.*

b) a diaconal invitation, that briefly indicates the subject or the beneficiaries of the petition; it is always omitted in *GaM*;

c) an oration.

4. Commentary

The heading alludes to readings between which these litiques are interpolated — at least in *VLO*. Tt is a point to which we will return.

A a Here we have a priestly 'apology', traditionally placed at the beginning of such a prayer.
The endings of the invitatories differ according to the manuscripts. *GaM* always adds *per dominum nostrum*, after the invitatories as well as the oration. *VL* ends the invitatories with a short doxology, for example, *cui est honor et gloria*, while *O* is content with a simple *Amen*. All this must have occurred later, so we have included it in the apparatus.

b The invitation made here does not make much sense

c The oration corresponds to the theme announced in 'a'.
The redactor of this litie likes to use the same word within a short interval for a particular literary effect that he is seeking. Here are some examples:

A c sanctifica ... sanctificatae

II c dona ... quam ... donasti

III c servientibus ... servire

VI c vivimus et vivemus
non quia non ... sed quia

VIII a per studium misericordiae ad suam misericordiam

IX a confitentes nomini suo suo iudicio iudicari

XII a abluendi ... abluti.
At the end of these orations *V* adds a short doxology, as it did after the invitatories. *L* refrains from this, as do both *O* and *GaM*.

I b The diaconal invitation comes very close to:
– M[1] IV '*pro pace ecclesiarium*, vocatione gentium *et quiete populorum*'; *Ha* Ib and *M*[1] IV are the only two texts to speak of the peace *of* the Churches;
– and *FG*[2] VI '*pro pace* regum *et quiete populorum*'.
As well, we find in *MGV* III 'pro regibus et pace';
Go IX 'pro pace regum';
Bo IX and *Hb* IX 'pro pace populi et regum'.

c The oration has nothing in common with the Gallican tradition.

II b once again takes up the pairing *sacerdotibus et ministris*.

III a Until now, we have only met the term *dux* in the later manuscripts in the Milanese tradition. *Barbaras gentes* matches with *barbaras nationes* in *OS* IV; cf. also the text of Ambrosiaster, Part One, Rome, T 3.

b The *principes* are named in *DG* V; Bernal (p. 330) notes that they would not have been qualified by *catholici* before the conversion of Recared I (586)
We note the link between the expression *et tranquillitatie temporum* and *Irl*[1] which has *pro altissima pace et tranquillitate temporum nostrorum*!

IV a 'pro his quos saeculi necessitas aut inquietudo detentat' matches with *DG* VIII–IX.

b Cf. *Bo* I.

V is missing in *VLO*, which explains the corrections made by these manuscripts in the preceding invitatory where they have added the sick to those who are absent. On the other hand, A, whose text is furnished only by *GaM*, proves the authenticity of this litique even though it is unfortunately incomplete; it is similar to *Go* VI and *Bo* VI, but the ending is different.

VI a This invitatory seems to take up several of the petitions from the litanies. The term *fructus* is found in *M*[1] VI and *Irl*[2] II; *aura* is found only in *DG* VI; *fecunditas et aeris(-um) temperies* appears in *M*[1] VI, *M*[2] VI, *FG*[1] VII, and *Irl*[2] III. The similarity between *aeris temperie* and *aera temperavit* certainly indicates a connection between the texts.

b By contrast, the terms of this invitatory have no exact correspondence in the preceding texts.
This petition does not exist in the Gallican tradition.

VII This is the first time that we have come across the *continentes*. No doubt it is an enlargement or adaptation of the prayer for virgins. *Irl*[2] prays 'pro continentia viduarum' and *Go* III speaks of *spadones* (eunuchs), who, in the light of Mt 19:12 are to be understood in the same sense as here.

VIII b Same heading as for *Bo* IV. Bernal points out (p. 330) that the diaconal | invitation proposes praying for those who are already giving alms while that at 'a' and 'c' asks the Lord to grant this spirit of giving to the faithful. He sees in this a sign of different origins for the priestly and diaconal formularies.

IX b To the penitents are added the *confitentes* (cf. *Go* VIIa). It is no longer a question of those who confess their faith (the *confessors* of the *OS* III), but of those who confess their sins; the spirituality has evolved.

c Here we have the reappearance of the term *emendatio*, as occurred in *FG*[1] IX, *FG*[2] VIII, and (*Irl*[2] VII); *DG* XIII used *emundatio*; *Hb* VIII had the verb *emundare*.

X a Same source as *Go* V and *Bo* V. All three have made revisions; we see that *GaM* uses the term *comes*, which is also found in *Go* V. Cf. p. 286, the comparison of these three texts.

b The deacon adds in the *navigantes*; cf. *OS* VI, *Irl*[1] VIII, *M*[1] VIII, and *Hb* VII.

XI a The priestly invitatory takes up the expression *pro spiritibus pausantium* which was the heading of *Go* X and *Bo* X.

b The diaconal invitatory on the other hand uses *pro defunctorum requie*, cf. *FG*[1] X and *Irl*[2] VIII; *et quiete* is added.
This petition does not exist in *MGV*.

XII This final litique features only in *GaM*; unfortunately it is incomplete.

II. Tradition B (Hb)

1. The Sources

TOLEDO Bibl. Capit. 35, 5, 'Officia et missae' of Toledo, end of 10th or beginning of 11th century. Description in Ferotin, LMS, 722–38. (Bourque 548 — Gamber 309).
We have not seen this manuscript. The section corresponding to our prayers has been reproduced almost exactly by the *Missale mixtum* of Cardinal de Cisneros, which appeared in Toledo in 1500 and was then printed in PL 85 according to the edition by Lesley (1755).

2. Text

The text reproduced below is that of PL 85, 448 ff. (indicated in the margin), but omitting the readings interpolated between the litiques. It takes place after the blessing of the paschal candle and after the prayer *Expectati temporis* which is found at the same place in *Ha* (*VLO*).

(448) A *Deinde dicatur prophetia — Lectio libri Genesis* (I–II)
Dicat diaconus: Pro solemnitate paschali
Flectamus genua
Levate.
Oratio
Pro solemnitate paschali flexis genibus te Pater omnipotens
obsecramus, ut mors unigeniti tui Domini nostri, qui vitam omni contulit
mondo, toti gratiam conferat populo christiano.
Resurrectio quoque ejus nos ad caelestia sublevet, et a corruptione
vitae hujus ereptos immortalitati aeternae consociet
Amen.
Per misericordiam tuam Deus noster qui es benedictus, et vivis et
omnia regis in saecula saeculorum
Amen.

I. *Lectio libri Genesis (V–VIII)*

(449) *Dicat diaconus*: Pro his qui variis necessitatibus detenti paschae
interesse non possunt
Flectamus genua

Levate.

Oratio

Deprecamur te, Pater aeterne omnipotens Deus, pro his qui diversis necessitatibus detenti solemnitate paschali interesse non meruerunt. Ut quia gaudio praesentium sunt exsortes, mereantur sanctorum meritis adesse participes. Ut sicut passio unigeniti filii tui Domini nostri pro multorum salute occurrit, ita et haec celebritas annuae festivitatis et presentibus tribuat gloriam et absentibus conferat veniam

Amen.

Per misericordiam tuam Deus qui vivis et omnia regis in saecula saeculorum.

Amen

II. *Lectio libri Genesis* (XXII)

(450) *Dicat diaconus*: Pro sacerdotibus ac ministris

Flectamus genua

Levate.

Oratio

Sacerdotes tuos, Domine, indue justitiam, et ministri tui laetentur. Illos doctrinis et vitae exemplis munifica, hos sanctitatis cultu officiique locupleta, ut dum utrique a te augmenta virtutum perceperunt, sine offensione tuis altaribus famulentur.

Chorus: Amen

Dicat presbyter: Per misericordiam tuam Deus noster qui vivis et omnia regis

in saecula saeculorum

Amen.

(451) III. *Lectio libri Exodi* (XII)

Postea dicat diaconus: Pro unitate fidei catholicae

Flectamus genua

Levate.

Oratio

Ecclesia tua, Christe, quae dilatata per universam terram diffusa est, omnis
tua gratia in unitatis gremio colligatur. Et quamvis semetipsam in gentium
varietate diffundat, fidei tamen divisionem non sentiat. Dissolve heresis schismata, quae subvertere cupiunt fidem, quae nituntur corrumpere veritatem. Ut sicut tu in caelis atque in terra unus atque idem dignosceris Dominis, ita tibi in unitate fidei serviat cunctarum gentium populus

Amen.

IV. *Lectio libri Exodi* (XIV)

(453) *Diaconus dicat*: ⟨Pro virginibus⟩[176]

Flectamus genua

Levate.

Oratio

Pro virginibus flectentes genua, te Pater omnipotens Deus postulamus, ut hanc

illustrem portionem ⟨gregis⟩[177] Christi tui, in qua maxime gaudet catholica
Ecclesia, ampliori fecunditate enutrias, ut quanto plus numerosior et
incorruptorum numerus exstat, tanto gaudium matrisEcclesiae augeatur.
Amen.

V. *Lectio libri Esayae Prophetae* (II)

(454) *Dicat diaconus*: Pro his qui elemosynas faciunt
Flectamus genua
Levate.

Oratio
Deprecamur te, Domine, pro his qui misericordiae fructibus egentium
subsidia conferunt, ut mereantur ex hac terrena dispensatione caelestem
percipere remunerationem. Et quicquid in usibus indigentium conferunt
proficiat illis ad fructum caelestium premiorum
Amen.

VI. *Lectio libri Ezechielis Prophetae* (XXXVII)

(455) *Dicat diaconus*: Pro peregrinantibus et navigantibus
Flectamus genua
Levate.

Oratio
Concede, Pater omnipotens, cunctos peregrinantes patriae fieri reduces.
Et[178] quoscumque turbulenti maris pervenit fluctus, ad tranquillitatis revoca
portum. Mereantur in hac solemnitate utrique et terrae exilium et maris
evadere exitium. Ut commune hujus laetitae votum, cunctis generale sit
gaudium
Amen

VII. *Lectio libri Habacuc prophetae* (I)

(456) *Dicat diaconus*: Pro egrotis
Flectamus genua
Levate.

Oratio
Miserere Domine his quos corporalis egritudinis valetudo involvit. Sana
cunctos in nobis mentis corporisque languores, atque omnibus indulgens,
solitam impertire medelam. Ut tibi cuncti in salute ministerium expleant
fidei, tibique referant laudes qui solus et peccata cordis emundas et
languorum corporum sanas
Amen.
Per misericordiam tuam Deus noster qui vivis et omnia regis in saecula
saeculorum
Amen.

VIII. *Lectio libri Jonae Prophetae* (I, IV)

(458) *Dicat diaconus*: Pro penitentibus
Flectamus genua
Levate.

Oratio

Cunctorum penitentium, Pater omnipotens, suscipe fletus, et quos hactenus
diabolus variis vitiorum sordibus inquinavit, respectu pietatis tuae purifica.
Tribue cunctis praeterita peccata deflere, et future non admittere. Ab illis
misericordia tua preveniente mundentur, ab istis tua custodiente gratia
liberentur
Amen.
Per misericordiam tuam Deus noster qui vivis et omnia regis in saecula
saeculorum
Amen.

IX. *Lectio libri Danielis Prophetae* (III)

(460) *Diaconis dicat*: Pro pace populi et regum
Flectamus genua
Levate.

(461) *Oratio*

Pro regibus saeculi hujus atque principibus tibi Pater flectentes genua
obsecramus ut tribuas illis moderamen justitiae, amorem pacis, virtutem
pietatis, studium bene regendae plebis. Ut in correptione et rectitudine eorum
pax simul et requies fidelium proveniat populorum
Amen

Psallendo: Sicut cervus.

Et prophetiis et orationibus cum tractibus dictis … letania.

(470) X *Et finito hymno angelorum diaconus dicat*:
Pro competentibus
Flectamus genua
Levate.

Et sacerdos dicat:

Oratio

Concede, Domine, omnes qui nunc fide meruerunt cognoscere veritatem
salutaris lavacri percipere innovationem. Sicque eos a cunctus peccatorum
sordibus baptismi unda purificet, ut ultra eos pravi operis inquinaqmenta
non maculent
Amen.
Per misericordiam tuam Deus noster qui vivis et omnia regis in saecula
saeculorum
Amen.

Dicat diaconus: Silentium facite.

Sequentia Epistolae Pauli Apostoli ad Romanos.

3. Liturgical Form

Hb is a litie made up of 11 litiques:

A is a general introduction, similar to those of the Gallican and Hispanic traditions (*Ha*);

I–X: 10 litiques, each comprising:
- a very brief diaconal invitatory;
- followed by the admonition, 'Let us kneel — Arise'
- a priestly oration.

4. Remarks

a) Each invitatory is followed by the invitation to kneel. Rather than being an influence of the Coptic liturgy,[179] it seems to be borrowed from the *OS*. The expressions *flexis genibus* or *flectentes genua* return three more times in the set (A, IV, IX).

b) The orations contain several phrases, which does not align with the style of Roman euchology; II even begins with a psalm verse! Several begin with *pro*, linking them directly to the invitatory formulary. VI alludes to the paschal solemnities.
All of this convinces us that we are in the presence of a text composed in Spain explicitly for the Easter Vigil, and not an ancient formulary of the *oratio fidelium*.

c) That the redactor of this litie was motivated by a literary concern is shown in the symmetry of the different elements of the sentence and in the use of the cursus. As this stylistic process was in use between the fourth and seventh centuries it does not provide us with any precise chronological indication.

d) The order of *Hb* corresponds to that of *Go-Bo* (cf. the synoptic table below); the only difference consists in the suppression of the prayer for the dead and in the anticipation of a petition for unity, situated here in third place. With regard to order, *Hb* is also quite similar to *GaM* which use the text of *Ha*.

In short, both the number of litiques and their internal structure once again point to the tendency to abridgement, a sign of a fairly late period, by which time this litie has undergone a major evolution.

---

176 pro virginibus *expl.* Lesley.
177 gregis *expl.* Lesley.
178 et] et ad *susp.* Lesley.
179 A Coptic Lenten litany contains the same admonitions in Greek, cf. Br. 159; supra, p. 134.

C. Study

It is immediately obvious that these Gallican and Hispanic texts are related, which justifies our treating them together, aided by the work of Bernal (pp. 324–47).

1. The Number of Litiques

The different formularies contain different numbers of litiques. Not counting the general introduction, we have:

12 in *GaM* and *MGV*,
11 in *A*, *Go*, *Bo*,
10 in *VL*(*O*) and *Hb*.

We actually have the trace of eleven litiques in *VL*(*O*) since the *Orationale* has in effect condensed into a single litique the prayer for those who are absent and that for the sick, which, in *GaM* and A, are separate. This combining is evident from the clumsiness in matching up the two petitions. Invitatory IV of *Ha* proposes praying 'pro his quos saeculi necessitas aut inquietudo detentat, *vel* pro his qui secundum carnis infirmitatem diversis egritudinem generibus afflictantur', and the oration begs 'praesta, ut famuli tui quorum necessitates *vel* infirmitates Ecclesiae sollicitudo commendat, pietatis tuae muneribus *vel* remediis perfruantur'. The diaconal invitatory mentioned only those 'qui huic sanctae festivitati interesse non possunt'; while, the text of the second part of the sentence, introduced each time by *vel*, is found literally in a supplementary litique (V) of *GaM*. Thus we do not hesitate to declare that the litie has been shortened. Following Baumstark,[180] Bernal several times notes this tendency to truncate the celebration.

We agree with the Spanish liturgist when he considers that the original number of litiques of *VL*(*O*)*A* was not eleven either, for they do not contain the petition *pro competentibus* that features in the Gallican tradition, *GaM* and *Hb*. It is therefore quite probable that early on, *VL*(*O*)*A* had twelve litiques, not counting the introduction.

2. Original Liturgical Form

a Distribution of the litiques between the readings in Spain

This phenomenon is a later development, since nothing in the content of the litiques makes reference to the readings. Moreover, the Gallican tradition is not aware of this fragmentation. Bernal thus rightly believes that the prayers and readings originally formed two distinct entities, a stage attested to by *GaM* and Gaul. When they interwove them, the petition *pro competentibus* was suppressed,

180 Baumstark (1957), 45.

'perhaps because it was outdated, considering the disappearance of the catechumenate', writes Bernal. In this way there would be the same number of litiques and readings. Later yet, the prayer for the sick was combined with that for those who were not present, thus reducing the number of litiques to ten, as witnessed by *VL*(*O*) and *Hb*.

b The tripartite structure of the litiques and their origin

Even though the diaconal admonition is lacking in *GaM* and in Gaul, (where its content is, nevertheless included in the form of a heading), Bernal considers that it was part of the original formulary. He bases this conclusion particularly on the Antiphonary of Léon (*A*) which contains neither invitatories nor orations, but only the admonitions, with music. This suggests to our author that the priestly formularies (invitatories and orations) were included in the sacramentary, and the parts for the deacon (admonitions) in another book — in this case the antiphonary. Thus the absence of these latter in *GaM* does not provide any argument against their antiquity.

Given our earlier enquiries, we think we can put these things into a more global perspective. We have seen that the headings (in Gaul) or the admonitions (in Spain) were clearly inspired by the Latin litanies. Bernal has noted this fact (pp. 343–46). He is even surprised (p. 345) to find a parallel with Book VIII of the CAp; in our opinion this does not prove any direct influence of the Syrian compilation on the Hispanic liturgy. An intermediary would have had to exist, namely, the Latin litanies that we have studied.

If these litanies were integrated only via the admonitions or headings, we could suppose that they were added to an already existing litie. But the priestly formularies themselves borrow these expressions from the litanies — we only have to cite the invitatory of *Go* I in Gaul and of *Ha* VI in Spain to see this. And so we think, as we previously suggested after the reading of *MGV*, that the Gallican and Hispanic liturgies must have formerly used the Latin litanies that we have published or others of the same kind. Then, probably under the influence of the *OS*, during the period of gradual infiltration of the Roman liturgy into these regions, these litanies would have been transformed into lities according to the taste of the day. Quite naturally their redactors would have incorporated the expressions they were accustomed to hearing in the ancient formularies, and even in Spain they would have liked the fact that the deacon summarised the priestly intention for the people, using formulas with which he was familiar. That would have been the pastoral way to get this reform accepted.

Can we say that the headings of these Gallian litiques were leftovers from ancient admonitions? Lowe has already suggested this.[181] Bernal has not considered the question. This explanation is probably the right one; otherwise these headings

181 Lowe (1923), 126.

would be merely rubrics for the use of the celebrant: there is scarcely any interest in that.

A second reason given by Bernal (p. 334–35) for attributing an archaic character to this tripartite structure of the litiques is the similarity with those of the *OS*, which are also based on three elements. We find this less convincing since, in the first place, as he himself has states, there is 'little difference' in the content of the diaconal admonition: in Spain, it summarises the petition; in the *OS* it invites the people to kneel. Moreover, we have already said that in the venerable Roman formulary, this admonition could have scarcely been original, and what is more, it does not feature in the Gallican form of the *OS* (*MGV*). In other words, while it is possible that the *OS* influenced the tripartite structure we think that this is highly improbable.

c The order of the litiques

Bernal has published a synoptic table on this subject. We have reproduced it below, with a few amendments, mostly concerning the numeration and the placement of the prayer for the sick in *VLA*.

Spain			Gaul		
GaM (= *Ha*)	*V + L + A* (= *Ha*)	*Hb*	*Go*	*Bo*	*MGV*
A. Introd.	Introd.	Introd.	Introd.	Introd.	Introd.
1. Pro clero	Pro unitate	Pro absent.	Pro absent.	Pro absent.	Pro unitate
2. Pro virgin.	Pro clero	Pro clero	Pro clero	Pro clero	Pro clero
3. Pro elem. fac.	Pro pace	Pro unitate	Pro virgin.	Pro virgin.	Pro pace
4. Pro absent.	Pro absent.	Pro virgin.	Pro elem. fac.	Pro elem. fac.	Pro virgin.
5. Pro egrot.	Pro ⟨egrot.⟩	Pro elem. fac.	Pro peregr.	Pro peregr.	Pro vid. et orph.
6. Pro peregr.	Pro fruct.	Pro peregr.	Pro egrot.	Pro egrot.	Pro egrot.
7. Pro poenit.	Pro virgin.	Pro aegrot.	Pro poenit.	Pro poenit.	Pro absent.
8. Pro unitate	Pro elem. fac.	Pro poenit.	Pro unitate	Pro unitate	Pro peregr.
9. Pro pace	Pro poenit.	Pro pace	Pro pace	Pro pace	Pro elem. fac.
10. Pro defunc.	Pro peregr.		Pro defunc.	Pro defunc.	Pro poenit.

SPAIN			GAUL		
11. Pro fruct.	Pro defunc.	Pro compet.	Pro compet.	Pro compet.	Pro neophit.
12. Pro compet.					Pro compet.

If a unique order existed, writes our author (p. 337), it is impossible to reconstruct it; however, certain facts can be recognised:

1 The correspondence in the order of *Go* and *Bo*, and the similarity with *Hb* and even with *GaM*;
2 The two other lities (*Ha* and *MGV*) each have a different order, without any correspondence;
3 However, a certain grouping of petitions is able to be discerned: litiques *pro virginibus, pro elemosinas facientibus, pro peregrinantibus, pro penitentibus* and *pro egrotantibus*, which tend to form the central petitions, more or less in the same order.

Let us summarise. The original litie (at least in the Easter Vigil) would have had the following form:

A an introductory litique, situating the prayer in relation to Easter;

I–XII Twelve litiques, whose order is not fixed. Each one comprises:
- a priestly invitatory,
- probably a diaconal admonition, summarising this invitatory with the help of a formula taken from the ancient litanies;
- an oration.

3. Link with Easter

It is not possible to confirm, writes Bernal (p. 333) with regard to these Hispanic formularies, that these formulae have been constructed on the basis of a paschal theme. In fact, at this point we must distinguish between the Gallican and Hispanic texts.

The Gallican texts make no reference to Easter night, beyond the first litique which places the whole prayer in context. But it could be that this was added later, being placed at the head of an existing litie that had no connection with Easter. The sole exception to this is the heading of *Bo* I, 'pro his qui … Pascha interesse non possunt'. We have already pointed out the evolution of this invitatory between *Go* and *Bo*. Perhaps this heading was introduced under Spanish influence.

The Hispanic formularies, on the other hand, contain — in addition to the introduction — clear references to the Feast, notably in the litique devoted to those who are absent (*Ha* IV and *Hb* I); cf. also *Ha* VII c (the parable of the 10 virgins from the prayers of the Lucernarium being given a paschal interpretation) and *Hb* VI and X (*nunc*). As we have already said, *Hb* seems to have been composed explicitly with the Easter Vigil in mind.

The presence of a prayer for catechumens does not prove that these lities were composed for the Easter Vigil, since they are also found in the *OS* and in certain litanies. This petition is, however, particularly well placed for this occasion.

4. Relations Between the Different Lities

After a 'meticulous examination', Bernal arrives at the following conclusions (pp. 337–38) which we will adopt, with a few additions of our own to complete them:

a all these formularies present with different texts. Most similar are *Go* and *Bo* while *MGV* and *Hb* are the most dissimilar. Sometimes even the ideas expressed are quite different.

b one invitatory — that for travellers — however, is comparable; the synoptic presentation of these three texts will allow us a little comparative examination:

***Go* V**	***Bo* V**	***Ha* X**
Caelestium et terrestrium	Caelestium et terrestrium	Caelestium et terrestrium
et infernorum dominum		
deum patrem omnipotentem	deum patrem	deum
fratres dilectissimi		fratres dilectissimi
deprecemur obsecrantes	supplices deprecemur	deprecemur
uti fratres nostros	ut omnes fratres nostros	ut fratribus nostris
ac sorores		
quicumque peregrinationum	qui peregrinationum	quicumque peregrinationis
necessitatibus subiacent	necessitatibus subiacent	necessitatibus subiacent
omnipotens deus auxilio	potentia auxilii	potenti auxilio
suo comes	sui	suo (comes *GaM*)
adiutor reducat	protegat	consolator
ac protegat	atque defendat	et redux esse dignetur…

With Bernal we consider that *Ha* would be closest to the original: 'potenti auxilio suo comes consolator et redux esse dignetur' offers a very satisfying meaning for a prayer intended for travellers, while the ending of *Bo* is more commonplace. As for *Go*, it gets confused and uses again the adjective *omnipotens* which has already been used to qualify *deum* at the beginning of the petition. It is hardly likely to be original. We note the presence of the term *comes* in *GaM* and *Go*.

The beginning, too, seems unsatisfactory in *Go*. Although the tripartite formula (with *et infernorum*) could recall Phil 2:10, it seems rather bombastic with regard to the bipartite expression of *Ha* and *Bo*, which is much more frequently found in the New Testament.

Addition of the word *obsecrantes* seems equally redundant, whereas the inclusion of *et sorores* is dear to *Go* (cf. supra). We could also look at the beginning of the invitatory for the sick, where again *Ha* seems to be better.

Does this mean that Gaul received these lities, or at least their influence, from Spain? Bernal believes that it is very probable that, in the specific case of the invitatory for travellers, the Hispanic text has influenced the Gallican via the *GaM*, a document which links the two traditions (namely by use of the Gallican order for the litiques, together with the term *praefatio*, which is typically Gallican, as heading of the invitatory for virgins, and *comes* in the invitatory for travellers). But according to the Spanish liturgist, the overall question of relationships between the two families remains open. It is a point on which a monograph would be most welcome.

5. *Original Function of the Lities*

The point that is of utmost importance for us is to know what relationship these formularies have with the *oratio fidelium*. The documents show that there is indeed a relationship, in the broad sense, except where they have been divided up and distributed between the readings. But do we detect, as with the *OS* for Rome, the trace of a Universal Prayer, customary in Gaul and Spain, and independent of the Easter Vigil?

Bernal (pp. 343–46) is willing to assert that here we do have vestiges of an *oratio fidelium*. In support of this opinion he offers the parallelism with the *OS*, the independence of the lities in relation to the readings, and the similarities with the ancient litanies.

These findings are accurate and in our view, give us permission to go even further. It is highly likely that the literary form of these prayers is due to influence of the *OS*,[1] but on the other hand the diaconal admonitions (in Spain) and the headings of the litiques (in Gaul) are borrowed from the litanies. And so we think that the litanies were customarily used in these regions for the Universal

1 In addition to all the similarities noted so far, it must be noted that they all bear the same name of *orationes* (*solemn* or *paschal*); was this a technical term for what we have called a 'litie'?

Prayer. Their existence is also proven by other traces (cf. the thesis of Ramos). Then, impressed by the breadth of the Roman *OS*, the litanies would have been remodelled to transform them into lities. A number of them which make no reference to Easter (the Gallican) could have served as an *oratio fidelium* before being reserved for the Easter Vigil. The Hispanic lities have closer relationships with Easter; *Hb* was even composed explicitly to be used on that night and therefore constitutes a regular formulary of the Universal Prayer.

D. Appendix: The '*Oratio Fidelium*' in the Hispanic Liturgy

We cannot leave the Hispano-Gallic domain without recalling the thesis of Fr Ramos on the existence of the *oratio fidelium* in Spain.[2] We have already referred to this in Part One, when studying St Augustine.

Its Place in the Celebration

The *missa*, first of ten variable elements in the Hispanic liturgy, sited (currently) between the Offertory chant and the *alia*, was, according to the Spanish Jesuit, originally a priestly invitatory to the Universal Prayer. He arrives at this conclusion from analysis of the texts on the one hand and the structure of this part of the Mass, between the readings and the anaphora on the other. This conclusion is confirmed by the testimony of St Isidore of Seville (*c*. 560–633) who wrote in his *De ecclesiasticis Officiis*:

> 'Prima (= missa) earundem oratio admonitionis est erga populum ut excitentur ad exorandum Deum.
> Secunda (= alia) invocationis ad Deum est, ut clementer suscipiat preces fidelium oblationesque eorum'.[3]

Thus, after the Offertory Chant (*sacrificium*) we have:

- The *missa* or *oratio admonitionis*; priestly invitatory,
- The Universal Prayer, properly so-called, composed of different (priestly?) invitatories,
- The *alia* or *oratio invocationis*: the conclusion by the priest.

This is what Ramos calls the 'euchological triptych'. The transposition of the Offertory Chant before this group comes at a later date and is due to the development of the rites of offering.

---

2 Ramos (1964) *Oratio admonitionis*...; and (1964) 'Rasgos de la "Oratio communis"...', 31–45. We have not been able to take into account the criticisms mounted against this study by P. Jaramillo, in a thesis presented at the Sant'Anselmo Institute, Rome. Its existence was pointed out by Fr Pinell, to whom we are most grateful.

3 Isidore of Seville, *De ecclesiasticis officiis*, 1, 15: *De missa et orationibus*, (PL 83), 752.

The Formularies

The texts of the *missa* are varied. Ramos distinguishes between those that are addressed to the people and those (later) addressed to God. He classifies them according to whether they are didactic or paranetic, or even on their insistence on the notion of offering. It is not always easy to know exactly which text fulfilled which function originally. Here is one as an example:

> 'Dei omnipotentis misericordiam cum omni supplicatione rogemus:
> ut Ecclesiae suae sanctae catholicae fidem augeat, pacem tribuat,
> nobis remissionem et indulgentiam peccatorum concedat.
> Infirmis salutem,
> lapsis reparationem,
> tribulatis gaudium,
> captivis redemptionem,
> oppressis relevationem,
> iterantibus prosperitatem,
> terrae suae pacem
> et defunctis fidelibus requiem sempiternam propitius tribuere dignetur.
> ℟: Praesta, aeterne omnipotens Deus'
>
> *Missa omnimoda,* LOrd., 234–35.

Is this an invitatory, or already the text of the Universal Prayer itself? The same question could be asked of the following formulary, that we cite because of its similarity with the litanies:

> 'Te deprecamur, Domine, ut adsis precibus cotidianis diebus ...:
> pro Ecclesia tua catholica, quam custodire digneris ab universis scandalis;
> pro serenitate regia, ut vitam tranquillam possideat;
> pro sacerdotibus in fungendis officiis, quos ab omni insidia diaboli facias liberos;
> pro clero et universo populo quos ... ab iminenti flagello propitius liberare digneris;
> pro spiritibus famulorum famularumque tuarum in pace quiescentium ut remissionem accipiant peccatorum'
>
> *Post Nomina* (III Dominico de Quotidiano), LMS 1355.[4]

But the *Missale mixtum* has preserved vestiges of the *oratio fidelium* itself. Here is the text, taken from the Ordinary of the Mass:

4 In Ramos (1964), *Oratio admonitionis,* 173–217, w2e find an inventory of 368 pieces, with indication of their sources. We can also add the references indicated by Dold (1964), note on p. 19.

With regard to the subsequent evolution of the *missa,* and its relationships with the final *Conversi* of the sermons of St Augustine, see what we have said above, when examining the texts of the Bishop of Hippo.

'Ecclesiam sanctam catholicam in orationibus in mente habeamus:
ut eam Dominus fide et spe et charitate propicius ampliare dignetur.
Omnes lapsos captivos infirmos atque peregrinos in mente habeamus:
ut eos Dominus propicius redimere sanare et confortare dignetur.
Chorus: Presta eterne omnipotens Deus'.[5]

Ramos, and many other liturgists before him, have pointed out the archaic character of these two invitatories. After our study of the litanies, this is even more clearly apparent. Without doubt we are in the presence of two lone invitatories that have survived from a set which would have been more important. Did they belong to a formulary that was already in existence at the time of Cardinal Cisneros? Let us analyse them.

Both have the same structure:

- The first example names the beneficiary in the accusative, depending each time on *in mente habeamus*. We have spoken at length about this expression in the course of Part One of this book and we have highlighted its antiquity. Ramos does the same (p. 72, note 46). This first sentence has a very ancient structure, equivalent to *pro sancta ecclesia catholica oremus.*
- The second example is based on the same schema:
  a final clause, whose subject is *Dominus*, and the verb *dignetur* with the infinitive. *Propicius* appears each time, together with a three-fold rhythm: 'fide et spe et charitate', forming a symmetry with 'redimere, sanare et confortare'.
  The content of the invitatories is very traditional:
  - The first recommends the Church to the faithful (with usual descriptor, but note the absence of *apostolicam*). In the final clause, however, we do not read the phrase 'toto orbe diffusa', despite its widespread use. The petition for the three theological virtues is original.
  - The second invitatory names those whom we have called the needy: captives, the sick, and travellers are cited in the numerous litanies, but none of them mention the *lapsi*. By contrast, these do figure in the lists of intentions of St Cyprian (T 3) and Tertullian (T 7).

  The response, on the other hand, has no chance of being ancient. As Ramos suggests (p. 73, note 48), we can assume that it was repeated after each petition.
  In short, we are inclined to see these invitatories, even if they are only preserved in recent sources, as very ancient vestiges of the *oratio fidelium.* They could date back to the third century.

---

5 *Missale mixtum*, (PL 85), 114 or 540.

And in Gaul?

In his inventory of texts, M. Ramos admits to being forced to point out the Gallican formularies as well, given their similarity of content and the parallel between the structure of the Mass in Spain and Gaul. But he is wary of extending to Gaul his conclusions on the existence of an *oratio fidelium* in Spain.

We think that there is room for research work to be undertaken here. The Spanish liturgist has pointed out and systematically classified (pp. 165–72) all the Gallican texts parallel to the Hispanic *missa*. The study of this material, compared with what we know about the Universal Prayer in Spain and what we have learnt from the ancient litanies, could well be the subject of a thesis and shed light on this still clouded domain of the *oratio fidelium* in Gaul.

Section Five

Subsequent Evolution

So far we have only considered traces and texts of the *oratio fidelium*, thereby limiting ourselves, by definition, to the Mass. However, a complete history of the liturgical genre of 'the common prayer' would also take into account the litanic prayers of the Office. This is a confusing domain that we cannot address here in its entirety,[1] but it is obvious that there were mutual influences between the Universal Prayer of the Mass and the litanic prayers of the Office. We will outline the subsequent evolution of our prayers in a way that will show the continuity of these different liturgical forms, but we cannot enter into all the problems posed by these texts.

A. The Psalm Verses

It seems that it is Gaul that acquires the habit of ending the prayer of the Hours with psalm verses that it often entitles *capitella de psalmis*. The expression is used in canon 30 of the Council of Agde in 506.[2] Perhaps the first example of it is in the *Regula monachorum* of Caesarius of Arles,[3] which dates from 503.[4] The Rule of St Columban, from around 600, tells us that the *seniores* have established that in the daytime Hours besides the three psalms, will be prayed

'cum versiculorum augmento intervenientium
pro peccatis primum nostris,
deinde pro omni populo christiano,
deinde pro sacerdotibus et reliquis deo
consecratis sacrae plebis gradibus,
postremo pro elemosinas facientibus,

1 Basic information can be found in the following works: Bäumer (1905), especially vol. 2, Appendix 2, 429–41; E. Bishop (1918), 116–36; Alfonso (1925), 'Verso le origini' 216 ff., 274 ff.; Fischer (1951), 55–74.

2 Council of Agde, ed. Munier, (CC 148), 206: 'et in conclusione matutinarum vel vespertinarum missarum post hymnos capitella de psalmis dici...'.

3 *Sancti Caesarii opera omnia*, vol. 2, ed. Morin (1942), 153, l. 16; or PL 67, 1102 (Clavis 1012). Sunday Lauds ends with 'Te Deum laudamus, Gloria in excelsis Deo, et capitellum'.

4 We note, however, as we have already said, that the most ancient manuscripts of the *Gloria in excelsis* (5th century) and the *Te Deum* (7th century) have these two hymns followed by psalm verses, intended for morning prayer; this usage, then could be older. The edition of the oldest examples of these hymns can be found in Warren (1895), 76–77 and 93–94.

postea pro pace regum,
novissime pro inimicis, ne illis deus statuat
in peccatum quod persecuntur et detrahunt nobis,
quia nesciunt quid faciunt'.[5]

We cannot fail to notice the similarity of these petitions with those of the ancient litanies! The Antiphonary of Bangor itself informs us on the form of this prayer, since it provides a text entitled *Oratio communis fratrum*[6] where one prays successively

'[pro peccatis nostris],
pro baptizatis,
[pro sacerdotibus],
pro abbate,
[pro fratribus],
pro fraternitate,
pro pace populorum et regum,
pro blasphemantibus,
pro impiis,
pro iter facientibus,
[pro gratias agentibus],
pro eleemosynariis,
pro infirmis,
[pro captivis],
[pro tribulantibus],
[pro poenitentibus]';

with each heading (except for the abbey, where three psalm verses but no prayer is indicated) being followed by one or two psalm verses, then a very short oration. Warren, the learned editor of this Antiphonary, dedicates a note[7] to them in which he publishes in parallel columns the sequence of these petitions and the passage of the Rule of St Columban cited above. He then compares them with the *Orationes maiores* for Lauds and Vespers in the Psalter of Rheims,[8] which begin with *Oremus pro omni gradu ecclesiae*. They are found in a number of manuscripts[9] and include a

---

5 *Sancti Columbani opera*, ed. Walker (1957), 130; (PL 80), 212C (Clavis 1108).

6 See *The Antiphonary of Bangor*, ed. Warren (1895), 22–24; (PL 72), 598–599 (Clavis 1938 — Gamber 150).

7 Warren (1895), 63–66.

8 CAMBRIDGE, Corpus Christi College 272, f. 171^{v}–172^{r}, dating from a little before 882. This piece is also edited by Bäumer (1905), vol. 2, 440–41, under the heading, 'Les Orationes maiores s. Preces'.

9 To the eight manuscripts cited by Bäumer on p. 439, we can add:

1. BRUSSELS, Bibl. Roy. IV, 41, f. 24^{r}–27^{r}. Processional from Liège, 1574. 'Preces maiores' following the Litany of the Saints.

2. BRUSSELS, Bibl. Roy. IV, 112, f. 13^{v}–14^{v}. Processional of Liège, 13th–14th century; for Ash Wednesday.

good number of local variants. Here is the text, taken from Bäumer, only partially complete:

Oremus pro omni gradu ecclesiae
℣. Sacerdotes tui induantur iustitiam et sancti tui exsultent
Pro pastore nostro
℣. 1. Beatus qui intelligit super egenum et pauperem
2. Dominus conservet eum et vivificet eum et beatum faciat eum in terra et non tradat eum in animam inimicorum eius
Pro rege nostro
℣. Domine salvum fac regem et exaudi nos in die qua invocaverimus te
Pro liberis eius (*rare petition*)
℣. Salvos fac servos tuos, Deus meus, sperantes in te
Pro antistite nostro (*in the monasteries*: Pro abate nostro)
℣. Dominus conservet eum et vivificet eum et beatum faciat eum in terra
Pro cuncto populo christiano (pro omni populo catholico)
℣. Salvum fac populum tuum, Domine, et benedic hereditati tuae (et rege eos et extolle illos usque in aeternum)
Pro pace (et unitate ecclesiae)
℣. Fiat pax in virtute tua et abundantia in turribus tuis
Pro fratribus et sororibus nostris
℣. Propter fratres meos et proximos meos loquebar pacem de te
Pro iter agentibus
℣. O Domine salvos fac eos; o Domine beneprosperare

---

3. CAMBRAI, Bibl. Mun. 55. f. 103. Psalter, 15th c.; following the Litany of the Saints.

4. CHANTILLY, Musée Condé 103 (not in folio form). Book of prayers, 16th century; 'preces et orationes dicendae post litanias'.

5. LONDON, Brit. Mus. Harl. 863, f. 111–12, at the end of a 12th c. Psalter, after the Litany of the Saints; ed. Dewick (1914), vol. 1, Appendix, col. 444–45.

6. MONTPELLIER, Bibl. Fac. Médecine MS 409, on the last folio (346) of the Psalter of Mondsee, after the litanies (around 800); ed. Unterkircher (1974), 515. After the first three intentions, it includes only 'pro senioribus nostris'; and 'pro defunctis'. It gives no biblical verses.

7. PARIS, B.N. lat. 1154, f. 21r–22. 'Liber precum', end of 9th c.; 'Capitula', following the Litany of the Saints.

8. PARIS, B.N. lat. 9467, f. 26–27. Clunian Processional, 17th c.; following the Litany of the Saints.

9. REIMS, Bibl. Mun. 304, f. 26r-v, Ritual of Saint-Thierry, first half of 10th c.; 'preces de quadragesima et adventu'.

10. REIMS, Bibl. Mun. 305, f. 91v–92r, Ritual of Saint-Bertin (Northern France), 11th c.; same heading.

11. VALENCIENNES, Bibl. Mun. 510, f. 88v (cover page). Collection of *Vitae* from the abbey of Saint-Amand, 10th c. No response.

12. VERDUN, Bibl. Mun. 132 (1–2–3), 15th c. Processional, at f. 6, 4 and 6 respectively.

13 VERDUN, Bibl. Mun. 132, 3, f. 25–26 (cover pages).

To which one can also add the *Processionnal* printed at COUTANCE in 1839, p. lxxviii ff., which is, however, missing the first petition 'pro omni gradu ecclesiae'.

(Benedictus qui venturus est in nomine Domini)

Pro (fidelibus) navigantibus

℣. Exaudi nos, Deus salutaris noster,

– et propter gloriam nominis tui, Domine, libera nos

– spes omnium finium terrae et in mari longe

Pro adversantibus (persequentibus) et calumniantibus nos

℣. Domine (Jesu Christe), ne statuas illis hoc peccatum, quia nesciunt quid faciunt

Pro discordantibus

℣. Pax Dei, quae exsuperat omnem sensum, custodiat corda eorum (et intelligentias eorum in pace)

Pro paenitentibus

℣. Convertere Domine usquequo et deprecabilis esto super servos tuos

Pro omnibus (nobis) eleemosynas facientibus (nobis bona facientibus)

℣. 1. Dispersit, dedit pauperibus, iustitia eorum maneat in saeculum saeculi

2. Retributor omnium bonorum, Deus, retribuere dignare omnibus nobis bona
facientibus propter nomen tuum vitam aeternam

Pro infirmis

℣. 1. Et clamaverunt ad Dominum, cum tribularentur, et desiderium eorum attulit eis

2. Mitte eis verbum tuum et sana eos de interitionibus eorum

Pro captivis (carceratis) et afflictis

℣. Libera eos, Deus Israel, ex omnibus tribulationibus suis

Pro peccatis et neglegentiis nostris

℣. 1. Domine, ne memineris iniquitatum nostrarum antiquarum, cito anticipent nos
misericordiae tuae (quia pauperes facti sumus nimis)

Pro fidelibus defunctis

℣. Requiem aeternam dona eis Domine, et lux perpetua luceat eis

Pro fratribus nostris absentibus

℣. Salvos fac servos tuos, Deus meus, sperantes in te

(Pro nobismetipsis

℣. Fiat misericordia tua Domine super nos, quemadmodum speravimus in te).

We can see that these prayers once again take up the expressions held dear by the ancient litanies; their influence was definitely exerted! We are very close to the *preces feriales* of the Roman Office.

According to Professor Fischer,[10] the development would have taken place in the following way. Gaul would have instituted the custom of concluding the

10 Fischer (1951), 57.

Hours with psalm verses. Ireland would have borrowed this custom and would then have transformed the ancient litanies, replacing the response with a psalm verse. This is the stage attested to by the Rule of St Columban (around 600) and by the texts that we have just cited, which would have spread to the continent in the course of the 7th century. These considerations allow him to distinguish the *preces feriales* of the Roman Office from the Gallican and Irish petitions (p. 58, note 21).

Soon a penitential character will be attached to these prayers; this is attested to by Amalarius (*c.* 775–850).[11]

B. The Hispanic Lenten 'Preces'

Another form in which this old base of litanies is developed and preserved is what the manuscripts call in an imprecise way the *preces*. Under this title fall the ancient litanies together with compositions that derive from them but which present a different literary genre.

Thus it is that on the first five Sundays of Lent, between the first two readings (Old Testament) and the last two (Apostle and Gospel) the *Missale mixtum* offers litanies, which are as follows:

- First Sunday: *Indulgentiam postulamus, Christi exaudi*
  ℟. *Placare et miserere* (PL 85, 298)
- Second Sunday: *Miserere et parce clementissime Domine populo tuo*
  ℟. *Quia peccavimus tibi* (PL 85, 318)
- Third Sunday: *Rogamus te rex saeculorum Deus sancta*
  ℟. Jam miserere peccavimus tibi (PL 85, 336).

This first sentence is found in the *preces* of the Aquitaine and Hispanic manuscripts. The petitions are not identical, but it is fundamentally the same text. It has been edited by M. Huglo.[12]

- Fourth Sunday: *Vide domine humilitatem meam, quia erectus est inimicus*
  ℟. *Miserere pater iuste, et omnibus indulgentiam dona* (PL 85, 354–55)

This text appears, somewhat shortened, in the *Bobbio Missal,* on Holy Saturday, without a response, under the heading: *Item alia de eodem die.*[13] The response is

11 Amalarius, *Liber officialis* IV, 4, 6 ff.; ed. Hanssens (1948), vol. 2, 424–25.

12 Huglo (1955), 374–75; philological and musical commentary is to be found 378–81. To the manuscripts cited can be added PARIS, B.N. nv. acq. lat. 3001, 13th c. monastic Processional from the south-west of France (Saint-Michel-de Gaillac?), f. 36v–37v. The music can be found in the *Variae preces,* Bénédictins de Solesmes (1896), 255–57.

13 *Bobbio Missal,* ed. Lowe, 66–67.

also found with the same function in Aquitaine manuscripts, but the petitions are different.[14]

– Fifth Sunday: *Insidiati sunt mihi adversarii mei gratis*
℟. *Tu pater sancta miserere et libera me* (PL 85, 372–73).

This piece is also in the *Bobbio Missal*, also for Holy Saturday, under the heading: *Incipit precis de eodem die.*[15]

The first three formularies are from actual litanies, whose petitions draw their vocabulary from the traditional arsenal, but their literary form is almost hymnic and announces the Sangallian *preces* of the 10th century.

The last two texts are quite different. They are no longer composed of petitions, but of cries in the first person put on the lips of Christ, as in the Impropria. Meyer, and De Bruyne after him,[16] have studied these two formularies. Contrary to Meyer, De Bruyne considers that the *Insidiati* was composed in Spain no later than the 7th century and that it was adopted by the *Bobbio Missal.*[17] He believes the other text to be by the same author.

We are willing to believe that the evolution would have taken place in the following way. The ancient litanies were at one time used in Spain, or at least they were known there. They underwent two mutations:

– the first transformed them into lities, delivered to us as the *orationes paschales*, commented on above;
– the second tended to turn them into hymns; this genre was very popular and will later find talented interpreters among the monks of St Gall. In the medieval Processionals there are numerous hymnic compositions (*Ardua spes, Clamemus omnes, Humili prece*, etc.) for the Rogation Days, where we also sometimes meet snippets from the ancient litanies.[18] But this no longer has anything to do with the Universal Prayer.

---

14 Cf. Huglo (1955), 365 and 376–77. Add to this manuscript 3001, f. 24v–26r.
15 *The Bobbio Missal*, ed. Lowe, 66.
16 Meyer (1913), 177–222. De Bruyne (1913), 421–36.
17 In his article, 'Bobbio (Missel de)', DACL 2, 939–62, Wilmart believes he can acknowledge that the *Bobbio* received its *preces* from Spain' (*c.* 947).
18 To read about these hymns see Stotz (1972).

C. The Litany of the Saints[19]

Apart from the *Kyrie eleison* that introduces it, the Litany of the Saints has preserved, in its fourth part, the petitions introduced by *ut*, where one can still sometimes recognize a distant echo from the ancient litanies. In any case they belong to the same wave as the litanies, or at least to the transformations they underwent. Once the *oratio fidelium* was suppressed, the need for intercessory prayer was reflected in a variety of ways.[20]

Its Origins

The origins of the Litany of the Saints are rather obscure. Some see it already in the Ordination ritual in the Old Gelasian sacramentary (between 628 and 715); at the time of the election,[21] after the Introit and Oration, the bishop addresses the participants, then 'incipiunt omnes *Kyrie eleison* cum laetania'.[22]

What formulary does *laetania* designate here? The question leaves us perplexed. The Old Gelasian, whose manuscript dates from around 750, obviously cannot be alluding to the Litany of the Saints such as was found everywhere from the 9th century. But that does not mean that this rubric does not have in mind an earlier stage of the litany, before it was fully developed. Since subsequently in the Ordination ritual we only ever find the Litany of the Saints, there is little chance that 'laetania' is directed at one of the ancient litanies, and even less at an ancient litany in its original form. But perhaps it is not necessary to put the two forms of litanies into opposition, since they have many common elements. The Litany of the Saints is a litany that begins by invoking the saints. If the specific character of this prayer is invocation of the saints, then when does this first appear?

The Psalter of Athelstan[23] is the first document to furnish any trace of it. On the final folio, this manuscript contains a 'litany of the saints' in Greek, which also features in a 12th century manuscript.[24] It is generally thought that this Psalter arrived in England around 690 and offers us the framework of a litany used in Rome. It may be the translation of a Latin original. These two Greek formularies

---

19 For information on the Litany of the Saints see the following: Baumstark (1904), 98–120; E. Bishop (1918), 137–63 and 314–332; Badcock (1932), 167–80; Moeller (1938), 80–86; Alfonso (1940), 206–13; Opfermann (1958), 306–19; Coens (1963), 131–332; Knopp (1970), 185–231.

Père Gy has studied this matter closely and is preparing an article on this subject; what we write here comes largely from exchanges we were able to have with him.

20 A further example is a translation (adapted) of Clement of Rome's great prayer, found in a manuscript of Troyes, edited by Wilmart, cf. L. Eizenhöfer (1972–1973), 223–40.

21 This *Ordo* of election was added in Gaul, cf. Chavasse (1958), 22–27.

22 Gelasian Sacramentary, ed. Mohlberg, no. 142, p. 24.

23 LONDON, Brit. Mus., Cotton MS Galba A XVIII, f. 200. According to Bishop, the manuscript dates from the 9th century, and according to Badcock and Knopp, the middle of the 10th.

24 LONDON, Brit. Mus., Cotton MS Titus D, XVIII, f. 12v; 12th c.

correspond to the first traces of Latin that come from an English manuscript from the first half of the 8th century,[25] the Stowe Missal and its parallel from Fulda.[26] On the basis of these five manuscripts, E. Bishop has edited in parallel columns the Greek and Latin texts of this schema of litanies of the saints, while G. Knopp provides a synoptic table of all the sources.[27]

According to Bishop, the litanies of the saints passed rapidly from the British Isles to the continent, where they are found for the first time in the Baptism ritual of the Gellone Sacramentary[28] and in OR 21 ('ordo letaniae maioris'),[29] both from the end of the 8th century. The way is then open for enlarging the litany by increasing the names of the saints (the Gellone Sacramentary gives only thirteen) and the introduction of invocations, newly composed or taken from the common fund of ancient formulas of intercession.

Bishop notes (p. 148) that if the Litany of the Saints arrives in England towards the end of the 7th century, its rapid spread would have been no surprise, given the religious spirit that prevailed at the time, and given the flexibility of this new devotion which combines both variety and freedom in the choice of saints with an essentially popular euchological genre.

According to Badcock, the Greek would have originated in Galatia or Capadocia, and would have dated back to the end of the 4th or beginning of the 5th century. This manuscript would have passed through Rome and reached Gaul, or a copy would have been made of it which was then used by the redactor of OR 21 and by Moelcaich. In the middle of the 8th century the manuscript found itself in England, where the litany is on the one hand translated into Latin, as in Royal 2 A XX, and on the other shortened into the copy that would serve as a model for Galba A XVIII in the 10th century and for Titus D XVIII in the 12th century. At the beginning of the 9th century, the original manuscript is in Ireland, which explains the presence of the Litany in the Stowe Missal, the manuscript of Fulda and in Saint-Gall 1359.

This bold reconstruction is not convincing on all points.

The Variety of Formularies

The very popular character of the Litany of the Saints undoubtedly explains why it does not exist in a single, unchanging formulary. *Angilbert's Ritual Order* is a

---

25 LONDON, Brit. Mus., Royal MS 2 A XX, f. 26; first half of the 8th c. This litany has been edited by Warren (1895), vol. 2, 89–90; and by E. Bishop in his Commentary on the *Book of Cerne*, ed. Kuypers (1902), 211–212.

26 *The Stowe Missal*, ed. Warner, p. 3. To this documentation furnished by Bishop, Badcock adds the manuscript SAINT-GALL, Stiftsbibl. 1359, f. 426–27; end of the 8th or beginning of the 9th century; it deals with a fragment of Irish manuscript edited by Warren (1881), 129–181.

27 E. Bishop (1918), 142–43; Knopp (1970), 203.

28 PARIS, B.N. lat. 12048, f. 173v ff. (Clavis 1905c — Bourque 22 — Gamber 855). While waiting for the edition promised by Dom Dumas, we can read the litany in Martene (1788), 66–67.

29 ed. Andrieu, vol. 3, 249.

document that describes for us the variety of litanies at the abbey of Saint-Riquier around the year 800;[30] but unfortunately it does not provide us with any texts. We learn that in the course of the Easter Mass, first the *letania septenaria* is sung, then the *quinaria*, and finally the *ternaria*. We cannot know exactly what this is about, since in later manuscripts these headings introduce very diverse formularies. However, some light is shed on the mystery by the 9th century Psalter of Corbie,[31] where, after the *Letania maior*, come the litanies of the Easter Vigil, which bear these same headings! Here they are:

– *prima septima*:	7 names of saints, preceded by *Kyrie eleison* and *Christe, audi nos*; followed by *Omnes sancti, orate pro nobis*.
– *secunda quina*:	5 names of saints, ending in the same manner as above;
– *tertia terna*:	3 names of saints *Omnes sancti, orate pro nobis,* *Propitius esto, parce nobis Domine.*

After a lacuna, *Angilbert's Ritual Order* describes the Rogation Days, in the course of which the *schola* sing on the three days a *letania generalis*, the *Laudes* ('Christus vincit'), then 'letanias … primo Gallicam, secondo Italicam, novissime vero Romanam'. Here too, we would love to read the formulary immediately under these headings! We must search further. Fortunately, a famous manuscript from the Bibliothèque Nationale has preserved a Psalter originating in that same abbey of Saint-Riquier,[32] dating to the exact same period (800). After the psalms and biblical canticles, we read there *Laudes* (f. 163–64), then:

letania ⟨romana⟩,[33] f. 164v–165;
letania gallica, f. 165v-r;
letania italica, f. 166r-v.

---

30 ROME, Bibl. Vat. Reg. lat. 235, f. 77v–82r; folios 74–84 relate to Saint-Riquier, dating (at least until f. 82r) from the 11th c. and have nothing to do with the beginning of the manuscript, which comprises the works of Guibert de Nogent and dates from the 12th century. Both the text and bibliography can be found in E. Bishop (1918), *Angilbert's Ritual Order…*, 321–29.

31 ZURICH, Zentralbibl. Car. C. 161, Corbie Psalter, 9th c., f. 180 ff.; ed. Coens (1963), 314–18.

32 PARIS, B.N. lat. 13159, Psalter of Saint-Riquier, year 800. Among the abundant bibliography concerning this manuscript, we note Leroquais (1941), vol. 2, 112–15, and Huglo (1952), 'Un tonaire du gradual de la fin du VIIIe s.', 176–86 and 224–33.

33 In fact, the manuscript reads *letania gallica*; the first two litanies actually receive the same heading. The litanies of Lobbes (BRUSSELS, Bibl. Roy. 7524–55 (3558), end of the 10th c., f. 79v ff.; ed. Coens (1963), 251 ff.) help us to resolve the difficulty, because they include three formularies: *letaniae*, f. 79v; *letania gallica*, f. 83v; and *letania italica*, f. 84r. The second begins in the same way as that of the Saint-Riquier Psalter, 'Pater de caelis Deus, miserere nobis'. We thus think that the copyist of this Psalter has made an error in the heading of the first litany; in his model, the word *letania* was probably not qualified by an adjective; or maybe it was, with the adjective *romana*. In this case we would recognise the three pieces indicated by Abbot Angilbert's Order.

The Three Traditions

1. Letania Romana

Angilbert mentions it without giving its contents. We have found it in only two other manuscripts:

- the Psalter of Saint-Riquier, where the copyist made an error in the heading of this litany,
- the Sacramentary of Senlis.[34]

This litany begins with *Kyrie eleison, Christe eleison,* ('Christe audi nos' *add* Senlis); then it moves directly to *Sancta Maria…;* there is no Trinitarian invocation. It is addressed to Christ. The Saint-Riquier Psalter moreover, adds the invocation *Filius Dei, te rogamus audi nos* before the final *Agnus Dei.* The *Kyrie eleison* completes the piece.

We point out that the current short Litany preserved in the Roman Ritual for the *Commendatio animae* has the same incipit.

2. Letania Gallica[35]

It begins with *Pater de caelis,* followed by invocations to the Son and the Holy Spirit and three Trinitarian invocations; these correspond perfectly with the Gallican type.

The ending is quite different to the preceding litany. The petitions end with various responses, which we find somewhat reminiscent of the ancient litanies. For example, 'Aeris temperiem bonam, concede nobis domine', is similar to *Irl*[2] III, manuscript *F.*

34 PARIS, Bibl. Sainte-Geneviève lat. BB 20, between 877 and 882, f. 23v ff.; ed. Delisle (1886), 363–66.

35 The *letania gallica* features in numerous manuscripts; principal and oldest among these, we cite:

PARIS, B.N. lat. 13159, f. 165r-v, Saint-Riquier Psalter, 800;

MONTPELLIER, Bibl. Fac. Médicine MS 409, f. 344v (without heading), in the appendices of the Psalter of Mondsee, *c.* 800; ed. Unterkircher (1974), 512; photograph table XI. Also ed. Coens (1963), 288;

BRUSSELS, Bibl. Roy. 7524–55 (3558), f. 83v, Litanies de Lobbes, 10th c., ed. Coens (1963), 256;

The manuscripts of OR 50, ed. Andrieu, vol. 5, 334–35 (without heading), Mayence, *c.* 950;

VIENNA, Nationalbibl. lat. 1888, f. 110r–111r, Rituel de Mayence, end of 10th c.; ed. Gerbert (1779), vol. 2, Saint-Blaise, 90 (= PL 138, 1086);

Knopp (1970), 215, also points out the manuscript BERLIN, theol. lat. F. 452 (9th c.), of Corvey.

3. *Letania Italica*

This is better known since the study dedicated to it by B. Opfermann.[36] He edited twelve texts: we ourselves have discovered still others. All the manuscripts that we have just cited contain this litany, apart from the second. It normally begins with *Exaudi Deus (Christe-Deus) R. Voces nostras*; often an *Agnus Dei* is added; the invocations to the saints follow. It ends with acclamations similar to those of *Laudes*. This has disappeared completely from current use.

In short, the Litanies of the Saints are situated in line with the litanic prayers that emerged in the 5th century. Thanks to the stroke of inspiration that thought to invoke the saints, the theme of the old litanies developed into a new liturgical form. It is always the same need for intercession that is expressed, and it is under this heading that we have presented these elements.

The litanies that we use today derive principally from the *letania romana*, whose structure they borrow. Their beginning, however, has been influenced by the *letaniea gallica*, from which comes the *Pater de caelis* and the Trinitarian invocations.[37]

D. The 'Laudes Regiae'

We noted, at the end of the *letania italica*, the presence of acclamations akin to those of the *Laudes* (*Christus vincit* …). These have absolutely nothing in common with the *oratio fidelium*. They consist of praise addressed to great personages (pope, emperor, officers …) and an invocation of the saints on their behalf, all the while being punctuated by several repeats of the chant, 'Christus vincit, Christus regnat, Christus imperat'. Their history seems to be close to that of the Litanies of the Saints and several of the manuscripts that we have just cited contain them. They have been the subject of a remarkable and very detailed study by E. Kantorowicz.[38] They are sometimes known as *Laudes regiae*, sometimes as *Laudes regales*, or yet *Laudes* carols, *regale carmen, laudes imperatoriae, triumphus.* Their Frankish origin seems beyond doubt.

---

36 Opfermann (1958), 306–19.

37 The recent revision of the Litanies of the Saints, made on the occasion of the new Liturgical Calendar, has eliminated this Gallican contribution, or rather considered it to be a doublet with *Kyrie, Christe, Kyrie*. A choice had to be made between the Roman and Gallican formulas. Cf. EL 83 (1969), 224 and the commentary by Jounel, 232.

38 Kantorowicz (1946), Cf. also Opfermann (1953).

Conclusion

The ancient litanies, or more precisely the phrases that they used, survived a surprisingly long time, despite being subjected to all sorts of vicissitudes and transformations. It is not rare, when consulting medieval liturgical sources, to come across a phrase that proves this. A single example: in manuscript 123 of the Angelica Library (which contains the Milanese *DG*), we find at f. 175ᵛ, under the heading *Pro quacumque tribulatione*, phrases very similar to the traditional prayers, such as: 'deprecamur te ut pacem aeris temperies bona [*sic*] celique serenitatem et fructus terrae largiaris nobis'.

There is still a good deal of research to do if one day we want to be able to follow step by step the evolution undergone by the formularies of the ancient litanies. We have somewhat cleared the ground in the case of the oldest sources. Fr Molin has published a number of texts of 'prayers of the prone' from the low Middle Ages[39] but between the two remains a great deal of uncultivated land! His study is likely to turn up some surprises, like the one we had when purely by chance we found a 10th century manuscript of the *oratio communis* comprising fifteen invitatories making use willy-nilly of all the materials we have mentioned.[40] But here we are venturing into another domain.

---

39 Molin (1967), 313–468.

40 SALISBURY, Cath. Library 180, f. 172ʳ–174, at the end of a 10th c. Psalter, following the Litany of the Saints; See *The Leofric Collectar*, ed. Dewick-Frere (1921), 631–33.

The *Leofric Missal*, ed. Warren (1883), 8, contains a similar formulary, but much shorter; it has been edited by Molin, (1967), 330.

We could also cite two formulations of the *Hanc igitur* cited by Ebner (1896), 415 and 417. The first comes from a sacramentary from Brescia, dating from the second half of the 9th century; at the end of the Canon, we read, 'Hanc Domnus Paulinus in canone addidit. Hanc igitur oblationem servitutis nostrae sed et cunctae familiae taue, quesumus Domine, ut placatus accipias, quam tibi offerimus

pro pace et unitate sanctae ecclesiae,
pro pace et caritate et unitate omnium christianorum,
pro fide catholica, ut eam inviolatam in meo pectore peccatori et in omnium fidelium tuorum iubeas conservare,
pro sancta tua scriptura, ut eam nobis per inluminationem sancti Spiritus et eius dona gratiae facias recte intelligere vel docere,
pro sacerdotibus tuis et omni grado ecclesiae,
pro regibus et ducibus et omnibus, qui in sublim[it]ate sunt constituti,
pro pauperibus, orfanis, viduis, captivis, penitentibus, it[in]erantibus, languidis, defunctis, qui de hac luce in recta fide et in tuo nomine confidentes migraverunt et pro omni populo catholico,
pro dissidentibus et discordantibus, ut ad caritatem et concordiam omnes revocentur [...]'.

This text is also cited by Cabrol, art. 'Aquilée (liturgie)', in DACL 1/2, 2690. The phrase 'in sublimitate' is found only in Irl^1 VI and in a variant of M^1 IV (cf. p. 152.) 'Dux' features only in manuscripts from Northern Italy. The list of the needy does not resemble any found in the known litanies.

The second formulary comes from a sacramentary from ROUEN, Cod. A 566, 10th c., whose text Ebner takes from Delisle (1886), 295: 'Hanc igitur oblationem servitutis nostrae, sed et cunctae familiae tuae, quaesumus Domine, placatus accipias, quam tibi devoto offerimus corde

pro pace et caritate et unitate s. Dei ecclesiae,
pro fide catholica, ut eam inviolatam in meo pectori peccatore et in omnium
fidelium tuorum iubeas conservari,
pro sacerdotibus Restoldo, Albuino, Tedo', Val. et omnium fidelium tuorum
et omni gradu ecclesiae,
pro regibus et ducibus et omnibus, qui in sublimitate sunt constituti,
pro familiaribus et consanguineis et omnibus nobis commendatis,
pro omnibus viventibus ac defunctis famulis et famulabus tuis, qui mihi
propter nomen tuum bona fecerunt et mihi in tuo nomine confessi
fuerunt; propitius sis illis Deus,
pro pauperibus, orfanis, viduis, captivis, it[in]erantibus, languidis, defunctis
(*11 names*) qui de hac luce in recta fide et in tuo nomine confitentes
migraverunt, etc.'

Clearly, these two texts are related.

Section Six

Universal Prayer Kyrie Eleison and Oratio super sindonem

Having methodically analysed the texts, we are now in a position to draw out the consequences for the history of the Mass. The information gained so far has indeed clarified it in a somewhat new way, especially with regard to the permanence of the *oratio fidelium* after the end of the 5th century and the appearance of the *Kyrie eleison*. Let us look first at the current position with regard to this latter element.

1. The State of the Question

It is Edmund Bishop who wrote the article that serves as a foundation for anyone who wishes to speak about the *Kyrie eleison*.[1] We have already referred to it several times. Following on from the work of Bishop, the eminent F. J. Dölger studied the use of this invocation in ancient culture.[2] The prevailing opinion of liturgists, before the work of Dom Capelle, was that the *Kyrie eleison* at the beginning of the Roman Mass was the vestige of an unknown litany, situated at this point of the Mass in imitation of Greek usage.[3] According to L. Eisenhofer, this initial litany was probably in use in the Roman Mass from the 4th century. Originally, the invocation *Kyrie eleison* would not have been part of it, but it would have entered some time in the 5th century, not as a response to petitions, but as an independent element. According to these authors, this litany fell into disuse for different reasons, notably the tendency to shorten the celebration, or because of competition from the Introit, or because of a stational litany.

The Contribution of Dom B. Capelle

It was in 1934 that Dom Capelle edited the *Deprecatio Gelasii* (*DG*). Unfortunately, in our opinion, he attributes the response *Kyrie eleison* to it on the basis of an altered manuscript.[4] According to him, 'the *Deprecatio* would be a text of the Roman *Kyrie eleison*'.(p. 129). Immediately Professor Klauser[5] replied that it

1 E. Bishop (1918), 'Kyrie eleison', 116–36.
2 Dölger (1920), 50–80.
3 Duchesne (1925), 174; E. Bishop (1918), 'Kyrie eleison', 124; Eisenhofer (1933), vol. 2, 87–88.
4 Capelle (1934). On the link between the *Kyrie* and the *DG*, cf. supra, Section Three, 1.
5 Klauser (1934), in JLW vol. 14, 443–44.

was unthinkable that the Roman Mass would ever have included, side by side, two such prolix and similar prayers of intercession (i.e. the *DG* and the *OS*). This criticism led the liturgist from Louvain to be more specific about the liturgical function of the *DG*.[6]

Struck by the number of sources indicating the presence of the *oratio fidelium* until Pope Felix III (483–492), and by the silence after this, the Abbot of Mont César came to believe that in order to introduce his *Deprecatio*, Gelasius suppressed the Roman *oratio fidelium* (identified at the time only with the *OS*). The pope introduced the *DG* instead and placed it with our current *Kyrie* before the readings. During the 6th century, then, the Mass would have included the *DG* with the response *Kyrie eleison* before the readings and would no longer have had the Universal Prayer after the Gospel. A century later, St Gregory removed from the *Kyrie eleison* of the daily Masses the 'alia quae dici solent', the *alia* that Capelle identifies with the invitatories of the *DG*. What remains is the sole response, *Kyrie eleison*, as we have today! But does this explanation truly square with reality? Truth to tell, the wise Benedictine had no proof of transference of the prayer of intercession from its ancient place (after the Gospel) to its subsequent place at the beginning of the celebration; he simply made reference to Greek usages.

Dom Capelle went on to complete this hypothesis. In a subsequent contribution,[7] he considers that Gelasius has remedied the deep trouble caused by the removal of the *oratio fidelium* and in its place introduced the *oratio super sindonem* that can be found for the greater part in the Sacramentary of Verona and most of the formularies of the Gelasian [sacramentary]. A meagre compensation that Gregory will withdraw a century later.

Therefore we now take up the three elements contained in the heading of this sixth section and consider how they are related.

The Work of A. Chavasse[8]

In the opinion of Abbot Chavasse, this thesis assumes more than it has the right to do, namely the transfer of the Prayer of Intercession from after the Gospel to the beginning of Mass. Taking advantage of work on the *oratio super sindonem* in the Milanese liturgy,[9] the professor from Strasbourg considers that this prayer would not have originally been an isolated piece, destined, on its own, to replace the *oratio fidelium*, but could well have been the priestly conclusion of the litany replacing the *OS*. The Litany and the *oratio super sindonem* would have formed the two parts of a whole, situated after the Gospel.

In the papal liturgy, however, the 'deprecatio' would have been displaced and introduced at the beginning of the Mass, taking place during the processional

6 Capelle (1939), 22–34; Tr. Lit., vol. 2, 135–45.
7 B.Capelle (1951), 129–144; Tr. Lit. vol. 2, 146–60.
8 Chavasse (1960), 313–23.
9 Borella (1958), 173–76.

litany that the OR describes for us on certain days, before the Introit. In this new place, the concluding prayer would have quickly disappeared, given its proximity to the Collect. In the presbyteral liturgy, however, such a transfer would not have been possible, since the place would have customarily been occupied by an entry litany. He thus explained that, in contrast to the Gregorian liturgy, the Gelasian liturgy would have generally retained the *oratio super sindonem*, except in the case of the Gregorian type of formularies that it later incorporated.

As for the current *Kyrie*, it is the remains of the 'deprecatio' of the papal liturgy; St Gregory abridged it to such an extent that it remains today a single invocation.

What are we to think of this? Mons Chavasse's argument is subtle, but rests on very precarious foundations. For example, he has deduced the existence of a customary entry litany in the Gelasian liturgy from its presence in this place during the Easter Vigil, while the rubric for Good Friday prescribes that the entry take place in silence, 'giving this prescription an insistence that would suggest that the exception was unique' (p. 319). Such arguments call for prudence. Moreover, the author links the *Kyrie* to the 'deprecatio', just as Capelle does, a link for which we would like to see some proof.

In short, this story is very complicated. The contribution of these last two authors is subject to a warning for caution. And so we are forced to take this inquiry along new paths. Let us look at the texts.

2. Study of the Texts

What elements can we be certain of?

a). The Triple Kyrie Eleison of M¹

If the triple *Kyrie eleison* that concludes *M¹* was part of this litany from the beginning, and if the dating that we have proposed is correct, then this triple invocation dates from the second half of the 5th century and is the oldest Western witness to the *Kyrie*. But how does it present itself to us? Not as the response to the litany, which we noted during analysis, but as an independent supplication. We could say that the redactor wanted to conclude his prayer with a certain stress.

This seemingly benign fact will, indeed, show itself to be important. In any case it calls into question those liturgists who 'evidently' see in the *Kyrie eleison* a response to the litany. Let us remember that we are not certain that *M¹* originated in Rome.

b). Canon 3 of the Council of Vaison (529)

This regional Council, convoked under the presidency of Caesarius of Arles, introduced the *Kyrie eleison* into the Churches of Provence. Here is the complete text of c. 3:

> 'Et quia tam in sede apostolica, quam etiam per totas Orientales adque Italiae provincias dulces et nimium salubres consuetudo est intromissa, ut Quirielieson frequentius cum grandi affectu et conpunctione dicatur, placuit etiam nobis, ut in omnibus ecclesiis nostris ista tam sancta consuetudo et ad matutinos et ad missas et ad vesperam Deo propitio intromittatur. Et in omnibus missis seu in matutinus seu in quadragensimalibus seu in illis, quae pro defunctorum commemorationibus fiunt, semper: "Sanctus, Sanctus, Sanctus" eo ordine, quomodo ad missas publicas dicitur, dici debeat, quia tam sancta, tam dulces et desideralilis vox, etiam si die noctuque possit dici, fastidium non poterit generare'.[10]

What did the Fathers of the Council have in mind in speaking of the *Kyrie eleison* in this way?

- It was in use at the Holy See just as much as it was in the East and in Italy (which many authors equate with Milan). This does not tell us anything very much; it could describe a litany with a *Kyrie eleison* response such as was already known in the East, or as a simple repetition of the invocation, as at the end of M^1.
- However, this custom is qualified by *intromissa*. Provided that we can rely on this dating, we are pushed towards a fairly recent usage, introduced not too long beforehand. But, in the East, litanies had been in used for at least a century and a half.
- this *consueto* is called *dulcis*, which seems a very strange word with which to qualify the response to a litany! This adjective inclines us towards something delightful or harmonious; we have already noted that in classical language, it could qualify a sound, a discourse or a song.[11]
- *frequentius* is imprecise. Does this term mean that the repetitions of the *Kyrie eleison* were numerous, or that they were used several times on the same day, during different Offices?

  Nevertheless, this word is, perhaps, the 'point' of this canon. For if 'to say *Kyrie frequentius*' means to use it as a response, then it would be hard to say that this usage, at least in the East, has just been introduced! But perhaps what is new, in the East as well as in Rome and Italy, is to repeat it, for its own sake, as a chant of supplication.

---

10 Council of Vaison, c. 3, ed. de Clercq (CC 148A), 79; Mansi 8, 727.

11 Thesaurus, vol. 5, 1, 2191–2, *dulcis* II, b, β.

- *cum grandi affectu et conpunctione*: is it conceivable that this somewhat romantic description is being applied to a litany with the response *Kyrie eleison*? Would it not be better to parallel this with a piece of chant with the same name, such as we find at the end of M^1? Bishop has already pointed out that the expression seemed to indicate that the *Kyrie eleison* was sung by the assembly of the faithful (p. 121).
- This innovation is introduced at Lauds, at Mass and at Vespers, but there is no precise indication of where it is placed.
- the second part of the canon deals with the widespread use of the Trisagion ('Aius') at all Masses — a further reason to believe that this canon decrees the introduction of two pieces of chant into the Provençale Mass.
- the verb *dicere* cannot be regarded as an objection to this hypothesis; it is used in reference even to public Masses where the 'Sanctus' was certainly sung.

In short, this canon makes more sense if, rather than seeing behind the expression *Kyrie eleison* a litany similar to the *DG* with the response *Kyrie eleison*, we see simply a piece of chant that seems to have been much appreciated in this period.

c). The Rule of St Benedict

St Benedict, whose rule dates from around 529, prescribed that Lauds on Sundays (ch. 12, 4) and weekdays (ch. 13, 11) as well as Vespers (ch. 17, 8) should conclude with a *litania*. Matins finished with a *supplicatio litaniae, id est quirie eleison* (ch. 9, 10), while Prime (ch. 17, 4), the Little Hours (ch. 17, 5) and Compline (ch. 17, 10) end with '*quirie eleison*'.[12]

Authors have widely discussed whether these three expressions were synonymous or if, given the precision of St Benedict, must be seen as different realities. What can we make of this?

Prime, the Little Hours and Compline all conclude with *Kyrie eleison*. We do not think that we must understand here a litany with the response, *Kyrie eleison*, but rather an independent piece of chant, similar to that which precedes the Our Father in the Benedictine Office tradition. This is corroborated by the rubric at Matins, which concludes with 'the supplication contained in the litany', that is, the *Kyrie eleison*. In other words, we believe that the expression *supplicatio litaniae* is not synonymous with *litania*, but rather with *Kyrie eleison*. It describes only a part of the litany, namely, this earnest supplication *Kyrie eleison* such as is found, for example, at the end of M^1. As for Lauds and Vespers, they conclude with a *litania*, which clearly refers to a complete litany.[13]

---

12 *Regula monasteriorum*, ed. de Vogüe, (SC 182), 512–29.

13 This is also the explanation given by de Vogüe, in his masterful commentary, *La Règle de saint Benoît*, vol. 2, (SC 182), 513, note 10 (concerning ch. 9, 10): 'The Litany is reduced to the "supplication", that is to say, to the response *Kyrie eleison* (cf. 17, 4): Roman usage' (with reference to Letter 9 of Gregory the Great); cf. also vol. 5 of de Vogüe's commentary, (SC 185), 451.

The expressions *supplicatio litaniae, id est Kyrie eleison* and *Kyrie eleison* do not describe a simple response to the petitions, but a particular supplication, probably sung. This interpretation is demanded by the existence of the triple *Kyrie eleison* ending of M^1 and by the subsequent Benedictine tradition. We do not think that these two varying points of reference should baffle us.

Certainly, it is not a question of the Mass but of the Office, but we cannot ignore any information when the documentation is so scarce. If the *Kyrie eleison* is indeed, as we suspect, a piece of chant that appeared (in the West) towards the end of the 5th century as a means of sincere appeal to the divine mercy, then we suppose that this 'mode' has entered not only the Eucharist but also the Office.

d). The Rule of Aurelian of Arles

The end of the *Regula ad monachos* composed by the archbishop of Arles consists of an *Ordo psallendi* that begins as follows:

'…ad tertiam ter *Kyrie eleison*, psalmi duodecim: …

Sic in omni opera Dei tertia vice *Kyrie eleison* dicite,

antequam incipiatis,

et psalmis perdictis,

et capitello perdicto'.[14]

This strongly confirms our hypothesis: the *Kyrie eleison* is said (sung) three times in a row, without any mention of a litany, and the expression certainly does not indicate an entire litany, as could have applied in the case of St Benedict. Just imagine an entire litany being repeated three times within the course of a single sung prayer! And this is made even clearer when we consider that the *Kyrie eleison* is repeated twelve times at Lauds on weekdays![15] We are at the beginning of the *Kyries*!

Are we familiar with the 'complete Litany' which ended Lauds and Vespers? Must we see in this a formulary of the type of litany that we analysed above, which would not have served as an *oratio fidelium* strictly speaking at the Mass, but would have exercised a similar function in the Office? De Vogüe does not ask this question. Lacking any documentation, the best we can conclude is that this litany would have had the liturgical form of those we have studied; this style of intercession would have passed from the Mass into the Office.

Perhaps this litany was subsequently reduced to the 'supplication' *Kyrie eleison*, following the example of what was done at the other Hours and which has continued on to current usage.

14 Aurelian of Arles, *Regula ad monachos*, (PL 68), 393 (Clavis 1844).

15 Aurelian of Arles, *Regula ad monachos*, (PL 68), 395: 'capitellum et *Kyrie eleison* duodecim vicibus'.

e). Evidence from St Gregory

The famous passage from the letter of Pope Gregory to John of Syracuse in 598 is well known. In order to situate it better, we will provide the context as well:

> 'Veniens quidam de Sicilia mihi dixit quod aliqui amici ejus, vel Graeci vel Latini, nescio, quasi sub zelo sanctae Romanae Ecclesiae, de meis dispositionibus murmurarent, dicentes: Quomodo Ecclesiam Constantinopolitanum disponit comprimere, qui ejus consuetudinem per omnia sequitur? Cui cum dicerem: Quas consuetudines ejus sequimir? respondit: Quia ... Kyrie eleison dici ...
>
> I. Kyrieleison autem nos neque diximus neque dicimus sicut a Graceis dicitur, quia in Graecis omnes simul dicunt, apud nos autem a clericis dicitur, a populo respondetur
>
> II. et totidem vicibus (vocibus) etiam Christe eleison dicitur, quod apud Graecos nullo modo dicitur.
>
> III. In cotidianis autem missis alia quae dici solent tacemus, tantum modo kyrieleison et Christe eleison dicimus, ut in his deprecationis vocibus paulo diutius occupemur'.[16]

The context could not be clearer. Gregory responds point by point to the accusation that he is imitating Greek usage. We note, however, that he is talking about the Mass, not the Office.

Customarily, it has been the understanding that the pope had a litany in mind. Since Capelle, there has been little hesitation in going further and naming the *DG*. This interpretation is based on III, where Gregory distinguishes the *Kyrie eleison* and the *alia quae dici solent*. This latter expression is referring to the invitatories of the *DG*; in suppressing them from daily Mass, Gregory retains only the response, *Kyrie eleison*.

But this interpretation does not harmonise with I. If the first word, *Kyrie eleison*, is referring to a litany, then the rest of the sentence doesn't make sense. It is not possible to see how among the Greeks a litany would be able to be said (sung) by all the faithful together. Similarly, in II, whether we understand the text to be *vocibus* (emphasis on the number of people, following on from I) or *vicibus* (emphasis on the repetition),[17] the text makes more sense if we are talking about an independent chant. Otherwise, it would probably mean alternation between the responses *Kyrie eleison* and *Christe eleison* to the invitatories of the litany which, in pastoral terms, is not very practical. Moreover, the expression *Christe eleison*, set in parallel with the phrase *Kyrie eleison* at the beginning of I, might

16 Gregory the Great, *Epistola* 9, 26, ed. Hartmann, MGH, 1988; or PL 77, 956. On the interpretation of this passage, the following can be consulted: Duchesne (1925), 174–75; E. Bishop (1918), *Kyrie*, 123–24; Callewaert (1942), 35–40.

17 On this variant, cf. Callewaert (1942), 37.

well suggest that this is not a technical term to designate the litany, as is generally supposed.

But if the pope had in mind a piece where *Kyrie eleison* and *Christe eleison* were chanted alternately, how can III be understood? What meaning is to be given to 'alia quae dici solent'? That is the nub of the question!

We believe that up to now liturgists have been a little premature in *a priori* assimilating the *Kyrie eleison* to a litany, or possibly to a response to it. But in M^1 we have found a triple *Kyrie eleison* that does not rank among either of these two models, and these early examples make good sense, if not more sense, when we suppose that in the West the *Kyrie eleison* was introduced as an independent piece of chant.[18]

Soon after, this chant was able to be linked to other formularies, as we see in M^1 and M^2, where it concludes the litany. And in fact, we find it:

- In the West
  - at the beginning and the end of the litanies of the saints, since the earliest manuscripts,
  - at the end of the *Laudes regiae*;
- In the East, in the Greek liturgy of St James, for example at the end of the litany before the gospel.[19]

Certainly, the facts that we have mentioned here in relation to the West, occur in a later period, but they direct us towards the same reality.

Also, we do not think that St Gregory gave the expression *Kyrie eleison* the same meaning throughout his response to John of Syracuse. In I and II he had in mind a *Kyrie eleison* sung on its own, alternating with *Christe eleison*; it was a matter of invocations to the divine mercy and not of a response.

But in III, the pope distinguishes between the solemnities where this chant would begin or conclude a litany of introduction to the Mass, and the daily Masses, where it stood alone, without litany, as subsequently was the case in the Roman Mass.[20] We would probably not be far from the truth in assuming that this last ordinance came from Gregory himself. This was the opinion of Bishop. An unwary reader, he wrote, would assume that Gregory himself introduced the *Kyrie eleison* into the Roman Mass.[21]

Thus we are led to a very similar position to that of Capelle. But while he considers that the current *Kyrie* had its roots in the response of the *DG* transferred to the beginning of Mass where it lost the invitatories ('alia quae dici solent tacemus'), we think that the *Kyrie* has been retained in the form in which it was

18 This insight is due to Fr. Botte, who has allowed us to report it, for which we are most grateful. The only way to test the strength of this intuition is by providing scientific justification.

19 Br 38, 1, 2–3; for more details concerning the East, cf. Ceriani (1913), 426.

20 This is also the understanding that we find in de Vogüe who writes, 'Gregory the Great here calls *deprecatio* what St Benedict called *supplicatio*'. (SC 185), 451, note 41.

21 E. Bishop (1918), *Kyrie*, 123.

introduced into the West, namely as a supplicatory chant, little altered by the addition of *Christe eleison*, perhaps by St Gregory himself.

3. The Introduction of the Kyrie into the West

Let us summarise our learnings and organise them into a table showing the progressive introduction of the *Kyrie*.

Following its introduction in the West at the end of the 5th or beginning of the 6th century, the *Kyrie* is an independent piece of chant. We understand that the *Kyrie* does not constitute an organic part of a wider whole, as the response to a litany, for example. It is introduced into Western liturgies (at least Roman, Milanese and Provençale) as a chant to invoke the divine mercy in the strongest possible way. Nevertheless, having taken root, it did not remain isolated but found itself joined to other more stable formulas, such as litanies.

A belief that the *Kyrie* did not belong to the litany from its first appearance, but arose from an independent source, is based on the following arguments:

a We know of several litanies that do not include the *Kyrie*;
b The Council of Vaison did not appear to assume that the *Kyrie* was joined to a litany;
c We quickly see it leading an independent existence: in the Rule of St Benedict, and certainly in that of Aurelian of Arles;
d Numbers I and II of the text of St Gregory are only comprehensible if referring to an isolated chant.[22]

On the other hand, the *Kyrie* was also used in combination with the litany; the invocative nature of these two elements predisposed their coming together. In *M*[1], the *Kyrie* concludes the litany. Saint Benedict, even if he included a stand-alone *Kyrie* for the Little Hours, did not ignore its connection with the litany since he spoke of *supplicatio litaniae, id est Kyrie eleison* in such a way that we can only interpret this expression to mean that the two elements are joined together. In the letter of St Gregory, these 'other things that one is accustomed to say' in combination with the *Kyrie* can only be a litany. Finally, a rubric in the ritual for Ordination in the Old Gelasian sacramentary (regardless of the metamorphoses this *Ordo* of election may have undergone)[23] prescribes that after the admonition of the pope, 'mox incipiunt omnes *Kyrie eleison* cum laetania'. It seems to us that this passage clarifies what Gregory said; effectively that at daily Mass only the single invocation *Kyrie* was sung, but on more solemn occasions — as for example Ordinations — the *Kyrie* was reunited to the litany, as no. III of Gregory's text

---

22 In assuming that the *Kyrie* originally consisted of simple repetition of this invocation, we align ourselves with the judgement of earlier liturgists like Alfonso (1925), 89–91 and Gastoue (1936), 109–11.

23 Chavasse (1958), 22–27. This *Ordo* was added in Gaul.

presumed. The redactor of the Gelasian puts it nicely: *Kyrie eleison cum laetania*. And in this we see the two ways in which the *Kyrie* was used.

In the course of history, these two uses have been preserved. The stand-alone *Kyrie* is sung at Mass, and in the Benedictine Office before the Our Father. But it also introduces or concludes a good number of litanies.

We must point out a third use, for this chant also came to serve as a response to litanies, as in the East. We find it being used this way in M^2 and FG^2. Thus this Eastern response, that the Latins had apparently translated as *Domine miserere*, has, via this convoluted route, ended up being included in Greek in the Western litanies themselves.[24]

We have witnessed the appearance of the *Kyrie* in the West, but several questions still remain unanswered: why is it located at the beginning of the Mass? What relationship does it have to the Universal Prayer and when was this suppressed? Let us look at this systematically.

4. The Suppression of the Universal Prayer

According to the works of Capelle and Chavasse, you would think that the *OS*, regarded as the customary formulary of the Universal Prayer in the Roman Church, fell into disuse after Pope Felix III (483–492), and that his successor, Gelasius replaced them with the *DG* — introduced at the beginning of the Mass by Gelasius himself, according to Capelle, a little after his pontificate, according to Chavasse.

This position needs to be reviewed, since we believe we have found, beyond the *OS*, other formularies for the Universal Prayer used in Rome. Indeed, the *DG* is part of a whole wave in which Latin texts were adapted for the *oratio fidelium*. Thus we cannot say that the *OS* disappeared simply because we can no longer find traces of it.

However, regardless of whether any of our sacramentaries retained a trace of the Universal Prayer in its traditional place or not, it was nevertheless suppressed.[25] When? By whom? For what reasons? We know nothing of this. So let us risk some attempts at answering this.

---

24 Jungmann (1960), 239–52, establishes a parallel (p. 248) between the *Kyrie eleison* and kneeling; both have the same penitential significance.

25 Certainly, we could imagine that the Universal Prayer existed without any trace being left in the sacramentaries. If its formulary was in the style of a litany, it could have fallen to the deacon, in which case the book of the celebrant would not have mentioned it since the priest had no role. In this sense, the presence of the *OS* in the Roman and Gallican sacramentaries is no argument, since the *orationes solemnes* included a role for the celebrant.

Nevertheless, we do not believe that such important collections as the Roman sacramentaries would not contain any allusion to the *oratio fidelium* if it constituted a customary ritual in the Mass of their epoch. We note that the detailed description of OR 1 (first part of the 8th century) does not breathe a word about it.

The date of its suppression must be during the 6th century. Indeed, the collection of *libelli missarum* that goes under the title of Sacramentary of Verona and which scholars agree reflects usage from the middle or end of the 6th century, includes no trace of the *oratio fidelium*. Therefore it had to have been suppressed prior to Saint Gregory, who is often accused of committing this liturgical crime. Moreover, its removal cannot be located too early in the 6th century; the *Deprecatio* of Gelasius (492–496) would have enjoyed at least a few years of use after its introduction.

Perhaps it is to Pope Virgilius (537–555) that the responsibility for this reform must be imputed. Placing it in the middle of the 6th century would explain why the sacramentaries were no longer familiar with the Universal Prayer and had not preserved the text of the *DG*.

What were the reasons for its suppression?

A number of authors, including Willis and Klauser,[26] propose the length of the formulary as the reason (here we understand they are referring to the *OS*). Others, such as Denis-Boulet, Hanon de Louvet and Kennedy,[27] insist that it was the disappearance of the catechumenate that led to the suppression of the Universal Prayer: since by that time everyone participated in the whole Mass it was no longer necessary to have a prayer reserved for 'the faithful' alone. Finally, these last authors, along with Callewaert, Jungmann and Bouman[28] believe that the Roman Mass renounced the *oratio fidelium* because its equivalent had been introduced into the Canon itself. This relationship between the Universal Prayer and the anaphoric intercessions, to which we will return, merits further study.

We think that among the causes for the suppression of the Universal Prayer we must include the development of the litanies. Their character fulfilled the aspirations of popular piety, their success led to their multiplication, and more and more often a litany was prayed before Mass. All of this contributed to the *oratio fidelium*'s particularity being overshadowed, and so it fell into disuse.

5. The *Oratio super Sindonem*

Let us recall that, thanks to the heading it bears in the Milanese liturgy, this is the description given to the prayer that precedes the oblation in the Gelasian-type formularies. According to Capelle, as we have already noted, its function was to replace the Universal Prayer once that had been transferred to the beginning of the Mass; this 'ersatz' quickly disappeared.[29] According to Chavasse, on the other hand, it functioned as a conclusion to the Prayer of the Faithful. In the papal liturgy, when the Prayer of the Faithful was transferred to the beginning of

26 Willis (1964), 25; Klauser (1975), 49.

27 Denis-Boulet, in Martimort (1965), 343; Hanon de Louvet (1929), 241; Kennedy (1963), 5.

28 Callewaert (1942), 24; Jungmann (1962), vol. 1, 509; Bouman (1959), 19–20.

29 Capelle (1951), 'L'oeuvre liturgique de S. Gélase', 129–1454; Tr. Lit. vol. 2, 158–59.

the Mass, the *oratio super sindonem* went with it, then quickly fell out of favour due to its proximity to the Collect. In the Gelasian liturgy on the other hand, it maintained its traditional place with the *oratio fidelium*, transfer being impossible since this presbyteral liturgy did not begin with a litany.[30]

We have not been able to look at the issue head on, and our research has not let us see any more clearly on the matter. We shall content ourselves with some remarks regarding these two positions.

Capelle's hypothesis must be seen in the light of Chavasse's work and the distinction between the two types of liturgy that were celebrated in Rome. Further, Capelle always identifies the *oratio fidelium* with the *OS*, which we dispute. Finally, if the *Kyrie eleison* was not part of the *DG*, there is no need to consider transferring it to the beginning of the Mass.

Chavasse's hypothesis rests, as we have already said, on fragile foundations. The deductions that he makes in order to reconstruct the entrance rites for the papal and presbyteral liturgies are subtle, but must be taken into account, considering the immense erudition of this master.

It is possible that the *oratio super sindonem* had been the conclusion of a Universal Prayer litany; the small number of similarities indicated by the author may make us think about it, but more research is needed. Furthermore, we have not found any rubric that links these two pieces, nor any external trace of a relationship. The professor of Strasbourg's construction explains the absence of the *oratio super sindonem* in the Gregorian liturgy and its presence in the Gelasian. Logically the latter would have maintained the Universal Prayer that this problematic prayer concluded, so how do we explain that neither this book, nor the old 'Leonine' (*Veronense*) breathe a word of it?

And so we think that the question remains open. The content of these prayers needs to be studied, starting from the end of Chavasse's article. Only this will teach us more.

6. The Opening Litany and the Kyrie Eleison

Finally we come to the ordinance for the beginning of the Mass. Originally the liturgy began with the readings. Then the Collect was added; it is to this stage of development that the entrance rite for Good Friday bears witness. Next came a long procession — accompanied by singing — that permitted the clergy to move from the sacristy at the rear of the church towards the sanctuary. The dates of these various additions are rather fluid but can generally be put around the 5th and 6th centuries. The *Gloria in excelsis*, originally sung only on Christmas day, was extended under Pope Symmachus (498–514) to Sundays and feasts of martyrs.[31]

30 Chavasse (1960), 316–19.
31 LP, vol. 1, 263.

Later again it was reserved to the bishop. But how did the *Kyrie* come to be inserted into the entrance rite?

Capelle considers that Gelasius suppressed the *OS* and ordered the singing of the *DG* at the beginning of Mass, imitating the Greek custom, with the response to this litany, *Kyrie eleison*, being the sole survivor when Gregory suppressed the invitatories. On the other hand, Chavasse thinks that the transfer of the litany of the Universal Prayer took place in the papal liturgy, to provide a parallel to the processional litany described in the *OR* as taking place — on certain days — before the Introit. In the presbyteral liturgy this transfer was neither necessary nor possible, for there already existed the normal entrance litany.

We have rejected Dom Capelle's explanation, but until now have not come up with more satisfactory one. Is Chavasse's more convincing? We have already pointed out its weaknesses. We point out again that if the litany of the *Kyrie* was put at the beginning of the Mass to match the stational litany described for certain days in the *OR*, the *Kyrie* that remained as a 'left over' would have been located before the Introit and not after, as is the case today.

Whatever the situation, the master liturgist has, in my opinion, done us a favour by drawing our attention to the entrance processions of the Mass. It is a fact that the processions met with increasing success and, no longer content with a procession to accompany the Introit, the need was felt to come to the church in procession; the OR testify to that. The litanies that accompanied these religious corteges met with the favour of the people and would lead in the 8th century to the Litany of the Saints.

Gregory of Tours († 594), for example, tells of the penitential procession ordered by Gregory the Great in 590, following an epidemic of the plague. Seven basilicas were designated as places of gathering (*collecta*); from there, seven processions, each including a group of priests, made their way towards St Mary Major to seek divine favours. This was known as the *litania septiformis*, during which the *Kyrie eleison* was sung.[32]

Chavasse is right to distinguish between the papal and presbyteral liturgies in Rome. If light has not yet been shed on this entrance rite, perhaps it is because we too quickly wanted to harmonise elements that in fact belonged to different celebrations.

Here too a monograph would be most welcome; we need to study the question for itself. The biggest difficulty is the lack of sources. Those we do have are rare, say very little, and are difficult to date. The only information we have on this litany before Mass comes from OR XX to XXIV (all dating from the end of the 8th century) for the papal liturgy, and from two rubrics in the Gelasian sacramentary (compiled in the course of the 7th century) for the presbyteral liturgy. What of any certainty can we draw from such documentation?

---

32 Gregory of Tours, *Libri historiarum decem*, 10, 1, ed. Krusch-Levison (1951), (MGH, Script. r. merov., 1, 1), 481 (PL 71, 529B): 'Veniebant utrique chori psallentium ad ecclesiam, clamantes per plateas urbis *Kyrie eleison*'.

7. Attempt at a Solution

Let us nevertheless take a risk at presenting some hypotheses. We have seen that the Universal Prayer must have disappeared in the course of the 6th century. This is also the period when the litanies met with success. While they were no doubt born in order to serve the Universal Prayer they would soon have found another function: that of accompanying the processions. The *Kyrie,* introduced in the West towards the end of the 5th century or the beginning of the 6th as a stand-alone piece of chant, was joined to the litanies and ended up being used as a response to a number of them.

We therefore do not think that the formulary of the Universal Prayer was 'transferred', as Dom Capelle says, from its traditional place towards the beginning of the Mass, nor, as Msgr Chavasse believes, that the stational litany that took place only on certain days drew the litany of the Universal Prayer to the beginning of the Mass to be used on those days when the stational litany was missing. Rather, we believe that the litany of the Universal Prayer fell into disuse for the reasons that we have outlined, and that its formularies, fashioned into an increasingly popular form, fulfilled a new function, that of accompanying processions, especially the one that took place before the Mass.

The *Kyrie* that concluded it remains as a representative witness, first of all for the days when there was no litany (the *OR* cited above indicate that when a litany preceded the Mass, the *Kyrie* was not sung), then for every day, once the litany disappeared.

That still does not explain why the *Kyrie eleison* follows the Introit instead of preceding it (and this still remains the case), unless the Introit, accompanying the procession of the clergy from the sacristy to the choir, was concluded with the *Kyrie* as had been done for the litanies. But this hypothesis is highly unlikely, since the *Gloria Patri* is already used to bring the Introit to a close.

Conclusion

Full light has not yet been shed on the evolution of the Entrance Rite, the suppression of the Universal Prayer and the *oratio super sindonem.* After studying the ancient litanies we find that the solutions we have reached are quite close to those of the liturgists from the beginning of the century, notably Eisenhofer whom we recalled at the start of this section. Apart from the dating that he proposed, we find his view of things to be very fair. In our opinion the hypotheses of Capelle and Chavasse are not at all certain, which in no way, we add, deprives these authors of the merit of their patient explorations.

Conclusions to Part Two

After this long excursion through the ancient liturgical texts, we must draw some conclusions about the Universal Prayer and its history.

A. The Thesis

The first thing to remember is that none of the texts studied in Part Two (apart from the *OS*) is presented in the sources as a formulary for the Universal Prayer. The most important assertion of our work is to maintain that they fulfilled this function. There is no shortage of arguments to prove this thesis:

- if the *oratio fidelium* existed, which Part One of our work has shown, (with certain nuances, we must remember), we need not be surprised that these texts have not been preserved, even if the sources no longer present them to us in their original function. This last fact holds when considering the disappearance of the Universal Prayer in the 6th century;
- the content of the pieces in question corresponds exactly to that of the Universal Prayer as defined by us in the introduction to this study;
- the litanies closely resemble the *OS*, even if they are expressed in a different liturgical form. But the litanies have served as the Universal Prayer, of this we are certain.
- the absence of penitential themes indicates to us that the primary purpose of these texts could not have been the penitential processions or the Rogation Days.

However, our assertion remains a thesis, whose value will be assessed by its critics. To throw doubt on it, one could point out the lack of indications in the manuscript tradition and on the place that these litanies occupy in the sources. The presence of biblical verses in certain of them (e.g. *Irl*[1] b/) could also lead down other paths.

B. The Evolution of the Universal Prayer in the First Six Centuries

Let us summarise the history of our prayer as it appears to us at the end of this study. We will not repeat here what we wrote at the end of Part One. Let us simply remember that from the literary sources we can affirm the existence of the Prayer of the Faithful during the first five centuries, but perhaps not everywhere nor, as we repeat continually, too readily. It is difficult to pinpoint its precise origin. We cannot claim that the admonitions of 1 Tim 2:1–2 formally 'institute' it, even if subsequently many texts refer to this passage as the basis of the practice. Jewish influences are not excluded, but it is not possible to establish a direct literary relationship with a Jewish prayer such as the Eighteen Benedictions and the Universal Prayer.

In formulas that were not fixed, the faithful prayed above all for the emperor and for the peace of the world, for the current situation in the Church, for the conversion of unbelievers and the faith of believers, for all people — especially the needy — and finally for enemies.

The first Latin formulary available to us is none other than the *OS*. In its primitive form, it consisted of invitatories alone, which appeared in Rome between 250 and around 320. At that time they may have been proposed by the deacon, but there is no external evidence to inform us about this. Towards the end of the 4th century a revision of these invitatories certainly took place; orations were added and the piece was reserved to the celebrant. It is the first and the most 'solemn' of those prayers that we entitled 'lities'. Its influence will be enormous, warranted by and proportionate to its theological and literary qualities.

It is in the same period, or at the beginning of the 5th century, that a liturgical form imported from the East appeared in the West: the litany. We use the phrase 'in the West' rather loosely, for the great difficulty is to know which Churches used these texts. This prevents us from accurately describing the history of the Universal Prayer in the ancient liturgies.

In this movement of Eastern texts we can detect two phases. The first, which lasts for the best part of the first three quarters of the 5th century, consisted in translating Eastern formularies. *Irl*^{1} and *M*^{1} are examples of this. If one or (and?) the other of these two pieces was Roman — and there are some indications in this direction — then we would have to revise the usual opinion of liturgists who believe that it was Gelasius (492–496) who introduced this liturgical form to Rome.

During the second phase, which began in the final quarter of the 5th century, these first Latin texts were adapted to the new circumstances and were cast into a literary form that better corresponded to the Latin language. The jewel of this series is the *DG*, which we owe to the pen of Pope Gelasius. We also include in this group *FG*^{1}, *M*^{2}, *FG*^{2}, and *Irl*^{2}. All these pieces are linked: we constantly find in them the same themes that we will detail below. According to the thesis of Dom Capelle, Pope Gelasius is generally credited with suppressing the Universal Prayer (or at least the *OS*), but this thesis must at least be called into question. More serious, in our opinion, is the absence of any allusion to the Universal Prayer in the sacramentary of Verona or in any of the other Roman sacramentaries. Moreover, we believe that it is towards the middle of the 6th century that the *oratio fidelium* fell into disuse — in Rome at least. The reasons for this suppression are not clear. Among other things are cited the disappearance of the catechemenate, the length of the formulary (for this, read *OS*), the fact that it resulted in a doubling up of the anaphoric intercessions, and, most importantly in our eyes, the evolution of the litanies.

Indeed, these adopted an increasingly popular form and enjoyed great success. By now M^1 and M^2 had joined the triple invocation, *Kyrie eleison,* to the end of their invocations. We see also that the texts were almost overrun with biblical verses, as is very apparent in M^2 and FG^2. This development will lead, in almost homogeneous fashion, to the *preces* of the Office and the Litany of the Saints, which came into being at the end of the 8th century.

Meanwhile, the litanies, which had spread to Spain and Gaul, were transformed into lities, probably under the influence of the prestigious *OS*.

We know from the work of Fr. Molin[1] that in the Middle Ages this whole subject, and in a certain sense, the existence of the Universal Prayer itself, was preserved under different forms. In Germany they were called *allgemeines Gebet,* in France *prières du prône,* in Spain *plegaria,* and in England *Bidding Prayers.* But that is another story.

C. The Content of the Formularies

As we did earlier for the prehistory of the *oratio fidelium,* we will here detail the contents of their petitions. We will include only the texts studied in the first three sections of Part Two, the others not being formularies of the Universal Prayer as such. However, given its antiquity, we will also include the remainder of the Hispanic text that we presented in the Appendix in the fourth section. Irl^2 comprises two parts, so that brings us to a total of ten texts.

Before examining the table below, it is worth highlighting the limitations associated with this task. First of all we point out that the range of examples is much reduced. If other texts had been available to us, the table would certainly be different. Any classification of this kind represents a certain shaping of reality, which could be done in other ways. Thus, while it is easy to classify litany petitions such as 'pro rege nostro', it is much more difficult to reduce to schematic form, something as rich as the *OS* where a number of themes appear. Unlike the litany, the litie names and details in the invitatory as well as in the prayer the graces that are being sought. Moreover, we cannot always know with any precision the meaning of certain words (e.g. *papa, senior, …*); peace is sometimes envisaged as a cease-fire and sometimes as the interior peace of the soul. This table, then, does not represent a photographic likeness of our materials. It can only furnish an indication, and recourse to the texts themselves remains indispensable.

1 Cf. especially Molin (1967), 313–468.

In order to judge the importance accorded to this or that petition, we have to take account of the place that it occupies within the formulary, and for this reason we have indicated each time its numerical place in the list of petitions. Moreover, we see that the most frequent petitions are also those that come at the beginning of the text, while those that deal with particular intentions and vary widely from one piece to another are generally found at the end.

The first table provides a synopsis of the ten formularies studied, with the themes contained in them listed alphabetically. The second offers a list of the petitions according to their frequency.

1. *Table of Themes*

	OS	*IRL*^{1}	*M*^{1}	*DG*	*FG*^{1}	*M*^{2}	*FG*^{2}	*IRL*^{2} *A*	*IRL*^{2} *B*	*ESP*
abbot (and his monastery)					IV		[VI]			
acolytes	III									
army		V	III	V	V	IV	[VI]			
ascetics				IV, XV?						
assembly (liturgical)				XII				VI		
benefactors		X	X	XI						
bishops	III	III	II	II	III	III	III		X	
catechumens	V	IX		VII						
charity/love		XIII		XVI						+
Christian people (≠ clergy)	III			II		III				
church (universal)	I	II	I	I	II	I	I			+
city		IV	V		[VI]	V	VII			
clergy/ orders	III	III	II	II	III	III	III	I	X	
confessors	III									
deacons	III	III								

	OS	*IRL*[1]	*M*[1]	*DG*	*FG*[1]	*M*[2]	*FG*[2]	*IRL*[2] *A*	*IRL*[2] *B*	*ESP*
death (Christian)		XII		XVII						
deceased				XIV	X			VIII	XIV	
Emperors and kings	IV	V	III	V	V	IV	IV	V	XI	
exiles			VIII							
exorcists	III									
faith and perseverance	I	XIV		XV						+
fruitfulness of the earth			VI		VII	VI		III		
heretics	VII			X						
holiness		XIV								
hope										+
hungry	VI									
Jews	VIII			X						
lapsi										+
neighbours									XII	
officials		VI								
orphans		VII	VII							
pagans	IX		IV							
peace	IV	I	IV		I		V	IV, V		
penitents		IX	VII		X					
pope	II		II			II	II		X	
porters	III									
possessed			IX							
preachers				III						
priests	III	III						I	X	
prisoners	VI		VII – VIII					V		+
readers	III									
remission of sins		XI		XIII	IX		VIII	VII		

	OS	***Irl***^{1}	***M***^{1}	***DG***	***FG***^{1}	***M***^{2}	***FG***^{2}	***Irl***^{2} ***A***	***Irl***^{2} ***B***	***Esp***
saints (commem. of)		XI		XVIII				VI		
schismatics	VII									
sick	VI		IX		VIII				XV	+
sub-deacons	III									
travellers (land)	VI	VIII	VIII	IX				IX	XIII	+
travellers (sea)/sailors	VI	VIII	VIII							
unity in the Church	I									
virgins	III	VII	VII					II		
weather (good)			VI	VI	VII	VI		III		
widows	III	VII	VII					II		

2. *Table of Frequency*

TOTAL: 10 formularies

No. of times		**Lacking in:**
9	ecclesiastical 'orders' or clergy	Spain
	emperor or king	Spain
8	universal Church	Spain, *Irl*^{2}*A-B*
	bishops	Spain, *Irl*^{2}*A(?)*
7	travellers (land)	*FG*^{1}, *M*^{2}, and *FG*^{2}
6	army	*OS, DG, Irl*^{2}*A-B*, Spain
	peace	*DG, M*^{2}, *Irl*^{2}*B*, Spain
5	city	*OS, DG, Irl*^{2}*A-B*, Spain
	sick	*Irl*^{1}, *DG, M*^{2}, *FG*^{2}, *Irl*^{2}*A*

No. of times		**Lacking in:**
	pope	Irl^{1}, DG, FG^{1}, Irl^{2}A, Spain
	remission of sins	OS, M^{1} M^{2}, Irl^{2}B, Spain
	good weather	OS, Irl^{1}, FG^{2}, Irl^{2}B, Spain

No. of times		**Features in:**
4	deceased	DG, FG^{1}, Irl^{2}A-B
	fruitfulness of the earth	M^{1}, FG^{1}, M^{2}, Irl^{2}A
	faith, its purity	OS, Irl^{1}, DG, Spain
	priests	OS, Irl^{1}, Irl^{2}A(?), Irl^{2}B
	prisoners	OS, Irl^{2}A, M^{1}, Spain
	virgins	OS, Irl^{1}, M^{1}, Irl^{2}A
	widows	OS, Irl^{1}, M^{1}, Irl^{2}A
3	benefactors	Irl^{1}, M^{1}, DG
	catechumens	OS, Irl^{1}, DG
	charity/love	Irl^{1}, DG, Spain
	Christian people (not the clergy)	OS, DG, M^{2}
	commemoration of the saints	Irl^{1}, DG, Irl^{2}A
	penitents	Irl^{1}, M^{1}, FG^{1}
	travellers (sea)/sailors	OS, Irl^{1}, M^{1}
2	abbot (and his monastery)	FG^{1}, FG^{2}
	assembly (liturgical)	DG, Irl^{2}A
	(a) Christian death	Irl^{1}, DG
	deacons	OS, Irl^{1}
	heretics	OS, DG
	Jews	OS, DG
	orphans	Irl^{1}, M^{1}
	pagans	OS, M^{1}
1	acolytes	OS
	ascetics	DG

No. of times		**Features in:**
	confessors	*OS*
	exorcists	*OS*
	exiles	M^{1}
	holiness	Irl^{1}
	hope	Spain
	(the) hungry	*OS*
	(the) *lapsi*	Spain
	porters	*OS*
	neighbours	$Irl^{2}B$
	officials	Irl^{1}
	(the) possessed	M^{1}
	preachers	*DG*
	readers	*OS*
	schismatics	*OS*
	sub-deacons	*OS*
	unity of the Church	*OS*

This analysis shows us that the Christians of the 4th to 6th centuries prayed first of all for the Church ('spread here and throughout the universe') and for its ministers. Prayer for civil authorities is also frequently indicated, but, as we noted in the conclusion of Part One, prayer for the emperor or king (and their army) is just as much a prayer for peace; indeed, the prayer for peace is sometimes attached to it.

We see that prayer for the deceased features only in the more recent texts; its first appearance is in *DG* XIV. The assembled community is mentioned only twice — in *DG* XII and Irl^{2} VI.

We see too a diminishment of perspectives the further we advance in time. While the patristic texts gathered in Part One were quite universalist, following 1 Tim 2:1, the later formularies reflect a narrower world view, where the universal Church is hardly mentioned. The Franco-Gallican 'pro … nostro' is typical of this attitude. We perceive in this the cultural collapse of the period.

D. Liturgical Form

In all this material, we have considered only two different liturgical forms: the litie and the litany.

Only the *OS* constitute a litie. Much later, their quality will influence the Gallic and Spanish liturgists who will give this form to their *orationes paschales*. But let us remember that originally the *OS* consisted of invitatories only, and was presented in a manner analogous to the Easter orations of *Bo* where a single *collectio* brought to a close eleven invitatories. Undoubtedly the prayer [following the invitatory] took place in silence then. If this is the case, then we would find ourselves in the presence of a third liturgical form, the oldest in the West, which would not be without links to some of the Eastern forms.[2]

All the remaining texts are cast in the form of a litany. For the most part they are of the invocative type (Irl^1, M^1, FG^1, M^2, FG^2), with only *DG* and Irl^2 being composed of invitatories. We point out, however, that Irl^1 and *DG* combine the two euchological types; the first part of Irl^1 is invocative, the second invitative (XII–XIV, with a clumsy transition in XI) and *DG* completes a series of invitatories with four invocations (XV–XVIII). The East was familiar with both types: in CAp, for example, the diaconal litanies are invitative while the anaphoric intercessions are invocative. Similarly, in the Greek liturgy of St James, the diaconal litanies are made up of two parts, as in Irl^1 and *DG*, but without passing from one type to another. The same occurs in the Byzantine liturgies.

The difference between these two euchological types is minimal and we often have to look closely to detect it. At the theological level they are equal. They are differentiated only by the subjects of the prayer. We therefore believe that the origin of these two types is clearly explained by the similarities with the Greek sources that we have just indicated. It is apparent that the diaconal forms consist of invitatories, since it is the role of the deacon in the liturgy to invite the participants to pray, whereas the priest formulates the prayer, in the name of the people, in order to address it to God.

While we have found very few indications with regard to the deacon (cf. conclusions to Part One), we think that these invitative formularies were pronounced by the deacons while the invocations were reserved to the priests. Later evolution favoured the priest. The *OS* themselves, in their original state, were, perhaps, a diaconal formulary. Their revision, at the end of the fourth century, turned them into a priestly formulary, with the addition of the Collects reserved to the celebrant. Only the *DG* (and the later Irl^2) retained invitatories. Was this for the sake of archaism, or from Eastern influence, or because of concern to distribute the ministries more equitably?

---

2 Cf. the Nestorian liturgy, Br 263–66.

E. Link with Eastern Sources

It is undeniable that the majority of themes that these texts offer us come from the East; the parallels that we have provided with the backing of other authors, remove any doubt. The Latin formularies do not seem to translate any one particular Eastern text, at least in the state in which we know the Eastern texts today; on the contrary, they draw their inspiration from different sources: the CAp, the Greek liturgies of Sts James and John Chrysostom, and yet others that we have pointed out in passing. They also cite other diaconal litanies and anaphoric intercessions. We might think that they had Brightman open in front of them!

We had to give up the idea of studying the entire Eastern domain, given its extent. We have limited ourselves to noting the Eastern parallels, well aware that the nub of the matter lies in the East. But before indulging in loose comparisons between the litanic texts of the East and the West, they must be studied in their own right. We have tried to do this with the Western texts. The Eastern domain remains. Whoever embarks on this task will need to be mindful on several points. First, in the East the Prayer of the Faithful is enshrined in a total liturgical structure. It is bound in a much stricter manner than in the West to the dismissal of the catechumens and other 'unworthies' and the prayer made on their behalf. Thus, it belongs to a different euchological system.

It would also be necessary to have a better understanding of the relations between the litanies and the priestly intercession prayed within the same liturgy, as well as the relationships between the prayers of the various Eastern liturgies. That alone will allow us to situate the origin of the liturgical form that is the litany and to know where the Latins sought their inspiration and their materials. Bishop thought that it was from Constantinople,[3] Capelle leant more towards Jerusalem[4] and Baumstark noted (without much probability in our opinion) Egyptian influences.[5]

Finally, it would be indispensable to pinpoint the age and history of these Eastern formularies that we have cited as parallels. Were they presented in the 4th–5th centuries in the manner that we know them today?

It is only then that we will be able to ask ourselves by what means they were exchanged between the two poles of the Mediterranean. It is a complex question that calls for detailed study. It can be divided into two sub-questions: that of sources and that of channels of influence.

a Must we assume the existence of a common source for both Eastern and Western formularies, a source that could have been used, for example, by the redactor of the CAp and by the reviser of the *OS*? We are wary of

3 E. Bishop (1911), 409.
4 Capelle (1934), 124.
5 Baumstark (1958), 71–80.

pronouncing on such a question. Here too a serious preliminary study of the Eastern texts is necessary.

b As for channels of influence, we will limit ourselves to just one comment. Duchesne argued that what he called the Gallican liturgy (i.e. all the non-Roman Latin rites) had very early been subjected to Eastern influence. He situated this influence in Milan in particular, thanks to the Cappadocian Auxence I, Arian bishop between 355 and 374, predecessor of Ambrose. This thesis has been contested by liturgists and historians of the quality of Wilmart, Brou and Griffe, who consider the Eastern influence to have occurred much later. But is seems to us that these authors, unlike Duchesne, are dealing with the Gallican liturgy in the strict sense, and this makes their argument somewhat flawed.

We know that quite recently M. Meslin has taken up Duchesne's thesis.[6] Even if the author is not a liturgist by profession, it seems to us that there is benefit in taking up the question with him. Indeed, it would have been necessary for the influence of the Eastern texts to have been exercised before the end of the 4th century to explain the sometimes literal similarities between them and the *OS* or Irl^1. On the other hand, it is not beyond the realms of possibility that M^1 and M^2, and even Irl^1, originated in Milan; this must at least be considered.

Let us also remember the conclusions reached in turn by W. Bousset.[7] He considered that the Eastern influence was exercised in two waves. The first he placed between the end of the persecutions and the definitive separation of the Empire, that is to say, in the course of the 4th century. A second, later, wave was, in his opinion, required in order to explain the similarities between the Latin litanies and the great Eastern liturgies, such as those of St James and St John Chrysostom.

In commenting on Irl^1, we cited among other channels of influence such people as Hilary of Poitiers (died around 367) and John Cassian (*c.* 360–434).

F. Universal Prayer, Anaphoral Intercessions and Diptychs

These are three different realities. We have spoken quite a lot about the first, which is situated at the transition point between the Liturgy of the Word and the Liturgy of the Eucharist. The anaphoric intercessions are the prayers of petition pronounced by the priest within the Eucharistic Prayer. The *Apostolic Tradition* is unaware of them, the CAp develops them at length, and the Greek liturgies of St James and St John Chrysostom introduce them with Μνήσθητι. As for the diptychs (also called *nomina*), they are the lists of persons, living or dead, that are named in the liturgy. Originally, these lists were read at the Offertory, then they were sometimes included in the anaphora itself.

6 Meslin (1967), Part Three.
7 Bousset (1916), 162–63.

The Roman Canon offers us the sequence of these two elements. In the *Te igitur* the priest announces the intentions of the offering:

'quae tibi offerimus
- pro Ecclesia tua sancta catholica, quam pacificare, custodire, adunare et regere digneris toto orbe terrarum,
- una cum famulo tuo papa nostro N.,
- et antistite nostro, N.,
- et omnibus orthodoxis atque catholicae et apostolicae fidei cultoribus'.

Then follows the reading of the *nomina vivorum* introduced by the *Memento*.

We have not ventured into the study of diptychs or anaphoric intercessions, but only touched on them in passing, since here we also find ourselves in the same field of intercessions.

- The difference between the *oratio fidelium* and the diptychs is clear; the latter are simple lists of names which are not shaped into a prayer formulary, while the former consist essentially of a petition together with a general indication of its aim and its beneficiary. We note that in the literary examples and the texts of the Universal Prayer that we have studied, there has never been any mention of a particular person; they may be described by their function (bishop, king) but they are never named as such.
- The distinction is much less clear between the Universal Prayer and the intercessions during the Eucharistic Prayer (anaphora). In the East the former is pronounced by the deacon, the latter by the celebrant; but we are not aware of any criteria that would make it possible to distinguish between the petitions expressed; sometimes they are even identical.

In the West the four intentions of the Roman *Te igitur* all feature prominently in the texts of the Universal Prayer. The first we find, even word for word, in *OS* I, in M^1 I and in M^2 I. What is more, a formulary such as Irl^2, that we think was initially composed to be used as the Prayer of the Faithful, is at the same time located within the 'canon papae gilasi' as if the two functions were interchangeable.[8]

We might object that our ancestors were not philosphers, the liturgists even less so than the others, no doubt. This doubling up did not disturb them as much as it does those of us who, re-shaped by the liturgical reform, do not support hearing prayed a second time an intention that has already been expressed in the same celebration.

---

8 In his article entitled 'De intercessiegebeden in het eucharistisch gebed' in *Tijdschrift voor liturgie*, vol. 56 (1972), 298–320, F. Sottocornola thinks however that the difference between the Universal Prayer and the anaphoric intercessions resides in their content. The Eucharistic Prayer necessarily includes, according to his historical research, a deprecative moment, which is a prayer for the Church and its unity from an eschatological perspective. The other intentions, which come later historically, are not essential to it. The petitions of the Universal Prayer, on the other hand, are much more diverse.

See also Grisbrooke (1966), 30–44 and 87–103.

We are not so sure of this. In our opinion the problem of the relationship between the *oratio fidelium* and the intercessions of the Eucharistic Prayer is bound to arise. The existence of this doubling up could well reveal to us important questions with regard to the history of the liturgy. We have not studied the anaphoric intercessions themselves, but after the study of the ancient *oratio fidelium*, we think that we can make some comments.

The Eucharistic Prayer of 'Hippolytus' does not contain any prayer of intercession. Since we consider that the *Apostolic Tradition* was familiar with the Universal Prayer, this situation seems quite satisfactory to us moderns: the anaphora expresses the ideas of offering and praise and is not weighed down with petitions. If the views of Dom Capelle[9] are correct, then the beginning of the Roman Canon has had the current structure since 416, under Innocent I. In other words, the *oratio fidelium* and the anaphoric intercessions co-existed for more than a century. But how did this come about? Several authors consider that the intercessions were inserted into the Canon because of the belief at the time that prayers were more efficacious the closer they were to the consecration. This explanation seems to us to demonstrate a poor modern theology rather than a historic reality. However, we do have to acknowledge that it was the Universal Prayer that disappeared while the intercessions were not removed from the Canon.

Other authors claim that the *oratio fidelium* and the anaphoric intercessions are quite different realities; the first pronounces petitions, the second cites the intentions for which the Eucharist is offered. The two prayers have thus co-existed without causing any problems.[10] We confess we cannot properly perceive the distinction; is the offering of sacrifice anything other than a form of prayer?

We wonder whether the following hypothesis should be seriously examined.[11] The Liturgy of the Word and the Liturgy of the Eucharist were once distinct, or at least could be separated in certain circumstances. We know this from Justin (T 5 and T 6), from 'Hippolytus' (Rome, T 1) and certain passages from the Old Gelasian sacramentary allude to this. Perhaps each of these elements included an intercession and the doubling up only became problematical when the readings and the Eucharist became definitively inseparable.

This hypothesis presumes that the Prayer of the Faithful belongs to the first part of the Mass, as it exists nowadays. But the description given by Justin clearly shows that, for him, the Universal Prayer began the Eucharist. It was the same for

9 Capelle (1952), 5–16; Tr. Lit., vol. 2, 236–47; cf. Also Capelle (1955), 181–91; Tr. Lit., vol. 2, 248–57.

10 This is the opinion of Dom. A. Nocent (1964), 948–64, who writes, 'The restoration of the *oratio fidelium* does not of itself lead to the suppression of intercessory prayers. Prayer for the Church, the pope, and the bishops at the end of the Liturgy of the Word is one thing; to offer sacrifice for them and to insert their name in Christ's offering and the commemoration of the 'mirabilia Dei' is another'. This quotation is taken from p. 963.

11 We owe the essence of this hypothesis to conversations that we had with Canon Houssiau, professor at the Catholic University of Louvain.

'Hippolytus' and in the East where, after all the dismissals, the *oratio fidelium* was reserves to the faithful alone and thus commenced the second part of the Mass.

But we think that this comment, accurate as it may be, does not constitute a serious objection to our own hypothesis; the Ancients, in effect, scarcely considered such questions of structure.

We believe, then, that these two formularies of intercession were able to co-exist because they each belonged to a liturgical function that was judged to be more or less independent of the other. From the time that they were definitively united with each other, the Universal Prayer fell into disuse, for all the reasons we have named above, most notably because of the growing popularity of processions in which these formularies found a new use.

We have also noted above that the clerical (priestly) movement that developed at the end of the 4th century is probably responsible for the transformation of the invitatories into invocative texts, and their reservation to priests at the expense of deacons. Perhaps this mutation also harmed the Universal Prayer, removing the diaconal character that could have been specific to it.

General Conclusions

After this long study of the Universal Prayer during the first six centuries, let us try to take stock of things.

1. Theological Problems of the Prayer

Despite interest in the enterprise, we will not proceed to a theological re-reading of the materials we have gathered. It would be exciting, for example to find out what conception of God and the world these formularies reflect, and what notion of prayer they embody. What should we think of Tertullian's statement in T 7 that 'only prayer can overcome God'. Is the purpose of prayer to harass the One who knows what we need even before we ask (Mt 6:8)? Or how are we to understand the canonical prescriptions charging penitents to assist at the whole of Mass but not to communicate?

It is beyond question that the Ancients sought from God objective things like the delaying of the end of the world (Tertullian T 1) or good weather (*pro aeris temperie*, in the litanies). Aristides wrote that it is thanks to the prayer of Christians that the world continues to exist. But it was not only to prayer that they attributed the subjective role of transforming the human heart to make it conform more fully to the Gospel. Such an objectivist notion of prayer presents problems for the contemporary Christian mentality which would regard study of the biblical and theological foundations as absolutely necessary.

Let us note also that in Eastern spirituality, the litanies and especially the numerous repetitions of the *Kyrie eleison*, whose appearance we have witnessed, are not unrelated to the use of the 'Jesus Prayer' which consists of continual repetition of the phrase, 'Lord Jesus, have mercy on me'. It is mentioned in the 6th century by Saint John Climacus. There would be benefit in researching the historical roots of this devotion and assessing its worth; we find the same spiritual approach expressed in it as in the multiplication of litanies.

2. '*Oratio Fidelium*' or Universal Prayer?

Modern liturgists use the expression *oratio fidelium* as a technical term to describe the prayer of intercession situated — in the Mass — between the readings and the Liturgy of the Eucharist. It has been translated as *Prayer of the faithful*. This title is in good part responsible for the initial success that the restoration of this prayer by the Second Vatican Council has experienced. The faithful feel involved.

We need to recognise, however, that this phrase is very ambiguous; let us examine its origin.

a) In the West

Scholars found the expression *oratio fidelium* in the letter of Felix III that we analysed and whose canonical background we have revealed. Let us recall that we read there that rebaptised clerics 'nec orationi non modo fidelium, sed ne catechumenorum omnimodis interesse' (Rome, T 18). We have shown, with a reasonable degree of certainty, that in the context, 'to participate in the prayer of the faithful' has nothing to do with taking part in the Universal Prayer, but concerns the right to join in prayer *with* the faithful. It would therefore be wrong to read any technical definition into this term.

This is corroborated by the fact that nowhere in the West have we found a heading that belongs directly to our prayer. The patristic texts are very fluid in this regard; only Augustine gives us some information, using the expressions *orationes Ecclesiae, orationes credentium* and *orationes fidelium* — although the one time that he uses the term *oratio fidelium* he is referring to the Our Father.[1] In other words, he too does not know any specific description. Later, the liturgical books use the terms *orationes*, a title perhaps reserved to the lities (*OS, orationes paschales*), *deprecatio* and *preces.*

b) In the East

Here the expression *oratio fidelium* has a precise and adequate meaning. In the East, as we may recall, the prayer is intimately connected with the sending forth of the 'unworthy'. In the CAp we see clearly that before the departure of the catechumens or penitents, etc., a prayer is prayed for them. When the faithful alone remain present, the εὐχὴ τῶν πιστῶν takes place. We understand clearly: this heading does not mean that the faithful have either composed the prayer or pronounced it. It merely indicates those who are authorised to pray it. Here we reach the origin of the expression 'prayer of the faithful' and its most fundamental meaning.[2]

---

1 On this, see Part One, Section 2, Augustine § 2.

2 We thus agree with the remarks made by E. Bishop (1918), 122, who writes, 'The *OS* cannot be called prayers *of* the faithful, rather, they are prayers *for* the faithful, which is quite different'. His caution has not been imitated, unless by A. Wilmart who noted: '... if the faithful participate in it in their heart, through their attitude and with a brief *Amen*, it is pronounced by the bishop in their name'. Art. 'Germain de Paris (lettres attribuées à saint)', DACL 6, 1075.

This is not the first time in history that the genitive, the most ambiguous of the grammatical cases, has played nasty tricks.

This primary meaning still prevails in the East, where the dismissals and the prayers that accompany them continue to exist. In the West it fits with the reality described by Justin and 'Hippolytus', the latter noting explicitly that this prayer is reserved to the faithful (Rome, T 1).[3] But subsequently this objection is no longer found in the West. Rome seems not to have known an *oratio catechumenorum*; instead a litique of the *OS* is dedicated to them. And the customary interpretation of the text by Felix III is not correct. The texts that we have studied pray for the needs of the Church and of society; the role of the faithful is no more important in them than in the 'priestly prayers', except in the case of the litanies, expressly constructed to favour participation of the people.

Personally, we consider that the expression *prayer of the faithful* should be erased from current vocabulary. It is understood only in the light of past culture and does not properly describe the current reality. If liturgists use *oratio fidelium* in a technical sense, so be it, provided that they know its meaning and do not attempt to draw deviant consequences from it. For our part, we prefer the term *universal prayer*, which seems much more appropriate to us. The true object of this ritual is to pray for the needs of all. The formularies we have studied all begin with the most universal petitions (the Church, peace) and end with more particular intentions. These latter are not excluded but they ought to be kept in reasonable proportions.

In the current terminology we speak again of *common prayer*; to us that seems adequate, since any prayer by the priests is made also in the name of the participants, in common with them. In this work, we have reserved the expression to describe the liturgical genre of a prayer aimed at including the participation of the people. The term is thus less evocative, less suggestive.

When article 53 of the *Constitution on the Sacred Liturgy* of the Second Vatican Council restored the Universal Prayer, it was referred to as the *oratio communis seu fidelium*. We are pleased to say that the *Institutio generalis missalis romani* of April 1, 1969 modified the official terminology and speaks of the *oratio universalis seu oratio fidelium* (n. 99 — cf. *Ordo Missae* n. 16).[4]

---

3 This prescription may appear to be juridical and to confer privileges whose meanings we do not fully understand. Perhaps it is susceptible to a richer interpretation; might it not suggest that Christian prayer is an activity 'sui generis', demanding the filial attitude laid down by the New Testament. If it is to be done 'in spirit and in truth' (Jn 4:23) it requires the one praying to have received the Holy Spirit and to know what has been revealed.

4 Further editions of the *General Instruction of the Roman Missal* have appeared since 1969. See Third edition of the *GIRM* (2001), no. 69. Ed.

3. The Contents — Problem of Fixed Formularies

The problem of the contents of the Universal Prayer arises somewhat sharply today. We do not think that, here as elsewhere, history can impose ready-made solutions on us, described — often a little too quickly — as traditional, in the theological sense of the word. We have some further remarks to make.

a) Absence of Connection with the Readings

We have not seen any connection between the readings proclaimed and the Universal Prayer. It could be objected that this is only natural when we are dealing with fixed formularies. But even prior to that, the literary sources do not in any way show us a close relationship with the Liturgy of the Word.

b) Prayer, Not Catechesis

We could claim, with almost as much certainty, the absence of any relationship between the homily and the Universal Prayer: there is no perceptible organic link between them. It is true that with Augustine, the formula *Conversi ad Dominum* does constitute a minimal link between the two realities, but even if they follow one after the other, they are not alike. The litanies never take the form of a mini-homily, and their invocations or invitatories are very clearly prayers or invitations to pray, and not catechesis.

The depth of content is obviously greater in the lities, whose invitatories and orations are more developed and almost always include a final clause detailing the graces sought, but the primary purpose is always to pray, not to teach.

c) The Problem of the Formularies

We have already detailed the contents of the petitions in the conclusions to Part One and Part Two. Fixed formularies present a problem since they do not allow the prayer to expand to include current concerns.[5] In fact, these texts express in a stereotypical fashion the needs of the Church and the world, written in a sufficiently general way to be continually useful. It should be noted here that the litanies have made the task easier for themselves by indicating the beneficiary of the prayer but never prescribing the graces being sought. In this way they avoid having to concretise the petition as we like to do nowadays.

---

5 But is there ever a 'reality' that is confined to a particular epoch? Or can the word reflect the same meaning from one era to another? We think that the existence of social communications today places us in a radically different situation in this regard.

d) Attempt at Explanation

We venture to propose two explanations for the appearance and maintenance of the formularies. The first deals with a fact, the second is no more than a line of thought.

1 Cultural decline

The 5th century saw the Germans established in the territory of the Empire. Already in 410 Rome had been pillaged by Alaric and his Goths. Both these events contributed to the fall of the Empire in 476 and had repercussions at the cultural level: from the 6th century a new world came into being, Antiquity was ended. The grand visions of the Fathers gave way to a moralising concern (cf. Caesarius of Arles), the horizons shrank, the world closed in on itself.

This cultural collapse was not without influence on the liturgy. We think that insufficient consideration has been given to the fact that the liturgical texts we still use today originated — or were compiled — at a time of cultural decline. Our explanatory hypothesis is this: ought we not make a connection between this fall in the level of culture and the fixing of formularies? In other words, were the texts compiled only because people were no longer skilled enough to create them and were only too happy to have a valid formulary in their possession?

This could explain why the litanies of the 5th century were preserved. Their redactors probably had no intention of handing on their works to future centuries since their chief intent was to help their contemporaries to pray. More significantly, this hypothesis could explain even the composition of the formularies, or at least their multiplication, since we cannot believe that before the 5th century no liturgical text had been put into writing! Even if our current concern is the Universal Prayer, we have to remember that the first redaction of the *OS* dates back to the 3rd century.

In any case — and this is certain — we find that the stereotyped formularies — sufficiently general so as to be applicable in other times and under other skies — have, over the ages, been modified and above all simplified in various ways, without creating new, updated forms. While their liturgical form may have been adapted, their content has not been enriched.

2 The formularies and the genius of the Latin language

In following the evolution of these pieces, we have been struck to see how formularies, originating in the West in the 5th century, have, after a degree of stylistic polishing (which gave rise to the second wave of litanies) traversed the ages without alteration, so that we find them, unaltered, fifteen centuries later.

On the other hand, as soon as these texts were translated into the vernacular languages of the 12th–13th centuries, we see a variety of expressions, a diversification resulting from place, circumstance and even the talent of the redactors.

Reflecting on these facts, we have wondered if the fixity of the Latin formulas did not have something to do with the genius of this language itself. Latin likes conciseness, and seems able to convey a great richness of meaning in a few words. Certain words, like *pietas* and *devotio,* are almost unable to be translated into another language without resorting to a paraphrase. Moreover, the language of Cicero is fond of rhythm and balanced phrases; once constituted they are often almost impossible to change either by adding or removing a word. Every element has its place and is needed for the balance of the formulary.

French (and English) proceed quite differently. There is far less sense of stereotypical formularies. This arises mainly from a lack of accent — an absence which imposes far less rhythm than for Latin.

In short, let us not too quickly describe as 'traditional' the use of formularies for the Universal Prayer. Let us discover the reasons that have led to our use of them, and let us be aware of the fact that we are living in another time and speak another language.

4. Evaluation

A. Contribution of this Study

1) Account of the Universal Prayer in the West in the First Six Centuries

The first contribution of this work has been the gathering of the documentation: initially the patristic sources, then the formularies themselves, edited and analysed.

This has shown that

- Christians have always been concerned about praying for the needs of the Church and the world;
- since the time of St Justin this preoccupation has been realised in the Universal Prayer;
- it existed in the early Church, but perhaps not from the very beginning, nor everywhere not at all times.

Thanks to these texts we are able to know its content and liturgical form (in large part taken from the East) and can reconstruct its history.

2) History of the Universal Prayer

Its pre-history takes on more precise contours, thanks to the critical study of the patristic sources. Its history is then clarified with regard to certain points. Without being able to repeat here all the nuances detailed in the course of our exposition, let us name in particular:

- the appearance in Rome of the *OS* between 250 and around 320, originally comprising invitatories only;

- the existence in the West, from the beginning of the 5th century (and so before Pope Gelasius) of litanies freely translated from Eastern texts, and reworked at the end of the century;
- the permanence of the Universal Prayer after Gelasius;
- its disappearance towards the middle of the 6th century;
- the survival of its formularies, adapted to new uses, in the Gallican and Hispanic *orationes paschales*, the processional litanies and the Litanies of the Saints.

3) Analysis Tool

Our study uses a tool that makes it possible to systematically classify liturgical forms, their constituent elements, and their style and attributes. Thanks to this method we have been able to analyse the texts and compare them with each other.

4) Terminology

The expression *oratio fidelium* assumes its full meaning only in the Eastern liturgy, where the Prayer of the Faithful takes place after the dismissal of the 'unworthy'. The liturgical realities of the West being different and, given the ambiguity of the phrase for our contemporaries, we prefer to use the expression 'Universal Prayer'.

B. Historical Issues Still Outstanding

Several questions remain to be clarified. Beyond purely historical interest, their study could shed light on certain pastoral issues:

1 Relationship with the East
Here it would be necessary:
– to research the origin of the litanic genre in the East;
– and to study the development of the formularies across the different liturgies.
Only then could we effectively compare the Eastern and Latin texts and discern the influences to which they were subjected.
2 Relationship between the Universal Prayer and the anaphoric intercessions.
3 Prescriptions regarding the beginning of the Roman Mass: processional litany, Introit, Kyrie.
4 Relationships between the Latin liturgies.

C. Prospects

In addition to the pastoral impact of research devoted to the problems noted above, we believe that one of the conditions necessary for the consistent and harmonious growth of the Universal Prayer in our present time is the theological study of the prayer of intercession. The people of today need to rediscover the justification for it and its conditions of legitimacy, based on its New Testament and traditional foundations.

Then they will be happy to believe in the Lord Jesus who tells them, 'Until now you have not asked for anything in my name. Ask and you will receive, so that your joy may be complete' (Jn 16:24).

Bibliography

This list is made up of three parts:

- The first indicates in alphabetical order the *signs and abbreviations* of the publications used, and the type of publication;
- The second cites the *sources* used; first the historical and literary sources, classified alphabetically; then the liturgical sources. Among these, those that are edited are set out in a systematic order. The unpublished manuscripts that we have used are cited in alphabetical order in the cities where they are to be found;
- The third part lists the *books and articles* that we have used. Among the works or articles on pastoral liturgy published since the restoration of the Universal Prayer, we have retained only the most important. Multiple contributions by the same author are listed in chronological order of publication.

1. Signs and Abbreviations

Altaner — B. Altaner, *Précis de patrologie*, ed. S. Mulhouse, Paris, 1961.

Bo — Bobbio Missal

Bourque — E. Bourque, *Etude sur les sacramentaires romains*, 3 vols, Rome — Quebec, 1948–1958. Number given refers to Bourque's numbers of the manusripts

Br — F. E. Brightman, *Liturgies Eastern and Western. I. Eastern Liturgies*, Oxford, 1896.

Bruns — H.Th. Bruns, *Canones apostolorum et conciliorum saeculorum IV–VII.* Vol. 1:Saeculum IV, Berlin, 1949.

CAp — Apostolic Constitutions, ed. F. X. Funk, *Didascalia et Consitutiones apostolorum*, Paderborn, 1905.

CC — *Corpus christianorum, series latina*, Turnhout, 1953-.

Clavis — E. Dekkers, and A. Gaar, *Clavis partum latinorum. Editio altera*, Bruges, 1961.

COD — *Conciliorum oecumenicorum decretal.* (*Istituto per le scienze religiose, Bologna*), Fribourg B., 1962.

CSEL — *Corpus scriptorium ecclesiasticorum latinorum*, Vienna, 1866-.

DACL — *Dictionnaire d'archéologie chrétienne et de liturgie*, Paris, 1904–1953.

Denzinger — H. Denzinger, and A. Schönmetzer Enchiridion *symbolorum: definitionum et declarationum de rebus fidei et morum*, 32nd edition, Barcelona, 1963.

DG — *Deprecation Gelasii.*

DHEE — *Dictionario de historia eclesiástica de España*, Madrid, 1972.

Diaz	M. C. Diaz y Diaz, *Index scriptorum latinorum medii aevi hispanorum*, (*Consejo Superior de Investigaciones cientificas*), Madrid, 1959. The number given refers to his numbering of the manuscripts.
Du Cange	C. du Cange, *Glossarium ad scriptores mediae et infimae latinatis*, 6 vols, Paris, 1733–6.
EL	*Ephemerides liturgicae*, Edizioni Liturgiche, Rome, 1887-.
FC	*Fathers of the Church. A New Translation*, Washington DC, 1947-.
FG^1	Franco-Gallican *Dicamus omnes*.
FG^2	Franco-Gallican *Kyrie eleison. Domine Deus omnipotens patrum nostrorum.*
Gamber	K. Gamber, *Codices liturgici latini antiquiores*, 2 vol., Fribourg S., 1968. The number given refers to his numbering of the manuscripts.
Go	*Missale Gothicum*, ed. L. C. Mohlberg, Herder, Rome, 1961.
Ha	*Orationes paschales*, Hispanic tradition A.
Hb	*Orationes paschales*, Hispanic tradition B.
HBS	Henry Bradshaw Society for Editing Rare Liturgical Texts, London, 1891-.
Irl^1	*Dicamus omnes* from the Stowe Missal.
Irl^2	Anaphoric intercessions from the Stowe Missal.
JWL	*Jahrbuch für Liturgiewissenschaft*, Aschendorff, Munster, 1921–1941.
JTS	*Journal of Theological Studies*, London, then Oxford, 1900-.
LMD	*La Maison-Dieu, Revue de pastorale liturgique*, Paris, 1945-.
LMS	M. Ferotin, *Liber mozarabicus sacramentorum*, Paris, 1912.
LOrd.	M. Ferotin, *Le Liber ordinum*, Paris, 1904.
LP	L. Duchesne, *Le Liber pontificalis. Texte, introduction et commentaire*, 3 vol., 2nd edition, ed. C. Vogel, Paris, 1955–7.
LQF	*Liturgiegeschichtliche* (then *Liturgiewissenschaftliche*) *Quellen und Forschungen*, Munster, 1919-.
LTK	*Lexikon für Theologie und Kirche*, 2nd edition, 10 vol., Fribourg B., 1958–1965.
LW	*Liturgisch woordenboek*, 2 vol., Roermond, 1958–1968.
M^1	*Divinae pacis* (Milanese)
M^2	*Dicamus omnes* (Milanese)
Mansi	J. D. Mansi, *Sacrorum conciliorum nova et amplissima collectio*, Florence, 1758–1798.
MGG	*Die Musik in Geschichte und Gegenwart. Allgemeine Enzyklopädie der Musik*, 14 vol., Cassel, 1949–1968.
MGH	*Monumenta Germaniae historica …*, Hanover-Berlin, 1826–2010.
MGV	*Missale gallicanum vetus*, ed. L. C. Mohlberg, Herder, Rome, 1958.
NRT	*Nouvelle revue théologique*, Louvain, 1868-.
OR	*Ordines romani*, ed. M. Andrieu, *Les Ordines romani du haut moyen âge*, (*Spicilegium sacrum lovaniense* 11, 23, 24, 28, 29), 5 vol., Louvain, 1931–1961.
OS	*Orationes sollemnes* of Good Friday.
PG	J. P. Migne, *Patrologiae cursus completus, Series graeca*, 161 vol., 1857–1866.

PL J. P. Migne, *Patrolgiae cursus completus, Series latina*, 221 vol., Paris, 1844–1864.
PRG C. Vogel and R. Elze, *Le Pontifical romano-germanique- de Xe siècle*, (*Studi e Testi* 226, 227, 269), 3 vol., Vatican City, 1963–1972.
QLP *Questions liturgiques et paroissiales*, Louvain, 1910–1969.
RB *Revue bénédictine*, Maredsous, 1884-.
RHE *Revue d'histoire ecclésiastique*, Louvain, 1900-.
RTAM *Recherches de théologie ancienne et médiévale*, Louvain, 1929-.
SC *Sources chrétiennes*, Paris, 1942-.
TA *Texte und Arbeiten. Beiträge zur Ergründung des lateinischen christlichen Schrifttums und Gottesdienstes*, ed. Archabbey, Beuron, 1917-.
Thesaurus *Thesaurus linguae latinae. Editus auctoritate et consilio Academiarum quinque germanicarum ...*, Leipzig, 1900-.
Tr.Ap. Apostolic Tradition, ed. B. Botte, *La tradition apostolique de saint Hippolyte. Essai de reconstitution* (LQF 39), Munster, 1963; see also ed. G. J. Cuming, Nottinham, 1976
Tr.Lit. B. Capelle, *Travaux liturgiques de doctrine et d'histoire*, 3 vol., Louvain, 1955–1967.
TU *Texte und Untersuchungen zur Geschichte der altchristlichen Literatur*, Leipzig then Berlin, 1882.

2. Sources

A. Historical and Literary Sources

Amalarius of Metz, *Amalarii episcopi opera liturgica omnia*, ed. J. M. Hanssens, 3 vol., (*Studi e testi* 138–40), Vatican City, 1948–1950.
Ambrose of Milan, *De Cain et Abel*, ed. C. Schenkl, (CSEL 32.1), Vienna, 1897.
———, *De fide*, ed. O. Faller, (CSEL 78), Vienna, 1962.
———, *De obitu Valentiniani*, ed. O. Faller, (CSEL 73), Vienna, 1955.
———, *De sacramentis*, ed. O. Faller, (CSEL 73), Vienna, 1955; ed. B. Botte (SC 25bis), Paris, 1961; ed. Thompson–Srawley, London, 1950.
———, *De virginibus*, ed. O. Faller, (*Florilegium patristicum* 31), Bonn, 1933.
———, *Expositio evangelii secundum Lucam*, ed. C. and H. Schenkl, (CSEL 32.4), Vienna, 1902.
———, *Expositio psalmi 118*, ed. M. Petschenig, (CSEL 62), Vienna, 1913.
———, *Opera*, ed. J. du Frische and N. le Nourry, 2 vol., Paris, 1686–1690 (= PL 14–16).
Ambrosiaster, *Ambrosiastri qui dicitur Commentarius in epistulas paulinas*, ed. H. J. Vogels, (CSEL 81, 3 vol.), Vienna, 1966–9.
Apollonius of Rome, *Der process und die Acta S. Apollonii*, ed. T. Klette, (TU 15, 2), Leipzig, 1897.

Aristides of Athens, *Die Apologie des Aristides. Recension und Rekonstruktion des Textes*, ed. E. Hennecke, (TU 4, 3), Leipzig, 1893.

Arnobius the Elder, *Arnobii adversus nationes libri VII*, ed. A. Reifferscheid, (CSEL 4), Vienna, 1875.

Athanasius of Alexandria, *Apologie à Constance*, ed. J. M. Szymusiak, (SC 56), Paris, 1958.

Athenagorus of Athens, *La supplica per i cristiani. Testo critic e commento*, ed. P. Ubaldi, (*Scrittori greci commentati* 3), Turin, 1921, 2nd ed., 1933.

———, *Supplique au sujet des chrétiens. Introduction et traduction*, ed. G. Bardy (SC 3), Paris, 1943.

Augustine of Hippo, *Augustins Enchiridion*, ed. O. Scheel, (*Sammlung ausgewählter Kirchen- und Dogmengeschichtlicher Quellenschriften*, 2, 4) Tübingen, 1930.

———, *De dono perseverantiae*, ed. the Maurists, Paris, 1679–1700, (PL 45), 993–1034; Eng. tr. ed. P. Schaff, (NPNF Series 1, vol. 5), Christian Literature Company, Buffalo NY, 1887.

———, *Enarrationes in psalmos*, ed. Dekkers–Fraipont, (CC 38–40), Turnhout, 1956.

———, *Epistulae*, ed. A. Goldbacher, (CSEL 34.1–2; 44; 57; 58), Vienna, 1895–1923.

———, *Saint Augustine, Letters, Vol. 1 (1–82)*, tr. W. Parsons, (FC 1), New York, 1951

———, *Saint Augustine, Letters, Vol. 3 (131–64)*, tr. W. Parsons, (FC 20), New York, 1953.

———, *Saint Augustine, Letters, Vol. 4 (165–203)*, tr. W. Parsons, (FC 30), New York, 1955.

———, *Saint Augustine, Letters, Vol. 5 (204–70)*, tr. W.Parsons, (FC 32), New York, 1956.

———, *S. Augustini sermones post Maurinos reperti*, ed. G. Morin, (*Miscellanea agostiniana* 1), Rome, 1930.

———, *Sermones de vetere testamento*, ed. C. Lambot, (CC 41), Turnhout, 1961.

———, *Sermons pour la Pâque*, ed. S. Poque, (SC 116), Paris, 1966.

———, *Opera*, ed. the Maurists, Paris, 1679–1700 (PL 32–47).

———, *The De Haeresibus of Saint Augustine*, ed. L. G. Müller, CUA Press, Washington, DC, 1956.

Aurelian of Arles, *Regula ad monachos*, PL 68, 393 ff.

Basil of Caesarea, *Saint Basile. Lettres*, ed. Y. Courtonne (*Collection des Universités de France — Les Belles Lettres*), 3 vol., Paris, 1957–1966.

Benedict of Norcia, *Regula monasteriorum*, ed. A de Vogüe and J. Neufville, 2 vol., (SC 181–82), Paris, 1972.

Boniface of Rome, *Epistola* 7 to Honorius, PL 20, 767 ff.

Burchard of Worms, *Decretorum libri XX*, PL 140, 537 ff.

Caesarius of Arles, *Sancti Caesarii arelatensis sermones*, ed. G. Morin and C. Lambot, (CC 103–04), Turnhout, 1953.

———, *Sancti Caesarii opera omnia*, vol. 2, ed. G. Morin, Maredsous, 1942.

Celestine of Rome, *Epistola* 23 to the Emperor Theodosius II, PL 50, 544 ff.

Clement of Rome, *Letter to the Corinthians*, ed. F. X. Funk, *Patres apostolici*, vol. 1., Tübingen, 1901; ed. A. Jaubert (SC 167), Paris, 1971; Also. L. J. *Johnson*, ed., *Worship in the Early Church*, vol. 1, Collegeville, MN, 2009.

Columban, *Regula monachorum*, in *Sancti Columbani opera*, ed. G. S. M. Walker, (*Scriptores latini Hiberniae*, 2), Dublin, 1957.

Concilia Galliae, 314–506, ed. C. Munier, (CC 148), Turnhout, 1963; 511–695, ed. C. de Clercq (CC 148A), Turnhout, 1963.

Cyprian of Carthage, *Saint Cyprien. Correspondance*, ed. L. Bayard (*Collection des Universités de France — Les Belles Lettres*), 2nd ed., 2 vol., Paris, 1961–2; For English tr. see *Saint Cyprian, Letters (1–81)*, ed. Rose Bernard Donna (FC 51), Washington, DC, 1964.

———, *Saint Cyprien. L'oraison dominicale*, ed. M. Reveillaud, (*Etudes d'histoire et de philosophie religieuses*), Paris, 1964; For English tr. see *St Cyprian on the Lord's Prayer: an English Translation with Introduction*, ed. T. H. Bindley, SPCK, London, 1904.

———, *Sancti Cypriani opera omnia*, ed. G. Hartel, (CSEL 3), 3 vol. Vienna, 1868–1871.

Didache, in F. X. Funk, *Patres apostolici*, vol. 1, Tübingen, 1901; See also *Worship in the Early Church*, ed. L. J. *Johnson*, vol. 1, Collegeville, MN, 2009.

Egeria, *Itinerarium Egeriae*, ed. A. Franceschini and R. Weber, (CC 175), Turnhout, 1965; See also *Egeria's Travels*, J. Wilkinson, (revised edition), Jerusalem–Warminster, England, 1981.

Eusebius of Caesarea, *Histoire ecclésiastique. Texte grec, traduction et annotations*, ed. G. Bardy (SC 31, 41, 55, 73), Paris 1952–1960.

Felix III of Rome, *Epistola* 7, PL 58, 925 ff.

Fructuosus of Tarragon, *Acta Fructuosi*, in *Acta Martyrum*, ed. T. Ruinart, Ratisbonne, 1859.

Fulgentius of Ruspe, *Sermons*, ed. J. Fraipont, (CC 91A) Turnhout, 1968.

Gaudentius of Braga, *Sermons*, ed. A. Glueck (CSEL 68), Vienna, 1936.

Gennadius of Marseilles, *De ecclesiasticis dogmatibus*, PL 58, 979 ff.

Gregory the Great, *Gregorii I papae registrum epistolarum*, ed. P. Ewald and L. Hartmann, (MGH *Ep.* 2), 2 vol., Berlin, 1891–1899.

Gregory of Nyssa, *Epistola canonica*, PG 45, 221 ff.

Gregory of Tours, *Libri historiarum X*, ed. B. Krusch and W. Levinson, (MGH, Scriptores rerum merovingicarum, vol. 1, part 1), Hanover, 1951.

Gregory Thaumaturgus, *Epistola canonica*, PG 10, 1020–1,

Hilary of Poitiers, *Ad Constantium imperatorem*, ed. A. Feder, (CSEL 65), Vienna, 1916.

———, *Tractatus super psalmos*, ed. A. Zingerle, (CSEL 22), Vienna, 1891.

Innocent of Rome, *Epistola* 20, ed. R. Cabie, *La lettre du pape Innocent 1er à Decentius de Gubbio*, (*Bibliothèque de la RHE*, 58), Louvain, 1973.

Isidore of Seville, *De ecclesiasticis officiis*, PL 83.

Jerome, *Commentarium in Ezechielem*, ed. F. Glorie, (CC 75), Turnhout, 1964.

———, *Commentarium in Ieremiam*, ed. S. Reiter, (CC 74), Turnhout, 1960.

———, *Commentarium in Titum*, PL 26.

John Cassian, *Collationes*, ed. M. Petschenig, (CSEL 13), Vienna, 1886; ed. E. Pichery, (SC 42, 54, 64), Paris, 1955–9.

———, *De institutis coenobiorum*, ed. M. Petschenig, (CSEL 17), Vienna, 1888; ed. J. C. Guy, (SC 109), Paris, 1965.

John Chrysostom, *Homily* 3 on the Letter to the Ephesians, PG 62, 1 ff.

Justin Martyr, *Apologies*, ed. L. Pautigny, (*Textes et documents pour l'étude historique du christianisme*), 2 vol., Paris, 1904; See also *Worship in the Early Church*, ed. L. J. Johnson, vol. 1, Collegeville, MN, 2009.

———, *Dialogue with Trypho*, ed. G. Archambault, (*Textes et documents pour l'étude historique du christianisme*), 2 vols, Paris, 1909; see also *Writings of Saint Justin Martyr*, tr. T. B. Falls, (FC 6), Washington, DC, 1965, 147–366.

Leo the Great, *Epistola* 167 to Rusticus of Narbonne, PL 54, 1203 ff.

Liber pontificalis, L. Duchesne, *Le liber pontificalis. Texte, introduction et commentaire*, 2nd ed. C. Vogel, 3 vol., Paris, 1955–7.

Marius Victorinus, *Commentarium in epistolam ad Ephesios*, PL 8, 1235–94.

Polycarp of Smyrna, *Ingace d'Antioche — Polycarpe de Smyrne. Lettres — Martyre de Polycarpe*, ed. T. Camelot, (SC 10), 3rd ed., Paris, 1958.

Prosper of Aquitaine, *Contra Collatorem*, PL 51, 213–76.

———, *De vocatione omnium gentium*, PL 51, 647–722.

———, *Praeteritorum sedis apostolicae auctoritates de gratia Dei et libero voluntatis arbitrio*, PL 51, 205–12.

———, *Pro Augustino responsiones*, PL 51, 170 ff.

Regino of Prüm, *Reginonis De synodalibus causis et disciplinis ecclesiasticis*, ed. F.G.A. Wasserschleben, Leipzig, 1849, Graz, 1964 (reprod. anast.).

Sidonius Apollinarius, *Letters*, ed. J. Sirmond, PL 58, 443–640.

Siricius of Rome, *Letter* to Himerius of Tarragon, PL 13.

Tertullian, *Ad Scapulam*, ed. E Dekkers, (CC 2), Turnhout, 1954.

———, *Apologeticum*, ed. E. Dekkers, (CC 1), Turnhout, 1954.

———, *De anima*, ed. J. H. Waszink, (CC 1), Turnhout, 1954.

———, *De oratione*, ed. G. F. Diercks, (CC 1), Turnhout, 1954.

———, *De praescriptione haereticorum*, ed. R. F. Refoule, (CC 1), Turnhout, 1954.

Timothy of Alexandria, *Responsa canonica*, PG 33, 1295 ff.

Vincent of Lerins, *Commonitorium*, PL 50, 635 ff.

Yves of Chartres, *Decretum*, PL 161, 9–1036.

B. Liturgical Sources

1. Published Sources

a) Eastern Liturgies

Apostolic Constitutions, F. X. Funk, *Didascalia et Constitutiones apostolorum*, vol. 1, Paderborn, 1905.

Didascalia of the Apostles, F. X. Funk, *Didascalia et Constitutiones apostolorum*, vol. 1, Paderborn, 1905.

Testamentum, Domini; I. Rahmani, *Testamentum Domini nostri Jesu Christi...*, Mayence, 1899.

Eucologe de Sérapion, F. X. Funk, *Didascalia et Constitutiones apostolorum*, vol. 2, Paderborn, 1905, 158–95; See also F. E. Brightman, 'The Sacramentary of Serapion', JTS 1 (1900), 88–113, 247–77.

The other Eastern sources that we have used are all taken from F. E. Brightman, *Liturgies Eastern and Western. I Eastern Liturgies*, Oxford, 1896.

b) Western Liturgies

1. Roman Liturgy

The Apostolic Tradition, B. Botte, *La tradition apostolique de saint Hippolyte. Essai de reconstitution*, (LQF 39), Munster, 1963. See also G. J. Cuming, *Hippolytus: A Text for Students*, 2nd edition, Grove Books Ltd., Nottingham, 1987.

SACRAMENTARIES:

'Leonine', ed. L. C. Mohlberg, L. Eizenhöfer and P. Siffrin, *Sacramentarium Veronense*, (*Rerum ecclesiasticarum documenta, Series maior, Fontes* 1), Rome, 1956.

'Old Gelasian', ed. L. C. Mohlberg, L. Eizenhöfer and P. Siffrin, *Liber sacramentorum romanae aeclesiae ordinis anni circuli*, (*Rerum ecclesiasticarum documenta, Series maior, Fontes* 4), Rome, 1960. See also H. A. Wilson, *Liber Sacramentorum Romanae Ecclesiae*, Oxford, 1894.

– 8th century Gelasian:

St Gall 348, ed. L. C. Mohlberg, *Das fränkische Sacramentarium Gelasianum in alamannischer Überlieferung*, (LQF 1–2), 2nd ed., Munster, 1939.

Rheinau 30, ed. A. Hänggi and A. Schönherr, *Sacramentarium Rhenaugiense, Handshrift Rh 30 der Zentralbibliothek Zürich*, (*Spicilegium friburgense*, 15), Fribourg S., 1970.

Angoulême, ed. P. Cagin, *Le sacramentaire d'Angoulême*, Angoulême, 1918.

Gregorian: J. Deshusses, *Le sacramentaire grégorien. Ses principales formes d'après les plus anciens manuscrits. Edition comparative*. Vol. 1: *Le sacramentaire, le supplement d'Aniane*, (*Spicilegium friburgense*, 16), Fribourg S., 1971.

Hadrianum: H. Lietzmann, *Das Sacramentarium Gregorianum nach dem Aachener Urexemplar*, (LQF 3), Munster, 1921.

Acluinianum: H. A.Wilson, *The Gregorian Sacramentary under Charles the Great*, (HBS 49), London, 1915.

ORDINES:

M. Andrieu, *Les Ordines romani du haut moyen âge*, (*Spicilegium sacrum lovaniense, Etudes et documents*, 11, 23, 24, 28, 29), 5 vol., Louvain, 1931–1961.

PONTIFICAL:

C. Vogel and R. Elze, *Le Pontifical romano-germanique du dixième siècle*, (*Studi e Testi* 226, 227, 269), 3 vol., Vatican City, 1963–1972.

ANTIPHONARY:

R. J. Hesbert, *Antiphonale missarum sextuplex*, Brussels, 1935.

2. Milanese Liturgy

SACRAMENTARIES:

Biasca: O. Heiming, *Das ambrosianische Sackramentar von Biasca. Die Handschrift Mailand Ambrosiana A24 bis inf. 1 Teil: Text*, (*Corpus ambrosiano liturgicum* 2, LQF 51) Munster, 1969.

Triplex: ———, *Das Sacramentarium Triplex. Die Handschrift Zürich Zentralbibl. C43. 1 Teil: Text*, (*Corpus Ambrosiano liturgicum*, 1, LQF 49), Munster, 1968.

Bergamo: A. Paredi, *Sacramentarium Bergomense*, (*Monumenta bergomensia* 6), Bergamo, 1962.

Aribert: A. Paredi, *Il Sacramentario di Ariberto*, (*Miscellanea A. Bernareggi*), Bergamo, 1958.

S. Simpliciano: J. Frei, *Das ambrosianische Sakramentuar D 3–3 aus dem mailändischen Metropolitankapitel. Eine textkritische und redaktionsgeschichtliche Untersuchung der mailändischen Sakramentartradition*, (*Corpus ambrosiano liturgicum* 3, LQF 56), Munster, 1974.

MISSAL:

A. Ratti and M. Magistretti, *Missale ambrosianum duplex. Ed. Puteo-bonellianae et typicae* (*Monumenta sacra et profana* 4), Milan, 1913.

ANTIPHONARY:

Antiphonale missarum juxta ritum sanctae Ecclesiae mediolanensis, Rome, 1935.

3. Gallican Liturgy

SACRAMENTARIES:

Gothicum: H. M. Bannister, *Missale Gothicum*, (HBS 52 and 54), 2 vols London, 1917–1919.

———, L. C. Mohlberg, *Missale Gothicum*, (*Rerum ecclesiasticarum documenta, Series maior, Fontes* 5), Rome, 1961.

Gallicanum Vetus: L. C. Mohlberg, *Missale Gallicanum vetus*, (*Rerum ecclesiasticarum documenta, Series maior, Fontes* 3), with Mone Appendix, Rome, 1958.

Bobbio; E. A. Lowe, *The Bobbio Missal. A Gallican Mass-book*, (HBS 53, 58, 61), 3 vol., London, 1917–1923.

M 12: A. Dold, *Das Sakramentar im Schabcodex M 12 Sup. Der Bibliotheca Ambrosiana mit hauptsächlich altspanischem Formelgut in gallischem Rahmenwerk*, (TA 43), Beuron, 1952.

Pseudo-Germain: E. C. Ratcliff, *Expositio antiquae liturgiae gallicanae*, (HBS 98), London, 1971.

4. Celtic Liturgy

SACRAMENTARIES:

Stowe; G. F. Warner, *The Stowe Missal* (HBS 31–32), 2 vol., London, 1906–1915.

(Fulda); G. Witzel, *Exercitamenta sincerae pietatis*, Mayence, 1555,

Mon; A. Dold, L. Eizenhöfer and D. Wright, *Das irische Palimpsestsakramentar in Clm 14 429 der Staatsbibliothek München*, (TA 43/54), Beuron, 1964.
ANTIPHONARY:
F. E. Warren, *The Antiphonary of Bangor*, (HBS 9–10), 2 vol., London, 1893–5.

5. Spanish Liturgy

SACRAMENTARIES:
M. Férotin, *Liber mozarabicus sacramentorum*, (*Monumenta ecclesiae liturgica*, 6) Paris, 1912.
———, Le Liber ordinum en usage dans l'Eglise wisigothique et mozarabe d'Espagne du cinquieme au onzième siècle, (*Monumenta ecclesiae liturgica*, 5), Paris, 1904.
A. Lesley, *Missale mixtum secundum regulam B. Isidori edictum mozarabes*, Rome, 1755 (PL 85).
ANTIPHONARY:
L. Brou and J. Vives, *Antifonario visigótico mozárabe de la Catedral de León*, (*Monumenta Hispaniae sacra, Series liturgica*, V, 1–2), 2 vol., Barcelona-Madrid, 1953–1959.
Various:
J. Vives, *Oracional visigótico*, (*Monumenta Hispaniae sacra, Series liturgica*, I), Barcelona, 1946.
F. Lorenzana, *Breviarium gothicum secundum regulam B. Isidori*, Madrid, 1804 (PL 86).

6. Different or later sources

Benedictines of Solesmes, *Paléographie musicale. Les principaux manuscrits de chant grégorien, ambrosien, mozarabe, gallican publiés en fac-similés photo-typiques*, Solesmes, 1889 ff.
———, *Variae preces e liturgia tum hodierna tum antiqua collectae aut usu receptae*, Solesmes, 1896.
Bishop, E., *Angilbert's Ritual Order for St-Riquier, Liturgica historica*, Oxford, 1918, 314–32.
Brou, L., *The Monastic Ordinale of St-Vedast's Abbey Arras*, (HBS 86–87), 2 vol., Bedford, 1957.
Cabrol, F. and Leclercq, H., *Relliquiae liturgicae vetustissimae*, (*Monumenta Ecclesiae liturgica* I, 1–2), 2 vol., Paris, 1900–1913.
Dewick, E. S., *The Leofric Collectar*, (HBS 45 and 56), 2 vol., London, 1914–1921.
Diehl, E., *Inscriptiones latinae christianae veteres*, 3 vol., Berlin, 1961.
Dold. A., *Die Zürcher und Peterlinger Messbuch-Fragmente aus der Zeit der Jahrtausendwende im Bari-Schrifttyp mit eigenständiger Liturgie*, (TA I, 25), Beuron, 1934.
Kuypers, A. B., *The Prayer Book of Aedeluald the Bishop, commonly called The Book of Cerne*, Cambridge, 1902.
Munier, C., *Les Statuta Ecclesiae antiqua. Edition, études critiques*, (*Bibliothèque de l'Institut de droit canonique de l'Université de Strasbourg*, 5), Paris, 1960.
Warren, F. E., *The Leofric Missal as used in the Cathedral of Exeter 1050–1072*, Oxford, 1883.
Wilmart, A., *Precum libelli quattuor aevi carolini. Prior pars*. Rome, 1940.

B. Liturgical Sources : 2. *Manuscript Sources*

Next to the symbol for the manuscript we indicate the formulary to which the manuscript attests, or the page in this study where reference is made to it.

AUTUN, Bibl. Mun.,	S 12	*FG¹–FG²*
	S 98	*FG¹*
	S 181	p. 117, note 11
	S 183	*FG¹–FG²*
	S 188	*FG²–FG²*
BERGAMO, Bibl. Civica,	Γ III 18	*M¹*
BESANÇON, Bibl. Mun.,	79	p. 117, note 11
	119	*FG¹*
	131	p. 117, note 11
	140	p. 117, note 11
BRUSSELS, Bibl. Roy.,	4836 (Cat. 641)	*FG¹–FG²*
	7524–55 (Cat. 3558)	Litany of the saints
	IV 41	p. 271, note 9
	IV 112	p. 271, note 9
CAMBRAI, Bibl. Mun.,	55	p. 117, note 11
		p. 271 note 9
	60	*FG¹–FG²*
	67	p. 117, note 11
	68	*FG¹–FG²*
	70	p. 117, note 11
	71	*FG¹–FG²*
	72 to 76	p. 117, note 11
	77	*FG¹–FG²*
	78	*FG¹–FG²*
	79	p. 117, note 11
	80	*FG¹–FG²*
	82	p. 117, note 11
	83	p. 117, note 11
	131	*FG¹–FG²*
	164 (olim 159)	*OS–Irl²*
CAMBRIDGE, Corpus Christi College,	272	p. 271, note 8
CARLSRUHE, Bad. Landesbibl.,	App. Aug. CLXVII	*Irl²*

CHANTILLY, Musée Condé,	103	p. 271, note 9
HAUTECOMBE, Abbey Sainte-Madeleine, Graduel de Valence,		p. 117, note 11
LANGRES, Grand Séminaire,	312	FG^1
LONDON, Brit. Mus.,	Add. 34.209	M^1-M^2
	Cotton MS Galba A XVIII	Litany of the saints
	Titus D XVIII	Litany of the saints
	Harl. 863	p. 271 note 9
	4951	FG^1-FG^2
	Royal MS 2 A XX	Litany of the saints
MADRID, Academia de la Historia,	18	p. 117, note 11
	45	FG^1-FG^2
	51	FG^1-FG^2
B.N., 136		FG^1
B.N., 1361		p. 117, note 11
Palacio Nacional, II. D. 3		p. 117, note 11
MILAN, Bibl. Ambr.,	A 24 Inf.	M^1-M^2
	D 87 Sup.	M^1-M^2
	I 127 Sup.	M^1-M^2
	Trotti 251	M^1-M^2
MONTPELLIER, Bibl. Fac. Médecine,	H 409	p. 271 note 9 and
		Litany of the saints
PARIS, Bibl. Mazarine,	512	*DG*
	541	FG^1
B.N. lat.,	776	FG^1-FG^2
	780	FG^2
	903	FG^1-FG^2
	909	FG^1-FG^2
	931	p. 117 note 11
	1086	p. 117 note 11
	1118	FG^2
	1120	FG^1-FG^2
	1121	FG^1-FG^2
	1122 to 1124	p. 117 note 11

	1132	p. 117 note 11
	1136	p. 117 note 11
	1153	*DG*
	1154	p. 271 note 9
	1210	p. 117 note 11
	1248	*DG*
	1331	p. 117 note 11
	1336	p. 117 note 11
	9467	p. 117 note 11
		p. 271 note 9
	9478	p. 117 note 11
	10517	p. 117 note 11
	10518	p. 117 note 11
	10581	p. 117 note 11
	12584	p. 117 note 11
	13159	p. 117 note 11
		Litany of the saints
	13256 to 13258	p. 117 note 11
	18050	p. 117 note 11
PARIS, B.N., nv. acq. lat.,	387	p. 117 note 11
	422	p. 117 note 11
	3001	FG^1–FG^2
Bibl. Sainte-Geneviève, lat.,	BB 20	p. 279 note 33
RHEIMS, Bibl. Mun.,	304	p. 271 note 9
	305	p. 271 note 9
ROME, Bibl. Angelica lat.,	123 (olim B. 3.18)	*DG* and M^2
Bibl. Vat. Palat. lat.,	489	p. 117 note 11
	506	M^1–M^2
Reg. lat.,	235	Litany of the saints
ROUEN, Bibl. Mun.,	222	p. 117 note 11
	223	p. 117 note 11
	224	p. 117 note 11
	242	p. 117 note 11
	253	p. 117 note 11
	255	p. 117 note 11
	773	p. 117 note 11

	3030	p. 117 note 11
SAINT-GALL, Stiftsbibl.,	15	p. 117 note 11
	97	p. 117 note 11
	339	p. 117 note 11
	349	p. 117 note 11
	360	p. 117 note 11
	395	p. 117 note 11
	443	p. 117 note 11
	473	p. 117 note 11
	1359	p. 276 note 25
VALIENCIENNES, Bibl. Mun.,	510	p. 271 note 9
VERCEIL, Arch. Capit.,	136	*M*[1]–*M*[2]
VERDUN, Bibl. Mun.,	12	p. 117 note 11
	127	p. 117 note 11
	130	p. 117 note 11
	131	p. 117 note 11
	132, 1–2–3	p. 117 note 9
	149 to 151	p. 117 note 11
	153	p. 117 note 11
VIENNA, Nationalbibl. lat.,	1888	*FG*[1] and Litany of the saints
ZURICH, Bibl. Centr. Car. C.	161	Litany of the saints

Books and Articles, Dictionaries and Instruments

Alfonso, P., 'Liturgia romana e liturgia ambrosiana: La litania *Dicamus omnes*', *Ambrosius* 1 (1925), 89–91.

———, 'Verso le origini delle preci dell'Ufficio', *Rivista liturgica* 12 (1925), 216 and 274.

———, 'Sallenda e salmodia', *Ambrosius* 2 (1926), 87–89.

———, *Oratio fidelium. Origine e sviluppo eucologico della prece dei fidedi*, Finalpia, 1928.

———, 'San Prospero di Aquitania e le *Orationes solemnes*', *Rivista liturgica* 17 (1930), 199–203.

———, 'Una redazione arcaica della litania romana', EL 54 (1940), 206–13.

Allard, P., *Histoire des persecutions du premier au quatrième siècle*, 3 vol., Paris, 1911–1924.

Andrieu, M., 'A propos de quelques sacramentaires récemment édités', *Revue des sciences religieuses* 2 (1922), 190–210.

Aucher, G., 'La versione armena della liturgia di S. Giovanni Crisostomo', *Chrysostomica*, Rome, 1908, 359–404.

Audet, J.-P., *La Didaché. Instructions des Apôtres*, (*Etudes bibliques*), Paris, 1958.

Bacha, C., 'Notions générales sur les versions arabes de la liturgie de S. Jean Chrysostome, suivies d'une ancienne version inédite', *Chrysostomica*, Rome, 1908, 405–71.

Badcock, F. J., 'A Portion of an Early Anatolian Prayer Book', JTS 33 (1932), 167–80.

Bannister, H. M., 'Some Recently Discovered Fragments of Irish Sacramentaries', JTS 5 (1904), 49–75.

Baronius, C., *Annales ecclesiastici*, ed. A. Theiner, 37 vol., Bar-le-Duc, 1864 ff.

Bastiaensen, A. A. R., *Le cérémonial épistolaire des chrétiens latins. Origine et premiers développements*, (*Graecitas et latinitas christianorum primaeva, Suppl.* 2), Nijmegen, 1964.

Bäumer, S., *Beiträge zur erklärung von 'Litaniae' und 'Missae' in der 'Regel' des H. Benedikt*, (*Studien und Mitteilungen aus dem Benediktinerorden, fasc.* 4), Raigern, 1881.

———, *Histoire du bréviaire* (tr. R. Biron), 2 vol., Paris, 1905 (German edition 1895).

Baumstark, A., 'Eine syrisch-melchitische Allerheiligenlitanei. Herausgegeben mit einleitenden Bemerkungen über orientalische Parallelen der *Litaniae omnium sanctorum*', *Oriens Christianus* 4 (1904), 98–120.

———, 'Liturgischer Nachhall der Verfolgungszeit', *Beiträge zur Geschichte des christlichen Altertums und der byzantinischen Literatur*, (Festschrift A. Ehrhard), Bonn-Leipzig, 1922, Amsterdam, 1969, 53–72.

———, 'Das Gesetz der Erhaltung des Alten in liturgisch hochwertiger Zeit', JLW 7 (1927), 1–23.

———, *Missale romanum. Seine Entwicklung, ihre wichtigsten Urkunden und Probleme,* Eindhoven-Nijmegen, 1929.

———, *Comparative Liturgy*. 3rd edition, rev. by B. Botte, Eng. tr. F. L. Cross, London, 1958. (Originally published in German, 1939).

———, *Nocturna laus. Typen frühchristlicher Vigilienfeier und ihr Fortleben vor allem im römischen und monastischen Ritus.* (Published from the estate of O. Heiming), (LQF 32), Munster, 1957.

Beck, H., *The Pastoral Care of Souls in South-East France during the Sixth Century,* (*Analecta Gregoriana* 51), Rome, 1950.

Beran, J., 'De ordine missae secundum Tertulliani *Apologeticum*', *Miscellanea liturgica Mohlberg* 2, Rome, 1949, 7–32.

Berger, R., *Die Wendung 'offere pro' in der römischen Liturgie,* (LQF 41), Munster, 1965.

Bernal, J. R., 'Los sistemas de lecturas y oraciones en la vigilia pascual hispana', *Hispania sacra* 17 (1964), 283–347.

Biehl, L., *Das liturgische Gebet für Kaiser und Reich. Ein Beitrag zur Geschichte des Verhältnisses von Kirche und Staat,* Paderborn, 1937.

Bingham, J., *Origines sive Antiquitates ecclesiasticae* (tr. Grischovius), 10 vol., Halle, 1724–1729.

Bishop, E., 'Kyrie eleison', *Downside Review,* 1899 and 1900; reprinted in *Liturgica historica. Papers on the Liturgy and Religious Life of the Western Church,* Oxford, 1918, 116–36.

———, 'The Litany of the Saints in the Stowe Missal', *Liturgica historica,* Oxford, 1918, 137–64.

———,'Liturgical Comments and Memoranda III-IX', JTS 11 (1910), 67–73; 12 (1911), 384–413; 14 (1913), 23–62.

———, 'Some Notes on the Litany', *Downside Review,* 39 (1921), 91–97.

———, Appendix to Connolly, R. H., *The Liturgical Homilies of Narsai,* (*Texts and Studies,* 8, 1), Cambridge, 1909. 117–21.

Bishop, W. C., 'The African Rite', JTS 13 (1912), 250–77.

———, *The Mozarabic and Ambrosian Rites,* London, 1924.

Blaise, A and Chirat, H., *Dictionnaire Latini-Français des auteurs chrétiens,* Strasbourg, 1954.

Blanchini, J., *Vindiciae canonicarum scripturarum vulgatae latinae editionis,* Rome, 1740.

Bonsirven, J., *Textes rabbiniques des deux premiers siècles chrétiens pour server à l'intelligence du Nouveau Testament,* (*Pontifical Biblical Institute*), Rome, 1955.

Borella, P., 'La "missa" o "dimissio catechumenorum" nelle liturgia occidentali', EL 53 (1939), 60–110.

———, 'La prece universale', *Ambrosius* 21 (1945), 70–74.

———, *Cenni storici sulla liturgia ambrosiana. La messa,* Milan, 1949.

———, 'L'*oratio super sindonem*', *Ambrosius* 34 (1958), 173–76.

———, '*Oratio fidelium* e dittici nelle segrete dell'offertorio', *Ambrosius* 36 (1960), suppl. to n. 3, [1]-[21].

———, *Il rito ambrosiano*, (*Biblioteca di scienze religiose* III, 10), Brescia, 1964.

———, '*Kyrie eleison* e prece litanica nel rito ambrosiano', *Jucunda laudatio* 2 (1964), 66–79.

———, 'L'*oratio fidelium* nelle sue varie forme strutturali', *Ambrosius* 41 (1965), 9–23.

Botte, B., *Le Canon de la Messe romaine*, Louvain, 1935.

———, 'Le ritual d'ordination des *Statuta Ecclesiae antiqua*', RTAM II (1939), 223–41.

———, 'Confessor', *Archivum latinitatis medii aevi* 16 (1941), 137–48.

Bouman, C., *Communis oratio. Problemen betreffende de vroegste geschiedenis van het christelijke smeekgebed*, Utrecht-Anvers, 1959.

Bousset, W., 'Zur sogenannten *Deprecatio Gelasii*', *Nachrichten von der Königlichen Gesellschaft der Wissenschaften zu Gottingen, Philologisch-historische Klasse*, Berlin, 1916, 135–63.

Bouyer, L., *Eucharist. Theology and Spirituality of the Eucharistic Prayer*, tr. C. U. Quinn, Notre Dame IN-London, 1968. (French publication, Tournai, 1966).

Brightman, F. E., *Liturgies Eastern and Western. I. Eastern Liturgies*, Oxford, 1896.

Bruylants, P., *Concordance verbale du sacramentaire léonien*, Louvain [1948].

Cabrol, F., 'Liturgie anténicéenee de l'Afrique', DACL 1, 591–619.

———, 'Liturgy postnicéenne de l'Afrique', DACL 1, 620–57.

———, 'Liturgie Diptyques', DACL 4.1, 1045–94.

———, 'Litanies', DACL 9.2, 1540–71.

Callewaert, C., 'Les étapes de l'histoire du Kyrie. Gélase, Benoît, Grégoire', RHE 38 (1942), 20–45.

———, 'Histoire positive du Canon romain. Une épiclèse a Rome?' *Sacris Erudiri*, vol. 2, 1949, 95–110.

Capelle, B., 'Le Kyrie de la messe et le pape Gélase', RB 46 (1934), 126–44' Tr. lit., vol. 2, 116–34.

———, 'Le pape Gélase et la messe romaine', RHE 35 (1939), 22–34; Tr. lit., vol. 2, 135–45.

———, 'L'oeuvre liturgique de s. Gélase', JTS 52 (1951), 129–44; Tr. lit., vol. 2, 146–60.

———, 'Innocent 1er et le canon de la messe', RTAM 19 (1952), 5–16; Tr. lit., vol. 2, 236–47.

———, 'Autorité de la liturgie chez les Pères', RTAM 21 (1954), 5–22.

———, 'L'intercession dans la messe romaine', RB 65 (1955), 181–91; Tr. lit., vol. 2, 248–57.

———, Méditation sur les *Orationes sollemnes* du vendredi saint', LMD 45 (1956), 69–75.

Cappuyuns, M., 'L'auteur du *De vocatione omnium gentium*', RB 39 (1927), 198–226.

———, 'L'origine des *Capitula* pseudo-célestiniens contre le semipélagianisme', RB 41 (1929), 156–70.

———, 'Les *orationes sollemnes* du vendredi saint', QLP 23 (1938), 18–31.

Ceriani, A. M., *Notitia liturgiae ambrosianae*, Milan, 1895. Reprinted in Ratti and Magistretti, *Missale ambrosianum*, Milan, 1913, 413 ff.

Chailley, J., 'Les anciens tropaires et séquentiaires de l'école de Saint-Martial de Limoges (Xe–XIe s.), *Etudes grégoriennes* 2 (1957), 163–88.

Chavasse, A., 'A Rome, le jeudi saint, au VIIe s., d'après un vieil Ordo', RHE 50 (1955), 21–35.

———, *Le sacramentaire gélasien (Vat. Reg. 316). Sacramentaire presbytéral en usage dans les titres romains au VIIe s.*, (*Bibliothèque de théologie* 4, 1), Tournai, 1958.

———, 'L'oraison *super sindonem* dans la liturgie romaine', RB 70 (1960), 313–23.

Chazelas, J., *Les livrets de prières privées du IXe s.* (*Mémoire dactylographié de l'Ecole nationale des Chartes*), Paris, 1959.

Clerici, L., *Einsammlung der Zerstreuten. Liturgieigeschichtliche Untersuchung zur Vor- und Nachgeschichte der Fürbitte für die Kirche in Didache 9, 4 und 10, 5*, (LQF 44), Munster, 1966.

Cneude, P., *Que faisons-nous à la messe?* Paris-Fribourg, 1969.

Coens, M., *Receuil d'études bollandiennes*, (*Subsidia hagiographica* 37), Brussels, 1963.

Congar, Y.-M., *L'ecclésiologie du haut Moyen-Age. De saint Grégoire le Grand à la disunion entre Byzance et Rome*, Paris, 1968.

Connolly, H., 'Liturgical Prayers of Intercession. The Good Friday *Orationes sollemnes*', JTS 21 (1920), 219–32.

Consilium ad exsequendam Constitutione de sacra liturgia.
De oratione communi seu fidelium. Eius natura, momentum ac structura. Criteria atque specimina ad experimentum coetibus territorialibus episcoporum proposita, Vatican, 1965. 2nd ed. 1966.

Danneels, G., 'De voorbede of het algemene kerkgebed', *Getuigenis* 2 (1966), 103–26.

Daras, M., 'Le *Kyrie eleison*', *Cours et conferences des semaines liturgiques*, 6, Louvain, 1928, 67–79.

De Bruyne, D., 'De l'origine de quelques textes liturgiques mozarabes', RB 30 (1913), 421–36.

———, 'L'origine des processions de la Chandeleur et des Rogations. A propos d'un sermon inédit', RB 34 (1922), 14–26.

De Clerck, P., *L'oratio fidelium dans les liturgies latines anciennes. Etat de la question. Sondage patristique*, Louvain, 1967 (typewritten).

Dekkers, E., *Tertullianus en de geschiedenis der liturgie*, Brussels-Amsterdam, 1947.

Delehaye, H., *Sanctus. Essai sur le culte des saints dans l'Antiquité*, Brussels, 1927.

Delisle, L., *Mémoire sur d'anciens sacramentaires*, (*Memoires de l'Institute National de France, Académie des Inscriptions et Belles Lettres*, vol. 32.1), Paris, 1886, 57–423.

Delle Torre, L., 'L'*oratio fidelium*, una preghiera dell'assemblea', *Rivista liturgica* 51 (1964), 214–24, and 52 (1965), 49–66.

Denis, H., 'La prière universelle', LMD 84 (1965), 140–65.

Deshusses, J., 'Le sacramentaire de Gellone dans son context historique', EL 75 (1961), 193–210.

Dewailly, L.-M., 'Mission de l'Eglise et apostolicité', *Revue des sciences philosophiques et théologiques* 32 (1948), 2–37.

———, 'Note sur l'histoire de l'adjectif *apostolique*', *Mélanges de science religieuse* 5 (1948). 141–52.

Dietz, O., 'Das allgemeine Kirchengebet', *Leiturgia*, (*Handbuch des Evangelischen Gottesdienstes*), vol. 2, Cassel, 1955, 417–51.

Dix, G., *The Shape of the Liturgy*, Westminster, 1945.

Dölger, F. J., *Die Sonne der Gerechtigkeit und der Schwarze. Eine religionsgeschichtliche Studie zum Taufgelöbnis*, LQF 14, (1919); 2nd ed. updated, 1971.

———, *Sol salutis. Gebet und Gesang im christlichen Altertum. Mit besonderer Rücksicht auf die Ostung in Gebet und Liturgie*, QLF 16/17, (1920).

———,'Das ungefähre Alter des *Ite, missa est. Zu Dominica sollemnia bei Tertullianus*', *Antike und Christentum* 6 (1940), 108–17.

Duchesne, L., *Origenes du culte chrétien. Etude sur la liturgie latine avant Charlemagne*. 6th edition, Paris, 1925. (1st edition, 1889).

Ebner, A., *Quellen und Forschungen zur Geschichte und Kunstgeschichte des Missale Romanum im Mittelalter. Iter italicum*, Fribourg B., 1896.

Ehrensberger, H., *Libri liturgici Bibliothecae Vaticanae manuscripti*, Fribourg B., 1897.

Eisenhofer, L., *Handbuch der katholischen Liturgik*, 2 vol., Fribourg B., 1932–3.

Eizenhöfer, L., *Canon Missae romanae. Pars altera: Textus propinqui*, (*Rerum ecclesiasticarum documenta, Series minor: subsidia studiorum* 7), Rome, 1966.

———, 'Das Gemeindegebet aus dem ersten Klemensbrief in einem karolingischen Gebetbuch', *Sacris Erudiri* 21 (1972–3), 223–40.

Federer, K., *Liturgie und Glaube. Eine theologiegeschichtliche Untersuchung*, (*Paradosis* 4), Fribourg S., 1950.

Fischer, B., '*Litania ad Laudes et Vesperas*. Ein Vorschlag zur Neugestaltung der Ferialpreces in Laudes und Vesper des Römischen Breviers', *Liturgisches Jahrbuch* 1 (1951), 55–74.

Fontaine, J., 'Martin v. Tours', LTK 7, 118–19.

Fortescue, A., *The Mass. A Study of the Roman Liturgy*, London, 1912. (French tr., A. Boudinhon, Paris, 1921).

Fransen, G, 'La tradition manuscrite du *Décret* de Burchard de Worms. Une première orientation', *Ius sacrum*, (*Festschrift K. Mörsdorf*) ed. A. Scheuermann and G. May, Munich, 1969, 111–18.

Funk, F. X., *Kirchengeschichtliche Abhandlungen und Untersuchungen*, 2 vols, Paderborn, 1897–9.

Gamber, K., *Liturgie übermorgen. Gedanken zur Geschichte und Zukunft des Gottesdienstes*, Friebourg B., 1966.

———, 'Die irischen Messlibelli als Zeugnis für die frühe römische Liturgie', *Römische Quartalschrift* 62 (1967), 214–21.

———, '*Conversi ad Dominum*. Die Hinweisung von Priester und Volk nach Osten bei der Messfeier im 4. und 5. Jahrhundert', *Römische Quartalschrift* 67 (1972), 49–64.

Gastoué, A., *Cours théorique et pratique de plain-chant romain grégorien d'après les travaux les plus récents*, Paris, 1904.

———, 'Les chants de la messe. Le Kyrie', *Revue Sainte-Cécile* 28 (1936), 109–11.

———, 'Le chant gallican', *Revue du chant grégorien*, 41 (1937), 101–06, 131–33, 167–76; 42 (1938), 5, 57, 107, 146, 171; 43 (1939), 7, 44.

Gerbert, M., *De cantu et musica sacra a prima ecclesiae aetate usque ad praesens tempus*, 2 vols, Saint-Blaise, 1774, ed. O. Wessely, Graz, 1968.

———, *Monumenta veteris liturgiae alemannicae*, 2 vol., Saint-Blaise, 1777–1779.

Göller, E., *Papsttum und Bußgewalt in spätrömischer und frühmittelalterlicher Zeit*, Fribourg B., 1933.

Gougaud, L., 'Liturgies Celtiques', DACL 2.2, 2969–3032.

Griffe, E., 'Aux origins de la liturgie gallicane', *Bulletin de littérature ecclésiastique* 52 (1951), 17–43.

———, *La Gaule chrétienne à l'epoque romaine*, 3 vol., 2nd ed., Paris, 1964.

Grisbrooke, W. J., 'Intercession at the Eucharist. II. The Intercession at the Eucharist Proper', *Studia Liturgica* 5 (1966), 20–44 and 87–103.

Grotz, J., *Die Entwicklung des Bußstufenwesens in der vornicänischen Kirche*, Fribourg B., 1955.

Gryson, R., *Le prêtre selon saint Ambroise*, (*Dissertatio ad gradum magistri in Facultate theological lovaniensi*, Series III, 11), Louvain, 1968.

Gülden, J., 'Das allgemeine Kirchengebet in der Sicht des Seelsorgers', *Die Messe in in der Glaubensverkündigung*, ed. F. X. Arnold and B. Fischer, Fribourg B., 1953, 337–53.

Gy, P.-M., 'Signification pastorale des prières du prône', LMD 30 (1952), 125–36.

———, 'Remarques sur le vocabulaire antique du sacerdoce chrétien', *Etudes sur le sacrament de l'Ordre*, (*Lex orandi* 22), Paris, 1957, 125–45.

———, 'Collectaire, ritual, processionnal', *Revue des sciences philosophiques et théologiques* 44 (1960), 441–69.

———, *Collectaires, rituels, processionnaux manuscrits des bibliothèques publiques de France*, (typewritten thesis), Le Saulchoir, 1960.

Hänggi, A. and Pahl, I., *Prex eucharistica. Textus e variis liturgiis antiquioribus selecti*, (*Spicilegium friburgense* 12), Fribourg S., 1968.

Hanon de Louvet, R., *En marge du missel romain. Commentaire historico-liturgique du propre du temps*, Wetteren, 1929.

Hanssens, J.-M., *Insitutiones liturgicae de ritibus orientalibus*, vol. 2–3, Rome, 1930–2.

Hierzegger, R., 'Collecta und Statio. Die römischen Stationsprozessionen im frühen Mittelalter', *Zeitschrift für katholische Theologie* 60 (1936), 511–54.

Hoppenbrouwers, H., '*Conversatio*. Une étude sémasiologique', (*Graecitas et latinitas christianorum primaeva, suppl.* 1), Nijmegen, 1965, 45–95.

Huglo, M., 'Un tonaire du Graduel de la fine du VIIIe s. (Paris, BN lat. 13159)', *Revue grégorienne* 31 (1952), 176–86 and 224–33.

———, 'Les preces des graduels aquitains empruntées à la liturgie hispanique', *Hispania sacra* 8 (1955), 361–83.

———, *Les tonaires. Inventaire, analyse, comparaison*, (Doctoral thesis), Paris, 1971.

———, 'Litany' *Dictionary of Music and Musicians*, ed. Grove, 6th edition, London, 1980.

Johanny, R., *L'Eucharistie, centre de l'histoire du salut chez saint Ambroise de Milan*, (*Théologie historique* 9), Paris, 1968.

Jungmann, J. A., *Die lateinischen Bußriten in ihrer geschichtlichen Entwicklung*, (*Forschungen zur Geschichte des innerkirchlichen Lebens* 3–4), Innsbruck, 1932.

———, 'Das Kyrie eleison in den Preces', *Liturgisches Erbe und pastorale Gegenwart*, Innsbruck, 1960, 239–52.

———, *Missarum Sollemnia. Eine genetische Erklärung der römischen Messe*, 2 vol., 5th ed., Vienna, 1962.

Kannengiesser, C., 'Enarratio in psalmum CXVIII: Science de la révélation et progrès spirituel', *Recherches augustiniennes* (Hommage au R.P.F. Cayré). vol. 2, Paris, 1962, 359–81.

Kantorowicz, E. H., *Laudes regiae. A Study in Liturgical Acclamations and Mediaeval Ruler Worship*, 2nd ed., Berkeley-Los Angeles, 1958.

Kennedy, V. L., *The Saints and the Canon of the Mass*, (*Studi de Antichità cristiana*, 14), 2nd ed., Rome, 1963.

Klauser, Th., *Abendländische Liturgiegeschichte*, 5th ed., Bonn, 1965.

———, *A Short History of the Western Liturgy*, 2nd ed., Oxford, 1979. (Published in German as *Kleine abendländische Liturgiegeschichte*, 1965).

Knoch, O., *Eigenart und Bedeutung der Eschatologie im theologischen Aufriß des ersten Clemensbriefes. Eine auslegungsgeschichtliche Untersuchung*, (*Theophaneia* 17), Bonn, 1964.

Knopf, R., *Der erste Clemensbrief untersucht und herausgegeben*, (TU 20, 1), Leipzig, 1899.

———, *Die Lehre der zwölf Apostel. Die zwei Clemensbriefe*, Tübingen, 1920.

Knopp, G., 'Sanctorum nomina seriatim. Die Anfänge der Allerheiligenlitanei und ihre Verbindung mit den *Laudes regiae*', *Römische Quartalschrift* 65 (1970), 185–231.

Koch, H., 'Die Büßerentlassung in der alten abendländischen Kirche', *Theologische Quartalschrift* 82 (1900), 481–534.

Lampe, G. W. H., *A Patristic Greek Lexicon*, Oxford, 1961-.

Lavorel, L., *La doctrine eucharistique selon saint Ambroise*, 2 vol., (typewritten thesis), Lyon, 1956.

Leclercq, H., 'Génuflexion', DACL, 6.1, 1017–21.

———, 'Papa', DACL 13.1, 1097–1111.

———, 'Pape', DACL 13.1, 1111–1345.

———, 'Pénitents (renvoi des)', DACL 14.1, 251–58.

Leroquais, V., *Les sacramentaires et les missels manuscrits des bibliothèques publiques de France*, 3 vol., Paris, 1924.

———, *Les psautiers manuscrits latins des bibliothèques publiques de3 France*, 2 vol., Mâcon, 1940–1.

Liddell, H. G., Scott, R. and Stuart Jones, H., *A Greek-English Lexicon*, 2 vol., Oxford, 1940, and 1 vol. *Supplement*, by E. A. Barber, Oxford, 1968.

Manz, G., *Ausdrucksformen der lateinischen Liturgiesprache bis ins elfte Jahrhundert*, (TA, I, 1), Beuron, 1941.

Marot, H., 'La collégialité et le vocabulaire épiscopal du Ve au VIIe siècle', *La collégialité épiscopale*, (*Unam sanctam* 52), Paris, 1965, 59–98.

Martene, E., *De antiquis Ecclesiae ritibus*, 4 vol., Bassano–Venice, 1788.

Martimort, A.-G., 'La liturgie de la messe en Gaule', *Bulletin du comité des études de Saint-Sulpice* 22 (1958), 204–22.

———, *L'Église en prière. Introduction à la liturgie*, 3rd ed., Paris, 1965.

Mateos, J., *La célébration de la parole dans la liturgie byzantine. Etude historique*, (*Orientalia christiana analecta*, 191), Rome, 1971.

Meslin, M., *Les Ariens d'Occident. 335–430*, (*Patristica Sorbonensia*, 8), Paris, 1967.

Meyer, W, *Gesammelte Abhandlungen zur mittellateinischen Rhythmik*, vol. 1–2, Berlin, 1905, vol. 3, Berlin, 1936.

———, 'Gildae Oratio rhythmica', *Nachrichten von der Königlichen Gesellschaft der Wissenschaften zu Göttingen. Philologisch-historische Klasse*, Berlin, 1912, 48–108.

———, 'Ueber die rythmischen Preces der mozarabischen Liturgie', *Nachrichten von der Königlichen Gesellschaft der Wissenschaften zu Göttingen. Philologisch-historische Klasse*, Berlin, 1913, 177–222.

———, *Die Preces der mozarabischen Liturgie*, Berlin, 1914.

Mikat, P., 'Zur Fürbitte der Christen für Kaiser und Reich im Gebet des 1. Clemensbriefs', *Festschrift für U. Scheuner*, Berlin, 1973, 455–71.

Milleres Carlos, A., *Manuscritos visigóticos. Notas bibliográficas*, Madrid-Barcelona, 1963.

Moeller, E., 'Litanies majeures et Rogations', QLP 23 (1938), 75–91.

Mohrmann, C., 'Quelques observations sur l'évolution stylistique du Canon de la messe romaine', *Vigiliae christianae* 4 (1950), 1–19.

Molin, J.-B., '*L'oratio fidelium*', ses survivances', EL 73 (1959), 310–17.

———, 'Comment redonner pleine valeur aux prières du prône?', *Paroisse et Liturgie* 42 (1960), 285–300.

———, '*L'oratio communis fidelium* au moyen âge en Occident du Xe au XVe siècle', *Miscellanea liturgica in onore di S. E. il cardinale G. Lercaro*, vol. 2, Rome, 1967, 313–468.

———, 'La prière universelle', J. *Dans vos assemblées. Sens et pratique de la célébration liturgique*, ed. J. Gelineau, Paris, 1971, vol. 1, 243–57.

———, 'Les manuscrits de la *Deprecatio Gelasii*. Usage privé des psaumes et dévotion aux litanies', EL 90 (1976), 113–48.

Molin, J.-B. and Maertens, Th., *Pour un renouveau des prières du prône*, (*Collection Paroisse et Liturgie*, 53), Bruges, 1961.

Morin, G., 'Que faut-il entendre par les confessores auxquels était adressé le traité de Macrobe le donastiste? (*Notes d'ancienne literature chrétienne* 1)', RB 29 (1912), 82–84.

Morin, J., *Commentarius historicus de disciplina in administratione sacramenti paenitentiae*, Venice, 1702.

Mouret, R., *Les fonctions liturgiques des diacres en Gaule avant la réforme carolingienne* (typewritten thesis), Paris, 1965.

———, *Propositions pour la prière universelle*, Paris, 1982.

Munier, C., *les Statuta Ecclesia antiqua. Edition. Etudes critiques*, (*Bibliothèque de l'Institut de droit canonique de l'université de Strasbourg* 5), Paris, 1960.
Nocent, A., 'La prière commune des fidèles', NRT 86 (1964), 948–64.
Oesterley, W. O. E., *The Jewish Background of the Christian Liturgy*, Oxford, 1925.
Opfermann, B., 'Um die Erneuerung des Fürbittengebetes in der Meßfeier', *Bibel und Liturgie* 18 (1951), 243–48.
———, *Die liturgischen Herrscherakklamationen im Sacrum Imperium des Mittelalters*, Weimar, 1953.
———, '*Litania italica*. Ein Beitrag zur Litaneigeschichte', EL 72 (1958), 306–19.
Paredi, A., 'La liturgia di sant'Ambrogio', *Sant'Ambrogio nel XVI. centenario della nascità*, Milan, 1940, 89–157.
Pinell, J., 'Liturgia hispánica', DHEE, vol. 2, 1303–20.
Pomares, G., *Gélase 1er. Lettre contre les Lupercales. 18 messes du sacramentaire léonien*, (SC 65), Paris, 1959.
Porter, W. S., *The Gallican Rite*, (*Studies in Eucharistic Faith and Practice*), London, 1958.
Poschmann, B., *Die abendländische Kirchenbuße im Ausgang des christlichen Altertums*, (*Münchener Studien zur historischen Theologie* 7), Munich, 1928.
———, *Die abendlandische Kirchenbuße im frühen Mittelalter*, (*Breslauer Studein zur historischen Theologie* 16), Breslau, 1930.
Pothier, J., 'Prières litaniales ou processionnelles', *Revue du chant grégorien* 9 (1900–1901), 113–20.
Probst, F., *Liturgie der drei ersten christlichen Jahrhunderte*, Tübingen, 1870.
———, *Liturgie des vierten Jahrhunderts und deren Reform*, Munster, 1893.
———, *Die abendländische Messe vom fünften bis zum achten Jahrhundert*. Munster, 1896.
Quasten, J., 'Oriental Influence in the Gallican Liturgy', *Traditio* 1 (1943), 55–78.
Ramos, M., *Oratio admonitionis. Contribución al studio de la antigua Misa española*, Grenada, 1964.
———, 'Rasgos de la *Oratio communis* según la *oratio admonitionis* hispánica', *Hispania sacra* 17 (1964), 31–45.
Rauschen, G., *Eucharistie und Bußsakrament in den ersten sechs Jahrhunderten der Kirche*, 2nd ed., Fribourg B., 1910; reprint, Amsterdam, 1971. French tr. *L'eucharistie et la penitence durant les six premiers siècles de l'Eglise*, Paris, 1910.
Renaud, B., *Eucharistie et culte eucharistique selon saint Cyprien* (typewritten thesis), Louvain, 1967.
Righetti, M., *Manuale di storia liturgica*, 4 vol., Milan-Genoa, 1950–1956.
Roetzer, W., *Des heiligen Augustinus Schriften als liturgiegeschichtliche Quelle. Eine liturgiegeschichtliche Studie*, Munich, 1930.
Ruinard, T., ed., *Acta Martyrum*, 3 vol., Ratisbonne, 1859.
Saxer, V., *Vie liturgique et quotidienne à Carthage vers le milieu du IIIe s. Le témoignage de saint Cyprien et de ses contemporains d'Afrique*, (*Studi di Antichità cristiana*, 29), Rome, 1969.
Schermann, T., *Die allgemeine Kirchenordnung, frühchristliche Liturgien und kirchliche Überlieferung*, (*Studien zur Geschichte und Kultur des Altertums* 3), 3 vol., Paderborn, 1914–1916.

Schmidt, H., *Introductio in liturgiam occidentalem*, Rome, 1960.

Schwartz, E., 'Bußstufen und Katechumenatsklassen', *Schriften der wissenschaftlichen Gesellschaft in Straßburg* 6 (1910), reprinted in *Gesammelte Schriften*, vol. 5, Berlin, 1963, 274–362.

Sejourne, P., *Le dernier Père de l'Eglise: Saint Isidore de Séville. Son rôle dans l'histoire du droit canonique*, Paris, 1929.

———, 'Saint Isidore de Séville et la liturgie wisigothique', *Miscellanea isidoriana*, Rome, 1936, 221–51.

Siffrin, P., *Kondordanztabellen zu den lateinischen Sakramentarien.*
II *Liber sacramentorum romanae aecclesiae — Sacramentarium Gelasianum*, (*Rerum ecclesiasticarum documenta, Series minor* 5), Rome, 1959.
III *Missale Gothicum* (*Rerum ecclesiasticarum documenta, Series minor* 6), Rome, 1961.

von Soden, H., *Das lateinische Neue Testament in Afrika zur Zeit Cyprians* (TU 33), Berlin 1901.

Sottocornola, F., 'De intercessiegebeden in het eucharistisch gebed', *Tijdschrift voor liturgie* 56 (1972), 298–320.

Stäblein, B., 'Gallikanische Liturgie', MGG 3 (1955), 1299–1325.

———, 'Saint-Martial', MGG 2 (1963), 1262–72.

Stiegler, A., 'Laienkommunion', LTK 6, 746.

Stotz, P., *Ardua spes mundi. Studien zu lateinischen Gedichten aus Sankt Gallen*, Berne, 1972.

Strittmatter, A., 'Notes on the Byzantine Synapte', *Traditio* 10 (1954), 51–108.

Stuiber, A., 'Die Diptychen-Formel für die *nomina offerentium* im römischen Meßkanon', EL 68 (1954), 127–46.

Thompson, T. and Srawley, J. H., *St Ambrose. On the Sacraments and on the Mysteries*, London, 1950.

Traube, L., 'Peronna Scottorum. Ein Beitrag zur Überlieferungsgeschichte und zur Paläographie des Mittelalters', *Vorlesungen und Abhandlungen*, vol. 3, Munich, 1930, 95–119.

Unterkircher, F., *Die Glossen des Psalters von Mondsee*, Fribourg, 1974.

Van de Paverd, F., *Zur Geschichte der Meßliturgie in Antiocheaia und Konstantinopel gegen Ende des vierten Jahrhunderts. Analyse der Quellen bei Johannes Chrysostomos*, (*Orientalia christiana analecta*, 187), Rome, 1970.

Vezzosi, A., ed., *Venerabilis viri J. M. Thomasii Opera omnia*, 7 vol., Rome, 1747–1754.

Vismans, T. A., 'Oud-gallicaanse liturgie', LW 2, 2084–94.

Vogel, C., *La discipline pénitentielle en Gaule des origins a la fin du VIIe siècle*, Paris, 1952.

———, 'L'orientation vers l'Est du celebrant et des fidèles pendant la célébration eucharistique', *L'Orient syrien* 9 (1964), 3–37.

———, *Introduction aux sources de l'histoire du culte chrétien au moyen âge* (*Biblioteca degli Studi Medievali*, 1), Spoleto, 1966. Translated and revised by W. Storey and R. Rasmussen, *Medieval Liturgy. An Introduction to the Sources*, Portland, OR, 1986.

von der Goltz., E., *Das Gebet in der ältesten Christenheit. Eine geschichtliche Untersuchung*, Leipzig, 1901.

Warren, F. E., *The Liturgy and Ritual of the Celtic Church*, Oxford, 1881.

Wasserschleben, F.G.A., *De sunodaibus causis et disciplinis ecclesiasticis*, Leipzig, 1840.
Willis, G. G., *Essays in Early Roman Liturgy*, (*Alcuin Club Collections* 46), London, 1964.
Wilmart, A., 'Bobbio (missel de)', DACL 2, 939–62.
———, 'Germain de Paris (lettres attribuées à saint)', DACL 6.1, 1049–1102.
———, 'Le manuel de prières de saint Jean Gualbert', RB 48 (1936), 259–99.
Wissowa, G., *Religion und Kultus der Römer*, (*Handbuch der klassischen Altertumswissenschaft von Iwan von Müller*, V, 4), Munich, 1912.
Wolfram, G., 'Der Einfluß des Orients auf die Kultur und Christianisierung Lothringens im frühen Mittelalter', *Jahrbuch der Gesellschaft für lothringische Geschichte und Altertumskunde*, 17 (1905), 318–52.

Notice

Unless otherwise stated, we take responsibility for the translations presented. The biblical citations are taken from the *New Revised Standard Version*, Nashville, 1989.

Index of *Incipits*

The *incipits* reproduced in this book are listed here in alphabetical order. For the litanies we do not give the beginning of each petition; for the table of themes, see p. 324. For the lities, we indicate the *initium* of each invitatory and each oration.

Index of Names*

* For a table of manuscuscripts, see Part Two of the Bibliography, where the manuscripts used in this work are cited in alphabetical order of the cities where they are preserved.

Prayer Exemplars

OS

I

Oremus, dilectissimi nobis, in primis pro ecclesia sancta dei, ut eam deus et dominus noster pacificare adunare et custodire dignetur toto orbe terrarum, subiciens ei principatus et potestates, detque nobis tranquillam et quietam vitam degentibus glorificare deum patrem omnipotentem.

OREMUS. Omnipotens sempiterne deus, qui gloriam tuam omnibus in Christo gentibus reuelasti, custodi opera misericordiae tuae, ut ecclesia tua toto orbe diffusa stabili fide in confessione tui nominis persueret. per dominum nostrum.

II

Oremus et pro beatissimo papa nostro, ut deus omnipotens qui elegit cum in ordine episcopatus saluum et incolumem custodiat ecclesiae suae sanctae ad regendum populum sanctum dei.

OREMUS. Omnipotens sempiterne deus, cuius aeterno iudicio uniuersa fundantur, respice propitius ad preces nostras et electum nobis antistitem tua pietate conserua, ut christiana plebs quae tali gubernatur auctore sub tanto pontifice credulitatis suae meritis augeatur. per.

III

Oremus et pro omnibus episcopis, presbyteris, diaconibus, subdiaconibus, acolytis, exorcistis, lectoribuis, ostiariis, confessoribus, uirginibus, uiduis, et pro omni populo sancti dei.

OREMUS. Omnipotens sempiterne deus, cuius spiritu totum corpus ecclesiae sanctificatur et regitur, exaudi nos pro uniuersis ordinibus supplicantes, ut gratiae tuae munere ab omnibus tibi gradibus fideliter seruiatur. per.

IV

Oremus et pro christianissimis imperatoribus nostris ut deus et dominus noster subditas illis faciat omnes barbaras nationes ad nostrum perpetuam pacem.

OREMUS. Omnipotens sempiterne deus, in cuius manu sunt omnium temporurm potestates et omnia iura regnorum, respice propitius ad Romanum benignus imperium, ut gentes quae in sua feritate confidunt potentiae tuae dextera conprimantur. per.

V

Oremus et pro catechumenis nostris, ut deus et dominus noster adaperiat aures praecordiarum ipsorum ianuamque misericordiae, ut per lauacrum regenerationis accepta remissione omnium peccatorum digni inueniantur in Christo Iesu domino nostro.

OREMUS. Omnipotens sempiterne deus, qui ecclesiam tuam noua semper prole fecundas, auge fidem et intellectum catechumenis nostris, ut renati fonte baptismatis adoptionis tuae filiis adgregentur. per.

VI

Oremus, dilectissimi nobis, deum patrem omnipotentem ut cunctis mundum purget erroribus, morbos auferat, famem depellat aperiat carceres, uinvula dissoluat, peregrinantibus reditum, infirmantibus sanitatem, nauigantibus portum salutis indulgeat.

OREMUS. Omnipotens sempiterne deus, maestorum consolatio, laborantium fortitudo, perueniant ad te preces de quacumque tribulatione clamantium, ut omnes sibi in necessitatibus suis misericordiam tuam gaudeant adfuisse. per.

VII

Oremus et pro hereticis et schismaticis, ut deus et dominus noster eruat eos ab erroribus uniuersis et ad sanctam matrem ecclesiam catholicam atque apostolicam reuocare dignetur.

OREMUS. Omnipotens sempiterne deus, qui omnes saluas et neminem uis perire, respice ad animas diabolica fraude deceptas, ut omni heretica prauitate deposita errantium corda resipiscant et ad ueritatis tuae redeant firmitatem. per.

VIII

Oremus et pro perfidis iudaeis, ut deus et dominus noster auferat uelamen de cordibus eorum ut et ipsi cognoscant Christum Iesum dominum nostrum.

OREMUS. Omnipotens sempiterne deus, qui etiam iudaicam perfidiam a tua misericordia non repellis, exaudi preces nostras quas tibi pro illius populi obcaecatione deferimus, ut agnita ueritatis tuae luce, quae Christus est, a suis tenebris eruantur. per.

IX

Oremus et pro paganis, ut deus omnipotens auferat iniquitatem a cordibus eorum, et relictis idolis suis conuertantur ad deum uerum et unicum filium eius Iesum Christum dominum nostrum, cum quo uiuit et regnat cum Spirito sancto.

OREMUS. Omnipotens sempiterne deus, qui non mortem peccatorum sed uitam semper inquiris, suscipe propitius orationem nostrum et libera eos ab idolorum cultura, et adgrega ecclesiae tuae sanctae ad laudem et gloriam nominis tui. per.

Irl[1]

a/ Dicamus omnes ex toto corde et ex tota mente:
Domine exaudi et miserere
⟨Domine exaudi et miserere⟩

b/ Qui respicis super terram et facis eam tremere
oramus te
Domini exaudi ⟨et miserere⟩

I Pro altissima pace et tranquillitate temporum nostrorum
oramus te
Domine ⟨exaudi et miserere⟩

II Pro sancta ecclesia catholica quae est a finibus usque ad terminus orbis terrae
oramus te
Domine ⟨exaudi et miserere⟩

III Pro patre nostro episcopo et omnibus episcopis et presbyteris et diaconis et omni clero
oramus te
Domine ⟨exaude et miserere⟩

IV Pro hoc loco et habitantibus in eo
oramus te
Domine ⟨exaudi et miserere⟩

V Pro piissimis imperatoribus et toto Romanorum exercitu
oramus te
Domine ⟨exaudi et miserere⟩

VI Pro omnibus qui in sublimitate constituti sunt
⟨oramus te
Domine exaudi et miserere⟩

VII Pro virginibus viduis et orphanis
oramus te
Domine ⟨exaudi et miserere⟩

VIII Pro peregrinantibus, iter agentibus ac navigantibus
oramus te
Domine ⟨exaudi et miserere⟩

IX Pro paenitentibus et catechumenis
oramus te
Domine ⟨exaudi et miserere⟩

X Pro his qui in sancta ecclesia fructus misericordiae largiuntur domine Deus virtutum exaudi preces nostras
oramus te
Domine ⟨exaudi et miserere⟩

Irl[1]

XI Sanctorum apostolorum et martyrum memores simus ut orantibus eis pro nobis veniam mereamur
oremus te
Domine ⟨exaudi et miserere⟩

XII Christianum ac pacificum nobis finem concedi
a domino comprecemur
praesta, Domine, praesta

XIII Et divinum in nobis permanere vinculum caritatis
sanctum dominum comprecemur
praesta, Domine, ⟨praesta⟩

XIV Conservare sanctitatem et catholicae fidei puritatem
sanctum Deum comprecemur
praesta, Domine, ⟨praesta⟩

c/ Dicamus omnes: Domine exaudi et miserere.

***M*[1]**

a/ Divinae pacis et indulgentiae munere supplicantes,
ex toto corde et ex tota mente
precamur te
Domine miserere

I Pro ecclesia tua sancta catholica
quae hic et per universum orbem diffusa est
precamur te
Domine miserere

II Pro papa nostro ·illo· et omni clero eius
omnibusque sacerdotibus ac ministris
precamur te
Domine miserere

III Pro famulo tuo ·illo· imperatore [et famula tua ··illa· imperatrice]
et omni exercitu eius
precamur te
Domine miserere

IV Pro pace ecclesarium, vocatione gentium
et quiete populorum
precamur te
Domine miserere

V Pro civitate hac et conversatione eius
omnibusque habitantibus in ea
precamur te
Domine miserere

VI Pro aerum temperie ac fructu
et fecunditate terrarum
Domine exaudi et miserere⟩

VII Pro virginibus, viduis, orphanis,
captivis et paenitentibus
precamur te
Domine miserere

VIII Pro navigantibus, iter agentibus, in carceribus,
in vinculis, in metallis, in exiliis constitutis
precamur te
Domine miserere

IX Pro his qui diversis infermitatibus detinentur
quique spiritibus vexantur inmundis
precamur te
Domine miserere

***M*[1]**

X Pro his qui in sancta tua ecclesia
fructus misericordiae largiuntur
precamur te
Domine miserere

b/ Exaudi nos Deus in omni oratione
atque deprecatione nostra
precamur te
Domine miserere

c/ Dicamus omnes: Domine miserere

d/ Kyrie eleison – Kyrie eleison –Kyrie eleison.

***M*[2]**

a/ Dicamus omnes: Kyrie eleison

b/ Domine Deus omnipotens partum nostrorum
Kyrie eleison

c/ Respice de caelo et de sede sancta tua

I Pro ecclesia tua sancta catholica quam conservare digneris
Kyrie eleison

II Pro papa nostro ·illo· et sacerdotio eius
Kyrie eleison

III Pro universis episcopis, cuncto clero et populo
Kyrie eleison

VI Pro famulo tuo ·illo· imperatore [et famula tua ·illa· imperatrice]
et omni exercitu eius
Kyrie eleison

V Pro civitate hac omnibusque habitantibus in ea
Kyrie eleison

VI Pro aerum temperie et fecunditate terrarum
Kyrie eleison

d/ Libera nos qui liberasti filios Israël
Kyrie eleison

e/ In manu forti et brachio excelso
Kyrie eleison

f/ Exurge Domine adiuva nos et libera nos propter nomen tuum
Kyrie eleison, Kyrie eleison, Kyrie eleison

DG

a/ Dicamus omnes: Domine exaudi et miserere
b/ Patrem unigeniti et Dei filium genitoris ingeniti
et sanctum domini spiritum fidelibus animis invocamus
⟨Domine exaudi et miserere⟩
I Pro inmaculata Dei vivi ecclesia ⟨per totum orbem constituta⟩
divinae bonitatis opulentiam deprecamur
⟨Domine exaudi et miserere⟩
II Pro sanctis Dei magni sacerdotibus et ministris
cunctisque Deum verum colentibus populis
Christum dominum supplicamus
⟨Domine exaudi et miserere⟩
III Pro universis recte tractantibus verbum veritatis
multiformen verbi Dei sapientiam peculiariter obsecramus
⟨Domine exaudi et miserere⟩
IV Pro his qui se mente et corpore propter caelorum regna
castificant et spirituali labore desudant
largitorem spiritalium munerum obsecramus
⟨Domine exaudi et miserere⟩
V Pro religiosis principibus omnique militia eorum
qui iudicium et iustitiam diligunt
domini potentiam obsecramus
⟨Domine exaudi et miserere⟩
VI Pro iocunditate ⟨serenitatis et opportunitate⟩ pluviae
atque aurarum vitalium blandimentis ac prospero diversorum
⟨temporum⟩ cursu
rectorem mundi dominum deprecamur
⟨Domine exaudi et miserere⟩
VII Pro his quos prima christiani nominis initiavit agnitio
quos iam desiderium gratiae caelestis accendit
omnipotentis Dei misericordiam obsecramus
⟨Domine exaudi et miserere⟩

DG

VIII Pro his quos humanae fragilitatis infirmitas et quos
nequitiae spiritalis invidia vel varius saeculi ⟨error⟩ involuit
redemptoris nostri misericordiam imploramus
⟨Domine exaudi et miserere⟩
IX Pro his quos peregrinationis necessitas
aut iniquae potestatis impietas vel hostilis vexat aerumna
salvatorem dominum supplicamus
⟨Domine exaudi et miserere⟩
X Pro iudaica falsitate ⟨ … ⟩ aut heretica pravitate deceptis
vel gentili superstitione perfusis
veritatis dominum deprecamur
⟨Domine exaudi et miserere⟩
XI Pro operariis pietatis et his qui necessitatibus laborantium
fraterna caritate subveniunt
misericordiarum dominum deprecamur
⟨Domine exaudi et miserere⟩
XII Pro omnibus intrantibus in haec sanctae domus domini atria
qui religioso corde et supplici devotione convenerunt
dominum gloriae deprecamur
⟨Domine exaudi et miserere⟩
XIII Pro emundatione animarum corporumque nostrorum
⟨et omnium⟩ venia peccatorum
clementissimum dominum supplicamus
⟨Domine exaudi et miserere⟩
XIV Pro refrigerio fidelium animarum praecipue sanctorum domini
sacerdotum qui huic ecclesiae praefuerunt catholicae
dominum spirituum et universae carnis iudicem deprecamur
⟨Domine exaudi et miserere⟩
XV Mortificatam vitiis carnem et viventem fide animam
praesta, Domine, praesta
XVI Castum timorem et veram dilectionem
praesta, Domine, praesta
XVII Gratum vitae ordinem et probabilem exitum
praesta, Domine, praesta

DG

XVIII Angelum pacis et solacia sanctorum
praesta, Domine, praesta
c/ Nosmetipsos et omnia nostra quae orta quae acta per dominum
ipso auctore suscipimus ipso custode retinemus
ipsiusque misericordiae et arbitrio providentiae commendamus
Domine ⟨exaudi⟩ et miserere
d/ Dicamus omnes: Domine exaudi et miserere
Domine ⟨exaudi⟩ et miserere.

***FG*[1]**

a/ Dicamus omnes: Domine miserere

b/ Ex toto corde et ex tota mente oramus te

Domine miserere

I Pro altissima pace et benigna constitutione invocamus te

Domine miserere

II Pro sancta ecclesia catholica quae est in toto orbe diffusa supplicamus te

Domine miserere

III Pro pastore nostro et omni clero eius imploramus te

Domine miserere

[IV Pro abbate nostro et omni congregatione eius flagitamus te

Domine miserere]

V Pro rege nostro et omni exercitu eius obsecramus te

Domine miserere

[VI Pro loco nostro et omnibus habitantibus in eo deprecamur te

Domine miserere]

VII Pro aeris temperie et fecunditate terrae precamur te

Domine miserere

VIII Pro his qui infirmantur ac diversis languoribus detinentur exoramus te

Domine miserere

IX Pro remissione peccatorum vel emendatione morum rogamus te

Domine miserere

X Pro requie defunctorum et indulgentia paenitentium imploramus te

Domine miserere

c/ Exaudi nos Deus in omni oratione nostra quia pius es

Domine miserere

d/ Dicamus omnes: Domine miserere.

FG[2] (B FAMILY)

a/ Kyrie eleison

b/ Domine Deus omnipotens partum nostrorum

Kyrie eleison

I Pro sancta ecclesia catholica quae est in toto orbe constituta

Kyrie eleison

II Pro papa nostro et omni plebe eius

Kyrie eleison

III Pro pastore nostro et omni clero eius]

Kyrie eleison

[IV Pro rege nostro et omni exercitu eius

Kyrie eleison]

V Pro pace regum et quiete populorum

Kyrie eleison

[VI Pro abate nostro et omni congregatione eius

Kyrie eleison

VII Pro loco nostro et habitantibus in eo

Kyrie eleison

VIII Pro remissione peccatorum et emendatione eorum

Kyrie eleison

d/ Libera nos qui liberasti filios Israël

Kyrie eleison

e/ Exaudi voces deprecantium te, Christe

Kyrie eleison

f/ Exaudi nos Deus in omni oratione ista

Kyrie eleison

Irl[2] A

I pro statu seniorum et ministrorum omnium puritate
II pro integritate virginum et continentia viduarum
III pro bona aeris temperie et fructum fecunditate terrarum
IV pro pacis redditu ac fine discriminum
V pro incolumitate regum et pace populorum ac redditu captivorum
VI pro votis adstantium et memoria martyrum
VII pro remissione peccatorum nostrorum et actuum emendatione
VIII pro requie defunctorum
IX pro prosperitate itineris nostri

Irl[2] B

X pro domino papa episcopo et omnibus episcopis et presbyteris et omni
ecclesiastico ordine
XI pro imperio romano et omnibus regibus christianis
XII pro fratribus et sororib us nostris
XIII pro fratribus in via directis
XIV pro fratribus quos de caliginosis huius mundi tenebris
dominus arcessire dignatus est ut eos in aeterna
summae lucis quiete divina pietas suscipiat
XV pro fratribus qui variis dolorum generibus affligantur
ut eos divina pietas curare dignetur.
Espagne
Ecclesiam sanctam catholicam in orationibus in mente habeamus:
ut eam Dominus fide et spe et charitate propicius ampliare dignetur.
Omnes lapsos captivos infirmos atque peregrinos in mente habeamus:
ut eos Dominus propicius redimere sanare et confortare dignetur.
Chorus: Presta eterne omnipotens Deus.